D1662974

The Theory of Functional Grammar
Part 1

Functional Grammar Series 20

Editors

A. Machtelt Bolkestein
Casper de Groot
J. Lachlan Mackenzie

Mouton de Gruyter
Berlin · New York

Simon C. Dik

The Theory of Functional Grammar

Part 1: The Structure of the Clause

second, revised edition

edited by

Kees Hengeveld

Mouton de Gruyter
Berlin · New York   1997

Mouton de Gruyter (formerly Mouton, The Hague)
is a Division of Walter de Gruyter & Co., Berlin.

♾ Printed on acid-free paper which falls within the guidelines of the
ANSI to ensure permanence and durability.

Library of Congress Cataloging-in-Publication-Data

```
Dik, S. C. (Simon C.)
    The theory of functional grammar / Simon C. Dik ; edited
by Kees Hengeveld. − 2nd, rev. ed.
        p.      cm. − (Functional grammar series ; 20)
    Includes bibliographical references (p.    ) and index.
    Contents: pt. 1. The structure of the clause.
    ISBN 3-11-015404-8 (v. 1 : alk. paper). −
    ISBN 3-11-015403-X (v. 1 : pbk. : alk. paper)
      1. Functionalism (Linguistics)    I. Hengeveld, Kees,
    1957−  .  II. Title. III. Series.
P147.D54   1997
415−dc21                                              97-29611
                                                           CIP
```

Die Deutsche Bibliothek − Cataloging-in-Publication-Data

Dik, Simon C.:
The theory of functional grammar / Simon C. Dik. Ed. by Kees
Hengeveld. − [Ausg. in Schriftenreihe]. − Berlin ; New York :
Mouton de Gruyter, 1997
   ISBN 3-11-015539-7
   Pt. 1. The structure of the clause. − 2., rev. ed. − 1997
   ISBN 3-11-015404-8

© Copyright 1997 by Walter de Gruyter & Co., D-10785 Berlin
All rights reserved, including those of translation into foreign languages. No part of this book may be reproduced in any form or by any means, electronic or mechanical, including photocopy, recording or any information storage and retrieval system, without permission in writing from the publisher.
Printing: Gerike GmbH, Berlin. − Binding: Lüderitz & Bauer-GmbH, Berlin.
Printed in Germany.

Preface

Preface to the first edition

Since the publication of Functional Grammar in 1978 many linguists have in one way or another responded to the ideas set forth in that book. Some have written reviews in various shades of sympathy; others have applied FG to a variety of different languages; yet others have challenged certain theoretical claims, sometimes suggesting alternative solutions for specific problems. All these reactions have obviously affected the 1978 framework. They have made it clear that certain modifications and extensions of that framework are called for. This work attempts to provide a new presentation of FG in which due attention is paid to these various contributions to the theory.

Just as important as the written and published reactions to FG were the countless discussions which took place in different kinds of groupings: introductory and advanced seminars on FG; weekly gatherings of our Amsterdam discussion group; the workshop held during the 13th International Congress of Linguists (Tokyo, 1982); the first conference on FG (Amsterdam, 1984); the symposium on predicate operators (Amsterdam, 1985); the second conference on FG (Antwerpen, 1986); the symposium on FG and the computer (Amsterdam, 1987); and the third conference on FG (Amsterdam, 1988). All these discussions taken together have probably been more influential in shaping and reshaping FG than the written literature, but they are less easy to acknowledge individually. I should therefore like to thank, in a general sense, all those who contributed to these discussions in one way or another. The final responsibility for the present work is of course my own.

This work will consist of two parts. Part I (referred to as *TFG1*) sets out the basic principles underlying the theory of FG, and discusses the structure of simple (that is, non-derived, non-complex) clauses. Part II (referred to as *TFG2*), which is in preparation, will contain a discussion of complex and derived construction types.

I have arranged the material in such a way that *TFG1* can be used as an independent introduction to FG. As such, it replaces *Functional Grammar* of 1978, although not all points discussed in that book are repeated in the same detail here. *TFG1* does not presuppose any antecedent knowledge of FG, nor does it otherwise depend on other sources for a proper understanding of its contents. *TFG2*, on the other hand, presupposes (and does not recapitulate) the contents of *TFG1*. *TFG2* can thus be used for advanced study of FG by those who already have a reasonable knowledge of the basic framework of the theory.

TFG1 and *TFG2* concentrate on the question of how the linguistic expressions of natural languages of any type can be described and explained in a way that is typologically, pragmatically, and psychologically adequate. FG in this sense is a theory of the organization of linguistic expressions. In the meantime I have developed a wider interest in the ways in which FG could be used as the grammatical component of an integrated model of the natural language user. One fundamental question in this context is how language users relate the content of linguistic expressions to their non-linguistic knowledge. In this connection I take the view that the underlying representations developed in FG for grammatical purposes might also be used for the representation of the non-perceptual part of this non-linguistic knowledge.

A model of the natural language user will not only require a linguistic and an epistemic capacity, but also a logic which enables it to derive new pieces of knowledge from the knowledge it already possesses, by applying rules and strategies of valid reasoning. If it is assumed that not only linguistic expressions, but also pieces of non-perceptual knowledge are coded in the form of underlying FG structures, it follows that the logic required for this task will have to operate on, and result in, such FG structures as well. We thus need a logic which takes the underlying FG structures for its syntax, and specifies how, given a certain knowledge base containing such structures, further structures of the same kind may be validly inferred. In *TFG1* and *TFG2* occasional reference will be made to this kind of logic, for which I use the term "Functional Logic" (FL). It is my intention to report on FL in a separate work.

Finally, I should like to thank Machtelt Bolkestein, Kees Hengeveld, Lachlan Mackenzie, and Jan Rijkhoff for comments which have led to improvements of both content and style of this book.

Holysloot, March 1989   Simon C. Dik

Preface to the second edition

This revised edition of *TFG1* appears together with *TFG2*. It differs from the first edition in the following respects:
 (i) Certain mistakes have been corrected.
 (ii) The explanation of certain topics has been improved.
 (iii) The whole text has been made compatible with the contents of *TFG2*, and cross-references to this second part have been made more precise.
 (iv) A number of theoretical developments have been integrated.
 (v) Experiences gained through computational implementation of FG in Prolog (cf. Dik 1992) have led to slightly different formulations at various points. Though the computer is hardly mentioned in the present work, it has become a source of inspiration for me both in generating ideas and possible analyses, and in testing their operational feasibility.
 Again, many reactions to *TFG1* have helped me to improve the first edition.

Holysloot   Simon C. Dik

Preface to the second edition by the editor

On 1 March 1995, Simon C. Dik died at the age of 55. The disease which led to his death had revealed itself three years earlier, and gradually prevented him from actively continuing his scientific work. When it had become apparent that it would not be possible for him to finish this two-volume *The Theory of Functional Grammar*, he asked me to assist him in preparing the manuscript for publication.

In this second, revised edition of the first volume, originally published in 1989, various modifications have been incorporated, as specified in the preface by the author. Chapters 6 and 7 have been revised most extensively in view of new developments with respect to the analysis of the term phrase. All revisions were discussed with the author. Since the text presented here is intended to reflect Simon Dik's views as closely as possible, references are made only to those publications that were known to the author, albeit sometimes in a preliminary version, at the time when I discussed the prefinal version of this volume with him.

Several persons and institutions have provided invaluable help while I was preparing this volume. The Faculty of Arts of the University of Amsterdam furnished financial support and exempted me from teaching duties during the academic year 1994-1995, which allowed me to advance much more rapidly than would otherwise have been possible. Lachlan Mackenzie read the entire text and provided many valuable comments. Hella Olbertz prepared the final camera-ready manuscript, including the indexes, and corrected numerous mistakes in the process. The Institute for Functional Research of Language and Language Use at the University of Amsterdam made their technical facilities available to me. Mouton de Gruyter and its staff gave technical and financial assistance throughout the editorial process. Finally, Matty Gaikhorst, Peter Kahrel, Lachlan Mackenzie, Harm Pinkster, Yvonne Sanders, and Willy van Wetter provided help of various kinds.

Amsterdam, May 1997   Kees Hengeveld

Table of contents

List of tables and figures xvii

Abbreviations used in FG-representations xix

1. Methodological preliminaries 1
   1.0. Introduction 1
   1.1. Functional Grammar 2
   1.2. The functional paradigm 4
   1.3. Some aspects of verbal interaction 8
        1.3.1. A model of verbal interaction 8
        1.3.2. The structure of pragmatic information 10
        1.3.3. Mutual knowledge 10
        1.3.4. Intention, meaning, and interpretation 12
   1.4. Standards of adequacy 12
        1.4.1. Pragmatic adequacy 13
        1.4.2. Psychological adequacy 13
        1.4.3. Typological adequacy 14
        1.4.4. The relations between the standards 15
   1.5. Abstractness, concreteness, and applicability 15
   1.6. Take languages seriously 17
   1.7. Constraints on the power of FG 18
        1.7.1. Avoid transformations 19
        1.7.2. Avoid filtering devices 21
        1.7.3. Avoid abstract semantic predicates 23
        1.7.4. Motivating these constraints 23

2. Some basic concepts of linguistic theory 25
   2.0. Introduction 25
   2.1. The importance of functional notions 25
   2.2. Linguistic universals 27
   2.3. Hierarchies 30
   2.4. Priorities 34
        2.4.1. Hierarchies and priorities 34
        2.4.2. An example 38
        2.4.3. On explaining priorities 39

x The Theory of Functional Grammar 1

  2.5. Markedness 41
    2.5.1. Marked construction types 41
    2.5.2. Markedness in oppositions 43
    2.5.3. Markedness shift 44

3. Preview of Functional Grammar 49
  3.0. Introduction 49
  3.1. The structure of the clause 49
  3.2. The structure of FG 56
    3.2.1. Notes on the mode of presentation 56
    3.2.2. Outline of the FG model 58
  3.3. The structure of this work 72

4. The nuclear predication 77
  4.0. Introduction 77
  4.1. The nuclear predication 78
  4.2. Predicate frames 78
    4.2.1. Predicate variables 82
    4.2.2. The form of the predicate 84
    4.2.3. The Type of the predicate 84
    4.2.4. Redundancy rules 86
    4.2.5. Arguments vs. satellites 86
    4.2.6. Selection restrictions 91
  4.3. Meaning postulates and meaning definitions 97
  4.4. Idioms 103

5. States of Affairs and semantic functions 105
  5.0. Introduction 105
  5.1. States of Affairs, predicates, and "Modes of Action" 106
  5.2. Semantic parameters for a typology of SoAs 106
    5.2.1. ± Dynamic 107
    5.2.2. ± Telic 108
    5.2.3. ± Momentaneous 111
    5.2.4. The interrelations between [dyn], [tel], and [mom]. . 111
    5.2.5. ± Control 112
    5.2.5. ± Experience 115
  5.3. Nuclear semantic functions 117
    5.3.0. Introduction 117
    5.3.1. First argument semantic functions 118
    5.3.2. Other nuclear semantic functions 120

		5.4.	Predication, State of Affairs, and "Reality" 124

6. On the function and structure of terms 127
    6.0. Introduction 127
    6.1. The nature of reference 127
        6.1.1. Entities are mental constructs 129
        6.1.2. Two ways of referring 130
    6.2. The structure of terms 132
    6.3. A typology of entities 136
        6.3.1. Different orders of entities 136
        6.3.2. Different types of first-order entities 137
            6.3.2.1. The insufficiency of set theory 138
            6.3.2.2. Types of entities 140
            6.3.2.3. Ensemble nouns and set nouns 142
        6.3.3. Referring to properties and relations 146
    6.4. Types of restrictors 147
        6.4.1. Some properties of underlying term structure 147
        6.4.2. Different surface forms of restrictors 151
    6.5. The representation of personal pronouns 152
    6.6. Types of relations between terms and predicate 154

7. Term operators 159
    7.0. Introduction 159
    7.1. Operators in FG 159
    7.2. Semantic domains of term operators 161
    7.3. Qualifying term operators 163
        7.3.1. Modes of being 163
        7.3.2. Sortal classifiers 164
        7.3.3. Collectivizing and individualizing operators 165
    7.4. Quantifying term operators 166
        7.4.1. Mensural classifiers 166
        7.4.2. Quantifiers and Numerators 168
            7.4.2.1. General principles of term quantification .. 169
            7.4.2.2. Referent ensemble, Domain ensemble, and
                     Universal ensemble 171
            7.4.2.3. A typology of quantifiers 171
            7.4.2.4. Universal quantification 175
        7.4.3. Genericity 176
        7.4.4. Ordinators 178

7.5. Localizing term operators 180
    7.5.1. Demonstratives 180
    7.5.2. Definiteness and indefiniteness 183
    7.5.3. Specificity 188

8. Non-verbal predicates 193
    8.0. Introduction 193
    8.1. Categorial differences between predicates 193
    8.2. Adjectival predicates 197
    8.3. Copula support 198
    8.4. Nominal predicates 202
    8.5. Adpositional predicates 206
    8.6. Possessive predicates 208
    8.7. Locative and existential constructions 209
        8.7.1. Initial analysis 209
        8.7.2. The role of pragmatic functions 212
    8.8. Differences in argument type 214

9. Nuclear, core, and extended predication 217
    9.0. Introduction 217
    9.1. From nuclear to core predication 218
        9.1.1. Predicate operators 219
        9.1.2. Aspectuality 221
            9.1.2.1. Perfective and Imperfective 222
            9.1.2.2. Phasal Aspect distinctions 225
        9.1.3. Level 1 satellites 225
    9.2. From core to extended predication 232
        9.2.1. Variables for states of affairs 232
        9.2.2. Predication operators 236
            9.2.2.1. Quantifying predication operators 236
            9.2.2.2. Localizing predication operators 237
                9.2.2.2.1. Tense 237
                9.2.2.2.2. Perspectival Aspect 238
                9.2.2.2.3. Objective mood and Polarity ... 241
        9.2.3. Level 2 satellites 243

10. Perspectivizing the State of Affairs: Subject and Object assignment 247
    10.0. Introduction 247
    10.1. Some differences with other approaches 248

    10.2. The FG interpretation of Subject and Object 250
    10.3. Subject/Object vs. semantic and pragmatic functions 254
    10.4. Accessibility to Subj/Obj assignment 258
        10.4.1. Criteria for the relevance of Subject and Object 259
        10.4.2. The Semantic Function Hierarchy 262

11. Reconsidering the Semantic Function Hierarchy;
    Raising; Ergativity 271
    11.0. Introduction 271
    11.1. Subj/Obj assignment and the layering of the clause 271
    11.2. Subj/Obj assignment to Loc and Temp 272
    11.3. First and second argument as targets for Subj 275
    11.4. A multi-factor approach to Subj/Obj assignment 277
    11.5. Raising phenomena 280
    11.6. Markedness shift 281
        11.6.1. Markedness shift and Obj assignment 282
        11.6.2. Markedness shift and Subj assignment: ergativity .. 284

12. Predication, proposition, clause 291
    12.0. Introduction 291
    12.1. States of Affairs and Possible Facts 292
    12.2. From predication to proposition 294
        12.2.1. The propositional content variable 294
        12.2.2. Proposition operators 295
        12.2.3. Attitudinal satellites 297
    12.3. From proposition to clause 299
        12.3.1. The illocutionary variable 299
        12.3.2. Illocutionary operators 300
        12.3.3. Illocutionary satellites 304

13. Pragmatic functions 309
    13.0. Introduction 309
    13.1. Extra-clausal and intra-clausal pragmatic functions 310
    13.2. Clause-internal pragmatic functions 311
    13.3. Topic and topicality 313
        13.3.1. Introducing a NewTop 315
        13.3.2. Maintaining a D-Topic 318
        13.3.3. Given Topic and Sub-Topic 323
        13.3.4. Resuming a Given Topic 325

13.4. Focus and focality 326
    13.4.1. Question-Answer pairs 328
    13.4.2. Different types of Focus 330
        13.4.2.1. Differences of scope 330
        13.4.2.2. Differences in communicative point 331
    13.4.3. The role of Focus in a grammar 335

14. Expression rules 339
    14.0. Introduction 339
    14.1. Interaction between different types of expression rules 340
    14.2. Productivity; rules and regularities 342
    14.3. Lexical priority 345
    14.4. The representation of non-productive forms 345
    14.5. The place of morphology in a Functional Grammar 348
    14.6. General format of form-determining expression rules 351
        14.6.1. Changes effected by expression rules 352
        14.6.2. Types of μ-operators 353
        14.6.3. Types of operanda 357
        14.6.4. Simultaneous application of μ-operators 360
        14.6.5. The sequential application of μ-operators 361

15. The operation of expression rules 365
    15.0. Introduction 365
    15.1. Expression rules affecting the form of terms 365
        15.1.1. Semantic, syntactic, and pragmatic functions 365
        15.1.2. Case marking 368
        15.1.3. The expression of term operators 372
        15.1.4. Agreement within terms 373
    15.2. Expression rules affecting the predicate 377
        15.2.1. Voice distinctions 377
        15.2.2. The effects of π-operators 380
        15.2.3. The expression of polarity 384
        15.2.4. The expression of illocutionary operators 386
    15.3. Agreement at the clause level 388

16. Principles of constituent ordering 391
    16.0. Introduction 391
    16.1. Some preliminary remarks 392
    16.2. Towards a multifunctional theory of constituent ordering ... 394
    16.3. Some auxiliary notions 396

   16.4. Constituent ordering principles 399
      16.4.1. General principles 399
      16.4.2. Specific principles 405

17. Constituent ordering: problems and complications 417
   17.0. Introduction 417
   17.1. Object-Subject languages 417
   17.2. Special positions 420
      17.2.1. The uses of P1 420
      17.2.2. Special positions other than P1 424
   17.3. Constituent ordering within term phrases 427
      17.3.1. Applicability of the principles to the term domain .. 428
      17.3.2. Hawkins' facts and their explanation 431
      17.3.3. Discussion of Hawkins' explanation 433
      17.3.4. Some conclusions 435
   17.4. Displacement phenomena 436
   17.5. Interactions between the ordering principles 439
      17.5.1. Preposings in Postfield languages 439
      17.5.2. Postposings in Prefield languages 441

18. Prosodic features 443
   18.0. Introduction 443
   18.1. Prosodic contours 443
      18.1.1. Tone 444
      18.1.2. Accent 446
      18.1.3. Intonation 448
      18.1.4. The form of prosodic contours 449
   18.2. The functions of prosody 452
      18.2.1. Distinctive function 452
      18.2.2. Characterizing function 453
      18.2.3. Predicate formation (derivation and composition) .. 454
      18.2.4. Inflectional expression rules 455
      18.2.5. Pragmatic functions 455
         18.2.5.1. Topicality 456
         18.2.5.2. Focality 457
      18.2.6. Articulation of the clause 461
      18.2.7. Illocutionary operators 462
      18.2.8. Conventionalized pragmatic effects 463
      18.2.9. Emotional expression 464
   18.3. On generating prosodic contours 464

References 467

Index of languages 493

Index of names 495

Index of subjects 499

List of tables and figures

Tables

1. Four types of universals 27
2. Incidence of Clitic Climbing in relation to features of Subject and Clitic 39
3. The process of markedness shift 46
4. Markedness shift in Dutch personal pronouns 46
5. Entity types designated by layers of underlying clause structure .. 55
6. Typology of States of Affairs 114
7. Feature combinations for States of Affairs 115
8. Types of entities as referred to by terms 137
9. Different types of entities 140
10. Different types of nominal predicates 142
11. Distinctions in operator systems 160
12. The twelve demonstratives in Lillooet 183
13. Semantic relations in non-verbal predications 205
14. Semantic relations in non-verbal predications (2) 214
15. Different orders of entities 215
16. Subj/Obj assignment possibilities across languages 267

Figures

1. A model of verbal interaction 8
2. Mutual knowledge of S and A 11
3. Overall model of FG 60
4. Possible derivative relations between predicate categories 196
5. Developmental stages of a State of Affairs 225
6. Perspectives on a State of Affairs 239
7. Focus types in terms of communicative point 332

Abbreviations used in FG-representations

Word classes

T	any word class
A	adjective
N	noun
V	verb

Syntactic functions

Obj	object
Subj	subject

Pragmatic functions

Foc	focus
GivTop	given topic
NewTop	new topic
Or	orientation
ResTop	resumed topic
SubTop	sub-topic
Top	topic

Semantic functions

Ø	zero
Ag	agent
Ben	beneficiary
Circ	circumstance
Comp	company
Dir	direction
Exp	experiencer
Fo	force
Go	goal (patient)
Instr	instrument
Loc	location
Man	manner
Po	positioner
Poss	possessor
Proc	processed
Rec	recipient
Ref	reference
So	source
Temp	time

Layers

f	predicate
x	term
e	predication
X	proposition
E	clause

Satellites

σ_1	any predicate satellite
σ_2	any predication satellite
σ_3	any proposition satellite
σ_4	any illocutionaty satellite

Π-operators

Π_1	any predicate operator
Π_2	any predication operator
Π_3	any proposition operator
Π_4	any illocutionary operator
Ant	anterior

Decl	declarative
Excl	exclamative
Gen	generic
Hab	habitual
Imp	imperative
Impf	imperfective
Int	interrogative
Neg	negative
Perf	perfect
Pf	perfective
Poss	possibility
Post	posterior
Pres	present
Progr	progressive
Req	request
Sim	simultaneous
Subs	subsequent

Term operators

Ω	any term operator
$\emptyset$	zero quantifier
1	singular
A	anaphoric
coll	collectivizing
d	definite
dem	demonstrative
g	generic
i	indefinite
ind	individuating
m	plural
$n°$	n-th
prox	proximate
Q	questioned
R	relative
rem	remote
-s	non-specific

1. Methodological preliminaries

1.0. Introduction

When one takes a functional approach to the study of natural languages, the ultimate questions one is interested in can be formulated as: How does the natural language user (NLU) work? How do speakers and addressees succeed in communicating with each other through the use of linguistic expressions? How is it possible for them to make themselves understood, to influence each other's stock of information (including knowledge, beliefs, prejudices, feelings), and ultimately each other's practical behaviour, by linguistic means?

A constructivist way of formulating this question is: how could we build a model of the natural language user (M.NLU) in such a way that M.NLU can do the same kinds of things that real NLUs can? What sorts of modules would have to be built into M.NLU, what sorts of relations would have to be established between these modules, and what kinds of processing strategies would be required to approximate the communicative performance of human NLUs?

As soon as one starts thinking about how to model NLU, one realizes that NLU is much more than a linguistic animal. There are many more "higher" human functions involved in the communicative use of language than just the linguistic function. At least the following capacities play essential roles in linguistic communication, and must thus be incorporated into M.NLU:

(i) a *linguistic* capacity: NLU is able to correctly produce and interpret linguistic expressions of great structural complexity and variety in a great number of different communicative situations.

(ii) an *epistemic* capacity: NLU is able to build up, maintain, and exploit an organized knowledge base; he can derive knowledge from linguistic expressions, file that knowledge in appropriate form, and retrieve and utilize it in interpreting further linguistic expressions.

(iii) a *logical* capacity: provided with certain pieces of knowledge, NLU is able to derive further pieces of knowledge, by means of rules of reasoning monitored by principles of both deductive and probabilistic logic.

(iv) a *perceptual* capacity: NLU is able to perceive his environment, derive knowledge from his perceptions, and use this perceptually acquired knowledge both in producing and in interpreting linguistic expressions.

(v) a *social* capacity: NLU not only knows what to say, but also how to say it to a particular communicative partner in a particular communicative situation, in order to achieve particular communicative goals.

From the formulations chosen it will be clear that these different capacities must interact closely with one another: each of them produces output which may be essential to the operation of the others. Within M.NLU, there will have to be efficient communication systems between the various modules which deal with the five essential capacities described.

It will also be clear that developing a fully adequate and operational M.NLU is an extremely complicated matter which must be broken down into a number of subtasks before we can even begin to approximate its completion. It is very important, however, that in breaking down the structure of NLU into different submodules, we do not lose sight of the integrated network in which these different submodules have their natural place.

1.1. Functional Grammar

This work develops a theory of Functional Grammar (FG), which is meant to reconstruct part of the linguistic capacities of NLU. FG is a general theory concerning the grammatical organization of natural languages.

As with any complex object of inquiry, the manner in which one conceptualizes a natural language, the questions one asks about it and the answers one seeks to find to these questions are heavily dependent on the basic assumptions which underlie one's approach. Together, these assumptions constitute one's basic philosophy, the *paradigm* (Kuhn 1962) or the *research tradition* (Laudan 1977) in which one operates. In linguistic theory one may discern quite a few distinct research paradigms, each with their own view of what a natural language is like, and how one should go about getting to grips with its structure and functioning.[1] Nevertheless, at a rather general level of abstraction, these various views can be grouped into two main paradigms, which have been vying for acceptance for the greater part of this century. For the sake of the argument, these two paradigms may be called the *formal paradigm* and the *functional paradigm*.

In the formal paradigm a language is regarded as an abstract formal object (e.g., as a set of sentences), and a grammar is conceptualized primarily as an attempt at characterizing this formal object in terms of rules of formal syntax to be applied independently of the meanings and uses of the constructions

---

1. See Dik (1985b) for a discussion of these different views.

described. Syntax is thus given methodological priority over semantics and pragmatics.[2]

In the functional paradigm, on the other hand, a language is in the first place conceptualized as an instrument of social interaction among human beings, used with the intention of establishing communicative relationships. Within this paradigm one attempts to reveal the instrumentality of language with respect to what people do and achieve with it in social interaction. A natural language, in other words, is seen as an integrated part of the communicative competence of NLU.[3]

Verbal interaction, i.e. social interaction by means of language, is a form of structured cooperative activity. It is *structured* (rather than random) activity in the sense that it is governed by rules, norms, and conventions. It is *cooperative* activity in the obvious sense that it needs at least two participants to achieve its goals. Within verbal interaction, the participants avail themselves of instruments which, in a general sense of the term, we shall call *linguistic expressions*. These expressions themselves are again structured entities, i.e. they are governed by rules and principles which determine their build-up.

From the functional point of view, then, linguistics has to deal with two types of rule systems, both ratified by social convention:

(i) the rules which govern the constitution of linguistic expressions (semantic, syntactic, morphological, and phonological rules);

(ii) the rules which govern the patterns of verbal interaction in which these

---

2. The formal paradigm is, of course, the basic view underlying Chomskyan linguistics since Chomsky (1957). It can be traced back to certain roots in earlier American linguistics, such as Bloomfield (1933) and Harris (1951), although it does not share the behaviourist tenets of these antecedents. Another source of inspiration for the formal paradigm lies in certain strongly formalist currents in modern logic (e.g. Carnap 1937). Along these various paths the formal paradigm can be traced back to the positivist philosophy fashionable in the first quarter of this century.

3. The functional paradigm can boast at least as long a history as the formal paradigm. The functional point of view can be found in the work of Sapir (1921, 1949) and his followers in the American anthropological tradition; in Pike's theory of tagmemics (Pike 1967); in the ethnographically oriented work of Dell Hymes (who introduced the notion of "communicative competence", Hymes (1972)); in the linguistic school of Prague, from its inception in the twenties up to the present day; in the British tradition of Firth (1957) and Halliday (1970a, 1973, 1985); and in a somewhat different sense also in the philosophical tradition which, from Austin (1962) through Searle (1969), led to the theory of Speech Acts.

linguistic expressions are used (pragmatic rules).

Rule system (i) is seen as instrumental with respect to the goals and purposes of rule system (ii): the basic requirement of the functional paradigm is that linguistic expressions should be described and explained in terms of the general framework provided by the pragmatic system of verbal interaction. And, as was argued in 1.0. above, verbal interaction itself must be seen as integrated into the higher cognitive functions of NLU.

FG is intended to be a theory that fulfils this requirement of the functional paradigm. This means, inter alia, that wherever possible we shall try to apply the following two principles of functional explanation:[4]

(i) a theory of language should not be content to display the rules and principles underlying the construction of linguistic expressions for their own sake, but should try, wherever this is possible at all, to explain these rules and principles in terms of their functionality with respect to the ways in which these expressions are used.

(ii) although in itself a theory of linguistic expressions is not the same as a theory of verbal interaction, it is natural to require that it be devised in such a way that it can most easily and realistically be incorporated into a wider pragmatic theory of verbal interaction. Ultimately, the theory of grammar should be an integrated subcomponent of our theory of NLU.

FG has been implemented in a computer program, called ProfGlot, which is able to perform the tasks of generating and parsing linguistic expressions in different languages, deriving certain logical inferences from these expressions, and translating them between the different languages. This program can be seen as a step towards exploiting the potential of FG within the wider context of a (computational) model of NLU. See Dik (1992).

1.2. The functional paradigm

A paradigm, in the sense in which this term is used here, is a composite structure of beliefs and assumptions which interlock and interact with each other. In order to give some more content to what I understand by the functional paradigm, I now present the basic conceptions of which it is composed, by answering a number of questions concerning the nature and functioning of natural languages.

---

4. For more detailed discussion of the notion "functional explanation", see Dik (1986).

(Q1) *What is a natural language?*
A natural language is an instrument of social interaction. That it is an instrument means that it does not exist in and by itself as an arbitrary structure of some kind, but that it exists by virtue of being used for certain purposes. These purposes concern the social interaction between human beings.

(Q2) *What is the main function of a natural language?*
The main function of a natural language is the establishment of communication between NLUs. Communication can be seen as a dynamic interactive pattern of activities through which NLUs effect certain changes in the pragmatic information of their communicative partners. Pragmatic information is the full body of knowledge, beliefs, preconceptions, feelings, etc. which together constitute the content of mind of an individual at a given time. Communication is thus not restricted to the transmission and reception of factual information.

It follows that the use of language requires at least two participants, a speaker S and an addressee A. Of course, there are situations in which some S uses language without there being another overt participant present in the situation. This is the case in speaking to oneself, in thinking, and in writing. These forms of language use, however, can be interpreted as derivative in relation to the interactive uses of language (Vygotsky 1962): in writing, one addresses an A who is not overtly present in the situation, but will be activated later when the written text is read; in speaking to oneself, one plays the roles of both S and A at the same time; and thinking can be interpreted as a covert form of speaking to oneself.

It is much easier to understand the individual uses of language as derivative from its communicative uses than it is to understand the communicative uses on the basis of the view that a language is first and foremost an instrument of self-organization and self-expression which, more or less as a by-product, can also be used for talking to others. On that view, the uniformity of language across individuals remains a mystery.

(Q3) *What is the psychological correlate of a language?*
The psychological correlate of a natural language is the NLU's "communicative competence" in the sense of Hymes (1972): his ability to carry on social interaction by means of language. The interpretation of "competence" as "communicative competence" does not mean that we cannot distinguish between "competence" (the knowledge required for some activity) and "performance" (the actual implementation of that knowledge in the activity). There certainly is a difference between what we can do, and what we

actually do in a given instance. When we use the term "communicative competence" rather than "grammatical competence" in the sense of Chomsky (1965), we mean that NLU's linguistic capacity comprises not only the ability to construe and interpret linguistic expressions, but also the ability to use these expressions in appropriate and effective ways according to the conventions of verbal interaction prevailing in a linguistic community. In fact, communicative competence even comprises the ability to use grammatically ill-formed expressions with good communicative results, a game at which most NLUs are quite proficient, as any transcription of spontaneous natural conversation reveals.

(Q4) *What is the relation between the system of a language and its use?*
Since a natural language is an instrument used for communicative purposes, there is little point in considering its properties in abstraction from the functional uses to which it is put. The system underlying the construction of linguistic expressions is a functional system. From the very start, it must be studied within the framework of the rules, principles, and strategies which govern its natural communicative use. In other words, the question of how a language is organized cannot be profitably studied in abstraction from the question of why it is organized the way it is, given the communicative functions which it fulfils.

This means that linguistic expressions can be understood properly only when they are considered as functioning in settings, the properties of which are codetermined by the contextual and situational information available to speakers and addressees. Language does not function in isolation: it is an integrated part of a living human (psychological and social) reality.

(Q5) *How do children acquire a natural language?*
The question of language acquisition has been hotly debated ever since language was considered as an object of scientific inquiry. The basic parameters of the discussion are the same now as they were centuries ago. They concern the ratio between the innate genetic factors and the social environmental factors which may be held responsible for the child's ability to acquire a natural language. Within the framework of the formal paradigm, Chomskyans have taken an extreme nativist standpoint in this matter. This is understandable, for when language is dissected from the natural social environment in which it is used and acquired, any form of language learning becomes a mystery, which can only be understood by assuming that language has been there all the time in the form of a genetically preprogrammed structure of the human mind.

From a functional point of view, on the other hand, it is certainly much more attractive to study the acquisition of language as it develops in communicative interaction between the maturing child and its environment, and to attribute to genetic factors only those underlying principles which cannot be explained as acquired in this interaction. Students of language acquisition who approach the problem from an environmental point of view have shown that the process of language acquisition is strongly codetermined by a highly structured input of linguistic data, presented to the child in natural settings, and adapted to its gradually developing level of communicative competence.

Note that a functional view of language does not preclude the existence of genetic factors guiding or facilitating the acquisition of a language. After all, natural language is a species-specific phenomenon. Such genetic factors, however, will be regarded as a last resort, to fall back upon when all other attempts at explaining the linguistic facts have failed (compare Hawkins 1983: 8).

(Q6) *How can language universals be explained?*
About the question why it is that natural languages have universal properties, similar things can be said. When languages are cut loose from their communicative purposes, the question naturally arises why they should have any common properties at all. After all, any arbitrary system would be just as good as any other. Again, in the functional approach to language one should like to be able to understand the pervasive common properties of languages in terms of the external factors which determine their nature. Any natural language can be considered as a particular solution to an extremely complex problem. As with any problem, the possible "space" for arriving at viable solutions is constrained by (i) the nature of the problem itself, (ii) the nature of the problem-solver, and (iii) the circumstances in which the problem must be solved. In the case of natural languages, these three factors can be specified as: (i) the establishment of high-level communicative relationships between human beings, (ii) the biological and psychological properties of natural language users, (iii) the settings and circumstances in which languages are used for communicative purposes.[5]

(Q7) *What is the relation between pragmatics, semantics, and syntax?*
It will now be evident that in the functional paradigm the relation between the different components of linguistic organization is viewed in such a way that

---

5. For a further development of this view, see Dik (1986).

8 Methodological preliminaries

pragmatics is seen as the all-encompassing framework within which semantics and syntax must be studied. Semantics is regarded as instrumental with respect to pragmatics, and syntax as instrumental with respect to semantics. In this view there is no room for something like an "autonomous" syntax. On the contrary, to the extent that a clear division can be made between syntax and semantics at all, syntax is there for people to be able to form complex expressions for conveying complex meanings, and such meanings are there for people to be able to communicate in subtle and differentiated ways.

The answers given to the seven questions posed above together constitute what I understand by the functional paradigm. This paradigm defines the basic philosophy which underlies FG. Each of the points mentioned would merit more detailed discussion. However, this work is to be a monograph on the theory of grammar rather than a treatise in linguistic philosophy. I therefore restrict myself here to the few remarks made, assuming that they sufficiently define the "key" to an understanding of the philosophical background of FG.

1.3. Some aspects of verbal interaction

1.3.1. A model of verbal interaction

So far I have used the term "verbal interaction" as if it were self-explanatory. This is not, of course, the case. I will therefore try to clarify some crucial aspects of what I understand by verbal interaction by means of Figure 1.

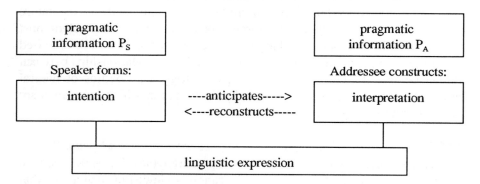

Figure 1. A model of verbal interaction

At any stage of verbal interaction both S and A possess a huge amount of pragmatic information, P_S and P_A, respectively. In saying something to A, S's intention is to effect a modification in P_A. In order to achieve this, S must form a communicative intention, a mental plan concerning the particular modification that he wishes to bring about in P_A. S's problem is to formulate his intention in such a way that he has a reasonable chance of leading A to the desired modification of his pragmatic information. S will therefore try to anticipate the interpretation that A is likely to assign to his linguistic expression, given the current state of P_A. This anticipation on the part of S thus requires that S should have a reasonable picture of the relevant parts of P_A. In other words, an estimate of P_A is part of P_S, a point to which I return in section 1.3.3.

A, on the other hand, interprets S's linguistic expression in the light of P_A and of his estimate of P_S, and thus tries to arrive at a reconstruction of S's presumed communicative intention. The interpretation arrived at may lead A to bring about that modification in P_A which corresponds to S's communicative intention.

If A does not arrive at an interpretation which has a reasonable match with S's communicative intention, there will be a misunderstanding between S and A. Many misunderstandings go unnoticed in everyday life. But when a misunderstanding concerns a point which is crucial to the further development of the interaction, it may be detected and resolved through further metacommunicative discussion between A and S about the nature of S's communicative intentions. Obviously, the roles of S and A switch whenever there is a change of turns.

It is important to stress that the relation between S-intention and A-interpretation is mediated, not established through the linguistic expression. From the point of view of A this means that the interpretation will only in part be based on the information which is contained in the linguistic expression as such. Equally important is the information which A already has, and in terms of which he interprets the linguistic information. From the point of view of S it means that the linguistic expression need not be a full verbalization of his intention. Given the information which S has about the information that A has at the moment of speaking, a partial verbalization will normally be sufficient. Often a roundabout verbalization may even be more effective than a direct expression of the intention.

Thus, the linguistic expression is a function of S's intention, his pragmatic information, and his anticipation of A's interpretation, while A's interpretation is a function of the linguistic expression, A's pragmatic information, and his conjecture about what may have been S's communicative intention.

1.3.2. The structure of pragmatic information

By pragmatic information I mean the full body of knowledge, beliefs, assumptions, opinions, and feelings available to an individual at any point in the interaction. It should be stressed that the term "information" is not meant to be restricted to cognitive knowledge, but includes any possible item which is somehow present in the mental world of individuals, including their preconceptions and prejudices. Pragmatic information can be divided into three main components:

(i) *general information*: long-term information concerning the world, its natural and cultural features, and other possible or imaginary worlds;

(ii) *situational information*: information derived from what the participants perceive or otherwise experience in the situation in which the interaction takes place;

(iii) *contextual information*: information derived from the linguistic expressions which are exchanged before or after any given point in the verbal interaction.

The pragmatic information of S and A will normally have a great deal in common (the *common* or *shared information*), but there will also be information which is only available to S, or only to A. The actual point of verbal interaction is typically located in this non-shared information; however, this point can be identified only against the background of the shared information.

We can now say that the primary function of verbal interaction is for S to effect changes in the pragmatic information of A. These changes may be *additions*, as when S provides A with some piece of information that A did not possess before; *substitutions*, as when S informs A that a certain piece of information should be replaced by some other piece of information; or *reminders*, when S makes A aware of some piece of information which A did possess before, but of which he was not aware at the moment in question. S may also intend to mainly effect a change in A's emotional information, as when he attempts to change A's presumed feelings about something.

1.3.3. Mutual knowledge

The pragmatic information of S will include a theory about the pragmatic information of A, and conversely: each participant usually has a rather structured and detailed idea about the other's properties, and this theory of the other plays an essential role in verbal interaction. As we saw in 1.3.1., it allows S to anticipate the possible interpretations of his expressions by A, and A to reconstruct the most likely communicative intention of S. This mutual relationship between S and A can be symbolized as in Figure 2. It is clear that the mutual relationship diagrammed in Figure 2 defines a structure of boxes within boxes within .. boxes: there is a theoretically infinite recursion as in (1):

(1) $(P_A)_S$ what S thinks about the pragmatic information of A[6]
     $((P_A)_S)_A$ what A thinks about what S thinks about the pragmatic information of A
     $(((P_A)_S)_A)_S$ what S thinks about what A thinks about what S thinks about A's pragmatic information

Some of the earlier steps in this recursion are of real importance for verbal interaction. For example, what I think you think about what I know can be very important if I want to get you to disclose some information which you would prefer to keep secret. But after a few steps in the recursion, further steps only have theoretical significance.

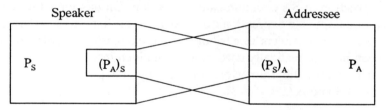

Figure 2. Mutual knowledge of S and A

Since participants have a theory about the pragmatic information of the other, they can also estimate what is shared and what is not shared between their own and the other's pragmatic information. This estimate of shared and non-shared information is of obvious importance for the success of verbal interaction. One rather common strategy is for S to start from estimated shared information, and to proceed from there to estimated non-shared information in order to have this added to, or substituted for, pieces of A's pragmatic information. This strategy, which has been termed the "Given-New Contract" in psycholinguistic work (Clark—Clark 1977), also has its impact on the pragmatically relevant structuring of linguistic expressions.

---

6. Brown (1984) aptly calls $(P_A)_S$ "the image of P_A in P_S".

1.3.4. Intention, meaning, and interpretation

In terms of the model of verbal interaction sketched in Figure 1, I shall reserve the term *meaning* (or *semantic content*) for the information which is in some way or other coded in the linguistic expression as such. Thus, semantic content is a feature determined by the language system, to be accounted for in the grammar of a language. Semantic content, however, is not identical to the initial communicative intention of S (which is only mediated by the linguistic expression), nor to the final interpretation arrived at by A (since A uses much more information than is coded in the expression as such). We may speak of a "scale of explicitness" of expression, in this sense that a communicative intention is coded in a relatively explicit manner when there is little difference between that intention and the semantic content of the expression, and in a relatively implicit manner when there is a great deal of difference between the intention and the semantic content. In terms of this scale of explicitness we must say that much of everyday verbal interaction is relatively implicit, and that much is left to the interpretive activity of A in order for him to arrive at a reconstruction of S's communicative intention. On this view the semantic content of a linguistic expression can be defined as that information which it is necessary and sufficient to attribute to that expression in order to explain how it can be systematically used in relating given intentions to given interpretations, within the framework defined by the pragmatic information available to S and A.[7]

1.4. Standards of adequacy

The aim of the theory of FG is to provide the means and principles by which functional grammars of particular languages can be developed. And the highest aim of a functional grammar of a particular language is to give a complete and adequate account of the grammatical organization of connected discourse in that language. Such a grammar should be able to specify all the linguistic expressions of a language by means of a system of rules and principles in which the most significant generalizations about the language are incorporated. Thus, a functional grammar should conform to the standards of adequacy (in particular, descriptive adequacy) such as have been formulated

---

7. The essential difference between semantic content and final interpretation was an important point in the teaching of Anton Reichling. See Reichling (1963).

for transformational grammars by Chomsky (e.g., 1965).

Given the different paradigm from which FG is conceived, however, we may expect differences with respect to what has been called "explanatory adequacy", i.e., with respect to the criteria which would allow us to determine which one of two or more descriptively adequate grammars would have to be preferred.

In this light, the following standards of adequacy are of particular importance for the theory of FG.

1.4.1. Pragmatic adequacy

We saw above that a functional grammar must be conceptualized as being embedded within a wider pragmatic theory of verbal interaction. Ultimately, it would have to be capable of being integrated into a model of NLU. We shall say that the degree of *pragmatic adequacy* of a functional grammar is higher to the extent that it fits in more easily with such a wider, pragmatic theory. In particular, we want a functional grammar to reveal those properties of linguistic expressions which are relevant to the manner in which they are used, and to do this in such a way that these properties can be related to the rules and principles governing verbal interaction. This means that we must not think of linguistic expressions as isolated objects, but as instruments which are used by a Speaker in order to evoke some intended interpretation in the Addressee, within a context defined by preceding expressions, and within a setting defined by the essential parameters of the speech situation.

1.4.2. Psychological adequacy

A grammar which strives to attain pragmatic adequacy in the sense described above is a grammar which is relevant to Ss and As, not a formal object cut loose from its users. It follows that such a grammar must also aim at *psychological adequacy*, in the sense that it must relate as closely as possible to psychological models of linguistic competence and linguistic behaviour. Psychological models naturally split up into production models and comprehension models. Production models define how Ss go about constructing and formulating linguistic expressions; comprehension models specify how As go about processing and interpreting linguistic expressions. A functional grammar which wishes to attain pragmatic and psychological adequacy should in some way reflect this production / comprehension dichotomy. This can be achieved by conceptualizing a grammar as a tripartite construct, consisting of (a) a production model (a generator in computational terms), (b) an interpretation model (a parser), and (c) a store of elements and principles used in both (a) and (b). A grammar taking such a form would be easier to integrate into models which are meant to simulate the linguistic behaviour of NLUs, and easier to evaluate through psychological testing methods or computational modelling.

Seen in this light, FG as presented in this work more closely approximates a production model than an interpretation model. The presentation follows a productive mode, laying out recipes for construing linguistic expressions from their basic building blocks. In order to attain psychological adequacy in the naturalistic sense intended here, the productive mode should be supplemented with an interpretive mode, consisting of rules and principles for arriving at an analysis and interpretation of given linguistic expressions.[8]

In the ProfGlot model (Dik 1992) it has been demonstrated how this view can be implemented by computational means. In particular, ProfGlot demonstrates how a parser can reconstruct the underlying structure of the clause by using the information contained in the input sentences on the one hand, and the contents of the lexicon and the rules of the FG generator on the other.

1.4.3. Typological adequacy

A third requirement to be imposed on the theory of FG (in fact, on any theory of language) is that it should be *typologically adequate*, i.e., that it should be capable of providing grammars for languages of any type, while at the same time accounting in a systematic way for the similarities and differences between these languages.

The requirement of typological adequacy obviously entails that the theory should be developed on the basis of facts from a wide variety of languages,

---

8. For discussion of such a tripartite model, see Des Tombe (1976). For its implications for a functional analysis of language change, Bossuyt (1983). Compare also Clark—Clark (1977) for a discussion of the various productive and analytic modules involved in the use of language. De Schutter—Nuyts (1983) and Nuyts (1988) have rightly called attention to the necessity of arriving at a "procedural" interpretation of FG.

and that its hypotheses should be tested on facts from yet further languages.

Through some unfortunate whim of the history of linguistics, theorists of language often pretend that they can restrict their attention to one or at most a few languages, while typologists of language often approach their research problems in a theory-neutral, quasi-inductive fashion. From the point of view of the requirement of typological adequacy, this state of affairs is rather counterproductive. Except in the heuristic "natural history" stage, typological work is mainly of interest if it is guided by theory-generated research questions. On the other hand, linguistic theory is of interest only to the extent that it reveals rules and principles which have potential crosslinguistic applicability.

1.4.4. The relations between the standards

At first sight, the standard of typological adequacy has little connection with the other two standards: pragmatic and psychological adequacy concern the degree to which the theory approximates a component of M.NLU; typological adequacy deals with the applicability of the theory to languages of diverse types. However, we can bridge this apparent gap if we consider that a typologically adequate theory reveals the most fundamental recurrent properties of natural languages, properties which have sedimented into the systems of languages through centuries of intensive use in verbal interaction. It is a reasonable working hypothesis, then, that those principles which are most generally characteristic of natural languages are at the same time the principles which have the most fundamental psychological and pragmatic significance. Through the intermediary of linguistic theory, then, typological research may be of ultimate relevance to psychology, just as psychological research may be relevant for the correct interpretation and explanation of the typological facts.

1.5. Abstractness, concreteness, and applicability

FG intends to be a general, typologically adequate theory of the grammatical organization of natural languages. If this intention is to be fulfilled, its rules and principles must be formulated at a sufficient level of abstraction to be applicable to any language, whatever its typological status. Wherever certain linguistic facts are such that they cannot naturally be handled by means of the principles of FG, it is the theory, not the language in question, which will have to be adapted.

In order to be applicable to languages of any arbitrary type, the theory must have a certain degree of abstractness. But in order to be practically applicable in the description of languages, the theory must be as concrete as possible: it must stay as close as possible to the linguistic facts as they present themselves in any language. This apparent paradox may also be formulated as follows: FG should strive for the lowest level of abstractness which is still compatible with the goal of typological adequacy. By "abstractness" I mean the distance (as measured in terms of rules and operations to be applied) between the actual linguistic expressions of a language on the one hand, and the underlying structures in terms of which these expressions are analysed on the other. Abstractness and typological adequacy interrelate in the following way: when the theory is too concrete in the description of particular languages, the notions used cannot be transferred to the description of other languages, and thus fall short of achieving typological adequacy. But when the theory is too abstract (= more abstract than is required for typological adequacy), it overshoots its mark of defining the most significant generalizations across languages, and thus loses in empirical import: it does not tell us very much about languages anymore.

Let us illustrate the abstractness issue with one rather simple example. Consider definiteness: in a language like English, definiteness is often expressed in the definite article *the*, as in *the house*. But proper names and personal pronouns are just as definite without carrying the definite article. And in languages such as Danish, definiteness may be coded in a suffix rather than in a definite article, as in *hus-et* 'the house'. Suppose, now, that we analyse the English phrase *the house* as follows:

(2)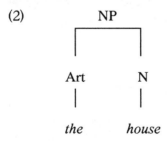

We would then need a quite different analysis for the definiteness intrinsic in proper nouns and pronouns, and another analysis again for the suffixal expression of definiteness, as in Danish. It will then be very difficult to generalize about definiteness, both within and across languages. The reason for this is that the notion "definite article" is too concrete, too close to the actual expression, to yield a typologically adequate account of definiteness. For this reason, FG uses a more abstract definiteness operator (d), which on the one hand captures the essential property common to all definite noun phrases, while at the same time allowing for different forms of expression, as in:

(3)　　English:　d [*house*]　　==> *the house*
　　　　　　　　d [*John*]　　==> ∅ *John*
　　　　Danish:　d [*hus-*]　　==> *hus-et*

We can then say that these various terms are alike in having the underlying definiteness operator, while differing in the way in which this operator is expressed. The differences are attributed to the different systems of expression rules which languages use to map underlying structures onto actual linguistic expressions.

1.6. Take languages seriously

There was a strong tendency in formal logic at the beginning of this century to regard natural languages as obscuring rather than revealing their true semantic or logical significance. The "logical form" of linguistic expressions was in many cases judged to be quite different from their grammatical form, and for this reason natural languages were regarded as unfit for the purposes of logical reasoning. The task of the logician was to define abstract formal languages, free from all the presumed obscurities and ambiguities of natural languages, in which the structure of logical reasoning could more adequately be reconstructed.

Unfortunately, this tradition of formal logic was not without influence on the theory of transformational grammar, especially in its initial phase, when the central thesis was that the deep structure of linguistic expressions was in crucial cases quite different from their surface structure. In the early seventies, many studies appeared with arguments to the effect that "X is really Y", trying to demonstrate that what at first sight looked like X (where X could be a category or a construction) was in fact only the outward manifestation of some "deeper" category or construction Y. Thus, there were arguments that "pronouns were really noun phrases", "articles were really pronouns", "quantifiers were really predicates", etc.

This idea, according to which languages are often not what they seem to be, easily leads to a non-empirical attitude towards linguistic analysis. Once it is assumed that languages often conceal rather than reveal their true underlying organization, one does not have to take actual surface structures very seriously anymore, and the road is clear for postulating all sorts of rather abstract and non-obvious analyses. This research strategy proved to be rather counterproductive. Time and again, the analyses proposed from this point of view turned out to be untenable. In many cases in which some construction X was supposed to be derivable from some underlying Y, closer inspection showed that X, after all, differed from Y in crucial respects, so that the analysis could not be maintained.

I believe that a simple lesson can be drawn from this situation: take languages seriously. Whenever there is some overt difference between two constructions X and Y, start out on the assumption that this difference has some kind of functionality in the linguistic system. Rather than pressing X into the preconceived mould of Y, try to find out why X and Y are different, on the working assumption that such a difference would not be in the language unless it had some kind of task to perform.

1.7. Constraints on the power of FG

A theory of grammar can fail in two quite different ways: it can be too weak (too concrete), so that it is unable to yield descriptively adequate grammars of particular languages, or it can be too strong (too abstract), in that it defines a class of grammars which widely exceeds the class of actual human languages. In the former case, it does not reach typological adequacy; in the latter, it does not define the notion "possible human language" in any interesting way. In order to avoid the latter danger, the power of the descriptive devices allowed by the theory should be constrained as much as possible. Within FG, this is achieved in three ways, discussed in the sections to follow. The kinds of descriptive devices to be avoided are illustrated by means of analyses which have been proposed at some point in the history of Transformational Grammar. Most of these analyses have later been discarded, and I do not wish to suggest that there is anyone who still endorses them. But the point I wish to make is that within the framework of FG these analyses should be excluded as a matter of principle.

1.7.1. Avoid transformations

FG avoids transformations in the sense of structure-changing operations. Structure-changing operations are operations which effect changes in pre-established structures through deletion, substitution, and permutation of constituents. In general, FG is based on the assumption that once a structure has been built up, this structure will be retained throughout the further derivation of the linguistic expression. In other words, a derivation is a matter of gradual expansion rather than a transformational mapping of one structure onto another. In order to clarify what sorts of operations are avoided in FG, it is useful to be a little more specific about these operations.

(i) *avoid deletion of specified elements*

Example 1. Compare:

(4) a. *I met a boy who was carrying a green uniform.*
     b. *I met a boy carrying a green uniform.*

On the basis of (i), any analysis which first produces (4a) and then derives (4b) by deleting *who was* will be avoided.

Example 2. Compare:

(5) a. *I consider John to be unfit for the job.*
     b. *I consider John unfit for the job.*

On the basis of (i), any analysis which first specifies (5a) and then derives (5b) by deleting *to be* will be avoided.

Example 3. Compare:

(6) a. *This is the book which / that I bought in Paris.*
     b. *This is the book I bought in Paris.*

On the basis of (i), any analysis which derives (6b) from (6a) by deleting *which* or *that* will be avoided.

In all these cases, FG will favour analyses which introduce the relevant elements only where they are required, and leave them out where they do not appear.

(ii) *avoid substitutions of one specified element by another specified element*

Example 1. Compare:

(7) a. *This is the book [I bought the book in Paris]*.
    b. *This is the book which I bought in Paris.*

On the basis of (ii), any analysis is to be avoided in which (7b) is derived from (7a) by substituting *which* for the embedded occurrence of *the book*.

Example 2. Compare:

(8) a. *Neg [I have some books]*.
    b. *I do not have any books.*

On the basis of (ii), one should avoid analyses in which (8b) is derived from (8a) by substituting *any* for *some*.

In these cases FG will try to immediately produce the target expressions in the conditions in which they appear, by-passing any other elements which may not appear in those conditions.

(iii) *avoid permutations of specified elements*

Example 1. Compare:

(9) a. *John doesn't like pancakes.*
    b. *PANCAKES John doesn't like.*

By virtue of (iii), any analysis will be avoided in which the order of constituents is first specified as in (9a), from which (9b) is then derived by moving the object to the initial position in the clause.

Example 2. Compare:

(10) a. *I believe that John is unfit for the job.*
     b. *I believe John to be unfit for the job.*

By virtue of (iii), (10b) will not be derived from (10a) by a rule which moves *John* from one specified position to another.

In cases such as these FG will favour solutions in which the relevant constituents are immediately placed in the position in which they actually occur in the final linguistic expression. In this particular case, this is achieved by not defining a linear order over the "deeper" constituents of the constructions involved, so that these constituents will finally be ASSIGNED A PLACE rather than being MOVED from one specified position to another.

There is one component of the FG model which does require transformations of a sort. This is the component of *predicate formation*. Predicate formation rules serve to derive predicate frames from other predicate frames, thus extending the set of predicate frames available in the lexicon by a set of derived predicate frames, which can then be input to the construction of predications.[9] Some types of predicate formation may effect changes in the categorial status of the input predicate frame, reduce or extend the number of arguments, incorporate arguments into the predicate, or modify the semantic functions of the argument positions of the predicate frame. Such transformations, however, are confined to the "Fund" of FG, the component which contains the set of predicates and the set of terms from which predications can be construed. Derived predicate frames serve to designate States of Affairs which are different from, but systematically related to, the States of Affairs designated by the input predicate frame. For example, if we have a verb of movement in English (*go, walk, run, drive*, etc.), there is a predicate formation rule which authorizes us to productively form modified predicates such as *go away, walk away, run away, drive away*, etc., which designate modified movements systematically related to the movements indicated by the basic predicates. Predicate formation rules thus have semantic import. The various operations which can be performed by predicate formation rules will be discussed in *TFG2*: chapter 1.

1.7.2. Avoid filtering devices

By "filtering devices" I mean descriptive strategies of the following form: with respect to a target set T of expressions to be specified by the grammar, one first specifies a more inclusive set T' (containing T as a proper subset), and then formulates conditions by means of which those expressions of T' which do not belong to T are rejected ("filtered out").

---

9. For the notions "predicate", "predicate frame", and "predication", see chapter 4.

This use of filtering devices leads to counterintuitive types of description, in which the grammar is allowed at some stage to generate structures which are produced only to be discarded later on. The rules underlying such a description cannot, of course, be taken to express significant generalizations about the well-formed expressions of a language.

Methodologically, the use of filtering devices provides excessive freedom for the formulation of grammatical rules, since the undesired output of such rules can always be filtered out later by applying the appropriate conditions. Psychologically, the filtering strategy would imply that NLUs are designed in such a way as to produce an enormous number of construction types which will go to the mental dustbin before they can be uttered. In crucial cases, the set of these misfires is even potentially infinite. Where this is the case, the use of filtering devices implies that the grammar fails to define an effective procedure for construing well-formed linguistic expressions.

One example of this type of filtering is the TG description of relative constructions as proposed in Chomsky (1965). This description assumed underlying structures of the following form:

(11)   This is the book [*I bought* Wh *the book in Paris*].

in which the embedded occurrence of *the book* was to be deleted under identity with the corresponding NP in the matrix clause. In that theory, however, the embedded sentence was developed independently of the matrix sentence. This meant, *inter alia*, that there was no guarantee that the embedded sentence was going to contain an occurrence of *the book* at all. In other words, a potentially infinite set of mismatches of the following kind could in principle be produced:

(12)   This is the book [*I bought* Wh *the shirt in Paris*].

All these mismatches were then to be filtered out by the conditions imposed on the relative transformation.

On the basis of the arguments given above, this type of filtering will be avoided in FG wherever possible. For any type of target structure FG will aim at defining rules which immediately generate only the set of well-formed target expressions without producing any "garbage" which will have to be discarded later on.

1.7.3. Avoid abstract semantic predicates

A third way in which the expressive power, and thus the degree of abstractness of FG is constrained lies in the treatment of lexical items. All basic contentive lexemes of a language are contained in the lexicon in the form in which they can actually appear in the expressions of the object language. This distinguishes FG from such approaches as Generative Semantics, in which underlying structures of the following form were postulated:

(13) $kill(x)(y) = \text{CAUSE}(x)(\text{BECOME}(\text{NOT}(\text{ALIVE}(y))))$

In such underlying structures the elements printed in capitals were judged to be drawn from a language-independent set of abstract semantic predicates. Such abstract predicates are avoided in FG, mainly because, once they are accepted, there is hardly any limit to the analyses which can be argued to underlie lexical elements. How one can nevertheless define the meaning of a predicate without using an abstract semantic vocabulary will be discussed in chapter 4 below.

The avoidance of an abstract vocabulary in the lexical domain does not apply to the grammatical domain of a language. In fact, most grammatical operations are captured in FG by means of abstract grammatical operators, functions, etc. Even abstract predicates may be recognized within the grammatical domain. But the dangers of accepting abstract predicates in that domain are much less serious than in the lexical domain. Since the grammatical domain is closed or finite as opposed to the lexical domain, there is no danger of an abstract analysis of the grammatical domain leading to an open-ended, more or less limitless, and thus ineffective linguistic description.

1.7.4. Motivating these constraints

Imposing the constraints discussed in the preceding sections on a theory of grammar can be motivated from several different points of view:

Methodologically, they impose limitations on the space within which the grammarian can set up his hypotheses concerning the structures underlying linguistic expressions.

Psychologically, they keep these underlying structures recoverable from their outward manifestations, and thus help us understand why it is at all possible for NLUs to produce and interpret linguistic expressions.

Computationally, they provide a basis for designing effective procedures for generating and parsing linguistic expressions.[10]

Obviously, it is an empirical question whether adequate grammars can be designed which obey all these constraints under all circumstances. In this area, however, it is better to fail through weakness than to fail through excessive strength.

---

10. The latter point is demonstrated in Janssen (1989).

2. Some basic concepts of linguistic theory

2.0. Introduction

In this chapter I introduce a number of basic concepts of linguistic theory which will prove to be important tools for FG as it develops through this work. Section 2.1. stresses the importance of functional as against categorial notions in the fabric of FG; 2.2. introduces the various types of universals which go into the making of a typologically adequate theory of language; 2.3. presents the concept of the typological "hierarchy", and the various phenomena connected with it; 2.4. discusses various kinds of "priority" which may affect the build-up of grammatical constructions; and 2.5. defines the notion of "markedness", as used in this work, and introduces the concept of "markedness shift", the modification of markedness relations across time.

2.1. The importance of functional notions

In the fabric of FG pride of place is given to functional or relational as opposed to categorial notions. Let us briefly note the basic differences between functions and categories. Compare the following two statements:

(1) a. *the old man* is a noun phrase.
    b. *the old man* is a subject.

Statement (1a) makes sense as it stands. A metalinguistic predicate such as "being a noun phrase" tells us something about the intrinsic properties of constituents, and can thus be predicated of such constituents considered in isolation. Once a noun phrase, always a noun phrase: categories such as "noun phrase" are non-relational notions.

Statement (1b), on the other hand, does not make sense as it stands. This is because "being a subject" is not a one-place predicate, but a two-place (relational) predicate telling us something about the relation between some constituent and the construction in which it occurs. Thus, it does make sense to say:

(2)   *the old man* is subject of *the old man ran away*.

On the other hand, it does not make sense to use a categorial expression in such a two-place statement:

(3)   *the old man* is a noun phrase in *the old man ran away*.

since the construction in which *the old man* occurs is irrelevant to its categorial status.

Generalizing from this we can say that categorial statements specify intrinsic properties of constituents, while functional statements specify the relations of constituents to the constructions in which they occur.

Linguistic expressions are complex networks, characterized by functional relations operative at different levels. Functions of different types are a powerful means for capturing these relations. Functions are also needed (alongside categories) because functions and categories do not stand in a one-to-one relation to each other. The same category may occur in different functions, and the same function may apply to constituents with different categorial properties.[1] FG recognizes functional relations at three different levels.

(i) *Semantic functions* (Agent, Goal, Recipient, etc.) specify the roles which the referents of the terms involved play within the State of Affairs designated by the predication in which these terms occur.

(ii) *Syntactic functions* (Subject and Object) specify the perspective from which a State of Affairs is presented in a linguistic expression.

(iii) *Pragmatic functions* (Theme, Topic, Focus, etc.) specify the informational status of a constituent within the wider communicative setting in which it occurs (that is, in relation to the pragmatic information of S and A at the moment of use).

From these rough definitions, which will be refined in later chapters, it will be clear why the terms "semantic" and "pragmatic" functions are used. The label "syntactic functions" is retained mainly in order to avoid unnecessary departure from traditional terminology: the concepts of Subject and Object are used to capture such oppositions as that between active and passive constructions, and these oppositions are usually described in terms of syntactic or

---

1. For this reason, functions cannot be reduced to (configurations of) categories. This was attempted both in structural linguistics and transformational grammar, in which categories were somehow regarded as more tractable, more reliable than functions. I believe this is simply another manifestation of the formalist conception of language underlying these theories.

grammatical relations. However, the notions Subject and Object as used in FG will undergo a reinterpretation in such a way that they will be regarded as making their own contribution to the semantics of the expression, a contribution consisting in defining different perspectives over the State of Affairs designated by the predication. For that reason, "perspectival functions" might be a better term to cover their essential nature.

As will be made clear in later chapters, there is reason to believe that semantic and pragmatic functions are universally relevant to natural languages, although not all languages necessarily make the same distinctions within the general domain of these functions. Syntactic functions, however, are not universal in this sense. There are many languages which can (and must) be described without making use of the functions Subject and Object. Nevertheless, these functions have universal properties in the sense that, once a language makes use of these functions at all, it will do so according to recurrent patterns which can be captured by language-independent principles. Thus, a general theory of syntactic functions is possible, although not all languages possess these functions.

The three types of function distinguished in FG determine crucial aspects of both the content and the form of linguistic expressions, and play a role in many of the rules which specify the formal and semantic properties of these expressions.

2.2. Linguistic universals

Linguistic universals are statements pertaining to the full set of natural languages. They embody hypotheses about universal properties of human languages. Since Greenberg (1963) four main types of universal have been distinguished, as indicated in Table 1.

Table 1. Four types of universals

	unconditional	implicational
absolute	Type A	Type C
statistical	Type B	Type D

28   *Some basic concepts*

Type A: *absolute unconditional universals* are statements of the form:

(4) a. All languages have property P.
    b. In all languages we find elements/rules of type Q.

Examples of type A universals would be such statements as:

(5) a. All languages distinguish vowels and consonants.
    b. All languages have yes/no questions.

Note that any linguistic universal is a hypothesis which must be tested against the full set of languages. In such testing we may find counterexamples by which the universal is falsified. The hypothesis will then have to be modified, supplemented by an auxiliary hypothesis, or rejected.

Type B: *statistical unconditional universals* are statements of the form:

(6) a. Almost all languages have property P.
    b. We find property P in n % of all languages.
        (where n deviates significantly from what could be expected on the basis of random distribution).

The following would be an example of such a universal:

(7)   99% of all languages have two or more distinct vowels.

It will be clear that statistical universals are more significant to the extent that they deviate more markedly from what could be expected on the basis of random distribution. Thus, statement (7), though not absolutely valid, does have a very high degree of significance. The at first sight contradictory notion of "statistical universal" may also be understood as implying that linguistic universals may have exceptions; the more exceptions, the less significant the principle.

Type C: *absolute implicational universals* take the following form:

(8) a. For all languages, if a language has P, then it also has Q.
    b. No language has P without having Q.

Such implicational universals capture a universally valid relation between P and Q. Note that they do not claim that all languages have P, nor that they all have Q; but if they have P, then they also have Q. To the extent that the hypothesis embodied in the universal is correct, we can predict the presence of Q from the presence of P. We can also say that this kind of implicational universal excludes languages with P but without Q, while allowing for all other logical possibilities with respect to the occurrence of P and Q:[2]

(9) P Q
     + + yes
     − − yes
     − + yes
     + − no

Since Q may occur without P but not P without Q, Q is a necessary condition for the occurrence of P, and in that sense is the more basic property of the two. For a concrete example of an absolute implicational universal, consider:

(10) If a language has the phoneme /m/, it also has the phoneme /n/.
(11) /m/ /n/
     +   +   yes
     −   −   yes
     −   +   yes
     +   −   no

To the extent that (10) is correct, we can predict the presence of /n/ from the presence of /m/; since /n/ may occur without /m/, but /m/ not without /n/, the /n/ is the more basic or fundamental nasal phoneme of the two.

Type D: *statistical implicational universals* are statements of the form of (10) for which no absolute validity is claimed to hold, but only a certain degree of statistical validity. They are thus tendencies bearing on the co-occurrence relations between different properties P and Q.

In the actual practice of typological research, many of the most interesting hypotheses take the form of statistical implicational universals, for which we will also use the term "tendency". Since this type of universal necessarily leaves a number of cases unaccounted for, their existence should be taken as

---

2. See the explanation in Comrie (1981).

a challenge to the linguist to find complementary principles accounting for these counterexamples to the initial universal. The interaction of the principles captured by the resulting set of universals should then account for all the cases under investigation. An illustration of this interaction between principles can be found in chapters 16 and 17, in which the various principles governing word order patterns are discussed.

2.3. Hierarchies

In certain interesting cases, implicational universals can be ordered in sequences. Consider the following pair:

(12) a.   If a language has P, then it also has Q.
     b.   If a language has Q, then it also has R.

Such universals can be ordered in a series of the following form:

(13)   P → Q → R

Thus, when we find P, we can predict Q, and from Q we can predict R. For a concrete example, consider:

(14) a.   If /ñ/, then also /m/.
     b.   If /m/, then also /n/.

(15)   /ñ/ → /m/ → /n/

Note that R in (13) (or /n/ in (15)) is to be regarded as the most fundamental property of the three: R may occur without Q or P, but the latter may not occur without R. For this reason, sequences such as (13) and (15) are often represented in the following format:

(16)   R > Q > P

(17)   /n/ > /m/ > /ñ/

where > can be interpreted as "is more central than", "is less conditioned than", "is more often to be found in a language than".
  Such sequences as (16) and (17) are called "hierarchies". A hierarchy is

thus a sequence of properties, claimed to be of absolute or statistical validity, such that a preceding property can occur without the following properties, but not the other way around.

One of the first significant hierarchies discovered in linguistic typology concerns the distribution of colour terms across languages. In a study of a great many languages, Berlin—Kay (1969) established the following hierarchy:

(18)   black >   red >   green > blue >   brown > purple
        white   yellow   pink
                                                       orange
                                                       grey

This hierarchy was further specified in the following rules:

(i) all languages have colour terms for 'black' and 'white' or 'dark' and 'light';

(ii) if a language has a colour term later in (18), it also has all the preceding colour terms;

(iii) no language has more than the eleven basic colour terms listed in (18).[3]

Hierarchies such as (18) epitomize in compact form the typological organization of a certain subdomain of the language system. They are powerful tools for capturing the underlying crosslinguistic pattern, while at the same time providing a systematic specification of how languages may differ from each other in the relevant subdomain. Hierarchies of this type have a number of important corollaries which can be briefly described as follows:

(i) *Possible language systems*. Hierarchies predict which language systems are possible and which are impossible with respect to the subdomain in question. For example, (18) predicts the following:

(19) a. possible:
         a language with only *black, white, red, green, yellow, blue*
     b. impossible:
         a language with only *red, blue, brown, pink*

---

3. Note that these rules concern basic (i.e. non-compound, non-derived, non-borrowed) colour terms of a language.

(ii) *Continuity*. If the hierarchy is correct, then a language can only have a continuous initial subsequence of the items specified in it. This allows us to predict the presence of earlier items from the presence of later items. For example, on finding a colour term for 'green' in a language, (18) allows us to also assume that terms for 'black', 'white', 'red', and possibly 'yellow' will occur in the language.

(iii) *Cut-off point*. We can easily characterize a language in relation to a given hierarchy by specifying up to what point that language proceeds in the hierarchy. The end-point in the hierarchy for a given language is called the "cut-off point" for that language. For example, if the term for 'blue' is the last basic colour term that a language has, then the cut-off point for that language in (18) is between the terms for 'blue' and 'brown'.

(iv) *Language change*. Hierarchies predict possible and impossible diachronic developments with respect to the properties involved. If the hierarchy is correct, the only possible changes are those through which the cut-off point either recedes or proceeds in the hierarchy. For example, if the cut-off point for a given language with respect to (18) is between 'blue' and 'brown', then the following two changes are the only possible ones: (a) the language acquires a basic colour term for 'brown'; (b) it loses its basic colour term for 'blue'. Any other change would lead to a language state which would be incompatible with (18). Hierarchies can thus also be seen as constraints on language change.

(v) *Linguistic insecurity*. Since the cut-off point defines the limit of the applicability of a hierarchy to a given language, as well as the pivot of linguistic change, we may expect a certain degree of linguistic insecurity around the cut-off point: there may be hesitations and varied judgments concerning the acceptability of items or constructions which just precede or just follow the cut-off point.

(vi) *Dialectal differences*. From points (iv) and (v) it follows that we may expect dialectal and idiolectal differences concerning the items which just precede or just follow the cut-off point.

(vii) *Frequency of occurrence*. Hierarchies are connected with two kinds of frequency distribution. First, they define differences of frequency of occurrence of the items involved across languages (typological frequency). For example, hierarchy (18) predicts that there are more languages with a basic colour term for 'red' than languages with a basic colour term for 'blue', etc. In general, given any hierarchy of this type, the typological frequency of the phenomena involved will decrease as we proceed through the hierarchy from beginning to end.

Second, hierarchies may also correlate with frequency differences of the relevant items within one and the same language. This means that even those items which do occur in a language (= the items preceding the cut-off point for that language in the hierarchy) will be used less and less frequently as we proceed through the hierarchy from left to right. For example, the frequency distribution of the eleven colour terms of (18) in Dutch is as follows:[4]

(20) 1. zwart   135   'black'
          wit   140   'white'
      2. rood   112   'red'
      3. groen   66   'green'
          geel   33   'yellow'
      4. blauw   53   'blue'
      5. bruin   40   'brown'
      6. grijs   50   'grey'
          oranje   16   'orange'
          paars   13   'purple'
          rose   13   'pink'

We see from (20) that by and large the frequency of the colour terms decreases through the hierarchy. This suggests a functional explanation for the existence of hierarchies of this type: the more frequent the need for referring to some colour, the higher the chance that there will be a separate lexical item for indicating that colour. Languages then differ as to the point up to which they afford themselves the "luxury" of having a special lexical item or construction type for the relevant lower-frequency positions in the hierarchy.

To the extent that the correlation between typological hierarchies and language-internal frequency distribution holds, it offers the interesting possibility of setting up potential typological hierarchies on the basis of language-internal frequency counts. Suppose, for example, that we were to find that (21a) is more frequent in English than (21b):

(21) a. *It is this man who bought the book.*
     b. *It is this book that the man bought.*

We could then tentatively set up the following hierarchy:

---

4. The figures represent absolute token occurrences of the colour terms in the Dutch corpus of 720,000 words compiled by Uit den Boogaart (1975).

34 *Some basic concepts*

(22)   Clefting of Subject > Clefting of Object

and hypothesize that there are languages which have their cut-off point after the first position in the hierarchy (i.e., languages in which constructions corresponding to (21b) are impossible), but no languages which do have Clefting of Object without having Clefting of Subject.

2.4. Priorities

2.4.1. Hierarchies and priorities

Hierarchies such as those discussed in 2.3. may also be described in terms of "priorities". For example, if (18) is correct, then having a basic colour term for 'black' has priority over having a basic colour term for 'blue'. And if (21) turns out to be correct, then the Subject has priority over the Object with respect to Clefting. There is evidence that a number of such priorities are operative both within and across languages. Sometimes such priorities can be described in terms of a kind of traffic rules by virtue of which certain items have priority over other items. Consider the following concrete example. Navajo has an opposition between two constructions somewhat similar to the active/passive opposition. The constructions in question are sometimes called the "direct" and the "inverse" constructions. Compare the following examples (from Platero 1974: 209):

(23) a.   hastiin   asdzáán   yi-zts'os.
          man   woman   dir-3:perf:3:kiss
          'The man kissed the woman.'
     b.   asdzáán   hastiin   bi-zts'os.
          woman   man   inv-3:perf:3:kiss
          'The woman was kissed by the man.'

Note that the verb is marked by *yi-* for 'direct', and by *bi-* for 'inverse'. For the pair of arguments 'man' / 'woman' we can have either construction. But if we took the pair 'man' / 'dog', as in 'The man saw the dog', then only the direct construction would be possible. On the other hand, for the pair 'dog' / 'man', as in 'The dog saw the man', only the inverse construction can be used (as if the only way to express this were 'The man was seen by the dog'). Thus, for any relation between 'man' and 'dog' to be expressed in constructions of type (23), 'man' will appear before 'dog'. This is only one instance of a more general priority hierarchy which monitors the choice of the direct versus the inverse construction type. This hierarchy can be represented as follows (cf. Hale 1973, Platero 1974):

(24)   human > other animate > inanimate force > other inanimate[5]

The priority rules for the choice of the direct and the inverse construction can be formulated as follows:

(25) a. If A > B in (24) and one wishes to express 'A pred B', then the direct construction must be used.
     b. If, in that condition, one wishes to express 'B pred A', then the inverse construction must be used.
     c. Only when A = B in (24), i.e. if A and B take the same position in the hierarchy, can a choice be made between the direct and the inverse construction.

Note that (25c) explains why, in the case of a pair such as 'man' / 'woman', both the direct and the inverse constructions can be used. We can now say that with respect to the choice of the direct / inverse construction in Navajo, 'human' has priority over 'other animate', 'other animate' over 'inanimate force', and 'inanimate force' over 'other inanimate'. We here see the contours of an ontology based on the following "pecking order":

(26)   man > dog > rain > harvest

However, before jumping to conclusions about a "Typical American Indian *Weltanschauung*", it would be good to study the frequency distribution of the corresponding constructions in English. We would then probably find that in each of the following pairs, the a-construction is more frequent than the b-construction:

---

5. "Inanimate force" refers to such entities as 'wind', 'storm', 'rain' etc. Thus, in expressing 'The rain destroyed the harvest', 'rain' has priority over 'harvest', and thus only the direct construction can be used.

(27) a. *The man saw the dog.*
b. *The dog was seen by the man.*
(28) a. *The enemy destroyed the harvest.*
b. *The harvest was destroyed by the enemy.*
(29) a. *The man was bitten by the dog.*
b. *The dog bit the man.*
(30) a. *The enemy was held up by the harvest.*
b. *The harvest held up the enemy.*

If this prediction should turn out to be correct, it would prove, again, that typological constraints which may lead to the exclusion of certain construction types in one language may be reflected in frequency differences in another. We could then conclude that the Animacy Hierarchy displayed in (24) is just as relevant in English as it is in Navajo, but that it affects the frequency of use rather than the (im)possibility of using certain construction types.

From a wide variety of phenomena in quite different languages it emerges that quite a few grammatical processes are monitored or codetermined by priority hierarchies of this kind. I shall here simply list the most important of these hierarchies. Their relevance will come up at various points in the further course of the discussion.[6]

(31) The Person Hierarchy
{1, 2} > 3   or:
Speech Act Participant > Non-Participant

---

6. There is a varied and rather disparate literature on priority hierarchies of this kind. Their relevance was first discovered with respect to the direct/inverse opposition in Amerindian languages (Hale 1973, Platero 1974, Allen—Frantz 1977, 1978). Hawkinson—Hyman (1974) pointed to their relevance for explaining voice phenomena in Bantu languages. Kirsner (1979) and García (1975) demonstrated the relevance of priority hierarchies with respect to frequency distributions of different constructions in Indo-European languages. Silverstein (1976) used priority hierarchies in explaining the phenomenon of "split ergativity", in particular in Australian languages. Kuno (1976) and Kuno—Kaburaki (1977) demonstrated the relevance of priorities for a number of grammatical phenomena in Japanese and English. Ertel (1977) discussed similar phenomena from a psycholinguistic point of view. Allan (1987) and Siewierska (1988) discuss their impact on constituent ordering. Indeed, in many cases the priorities result in linear orders in which the more prominent constituents precede the less prominent ones.

First and second person (the speech act participants) have priority over third person (non-participants); if there is any priority between first and second person, this may now be 1 > 2, now 2 > 1; that seems to be a language-dependent matter.

(32) The Animacy Hierarchy
human > other animate > inanimate force > inanimate

(33) The Gender Hierarchy
Masculine > Feminine > Other

(34) The Definiteness Hierarchy
definite > other specific > non-specific

(35) The Semantic Function Hierarchy
Agent > Goal > Recipient > Beneficiary > Instrument > Location > Time

This hierarchy says, for instance, that Agents have priority over non-Agents. The hierarchy will be discussed in detail in chapter 10.

(36) The Syntactic Function Hierarchy
Subject > Object > terms without Subj / Obj function

(37) The Pragmatic Function Hierarchies
a. Topic > non-Topic
b. Focus > non-Focus

Note that these different hierarchies are not completely independent of one another. For example, since first and second person necessarily refer to human entities, the Person Hierarchy and the Animacy Hierarchy can be conflated into:

(38) The Person / Animacy Hierarchy
{1, 2} > 3 human > animate > inanimate force > other inanimate

And since first and second person are necessarily definite, the Person and Definiteness Hierarchies can be conflated into:

(39) The Person / Definiteness Hierarchy
{1, 2} > 3 definite > other specific > non-specific

2.4.2. An example

An interesting example of the influence of priority hierarchies on grammatical processes was presented in Myhill (1988). Myhill studied the factors which influence the choice between the following alternative constructions in Spanish:

(40) a. *Voy a ver-lo.*
    I-go to see-him
    'I'm going to see him.'
  b. *Lo voy a ver.*
    him I-go to see
    'I'm going to see him.'

In (40a) the clitic *lo*, which is the direct object of *ver* 'see', appears in the position immediately after *ver*; in (40b) the clitic is placed before the main verb *voy*; it has in a sense been raised into the main clause, which explains why the phenomenon is known as "clitic climbing" (CC). One factor which influences CC is the degree of "auxiliarity" of the main verb: the more auxiliary this verb is, the greater the chance that CC will occur. Another factor, however, is the relation between the clitic and the subject of the main verb as regards the following hierarchy:

(41)   2 > 1 > 3 human singular > 3 other

Note that this hierarchy comprises features of Person, Animacy, and Number.[7] The figures in Table 2, which Myhill found in a corpus of a few hundred examples culled from written South-American Spanish texts, display the influence of this hierarchy on Clitic Climbing.

As these figures show, the general rule seems to be that the higher the degree of priority of the clitic over the subject in terms of hierarchy (41), the greater the chance that the CC-construction will be chosen. Note that the

---

7. I have not included the category of Number in the hierarchies given in (31)-(39), because there is a lack of data on the role of Number in the relevant priorities.

figures distribute rather evenly between the two extremes 'You are going to see them' (only 9% chance of CC) and 'They are going to see you' (83% chance of CC). Intuitively, one gets the feeling that the more important the embedded clitic is as compared to the subject of the main verb, the greater the pressure to place it in the more prominent main clause position, where it also "beats" the subject in surface structure prominence.

This raises the question of how the influence of these priorities can be explained.

Table 2. Incidence of Clitic Climbing
in relation to features of Subject and Clitic[8]

↓ Clitic I Subj →	2	1	3humsg	3other
2	—	62%	75%	83%
1	34%	—	52%	56%
3humsg	22%	21%	—	56%
3other	9%	24%	21%	—

2.4.3. On explaining priorities

The various priority hierarchies briefly presented in 2.4. can be used to explain a wide variety of grammatical phenomena in quite divergent languages, as was illustrated in 2.4.1. The hierarchies themselves, however, are also in need of a (higher-order) explanation. Why are these priorities potentially relevant for the application of grammatical rules, as well as for frequency distributions both within and across languages?

Different attempts have been made at explaining the relevance of these hierarchies in terms of underlying pragmatic or psychological principles. Hawkinson—Hyman (1974) have suggested that they reflect the "naturalness" by which some entity is taken as the topic of discourse. Kuno (1976) and Kuno—Kaburaki (1977) explain the priorities in terms of "empathy", by which they understand the relative ease with which a speaker identifies with

---

8. The construction does not occur with coreferential subject and clitic.

a person or thing involved in a given state of affairs. Other linguists point to the "egocentric" nature of linguistic communication: the closer to the speaker an entity is, the more important it is and the higher its degree of priority. It is to be noted, however, that the Speaker does not universally take the most prominent position in the Person Hierarchy (31): in some languages, with respect to certain grammatical processes, the Addressee takes that position, while sometimes S and A, as participants in the speech situation, have *ex aequo* priority with respect to non-participants. In general, then, it is the participants rather than just the Speaker who seem to take the central position in the "pragmatic universe".

I believe that the various factors mentioned above do not necessarily exclude one another, and that each of them highlights a particular feature that contributes to the degree of communicative importance of constituents.

We can say that our cognitive world, as it reveals itself in linguistic communication, is built around a "deictic centre" defined by the basic parameters of the speech situation.[9] These parameters are the participants S and A, the moment of speaking t_0 and the place of speaking l_0. The deictic centre can thus be defined as follows:

(42)   Deictic Centre = $\{S, A, t_0, l_0\}$

From the deictic centre, the pragmatic universe extends in all directions. Some items in that space are closer to the centre, and thus easily accessible; others lie further away and are more difficult to access. Obviously, distance should here be understood in a cognitive sense: that distance is greater to the extent that an item is cognitively less close or familiar to the participants.[10]

Since distance from the deictic centre is a cognitive matter, it will also be culturally and psychologically determined. What is relatively close in one culture may be relatively distant in another; what is relatively familiar to one person may be relatively unfamiliar to another. Distance in pragmatic space is thus a feature of the culturally and psychologically defined cognitive world of natural language users.

That such a cognitive factor as "relative distance in pragmatic space" has worked itself into the conditions which monitor the application of apparently formal morphosyntactic rules is just another instance of the fact that the rules

---

9. For this notion of "deictic centre", see Brown—Yule (1983: 52-53), and Comrie (1985).

10. On this usage of "familiarity" see Allan (1987) and Siewierska (1988).

of grammar are ultimately subservient to pragmatic goals. It is only in a functionally oriented conception of grammar that such facts as these find their natural place.

In grammatical theory the term "accessibility" has been introduced in the sense of a constituent's ability to be subjected to some grammatical rule or process (e.g. in Keenan—Comrie 1977). In *TFG2*: chapter 16 we will discuss the status of such accessibility constraints from the point of view of FG. There it will be argued that there are connections between grammatical and cognitive accessibility in the sense that, to a certain extent, those constituents which are most accessible to grammatical processes are at the same time most accessible in the cognitive sense.

2.5. Markedness

Closely related to the hierarchies and priorities discussed in 2.3. and 2.4. is the concept of "markedness". This concept has come to be used in several different (though not totally unrelated) senses. The term was originally introduced by Jakobson (1936) and Trubetzkoy (1939) to indicate certain relationships within phonological and morphological oppositions. This concept of "markedness in oppositions" will be briefly discussed in section 2.5.2. More recently, the term has also been used to indicate "marked" and "unmarked" construction types, both within and across languages. Let us first consider this usage in more detail.

2.5.1. Marked construction types

A construction type is more marked to the extent that it is less expectable, and therefore commands more attention when it occurs. In general, the less frequent, the more rare a linguistic item is, the higher its markedness value. Let us first illustrate this with the following abstract example:

(43) a. − − − − − − − − − − + − − − − − − −
     b. − − + − − − − + − − − + − + − − + −
     c. − + − − − + + − + − − + + − + − + +
     d. + + + − + + − + + + − + + − + − + +
     e. + + + + + + + + − + + + + + + + + +

42   *Some basic concepts*

In (43a) there is only a single plus in a whole series of minuses. The occurrence of the plus, then, is highly marked (it has a high degree of information value in terms of information theory); in (43b) there is still a higher chance of meeting a minus than a plus: the plus is the marked item, but it is less marked than in (43b). In (43c) there is an equal number of pluses and minuses: neither item is especially marked in relation to the other. In (43d) it is the minus which has a higher degree of markedness, and in (43e), finally, the minus is highly marked. We see, then, that markedness in this sense correlates inversely with frequency of occurrence.

Let us now consider some examples in terms of some of the phenomena discussed in 2.3. and 2.4. Consider first the colour term hierarchy given in (18). We saw that 'black' and 'white' are the most common both within and across languages, whereas 'purple', 'pink', 'orange', and 'grey' are the least frequent. Thus, the occurrence of the former is most unmarked, that of the latter most marked. Saying that something is orange is, in this sense, to command more attention than saying that something is black or white.

Next, consider the example given in section 2.4.2. We saw there that if the subject of the main verb is "third person non-human, non-singular" and the clitic "second person", there is an 83% chance that the clitic will be placed before the main verb. From this it follows that the 17% cases in which this does not occur are rather highly marked constructions; they might lead us to look for special factors which determine why this marked construction rather than the unmarked construction is used. Conversely, when the subject is "first person" and the clitic is "third person, non-human, non-singular", there is only a 9% chance that the clitic will "beat" the subject in terms of prominence in the clause. If this happens, then, the resulting construction will be highly marked.

For a third example, consider the following constituent order phenomena in English and Dutch. In both languages the dominant main clause order is at first sight S Vf X: subject, finite verb, other constituents.[11] In both languages, however, there is a possibility of placing "other constituents" in front of the subject, as in:

(44) a.   *John likes the Odyssey, but* the Iliad *he does not appreciate.*
     b.   *Jan houdt van de Odyssee, maar* de Ilias *waardeert hij niet.*

---

11. In chapter 17 we will see that, as far as Dutch is concerned, this is a gross oversimplification.

Note that in English this leads to X S Vf, in Dutch to X Vf S order. In both English and Dutch, this X-initial pattern is less frequent than the S-initial pattern, and thus constitutes a marked construction type with extra attention-commanding value. In English, however, the markedness value of X-initial patterns is much higher than in Dutch. To demonstrate this, consider the ratio between the two patterns in the first 100 main clauses of an American and a Dutch novel:[12]

(45) a. English: S Vf X: 90%   X S Vf: 10%
     b. Dutch: S Vf X: 58%   X Vf S: 42%

We see that in English the X S Vf order occurs in only 1 out of 10 cases, whereas in Dutch we find it in 4 out of 10 instances. Clearly, the preposing of "other constituents" is a much more highly marked option in English than it is in Dutch. In fact, the X-initial order in Dutch can hardly be called a marked option at all.

We see from these various examples that not only the existence of alternative constructions, but also the frequency with which these are chosen, are essential for determining the markedness value, and hence the degree of "expressiveness" of these alternatives.

2.5.2. Markedness in oppositions

As noted above, the notion of markedness was first introduced to characterize certain properties of phonological and morphological oppositions. Consider, first of all, the following simple example:

(46)   singular: *book*   plural: *book-s*

Note that the plural form is characterized by the explicit presence of a plural ending, where the singular is characterized by the absence of any ending. This presence vs. absence of a formal marker corresponds, in a sense, to a semantic difference: the plural form is used when explicit reference is to be made to

---

12. J.D. Salinger, *The catcher in the rye*, Harmondsworth: Penguin, 1951; and Cees Nooteboom, *Philip en de anderen*, Amsterdam: Querido, 1972. I have not included initial constituents which are marked off from the main clause by a comma, since these are better considered as being outside the clause proper.

more than one entity of the type 'book'; but the use of the singular form is not restricted to indicating just one entity of the type 'book', since in those cases in which the number of "book-entities" is irrelevant (i.e. may be one or more) we also find the form *book*, as in *book jacket, book market, book production, book collector, book-ish*, etc. Rather than say that *book* signals 'singular', it would thus be more appropriate to say that it signals 'non-plural', in the sense that it does not explicitly inform us about plurality, although it is not incompatible with a plural interpretation. The opposition can now be represented as follows:

(47) | | *book* | *book-s* |
| --- | --- | --- |
| markedness: | unmarked | marked |
| form: | absence of suffix | presence of suffix |
| meaning: | 'non-plural' | 'plural' |

In a situation where the opposition between 'singular' and 'plural' is not important, we say that this opposition is "neutralized". The general principle is then that in conditions of neutralization, it is the unmarked rather than the marked member of the opposition which appears.

Since the unmarked member covers all the ground that is not covered by the marked member (in this case: both singularity and non-relevance of number), it will also occur more frequently than the marked member (see Greenberg 1966). This is one point in which "marked constructions" and "marked members of oppositions" are alike: they occur less frequently than their unmarked counterparts and correspondingly have more "explicit", more "expressive" communicative value.

2.5.3. Markedness shift

The markedness value of a linguistic item is not a fixed, immutable property of that item. It may vary with the environment in which it is used, and with the frequency with which it recurs.

For the environmental factor, consider the following non-linguistic example: if I go to a formal dinner without wearing a tie, I will be a highly marked phenomenon: I will be "the odd man out" for not wearing a tie; on the other hand, if I go jogging in the park with a couple of friends during our lunch break while wearing a tie, I would certainly be the marked jogger for wearing the tie. Thus, the same behaviour may be marked in one circumstance, unmarked in another.

For the frequency of recurrence factor, consider what happens when in both situations I persist in my odd behaviour: my markedness value will gradually decrease, until finally nobody notices anymore: I will be that fellow who goes to dinner without a tie, and jogs with his tie on. I will be placed in a niche of unmarked oddness.

Similar things may be said about the markedness of linguistic items: (i) what is marked in one environment may be unmarked in another; and (ii) when frequent use is made of marked forms, they gradually lose their markedness.

One type of loss of markedness is involved in what I call markedness shift. By this I mean a historical process through which an originally marked item loses its marked character (gets "demarked"), and thus makes room for the creation of a new marked form. Let us illustrate the working of markedness shift by the parable of the "Sunday suit". Suppose Mr. Brown buys himself a new suit for Sundays and festive occasions. At first, the Sunday suit is only used for such occasions: it is a marked suit which gives Mr. Brown and others the idea that he really dresses up for those occasions. Then, Mr. Brown starts wearing his Sunday suit on certain ordinary workdays. The suit becomes less "special", less "marked", and loses its capacity to really symbolize a "Sunday" appearance. In the end, then, Mr. Brown will need a new marked Sunday suit for the festive occasions.

For a second, more linguistic example, consider the expressions that we use to indicate that something is really very good or nice: *wonderful, fantastic, terrific, amazing, gorgeous*, all these expressions started their life as very strong, marked symbols of positive evaluation. But all of them, through overexploitation, underwent a process of inflation which made them lose much of their markedness. This explains why each new generation seems to need its own brandnew terminology for expressing positive evaluation.

We can now see that two principles appear to underlie such processes of markedness shift: (i) the need for especially expressive linguistic items to achieve special effects in communication; (ii) the tendency to overexploit such items and thus subject them to a process of inflation.

The process of markedness shift often takes the form symbolized in Table 3. In Stage 1 there is an opposition between an unmarked form E_1 and a marked form E_2. In Stage 2 the marked form E_2 has lost its markedness, and has pushed E_1 out of business; E_1 may either remain in use as an archaic variant of E_2, or it may disappear altogether. In Stage 3, a new marked form E_3 has been created; from that stage on, the process may start anew.

Table 3. The process of markedness shift

	marked	unmarked	obsolete
Stage 1	E_2	E_1	—
Stage 2	—	E_2	(E_1)
Stage 3	E_3	E_2	—

For an example of a markedness shift according to the pattern of Table 3, consider the (simplified) representation of the historical development of second person pronouns in Dutch in Table 4. In Stage 1 we have the unmarked form *du* 'you-sg' whereas the second person plural pronoun *ghi* was used for polite address. In Stage 2 the originally marked form has become the unmarked second person singular pronoun (losing its plurality in the process), and *du* has disappeared. In Stage 3 a new polite form *U* (abbreviated from a form meaning 'your honour') was introduced for polite address.

Table 4. Markedness shift in Dutch personal pronouns

	marked	unmarked	obsolete
Stage 1	ghi	du	—
Stage 2	—	ghi	(du)
Stage 3	U	jij	—

Observe that a similar process occurred in English (*du* corresponds to the older English form *thou*), but that English is still in Stage 2, since no new marked form for polite address has been created.

Just as is the case with expressions of "positive evaluation", politeness is typically in need of marked forms of expression which, however, are liable to lose their markedness over time: once we have become accustomed to addressing important people as 'your honour', we may be in need of even more marked expression types for even more important persons. In the area of politeness, then, we may expect a continuous process of devaluation of old expressions, and of introduction of new, ever more marked expression types.

The process of markedness shift is not, however, restricted to such forms of lexical organization as exemplified above. It also has explanatory power with respect to certain developments in the grammatical structures of natural languages. Several examples of this will be discussed in the further course of this work.

3. Preview of Functional Grammar

3.0. Introduction

In this chapter I give a preview of FG by sketching (i) the abstract underlying structure of the clause according to FG, (ii) the lay-out of the FG clause model, and (iii) the structure of this work. All the notions introduced in this preview return for more thorough discussion in later chapters and in *TFG2*.

3.1. The structure of the clause

Any natural language text can be exhaustively divided into *clauses* and *extra-clausal constituents*. By "clauses" I mean the main and subordinate clauses of traditional grammar. Extra-clausal constituents are constituents which are neither clauses nor parts of clauses. In a construction such as:

(1)   Well, John, *I believe that your time is up.*

the constituents *well* (an "Initiator") and *John* (an "Address" or "Vocative") are extra-clausal constituents; *I believe that your time is up* is a main clause; and *that your time is up* is a subordinate clause. In *TFG1* we mainly concentrate our attention on the structure of main clauses; extra-clausal constituents and subordinate clauses will be treated in *TFG2*.

In order to do justice to the formal and semantic properties of clauses in a typologically adequate way, we assume that each clause must be described in terms of an abstract *underlying clause structure*, which is mapped onto the actual form of the corresponding linguistic expression by a system of *expression rules*, which determine the form, the order, and the prosodic contour of the constituents of the underlying clause structure, given their status within the underlying structure:

(2)   Underlying Clause Structure
                                  |
                             Expression Rules
                                  |
                           Linguistic Expressions

The underlying clause structure is a complex abstract structure in which several "layers" of formal and semantic organization can be distinguished.[1] As a first approximation to this structure, we can represent it as in (3).

(3)
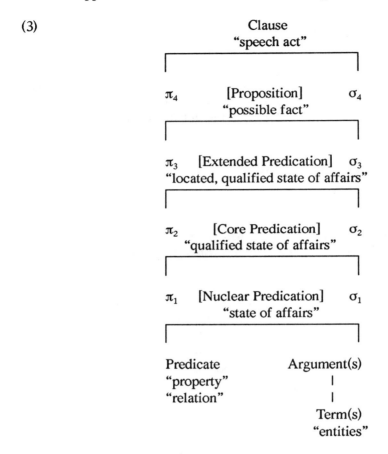

Let us describe this abstract clause model from bottom to top. The construction of an underlying clause structure first of all requires a *predicate* which is to be applied to an appropriate number of *terms* of the appropriate types, functioning as *arguments* to the predicate. Predicates designate properties or relations, while terms can be used to refer to entities. As an example of a predicate we may take the verb *write*. This predicate takes two

---

1. For this idea of "layering" I am indebted to Foley—Van Valin (1984) and to its elaboration in the context of FG by Hengeveld (1989).

arguments: it designates a two-place relation between two entities in the roles of a 'writer' and 'something written', and thus is necessarily applied to two terms, for example, the terms (John) and (a letter). When a predicate is applied to an appropriate set of terms, the result is a *nuclear predication*. In this example the resulting nuclear predication can be provisionally represented as:

(4)   write (John) (a letter)

Such a nuclear predication can be interpreted as designating a set of states of affairs (SoAs), where an SoA is "the conception of something that can be the case in some world". If we assume a world in which it is the case that a person called 'John' writes something of the type 'letter', then we can say that (4) correctly describes that SoA in that world. Note that an SoA need not exist or be the case in "reality" in order to be designated by a predication: the SoA can just as well be created in a "mental world" of S and A, and then be properly described by a predication.

An SoA is something that can be said to occur, take place, or obtain in some world; it can be located in time and space; it can be said to take a certain time (have a certain duration); and it can be seen, heard, or otherwise perceived.

Starting from the nuclear predication, the full structure of the clause can be built up layer by layer, by specifying grammatical operators "π" and lexical satellites "σ" appropriate to the given layer. Operators concern distinctions which are grammatically expressed in the language concerned, satellites are modifications which are lexically expressed. Satellites largely coincide with "adverbial modifiers".

At the first layer, the nuclear SoA is qualified by predicate operators π_1 and predicate satellites σ_1 which provide further specification of the kind of SoA designated. An aspectual distinction such as "Progressive" would be an example of a predicate operator, a Manner adverb such as *carefully* of a predicate satellite. Both qualify the nuclear SoA with certain finer distinctions. The resulting "core predication" can be provisionally represented as:

(5)   Prog [write (John) (a letter)] (carefully)
        'John (was) writing a letter carefully.'

At the next layer, the qualified SoA expressed in the core predication can be located in space and time by predication operators π_2 and predication satellites σ_2. For example, we can locate the SoA designated by (5) in space and time in the following way:

(6)   [Pres [Prog [*write* (*John*) (*a letter*)] (*carefully*)] (*in the library*)]
        'John is carefully writing a letter in the library.'

An element such as "Pres(ent)" represents a grammatical means for locating an SoA in the time interval overlapping the moment of speaking. A constituent such as (*in the library*) represents a lexical means for locating the SoA designated by the predication in space. Note that internally it has the structure of a term, which can be used to refer to an entity, namely the library. Thus, by adding a predication operator Pres and a locative satellite (*in the library*) to core predication (5), we situate the qualified SoA designated by (5) in time and space. The result is called an *extended predication*, designating a located, qualified SoA.

This completes the descriptive or representational part of the clause structure. The SoA that the Speaker wishes to communicate about has now been described, qualified, and situated. At the next layer, the Speaker can now specify the attitude he takes with respect to this SoA. This can be done by specifying propositional operators π_3 and propositional satellites σ_3, both designating subjective attitudinal or modal evaluations on the part of S. For example, (6) might be modalized as follows:

(7)   [Poss [Pres [Prog
        [*write* (*John*) (*a letter*)]
        (*carefully*)] (*in the library*)] (*as far as I know*)]
        'As far as I know, John may be carefully writing a letter in the library.'

The proposition operator Poss indicates that S judges it possible that the SoA is indeed the case. The satellite (*as far as I know*) specifies something about the quality of the information that S transmits. The result is a *proposition*, designating a possible fact, presented through the eyes of S.

Propositions are things that people can be said to believe, know or think about; they can be reason for surprise or doubt; they can be mentioned, denied, rejected, and remembered; and they can be said to be true or false.[2] We can now say that a predication, which designates an SoA, can be built into a higher-order structure: the proposition, which designates a "propositional content" or a "possible fact".

Let us now return to the clause:

---

2. Compare Vendler (1967).

(8)   As far as I know, John may be carefully writing a letter in the library.

The structure given in (7) does not provide us with a full analysis of (8): the analysis does not account for the speech act status or the *illocutionary force* of the clause as a whole: (8) is a declarative rather than an interrogative or an imperative sentence. We will assume that those items to which illocutionary forces apply are typically propositions rather than predications: we declare and question propositional contents rather than SoAs.[3] In the second place, the illocutionary force of (8) is signalled by grammatical rather than lexical means: it is the sentence form plus the intonation which informs us that (8) is a statement rather than a question. We shall therefore analyse illocutionary forces, as coded in sentence types, by means of illocutionary operators π_4 which apply to propositions. In this way, we arrive (roughly speaking)[4] at an analysis of the following form for (8):

(9)   [Decl [Poss [Pres [Prog
        [*write*(*John*)(*a letter*)]
        (*carefully*)] (*in the library*)] (*as far as I know*)] σ_4]

The illocutionary satellite σ_4 could also be specified, this time by some adverbial which in some way modifies or specifies the illocutionary value of the clause as a whole. *Frankly* would be an example of such a satellite, since it designates the "way of speaking" in which the clause is produced:

(10)   [Decl [Poss [Pres [Prog
        [*write*(*John*)(*a letter*)]
        (*carefully*)] (*in the library*)] (*as far as I know*)] (*frankly*)]
        'Frankly, as far as I know John may be carefully writing a letter in the library.'

Just as an extended predication can be built into a proposition, therefore, the proposition in turn can be built into an illocutionary frame, resulting in the underlying structure of the full clause, which designates a speech act (in this case, a declarative speech act) with respect to a proposition, which contains

---

3. This does not hold for imperatives. See *TFG2*: chapter 11.
4. The analyses presented here by way of examples will later be refined and more formally represented.

an extended predication which is itself construed from a core predication, which in turn contains a nuclear predication defined by a predicate, as applied to an appropriate set of terms.

Fortunately, not all clauses are as complex as (10). Many of the operators and all the satellites can be left unspecified, so that we may get structures such as:

(11) a. *John laughed.*
     b. [Decl [∅ [Past [∅ [*laugh (John)*)] ∅] ∅] ∅] ∅]

However, the empty elements ∅ are relevant even for this structure, since they indicate operator and satellite positions which, in suitable circumstances, may be specified, and therefore indicate "neutral" values when they are not so specified.

The layered structure of the clause allows us to correctly specify the various scopes of the operators and satellites of the different levels. For example, since Decl is an illocutionary operator of Level 4, it will have the whole remainder of the clause, i.e., the proposition and everything below it, in its scope. Likewise a predication operator such as Past will have the whole core predication, including its predicates and terms, in its scope.

It will prove useful, in the further development of this work, to employ various types of variables to indicate the various things which are designated by structural elements of different levels of the underlying clause structure. Where this is relevant, we shall use the variables presented in Table 5. The precise way in which these variables will be used in a more formal elaboration of the underlying structures of various levels will be clarified in the further course of our discussion.[5]

---

5. The elaboration of the higher levels of underlying clause structure owes much to the contributions of a number of scholars. Vet (1986) suggested the use of event variables e_i, e_j,... at the predication level, and demonstrated that they can be used for properly defining the scope of predication operators and satellites. The idea of using "typed" variables of this kind was earlier suggested by Reichenbach (1947) in a logical context. Hengeveld (1987, 1988, 1989) developed the idea of distinguishing between the predication and the proposition within the structure of the clause, and demonstrated the usefulness of this idea with particular reference to the analysis of different types of modalities. In doing so he incorporated certain ideas from Foley—Van Valin (1984), Bybee (1985), and Lehmann (1987). The distinction between predication and proposition can be used to capture the semantic difference between "events" and "facts" as discussed in Vendler (1967), and the

Table 5. Entity types designated by layers
of underlying clause structure

STRUCTURAL UNIT	DESIGNATION	VARIABLE
Clause	Speech Act	E
Proposition	Possible Fact	X
Predication	State of Affairs	e
Predicate	Property / Relation	f

As noted above, *terms* are expressions which can be inserted into the argument and satellite positions of underlying clause structures. Terms can be used to refer to entities in some (mental) world. Prototypically, terms refer to entities such as 'John', 'a letter', and 'the library', which can be conceived of as existing in space. These will also be called "first-order entities", and they will be represented by means of the variable "x". The terms used to refer to first-order entities will be called "first-order terms". However, terms can also be used to refer to any of the entity types designated by the different layers of underlying clause structure, as indicated in Table 5. Thus, we can use terms to refer to properties and relations (zero-order entities), to States of Affairs (second-order entities), to possible facts (third-order entities), and to speech acts (fourth-order entities). Terms which are used to refer to other than first-order entities usually have a derived or complex structure. They will be discussed at appropriate places in this work. Pending such discussion "term" will be used in the more restricted sense of "first-order term", unless indicated otherwise.

---

difference between first-order, second-order, and third-order entities as presented in Lyons (1977). The incorporation of the illocutionary level into the FG model builds on suggestions made by De Jong (1981), Peres (1984), and Moutaouakil (1986). The status of the predicate variable "f" was clarified by Keizer (1991, 1992) and Hengeveld (1992a), and the relationships between levels of clause structure, types of entities, and types of terms has been elaborated on the basis of Keizer (1991).

3.2. The structure of FG

3.2.1. Notes on the mode of presentation

We saw in section 3.1. that the underlying structure of the clause according to FG is a complex layered network in which a great number of different elements may operate at different levels, creating all sorts of dependencies through the network. The expression rules, which mediate between this underlying network and the actual form of linguistic expressions, again form a complex interface, in which different types of rules, in interlocking fashion, determine the form and the order of constituents, as well as their local and global prosodic properties. This overall complexity poses certain problems for the mode of presentation of the theory, for two main reasons.

First, there are both top-down and bottom-up dependencies in linguistic structure: hierarchically higher choices may constrain lower options (top-down), and lower choices may constrain higher options (bottom-up). There is a top-down dependency in the creation of a clause structure if some high-level decision constrains the choices which can be made at lower levels in the hierarchy. For example, if we take the high-level decision to create an imperative clause, the type of SoA to be specified in the nucleus of that clause is subject to certain constraints: it must be a "controllable" SoA of which the Addressee takes the first argument position. There is a bottom-up dependency in the creation of a clause structure if a lower-level choice constrains certain higher-level options. For example, if we start by choosing a non-controllable nuclear predicate from the lexicon, then we can no longer choose "imperative" at the illocutionary level.

In the second place, a model of grammar that is to be psychologically adequate will have to cater for both the productive and the interpretive capacities of natural language users. In the productive mode, speakers are able to construe underlying clause structures and map these onto linguistic expressions; in the interpretive mode, they are able to take in a linguistic expression and reconstruct its underlying structure in such a way as to be able to understand its semantic and pragmatic import. In computational terms, a model of the natural language user will have to contain both a generator and a parser which, as far as this is possible, will have to operate in terms of the same rules and principles.

It is very difficult, however, to start the presentation of FG with the full complexity of linguistic expressions in context, and then decompose this complexity until finally we arrive at the basic building blocks. This is difficult because the higher levels of grammatical organization presuppose all the lower levels of structure in order to be properly understood and evaluated.

For these various reasons, our presentation follows a bottom-up course, in which we present the various modules of FG in a quasi-productive mode, "as if" building up the full complexity of linguistic expressions from what we consider to be their most basic building blocks at the morphosemantic level, the predicates. From there, we add more complexity in a step by step fashion, until ultimately we are in a position to grasp the full complexity of linguistic expressions, as regards both their underlying structure and their expression properties.

Although the model of FG is presented in a quasi-productive mode, I do not wish to suggest that this order of presentation necessarily simulates the various steps that a speaker takes in producing linguistic expressions. This is not plausible, for the following reasons:

(i) speakers do not randomly generate linguistic expressions "out of the blue": they start from a richly articulated knowledge base, and (usually) have some piece of knowledge to convey when they say something. Producing a linguistic expression thus consists of moulding a certain piece of knowledge into an appropriate linguistic form. A full psychologically adequate production model will thus contain at least a knowledge base, a facility for producing linguistic expressions, and an interface for interrelating these two components. In the present work, we mainly restrict our attention to the linguistic capacity.[6]

(ii) the actual order of sentence production is not necessarily uniquely determined. For example, a speaker might start by selecting a predicate frame, and then specify the terms required by that predicate frame to produce a full predication; or he might start by forming one or more terms, and then select a predicate frame to arrive at an appropriate predication. In general, the speaker may run through the components of the grammar in different ways, depending on the context, on his memory of certain bits and pieces of knowledge, and on his flow of attention either from communicative intentions through facts and states of affairs to properties / relations and entities, or the other way around, from entities and properties / relations to states of affairs, then to facts and ultimately to communicative intentions.

(iii) the order of actual production is not even necessarily organized in a

---

6. In several studies, however, I have argued that FG might also have something to offer for the construction of a more encompassing cognitive model of NLUs. See Dik (1987a, 1987b, 1989a).

sequential way. Psychological studies of sentence production (and interpretation!) make it plausible that natural language users have rather strong capacities for the parallel processing of information. This means that one section of the speaker's production facility may be working on the construction of terms, while another section is already looking around for suitable predicates, and a third section is active in deciding what the illocutionary force of the clause is going to be.

For all these activities, however, the natural language user needs some equivalent of the different modules that are incorporated in the theory of FG, no matter how he runs through these modules in the actual production and interpretation of linguistic expressions. In a sense we could say that the theory defines a complex instrument, and that additional psycholinguistic theories of text production and interpretation are required in order to specify in what different ways natural language users can play on that instrument. Our requirement of psychological adequacy says that the theory of the instrument may not be incompatible with what is known about the ways people play on it.

Through computational implementation (Dik 1992) it has been demonstrated that a model which contains an FG generator as described in this book can very well be put to procedural tasks such as producing and parsing sentences, translating them from one language to another, and drawing certain logical inferences from them. The reverse would be much more difficult to achieve. This is an extra argument for considering the generator as a central component of the linguistic module of communicative competence.

3.2.2. Outline of the FG model

When we look at the construction of linguistic expressions in a quasi-productive way, as in the overall model of FG represented in Figure 3, the first thing we must be able to do is construct nuclear predications. For the construction of nuclear predications we need a set of predicates and a set of terms. The component that contains all the predicates and terms from which predications can be construed is called the "Fund" of the grammar.

As will become clear below, the underlying structures of terms are themselves construed from predicates. Therefore, predicates constitute the most basic building blocks at the morphosemantic (as opposed to the phonological) level of linguistic organization. Concerning these predicates, FG starts from the following assumptions:

— All lexical items of a language are analysed as predicates.

— Different categories and subcategories or types and subtypes of predicates are distinguished, according to their different formal and functional properties. Thus, many languages have at least verbal (V), adjectival (A), and nominal (N) predicates, and various subtypes within these categories.

— All predicates are semantically interpreted as designating properties or relations.

— Predicates may be *basic* or *derived*. They are basic if they must be known as such in order to be used in appropriate ways. They are derived if they can be formed in regular ways by synchronically productive rules of *predicate formation* (see *TFG2*: chapter 1).

— Basic predicates may be stems, words, or combinations of words. If a basic predicate consists of a combination of words, it will be an *idiom*: although it consists of different words, it cannot be semantically derived by productive rule.

— All basic predicates are listed in the *lexicon*. The lexicon thus contains the full stock of basic predicates of the language.

— Predicates are not regarded as isolated elements, to be inserted into independently generated structures of some kind; they are considered to form part of structures called *predicate frames*, which contain a kind of "blueprint" for the predications in which they can be used. The structure of the predication is built up around the predicate frame.

— An example of a predicate frame would be the following:

(12) *give* [V] $(x_1: \text{<anim>}(x_1))_{Ag} (x_2)_{Go} (x_3: \text{<anim>}(x_3))_{Rec}$

Each predicate frame specifies the *form* (here *give*), the *type* (here V), and the *valency* or *argument structure* of the predicate. The argument structure of the predicate *give* is here specified as consisting of three argument positions, indicated by x_1, x_2, x_3, carrying the *semantic functions* of Agent (Ag), Goal (Go), and Recipient (Rec), where the first and the third argument are constrained by the *selection restriction* <animate>.

— Each basic predicate frame in the lexicon is associated with a number of *meaning postulates*, through which the predicate is semantically related to other predicates of the language. If these meaning postulates add up to a full specification of the meaning of the predicate, they may be termed *meaning definitions*. For derived predicates, the meaning resulting from the application of some predicate formation rule will be specified in that predicate formation rule itself.

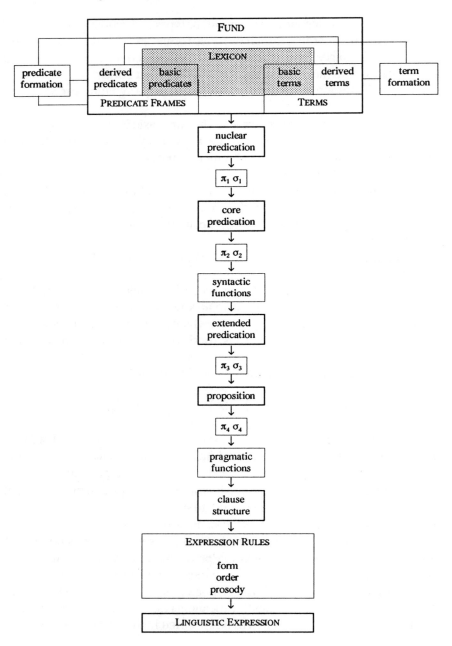

Figure 3. Overall model of FG

— Derived predicates will likewise consist of (derived) predicate frames. From this it follows that rules of predicate formation will take the form of mappings of predicate frames onto (derived) predicate frames.
— Predicate frames are supposed to have no linear order: the order in which they are presented (predicate first, then argument positions) is purely conventional. Any other order, or even a two- or three-dimensional structure, would do just as well. The actual linear order will only be defined at the level of the expression rules.

The other half of the Fund consists of *term structures*. For these structures we start from the following assumptions:
— All linguistic expressions which can be used to refer to entities in some world are analysed as terms.
— Terms range from very simple items such as pronouns (*he, she, they*) and proper names (*John, Mary*) to extremely complex noun phrases such as:

(13)   *a book that Jim told me nobody reads in the Western world, although it is rightly considered to be a masterpiece of Chinese literature*

— Terms may also be used to refer to higher-order entities such as SoAs (*the defeat of the enemy*), possible facts (*that John sold the car*) or speech acts (*John's question what he should do*). Such terms will often contain *embedded predications, embedded propositions,* or *embedded speech acts*.[7]
— Just as in the case of predicate frames, we distinguish between basic and derived term structures. Basic term structures are those items that can only be used as terms, and which one has to know as such if one is to use them correctly. Examples are personal pronouns and proper names. Basic term structures are contained in the lexicon. The vast majority of term structures, however, are derived through productive rules of *term formation*.
— Term formation rules produce (first-order) term structures conforming to the following general schema:

(14) $(\omega x_i: \varphi_1(x_i): \varphi_2(x_i): ... : \varphi_n(x_i))$

in which ω stands for one or more *term operators*, x_i symbolizes the intended referent, and each $\varphi(x_i)$ is a "predication open in x_i" (i.e. a predicate frame of which all positions except that occupied by x_i are filled by term structures),

---

7. See *TFG2*: chapter 5.

which acts as a "restrictor" on the possible values that x_i may have. For one example of a term structure, consider:

(15) a. *the big elephant that lives in the zoo*
 b. (d1x_i: *elephant* [N] $(x_i)_\varnothing$: *big* [A] $(x_i)_\varnothing$:
  live [V] $(x_i)_{Pos}$ (d1x_j: *zoo* [N] $(x_j)_\varnothing)_{Loc}$)

This term structure can be paraphrased as follows: "definite (d) singular (1) entity x_i, such that (:) x_i has the property 'elephant', such that x_i has the property 'big', such that x_i has the property that it lives in the definite singular entity x_j such that x_j has the property 'zoo'. This example, the details of which will obviously be discussed below, gives us a first impression of what it means to say that term structures are construed from predicate frames: the first restrictor in (15b) is the predicate frame for 'elephant', the second restrictor is the predicate frame for 'big', and the third restrictor is made from the predicate frame of 'live' by inserting the term structure for 'the zoo' into the second argument position of this predicate frame.

— The order imposed on term structures according to schema (14) is not supposed to reflect actual surface order (which may be rather different across languages), but the "semantic" order in which the various operators and restrictors make their contribution to the definition of the intended referent. Again, the actual surface order will be determined by the expression rules.

We have now given an impression of the contents of the Fund and of the lexicon which is embedded in it. Since both term formation and predicate formation have certain recursive properties, the Fund offers a practically unlimited store of predicate frames and term structures for the construction of nuclear predications. Such nuclear predications result when appropriate term structures are inserted into the argument slots of predicate frames. For a simple instance of this, consider:

(16) a. *The hen laid an egg.*
 b. *lay* [V] (d1x_i: *hen* [N] $(x_i)_\varnothing)_{Ag}$ (i1x_j: *egg* [N] $(x_j)_\varnothing)_{Go}$

Such a predication designates the SoA of "definite hen laying indefinite egg". Note that so far this SoA has not been defined for any parameters of time and space. For example, the Past tense of *laid* is not captured at this level of analysis.

Into the representations presented so far I shall now introduce some simplifications which, without loss of information, make these representations easier to read. In (15b) and (16b) I have used term representations following the schema:

(17) a. $(x_i: f(x_i))$
'an x_i such that x_i is f'
b. $(x_i: f(x_i)(x_j))$
'an x_i such that x_i has the relation f to x_j'

In structures of the form (17b) the argument structure of f is useful, since we can now see which argument of f corresponds to the intended referent symbolized by x_i. For example, the following two (simplified) structures have quite different meanings:

(18) a. $(x_i: man(x_i): love(x_i)(Mary))$
'man who loves Mary'
b. $(x_i: man(x_i): love(Mary)(x_i))$
'man who Mary loves'

In cases such as (17a), however, in which f represents a simple one-place property of the intended referent, the presence of the argument variable is redundant, and in fact leads to unnecessarily complex representations. We shall therefore simplify (17a) to:[8]

(19) $(x_i: f)$
'x_i such that x_i has the property f'

This means that the structure (20a) will be simplified to (20b):

(20) a. $lay\ [V]\ (d1x_i: hen\ [N]\ (x_i)_\emptyset)_{Ag}\ (i1x_j: egg\ [N]\ (x_j)_\emptyset)_{Go}$
b. $lay\ [V]\ (d1x_i: hen\ [N]\ \quad)_{Ag}\ (i1x_j: egg\ [N]\ \quad)_{Go}$

I shall interpret these two representations as meaning exactly the same thing, and from now on use the simplified notation of (20b).

As we saw in 3.1. above, a nuclear predication such as (20b) can be further specified by predicate operators π_1 and predicate satellites σ_1:

— *Predicate operators* π_1 are grammatical operators which in one way or another specify the internal dynamics of the SoA. Some examples are such

---

[8]. Mackenzie (1987) claims that there are principled reasons to represent terms this way.

aspectual oppositions as those between "Progressive" and "Non-Progressive", or between "Perfective" and "Imperfective".[9]

— *Predicate satellites* σ_1 include satellites for Manner, Speed, Instrument, Direction, and Beneficiary, which tell us something more specific about what kind of SoA we are dealing with.

The result of these Level 1 extensions, the *core predication*, can thus be represented as:

(21)   core predication = π_1 [nuclear predication] σ_1

Note that the relevance of predicate operators such as Progressive or Perfective / Imperfective depends on the grammatical organization of the language involved, and that the specification of Level 1 satellites is optional. It is often the case, therefore, that the core predication is identical to the nuclear predication.

The core predication can now be provided with an SoA variable, so that we get structures of the form:

(22) e_i: [core predication]
        'State of Affairs e_i having the properties specified by the core predication'

where e_i is a variable symbolizing the SoA involved, and the [core predication] specifies the nature of this SoA. In a sense, the core predication is used as a predicate over the SoA variable.

The core predication appears to be the level where the "syntactic" or "perspectivizing" functions Subject and Object come into play. Subject and Object function are used in FG to capture the different "points of view" from which the SoA coded in a given predication can be presented. Formally, such different perspectives are coded through differential assignment of Subject and Object function to the terms of the predication. Through the expression rules, this finally leads to such alternative constructions as active vs. passive, as in (23), or to pairs related through what is sometimes called "dative shift", as in (24):

(23) a.   *John* (AgSubj) *gave the book* (GoObj) *to Mary* (Rec).
     b.   *The book* (GoSubj) *was given to Mary* (Rec) *by John* (Ag).

---

9. Compare Comrie (1976), Hengeveld (1989).

(24) a.   *John* (AgSubj) *gave the book* (GoObj) *to Mary* (Rec).
     b.   *John* (AgSubj) *gave Mary* (RecObj) *the book* (Go).

Note that these alternative construction types differ in the distribution of Subject (= primary vantage point) and Object (= secondary vantage point) over the terms of the predication. In chapters 10 and 11, the mechanism of Subject and Object assignment will be discussed in detail. In chapter 11 it will be argued that, apart from a few counterexamples, the assignment of Subject and Object function is limited to arguments and Level 1 satellites.

Core predications can now be further specified by Level 2 operators and satellites:

— *Predication operators* π_2. These are Level 2 operators which represent the grammatical means by which the SoA can be located with respect to temporal, spatial, and cognitive coordinates. These are therefore operators which leave the internal structure of the SoA intact, but locate it with respect to the different dimensions mentioned. For example, a Tense operator Past locates the SoA in the time interval preceding the moment of speaking.

— *Predication satellites* σ_2. These represent the lexical means by which an SoA can be located with respect to the parameters mentioned. Thus, a satellite such as *yesterday* locates the SoA in the time interval consisting of the day preceding the day of speaking; and a satellite such as *in Africa* locates the SoA in the continent of that name.

These further specifications result in the *extended predication*, which can now be represented as follows:

(25)   extended predication = π_2 e_i: [core predication] σ_2

For a simplified example, consider:

(26) a.   Past e_i: [*lay* (*the hen*) (*an egg*)] (*in the garden*)
     b.   *The hen laid an egg in the garden.*

We are now at the level at which fully developed extended predications of type (26a) have been specified. These can in turn be built into a propositional structure, in which the extended predication is used to specify a possible fact, i.e. something which can be known, believed, mentioned, remembered, etc. The propositional structure (or briefly "proposition") can be represented as follows:

(27)   proposition: π_3 X_i: [extended predication] σ_3

In this structure, then, the extended predication is used as a predicate over a variable X_i, which symbolizes the possible fact involved. This structure can again be extended by two types of elements, which operate at Level 3:

— *Proposition operators* π_3. These are operators capturing the grammatical means by which the speaker can express his personal evaluation of or attitude towards the propositional content. These include "subjective" modalities through which the speaker expresses his belief or disbelief in the content of the proposition, his hope or wish that the proposition may come true, or the source through which he has obtained the information contained in the proposition. All these operators thus relate the content of the proposition to the subjective world of the speaker.

— *Proposition satellites* σ_3. These are satellites which capture the lexical means by which a speaker can specify his evaluation of, or his attitude towards the content of the proposition. For example, when we have an expression such as:

(28)   *In my opinion, John is a fool.*

it is clear that the expression *in my opinion* does not change anything in the SoA expressed by the predication, nor does it locate the SoA with respect to "objective" coordinates of time, space, or cognition; rather, it restricts the value which the speaker himself wishes to be attached to the content of the proposition. The truth of the possible fact expressed in that proposition is explicitly restricted to the subjective world of the speaker.[10]

The proposition, in turn, can be built into a schema for the full clause, which designates the particular speech act expressed in the linguistic expression. As a first approximation, we can thus write:

(29) E_i: [proposition]

The proposition now acts as a predicate over the speech act variable E. And at this level, again, the clause structure can be modified and specified by operators π_4 and satellites σ_4, for which we will use the terms *illocutionary operators* and *illocutionary satellites*. Just as at the other levels, we shall use

---

10. This is the category of modifiers for which Greenbaum (1969) coined the term "attitudinal disjuncts"; *disjuncts* because of their comparatively loose connection with the rest of the sentence; *attitudinal* because of their semantic connection with the personal attitude of the speaker.

operators for the more grammatical specifications of the character of the speech act, and satellites for the more lexical modifications:

— *Illocutionary operators* π_4. These operators specify the basic illocutionary force of the clause (such as Decl(arative), Int(errogative), Imp(erative), etc.), or modifications of these basic values.

— *Illocutionary satellites* σ_4. These satellites specify how the Speaker wishes the speech act to be taken or understood by the Addressee. Consider the following example:

(30)   *Briefly, John is a fool.*

Here the basic illocutionary force of the expression is Decl, and *briefly* is an illocutionary satellite specifying a certain qualification of the speech act as such (and not of the proposition, let alone of the predication contained in it).[11]

The full clause structure can thus be represented as follows:

(31)   clause = π_4 E_i: [proposition] σ_4

It will now be clear that the full structure of the clause can be represented as follows:

(32) $[\pi_4\ E_i: [\pi_3\ X_i: [\pi_2\ e_i: [\pi_1\ [\text{pred}\ [T]\ \text{args}]\ \sigma_1]\ \sigma_2]\ \sigma_3]\ \sigma_4]$
          [.....nucleus....]
         [...core predication...]
        [........extended predication........]
       [......................proposition.......................]
      [...................................clause..................................]

This structure is equivalent to that which was given in (3) above, with this difference that the relevant layers have now been provided with the relevant variables for speech acts (E), propositions (X), and SoAs (e). Note that the core predication has no variable of its own, since the SoA has only been fully defined when the predicate operators π_1 and the predicate satellites σ_1 have been specified. The "[T]" in the nucleus stands for the "Type" of the predicate.

Once we have reached this highest level of the organization of the clause,

---

11. This is the type of modifier which Greenbaum (1969) termed "style disjunct", since it pertains to the style rather than to the content of speaking.

we are ready to assign *pragmatic functions* to the various constituents of the clause. Pragmatic functions specify the informational value of different parts of the clause, in relation to the speaker's estimate of the pragmatic information of the addressee. We divide pragmatic functions into those which relate to the dimension of *topicality* and those which have to do with the dimension of *focality*.

By topicality we understand everything pertaining to "what the clause is about", given the informational setting in which it occurs. Topical functions can only be assigned to terms. Certain terms may introduce New Topics, others have the function of referring to Given Topics, Sub-Topics, or Resumed Topics. Each of these pragmatic functions may, depending on the organization of the language in question, have certain consequences for the formal expression of the underlying clause structure. These consequences may consist of the insertion of special Topic markers, of special positions assigned to Topics in the linear order of the expression, or of special prosodic features assigned to topical constituents.

Focality is interpreted as signifying which constituents of the clause are communicatively the most important or "salient", given the speaker's estimate of the pragmatic information of the addressee. Focal functions are attached to those constituents on which special emphasis is placed, or which are presented as being in contrast with other pieces of information which are either explicitly mentioned in the context, or are to be understood from that context. In contrast to Topic functions, Focal functions can in principle be assigned to any part of the underlying clause structure, not just to terms. Focal functions, again, have their consequences for the form, the order, and the prosodic contour by which the relevant constituents are expressed through the expression rules.

Once the pragmatic functions have been assigned, we have reached the fully specified underlying clause structure which can now be input to the expression rule component. The idea is that this fully specified clause structure should contain all those elements and relations which are essential to the semantic and pragmatic interpretation of the clause on the one hand, and to the formal expression of the clause on the other.

As far as the expression rules are concerned, these take care of three main features of linguistic expressions: the *form* of constituents, the *order* in which they are to be expressed, and the *prosodic contours* (tone, accent, and intonation) with which they have to be provided.

As for the form of constituents, remember that, as far as content is concerned, underlying clause structures only contain basic and derived predicates, that is, lexical items and combinations of lexical items. All the "grammatical" elements of linguistic expressions, such as inflectional affixes, adpositions (pre- and postpositions), and grammatical particles, will be spelled out by the expression rules as the result of the application of operators and (semantic, syntactic, and pragmatic) functions on these predicates. For the purposes of formal expression, all the elements in the underlying clause structure which have some influence on the form of constituents will be treated as *morphosyntactic operators*; this includes both the operators and the functions in underlying clause structure. Formal expression rules will then take the following form:

(33)   operator(s) [input form] = output form

In other words, the impact of one or more operators on an input form yields a certain output form. The "input form" may either be a predicate from the underlying clause structure, or an output form of an earlier formal expression rule. The output form may contain auxiliary morphosyntactic operators which are introduced by the rule, and which trigger further rules of formal specification. For a simple example, consider the form of the verb in (34):

(34)   *John* had cooked *the potatoes.*

For this form, the underlying clause structure contains the following material:

(35)   Past Perf *cook* [V]

in which Past and Perf represent the predication operators, and *cook* occurs in stem form. The relevant expression rules will take the following form:

(36) a.   Perf [pred [V]]   =   *have* [V] PaP pred [V]
     b.   PaP [pred [V]]   =   pred-ed [Vi]
     c.   Past [*have* [V]]   =   *had* [Vf][12]

In (36a) the Perf operator on the predicate is expressed by the auxiliary verb *have*, while at the same time an auxiliary operator PaP ("past participle") is placed on the original lexical predicate. In (36b) this auxiliary operator triggers the formation of the form *cook-ed*, which is characterized as a non-

---

12. As we will see in chapter 14, the matter is a little bit more complicated, since *had* cannot be productively derived from *have*.

finite verbal form Vi. The Past operator now works on the auxiliary verb *have* to produce *had*, which is at the same time characterized as a finite verbal form Vf. (36a-c) will thus effect the following derivation:[13]

(37) 1. Past Perf *cook* [V]
       2. Past *have* [V] PaP *cook* [V]
       3. Past *have* [V] *cook-ed* [Vi]
       4. *had* [Vf] *cook-ed* [Vi]

With respect to constituent order it should be remembered that the underlying clause structure is not linearly ordered, at least not in the sense of specifying the actual order of constituents in the surface structure of the linguistic expression. The ordering rules thus assign a linear position to constituents which do not yet have such a position. Therefore, these linearization rules are called *placement rules*. The formal nature of placement rules can be symbolized as follows:

(38) underlying structure: {a, b, c, d}
      ordering template: 1 2 3 4
      placement rules: a := 4
                            b := 2
                            c := 1
                            d := 3
      output sequence: c b d a

We thus start with an unordered set of constituents in underlying structure. Then, we have an ordering template consisting of a sequence of positions which are numbered or otherwise characterized. The placement rules tell us which constituents go to which positions under which conditions. The result is an ordered sequence of constituents. Let us apply this to example (34):

---

13. This type of derivation has now been worked out in great detail in the computational version of FG (Dik 1992).

(39)   underlying structure:
       {had [Vf], cook-ed [Vi], John$_{Subj}$, the potatoes$_{Obj}$}
       ordering template: 1 2 3 4
       placement rules: Vf := 2
                             Vi := 3
                             Subj := 1
                             Obj := 4
       output sequence: *John had cooked the potatoes.*

Note that the placement rules here work on the assumption that the constituents occur under the scope of the Decl operator. If the illocutionary operator were Int instead, a slight modification of the placement rules would yield the desired sequence:

(40)   *Had John cooked the potatoes?*

Note further that if languages have different constituent ordering patterns, their underlying clause structures can nevertheless have the same form: the ordering differences will be taken care of by the placement rules.

The prosodic contours of linguistic expressions will be sensitive to the following main features of the underlying clause structure:

— lexically distinctive tone differences (if there are any, as in tone languages);
— lexically distinctive accent differences (if there are any) and "characteristic accent positions" of lexical items;
— possible modifications in tone and accent effected by the formal expression rules (e.g. tone or accent shifts effected by inflectional rules);
— the pragmatic functions assigned to the constituents of the underlying clause structure;
— the illocutionary operators, to the extent that these are expressed in prosodic contours.

These appear to be the main features that contribute to the final prosodic contour of linguistic expressions, which will have to be described as the resultant of the different contributions of these various features.

3.3. The structure of this work

The further contents of this work can be briefly sketched as follows:

Part I

Chapter 4 discusses the properties of the basic (lexical) predicate frames which underlie the construction of nuclear predications. The concepts treated here are predicate frame, argument (as opposed to satellite), selection restriction, and meaning postulate / definition.

Chapter 5 treats the different types of States of Affairs which may be designated by nuclear predicate frames, and in relation to this, the semantic functions which may be attached to the argument positions of nuclear predicate frames.

Chapter 6 discusses the nature of "referring" (which is interpreted as a cooperative action of speaker and addressee), the principles of term formation, and the structural and functional properties of term structures. This leads to a typology of entities, a subcategorization of the types of things that can be referred to by means of terms, and to a typology of restrictors, a classification of the types of expression that can be used to constrain the creation or the retrieval of the intended referent. The chapter ends with a discussion of the nature of appositional terms.

Chapter 7 treats the various types of term operators which may go into the construction of term structures: definiteness, specificity, genericity, demonstratives, quantifiers (including cardinals), ordinals, and the operators used for specifying questioned, relativized, and anaphoric terms.

Chapter 8 discusses the treatment of non-verbal predicates (= predicates consisting of an adjective, a noun, a term, an adpositional phrase) in FG. In connection with this, the notion of "copula support" is introduced. The chapter ends with a discussion of locative and existential sentence types.

Chapter 9 shows how the nuclear predication can be extended by predicate operators and predicate satellites, so as to result in a core predication. From the core predication we go on to the construction of the extended predication through the specification of predication operators and predication satellites, by means of which the State of Affairs designated by the core predication is located in the spatial, the temporal, and the cognitive dimensions.

Chapter 10 treats the mechanism of Subject and Object assignment, interpreted in terms of the notion of perspective (= the point of view from which the SoA is presented in the linguistic expression). It is argued that Subj/ Obj assignment possibilities are sensitive to a crosslinguistically valid Semantic Function Hierarchy.

Chapter 11 re-examines the Semantic Function Hierarchy in the light of the present version of FG, and considers whether the hierarchy could be interpreted as an epiphenomenon of the operation of more basic factors, notably the different "priorities" discussed in chapter 2. There is a brief discussion of "Raising" phenomena and of "markedness shift" with respect to Subj / Obj assignment, and its relation to ergativity.

Chapter 12 shows how the extended predication can be built into a propositional structure, how this structure can be extended by propositional operators and satellites, and how the resulting proposition can be built into a clause structure at the speech act level. Then, it discusses the specification of the clause structure with illocutionary operators and satellites.

Chapter 13 treats the mechanism of pragmatic function assignment, introduces the notions of topicality and focality, and distinguishes a number of Topic and Focus functions, which are shown to have a variety of effects on the organization of linguistic expressions in different languages.

Chapter 14 discusses some general properties of expression rules, and sketches a theory of those rules which determine the form of the constituents of the underlying predication.

Chapter 15 shows what sorts of formal effects are brought about by the different operators and functions which characterize the constituents in the underlying structure of the clause.

Chapter 16 discusses the "placement rules" which are responsible for the order of constituents in the final linguistic expression. It introduces the notion of a "multifunctional" account of constituent ordering, and formulates a number of general and specific principles which, in mutual interaction and competition, determine the actual constituent ordering patterns of a language.

Chapter 17 then considers a number of difficulties and complications in the domain of constituent ordering, some of which can be understood in terms of interactions between the constituent ordering principles, whereas others remain unexplained.

Chapter 18 outlines how the expression rules define the prosodic contours of linguistic expressions, taking into account the intrinsic tonal and accentual properties of predicates, the possible influence exerted on such properties by the formal expression rules, and the prosodic effects of pragmatic functions and illocutionary operators.

Part II

Chapter 1 describes how predicate formation rules operate within the model of FG. These rules derive new predicates from given predicates, thus extending the lexical inventory of a language. Predicate formation rules may affect the type of a predicate, the quantitative valency of a predicate, and the qualitative valency of a predicate.

Chapter 2 introduces the notion of "verbal restrictor". This notion covers all restrictors at the level of the term which are based on verbs, and thus generalizes across relative clauses and participial restrictors. Some general properties of verbal restrictors are presented and their treatment in Functional Grammar is explained.

Chapter 3 then discusses the various types of verbal restrictor from a typological perspective. Postnominal, prenominal, and circumnominal verbal restrictors are shown to display a number of recurrent properties.

Chapter 4 offers explanations for a number of these recurrent properties in terms of their relation to the basic Prefield of Postfield orientation of a language on the one hand, and the historical scenarios that lead to the creation of verbal restrictors on the other.

Chapter 5 introduces the notion of "complex term". These are terms which are formed on the basis of a predication, a proposition, or a clause, and thus represent embedded constructions either in argument position ("complement clauses") or in satellite position ("adverbial clauses"). The chapter furthermore discusses the semantic properties of complex terms.

The structure of this work 75

Chapter 6 discusses the functional and formal properties of embedded constructions. The functional properties of embedded constructions concern the semantic, syntactic, and pragmatic functions assigned to them. The formal properties of embedded constructions concern their position in the main clause, the presence of subordination markers, and the internal structure of the embedded construction.

Chapter 7 classifies types of embedded constructions on the basis of the various parameters discussed in chapter 6, and discusses their treatment in Functional Grammar. Some recurrent properties of finite and non-finite constructions and their various subclasses are presented.

Chapter 8 deals with the treatment of polarity distinctions in FG. It is claimed that polarity is operative at various levels of the structure of the clause, which is reflected in the formal expression of negative polarity in particular.

Chapter 9 takes up the topic of coordination and shows that for the treatment of coordinate structures a hierarchical approach to clause structure is required as well, since units of all levels of structure may be coordinated.

Chapter 10 discusses the way in which anaphorical relationships can be handled in FG. Special attention is paid to the nature of the entities to which anaphoric reference can be made and to the ways anaphorical elements are formally expressed.

Chapter 11 goes into the question of how illocutionary distinctions can be treated in FG. The chapter takes basic illocutions, as reflected in sentence types, as its point of departure and then studies the the ways in which these basic illocutions may be adapted to more specific communicative needs via the application of specific grammatical and lexical strategies.

Chapter 12 studies the treatment of various types of question in FG. Q-word questions are studied in most detail, since they relate in interesting ways with verbal restrictors (chapters 2-4) on the one hand, and focus constructions (chapters 13-14) on the other.

Chapter 13 shows the basic patterns that focus constructions may display, and describes their treatment in FG. Special attention is given to Cleft and Pseudocleft constructions, which are interpreted as expression variants of one underlying structure.

Chapter 14 goes into a number of specific topics related to the treatment of focus constructions. Firstly, the status of predicate clefts is discussed. Secondly, the relation between focus constructions and Q-word questions is studied. Finally, the process of markedness shift which leads to the demarking of focus construcions is dealt with.

Chapter 15 studies a number of construction types in which the surface form deviates from the postulated underlying structure, as in the case of Raising. Both formal and positional discrepancies are studied, and their treatment in FG is described.

Chapter 16 picks up various points made in earlier chapters which together contribute to the formulation of a general theory of accessibility, i.e. the extent to which constituents may be subjected to syntactic operations. This theory is defined in terms of relative distance in cognitive space, as measured from the deictic centre.

Chapter 17 deals with the way in which extra-clausal constituents are accounted for in FG. These constituents can neither be analysed as clauses nor as fragments of clauses and are generally only loosely associated with the main clause they precede, follow, or interrupt.

Chapter 18 sketches a number of aspects of the structure of discourse that FG should be capable of accounting for in the long run.

4. The nuclear predication

4.0. Introduction

We saw in the preceding chapter that the kernel of the underlying clause structure is formed by the predication. The predication itself can be divided into three different levels: the nuclear predication, the core predication, and the extended predication. The relationships between these three levels of structure can be symbolized as follows:

(1)   [π_2 e_i: [π_1 [pred [T] (args)] σ_1] σ_2]
            [...nucl. pred....]
          [.....core predication....]
      [.........extended predication........]

Thus, the nuclear predication consists of a predicate of Type T^1, together with the arguments associated with the predicate; the core predication consists of the nuclear predication, extended by predicate operator(s) π_1 and predicate satellites σ_1; the extended predication consists of the core predication, provided with an SoA variable (e_i) and modified by predication operator(s) π_2 and predication satellites σ_2.

We start with the central component of the whole system, the nuclear predication, which itself is formed from predicate frames. We restrict ourselves for the time being to verbal predicates; non-verbal predicates will be treated in chapter 8.

Throughout this chapter, we disregard the internal structure of the terms which may fill the argument (and satellite) positions within the predication. The internal structure of terms is discussed in chapter 6.

---

1. In earlier work on FG the type of the predicate was represented by means of the symbol β.

4.1. The nuclear predication

The fundamental structure of the nuclear predication is determined by the combinatorial possibilities (the *valency*) of the predicate, as defined in the predicate frame. We saw that predicates can be basic or derived. In the former case they are contained in the lexicon, in the latter they are produced through predicate formation rules (see *TFG2:* chapter 1). Here, we mainly restrict our attention to basic predicates.

All predicates are lexical items of the language. In principle FG does not recognize abstract predicates (cf. section 1.7.3.). This means that predicates are forms which can occur in actual linguistic expressions of the language.

When a predicate is basic, this means that the speaker must learn and know it as such in order to be able to use it correctly. It does not mean that the predicate has no internal semantic structure. Indeed, the meaning of most basic predicates is such that it can at least in part be analysed in terms of combinations of the meanings of semantically simpler predicates. Thus, the English predicates *die*, *kill*, and *murder* are basic predicates, since there is no rule of English by means of which they could be formed; they therefore belong to the lexicon of English. Their meanings, however, are structured in the sense that they can be analysed in terms of more elementary predicates.

In order to account for the semantic properties of predicates and the semantic relations that hold between them, each predicate frame in the lexicon is provided with a number of *meaning postulates*. Meaning postulates specify what (combinations of) predicates are entailed by a given predicate frame; in certain cases the meaning postulates associated with a predicate frame add up to a full specification of its meaning, which can be read both ways. In that case the combined meaning postulates provide a *meaning definition* for the predicate in question.

4.2. Predicate frames

The general format of predicate frames can be illustrated with the predicate frame for the English verb *give*:

(2) $(f_i: give)$ [V] $(x_1: \text{<animate>})_{Ag}$ $(x_2)_{Go}$ $(x_3: \text{<animate>})_{Rec}$

The predicate frame specifies the following types of information concerning the predicate:

— the *predicate variable* f_i, symbolizing the property or relation designated by the predicate (see 4.2.1.).
— the *form* of the predicate, here *give* (see 4.2.2.).
— the *Type* of the predicate, here V (verbal) (see 4.2.3).
— the *quantitative valency*: the *number* of arguments that the predicate takes to form nuclear predications. The argument positions are symbolized by the variables $x_1, x_2, ..., x_n$ which mark the argument slots. In terms of quantitative valency, we distinguish one-place (or monovalent), two-place (or bivalent), three-place (or trivalent), and in general n-place predicates. In natural languages, however, the maximum quantitative valency of basic predicates seems to be three, and that of derived predicates four.[2]
— the *qualitative valency*: the *types* of arguments that the predicate takes, as specified by the semantic functions of the arguments, and the selection restrictions imposed on them. The semantic functions tell us which roles are played by the argument entities in the State of Affairs (SoA) designated by the predication. In the case of predicate frame (2), they tell us that the arguments of *give* play the roles of Agent, Goal (or Patient), and Recipient. At the same time, the first argument semantic function (Agent) informs us about the type of SoA involved: an Action, as opposed to a Process, a Position, or a State. This interaction between semantic functions and SoA typology will be discussed in chapter 5. The selection restrictions, such as <animate> in (2), inform us about the semantic type of the terms which can be inserted into the argument positions if one is to arrive at a "normal", non-metaphorical type of predication (see 4.2.6.).

We see that the predicate frame codes a considerable amount of information concerning the semantic and syntactic combinabilities of the predicate. The predicate thus provides a "blueprint" for the types of predication that can be formed around it. Note that when two predicate frames differ in any of the features described above they are, by definition, two different predicate frames. Let us note the following further points about predicate frames:

(i) We saw that the predicate frames themselves define the kinds of structures in which they can be used: we get a nuclear predication when the argument slots of the predicate frame are filled with term structures. There is no need, therefore, for independently generated structures such as constituency or dependency trees for lexical items to be inserted into. The structures are instead directly formed from the lexical items. This makes for parsimony in

---

2. For example, derived causative predicates as in *John let Mary give the book to Peter* may have four arguments. See *TFG2:* chapter 1.

the storage of the relevant information: no such information will be unnecessarily duplicated. Also, it secures the integrity of the argument structure all through the derivational history of any given construction.

(ii) The order in which the predicate and the arguments are given in the predicate frame has no direct or necessary relation to the linear order in which these constituents will finally be expressed. Predicate frame (2) could just as well be written as (3) or (4), without any loss of information:

(3) $(x_3: \text{<animate>})_{Rec} \ (x_2)_{Go} \ (x_1: \text{<animate>})_{Ag} \ (f_i: give) \ [V]$

(4)

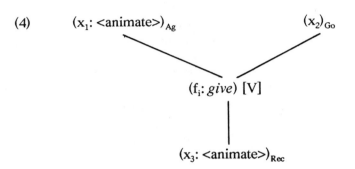

Thus, predicate frames are order-free structures, the constituents of which will finally be linearized by the placement rules. This implies that languages with quite different constituent ordering patterns can nevertheless be described in terms of the same format of predicate frames. This is appropriate, since two predicates of 'giving' from languages with widely divergent constituent orders do not appear to be semantically so different from each other. The notion of the predicate frame thus contributes considerably to the typological adequacy of the theory.

Since the constituents of the predicate frame have no linear order to begin with, they cannot be reordered or moved from one position to another. In this way we avoid permutations of specified elements, a constraint discussed in 1.7.1. above. Note that the numbering of the argument positions $x_1, x_2, x_3,...$ does indeed define an ordering over these positions; but again, this ordering has no direct relation to linear order in the clause: rather, it reflects a priority hierarchy defined over the semantic functions (see 2.4. above), in the sense that Agent arguments are more central to the predication than Goals, and these more central than Recipients. In terms of such differences as these, we shall have reason to distinguish "first arguments" (such as Agent), "second arguments" (such as Goal), and "third arguments" (such as Recipient).

(iii) Predicate frames can be called "open predications" in the sense that they provide structures from which predications can be formed through the insertion of term structures.[3] The term "open predication" can be used for any predicate frame which has at least one term position which has not been filled with a term structure. When all term positions of a predicate frame have been filled by terms, we speak of a "closed predication". Thus, all predicate frames are open predications by definition. But there are also open predications which result from partially filling in the argument positions of a predicate frame. Of special importance are open predications in which all argument positions except one have been filled in with terms. When the remaining slot of such "1-open predications"[4] is marked by x_i, we speak of a "predication open in x_i". The following examples illustrate this terminology:[5]

(5) a. predicate frame (2):
   give [V] $(x_1)_{Ag}$ $(x_2)_{Go}$ $(x_3)_{Rec}$
   = an open predication in x_1, x_2, x_3
   b. open predication in x_1:
   give [V] $(x_1)_{Ag}$ *(the book)*$_{Go}$ *(the girl)*$_{Rec}$
   open predication in x_2:
   give [V] *(the boy)*$_{Ag}$ $(x_2)_{Go}$ *(the girl)*$_{Rec}$
   open predication in x_3:
   give [V] *(the boy)*$_{Ag}$ *(the book)*$_{Go}$ $(x_3)_{Rec}$
   c. closed predication:
   give [V] *(the boy)*$_{Ag}$ *(the book)*$_{Go}$ *(the girl)*$_{Rec}$

Where a many-place predicate defines a relation between its arguments, a 1-open predication in x_i may be interpreted as specifying a property of x_i. Thus, the open predications of (5b) can be said to specify the following properties:

(6) a. the property of 'giving the book to the girl'
    b. the property of 'being given to the girl by the boy'

---

3. Logicians would here speak of "predicational functions": they are functions which take term n-tuples and deliver predications.
4. See Kwee (1979).
5. Note that in giving such examples as in (5), we often leave out details which are not relevant to the point under discussion. As will become clear in chapter 6, the internal structure of terms is much more complex than is suggested by these examples.

c. the property of 'being given the book by the boy'

Because of this property-specifying character, 1-open predications play an important role with respect to a number of grammatical processes. To get a first impression of this, consider a complex term such as:

(7)   the book which was given to the girl by the boy

This term designates an entity which must have the property 'book' and the property of 'having been given to the girl by the boy'. This second property is precisely the property defined by the open predication in x_2 in (5b), as paraphrased in (6b). This explains why the term structure underlying (7) will have roughly the following form:

(8)   (d1x_i: *book* [N]: *give* [V] (*the boy*)$_{Ag}$ (x_i)$_{Go}$ (*the girl*)$_{Rec}$)

The structure of terms will be discussed in detail in chapter 6. The analysis of relative clauses is treated in *TFG2:* chapters 2-4.

4.2.1. Predicate variables[6]

Predicates designate properties of, or relations between the entities referred to by the argument terms. In certain conditions it is possible to anaphorically refer back to such properties or relations, as in:

(9) a. *Jean est intelligent mais Pierre ne l'est pas.*
    b. *Jan is intelligent maar Piet is* het *niet.*
    c. *John is intelligent but Peter isn't* ø.

In French and Dutch the property 'intelligent' is anaphorically referred to by the pronominal elements *le* and *het*, respectively. In English we do not find such a pronominal element, but nevertheless it is understood that it is the property of being intelligent which is denied of Peter. We could say that (9c) is a form of zero anaphora.

Whenever there is an anaphorical relationship of this kind we assume that

---

6. The notion of the predicate variable has been elaborated in Hengeveld (1992a) and Keizer (1992), to which I refer for more detailed argumentation.

the item referred to is represented by a variable in the underlying structure. This variable is then taken up again by the coindexed anaphorical element, which may be marked by the anaphorical operator A.[7] We thus get such relationships such as:

(10)   *John likes Mary* (x_i), *but Peter doesn't like her* (Ax_i)

This approach to anaphora has the virtue of not requiring any kind of deletion or ellipsis in order to correctly specify the anaphorical element. If we follow this line of thought, the fact that properties or relations can be the antecedents of anaphorical elements leads to the recognition of *predicate variables*. Parallel to (10) we should like to analyse (9a) as:

(11)   *Jean est intelligent* (f_i), *mais Pierre ne l'* (Af_i) *est pas.*

This can be achieved if we analyse *Jean est intelligent* as:

(12)   (f_i: *intelligent* [A]) (d1x_i: *Jean*)$_\varnothing$
         'definite single entity x_i such that Jean has property f_i such that intelligent'

Using the variable f_i, we can now analyse constructions such as (11) in the following way:

(13)   (f_i: *intelligent* [A]) (d1x_i: *Jean*)$_\varnothing$ *mais* neg ((Af_i) (d1x_j: *Pierre*)$_\varnothing$)

We can then say that (Af_i) in this type of construction is expressed by a pronominal element in French and Dutch, and by zero in English.

Since anaphorical reference to properties or relations is in principle always possible, a predicate must be understood to always have an associated predicate variable. However, when the predicate variable is not in any way at stake we shall, for the sake of simplicity, write (14a) rather than (14b).

(14) a.   *give* [V] (x_1: <animate>)$_{Ag}$ (x_2)$_{Go}$ (x_3: <animate>)$_{Rec}$
     b.   (f_i: *give*) [V] (x_1: <animate>)$_{Ag}$ (x_2)$_{Go}$ (x_3: <animate>)$_{Rec}$

---

7. Anaphora is discussed in *TFG2*: chapter 10.

4.2.2. The form of the predicate

The form of the predicate must be thought of as coded in some standard type of phonological representation. By convention, where phonological detail is not at stake, we represent the form of the predicate by the written form of the infinitive (in the case of verbs) or the singular form (in the case of nouns). This is, in several respects, a simplification. First, for many languages we will need the *stem* or *root* rather than the infinitive or any other inflected form of the predicate. Second, the predicate may have irregular forms (such as *gave* and *given* for *give*). Since by general principle all forms which cannot be productively derived must be contained in the lexicon, these irregular forms must be stored with the predicate frame in the lexicon. Later we will see that this can be done by storing the irregular forms in a "paradigm" which is associated with the predicate frame. For example:

(15)   paradigm(*give*) = {Past *gave*, Past Participle *given*}

where each of the irregular items must again be thought of as being coded in phonological form. The expression rules will then first consult the lexical paradigms, and choose the relevant form if they find it there; if not, the relevant productive expression rule will be applied (see chapters 14/15 for details).

4.2.3. The Type of the predicate

The Type of the predicate is a receptacle for all those semantic and morpho-syntactic properties of the predicate which in one way or another codetermine the behaviour of the predicate in the construction of linguistic expressions. So far I have only indicated the basic categories V (verbal), A (adjectival), and N (nominal) in the predicate Type. Various subcategories of such categories must be distinguished. Such subcategorial information can then be coded in the Type. Many of the subcategorization and selectional properties of the predicate need not be explicitly coded in the predicate frame, since they can be "read off" from the structural properties of the frame as such. For example, that *give* is ditransitive is clear from the fact that it takes three arguments, that it is agentive is clear from the semantic function on the first argument position, and that it is selectionally restricted to <animate> Agents and Recipients is clear from the selection restrictions on the argument positions.

Other Type features, however, cannot be read off from the predicate frame. Consider some examples. For nouns such as *boy* and *girl* we must know that the former designates male, the latter female entities, in order to account for such phenomena as:

(16) a.   *The boy hurt* him*self.*
     b.   *The girl hurt* her*self.*

In order to be able to account for the correct choice of the reflexive pronoun we can code the relevant information in the Type of these nominal predicates:

(17) a.   *boy* [N,masc]
     b.   *girl* [N,fem]

In other languages such information on the Gender of the noun may have a wider impact on the expression of the relevant constructions. In French, for example, the correct choice of the articles and the formal expression of the adjective need this information:

(18) a.   Le *garçon* *est* beau.
          the boy   is   beautiful
     b.   La *fille est* belle.
          the girl is   beautiful

Just as in the case of nouns, semantic and morphosyntactic Type features may be essential to the behaviour of verbal predicates. For example, only predicates designating a movement may be combined with satellites of Direction:

(19) a.   *John walked* to his house. (Direction)
     b.   **John sang to his house.*

The fact that *walk* designates a movement can be coded in the predicate frame:

(20)   *walk* [V,move] $(x_1: <\text{animate}>)_{Ag}$

and the feature "move" can then be used to open up the possibility of adding a Direction satellite.

Other uses of the Type slot of predicate frames will be given in the further course of this work.

4.2.4. Redundancy rules

There may be certain redundancies between the various properties of a predicate frame. For example, our analysis of States of Affairs and semantic functions in chapter 5 will embody the following claims:

(21) a. all action predicates have the Type features +control and +dynamic
 b. all action predicates have a first argument with semantic function Agent

Thus, the predicate frame (22a) could be more fully specified as (22b):

(22) a. (f_i: *give*) [V] (x_1: <animate>)$_{Ag}$ (x_2)$_{Go}$ (x_3: <animate>)$_{Rec}$
 b. (f_i: *give*) [V,action,+con,+dyn]
    (x_1: <animate>)$_{Ag}$ (x_2)$_{Go}$ (x_3: <animate>)$_{Rec}$

In view of the rules in (21) predicate frame (22b) contains several redundancies. Nevertheless, if might be useful to have such redundant structures available at certain points in the grammar. For example, certain rules might apply to all predicate frames with the feature +con, while other rules might apply to all predicate frames of Type "action". To the extent that this is the case, we can enter some non-redundant type of representation in the lexicon. In this case, the non-redundant representation will contain one of the following pieces of information:

(23) a. the Type contains "action";
 b. the Type contains "+con, +dyn";
 c. the semantic function of the first argument is Agent.

Starting from any of these pieces of information, the other pieces of information can be filled in automatically by redundancy rules.

4.2.5. Arguments vs. satellites

Within the structure of the clause we distinguish two types of term positions: *argument positions* and *satellite positions*. The terms filling these positions may be called arguments and satellites. *Arguments* are those terms which are required by some predicate in order to form a complete nuclear predication.

They are essential to the integrity of the SoA designated by the predicate frame. If we leave them out, the property/relation designated by the predicate is not fulfilled or satisfied. *Satellites* are not in this sense required by the predicate; they give optional further information pertaining to additional features of the SoA (Level 1), the location of the SoA (Level 2), the speaker's attitude towards or evaluation of the propositional content (Level 3), or the character of the speech act (Level 4).

Arguments relate to the predicate; satellites relate to the nuclear predication (Level 1), the core predication (Level 2), the proposition (Level 3), or the clause (Level 4). Arguments have a more central position in the clause, satellites a more peripheral one. We assume that both arguments and satellites are terms, i.e. expressions which can be used to refer to entities.[8]

In many cases this is rather straightforward: the satellite *in the garden* clearly contains a term referring to a particular garden; and *at three o'clock* can be used to refer to that moment of time that, by convention, we call 'three o'clock'. In other cases the term status of satellites may be less clear. For example, is a Manner satellite such as *gracefully* used to refer to an entity of any kind? One indication may be that when we try to paraphrase such adverbial constituents, we usually end up with a term-like expression (e.g. *with grace, in a graceful way/manner*). We return to such questions as these in later sections in which the different types of satellites are discussed.

The distinction between arguments and satellites would be an easy matter if we could simply say: arguments are obligatory, satellites are optional constituents of the clause, and: arguments are characterized by one set of semantic functions, satellites by another set, and these two sets do not overlap. In fact, however, matters are less straightforward than this, so that in certain cases it may be difficult to decide whether a given term has the status of an argument or a satellite. This is especially true of the borderline between arguments and predicate satellites (Level 1), since both types of terms tell us something about the internal properties of the SoA designated by the core predication.

To start with the semantic functions: there is a certain degree of overlap

---

8. Some such distinction as between argument and satellite is made, in one form or another, in different grammatical theories. Thus, Tesnière (1959) distinguishes between *actant* (= argument) and *circonstantiel* (= satellite). In German grammars we find the terms *Ergänzung* ('completion') and *freie Angabe* ('free adjunct'). See also Pinkster (1972) for the distinction between "nucleus" and "periphery".

between argument and satellite functions. In other words, certain semantic functions may sometimes mark a satellite, sometimes an argument.[9] Consider the following pair of constructions:

(24) a. *John bought a car in Amsterdam.*
b. *John lives in Amsterdam.*

In each of these constructions the constituent *in Amsterdam* has the semantic function of Location. However, in (24a) it has the status of a Level 2 satellite, which locates the whole SoA of John's buying a car in the spatial dimension, while in (24b) it is an essential argument of the predicate *live*. Indeed, *live* in this sense designates a relation between an animate being and a Location, and the SoA is not complete if the Location term is left out. Compare:

(25) a. *John bought a car.*
b. *John lives.*

(25b) is certainly grammatical, but with a rather different interpretation of *live* ('be alive') than is appropriate in (24b). Indeed, we can find such constructions as:

(26) *In Amsterdam, John really lives.*

in which *lives* is used in a pregnant intransitive sense, and *in Amsterdam* is, again, a Level 2 satellite. For a similar difference, consider:

(27) a. *They discussed the matter politely.*
b. *They behaved politely.*

In both constructions *politely* has the semantic function of Manner. But in (27a) it provides an optional addition to the predication, in (27b) it is an essential argument of the predicate. And indeed, the predicate *behave* designates a relation between an entity (usually a person) and a way of behaving, whereas *discuss* in (27a) designates a relation between two or more persons and some topic of discussion, the whole of which can be said to be carried out in a certain manner.

---

9. See the discussion in Pinkster (1972: 79-82), from which some of the examples in this section have been borrowed.

Similar pairs can be construed for such semantic functions as Direction and Source, which usually mark satellites. But Direction is a nuclear argument of the predicate *go*, and Source a nuclear argument of the predicate *expel* (somebody [Goal] from something [Source]).

A general test, then, for distinguishing arguments from satellites is the following: a satellite can be left out without affecting the grammaticality or the meaning of the remaining construction, whereas leaving out an argument will either render the remainder ungrammatical or change its semantics. Even this criterion, however, cannot be applied mechanically, for the following reasons:

(i) *Arguments may be left unspecified in certain settings.*
If the setting (= context and situation) is sufficiently specified, even arguments may be left out without affecting the acceptability or the meaning of the remainder, as in:

(28) a. *What shall we do? Buy or sell?*
     b. *Jump!*

Nobody will contend, on the basis of (28a-b), that *buy*, *sell*, and *jump* are zero-place predicates (= predicates without argument positions). But this implies that even conceptually necessary arguments need not be overtly present in the actual linguistic expression, provided they can be reconstructed from the setting in which that expression is used. In the case of imperative speech acts such as (28b) it is even the general rule that the Agent is left unspecified, no doubt because it is evident from the illocutionary act of 'ordering' itself that the Addressee is the intended Agent of the predication.

(ii) *Predicates can be put to so-called "absolute" uses.*
Compare the following constructions:

(29) a. *John was drinking a glass of milk.*
     b. *John was drinking.*
     c. *John drinks.*

In (29a) *drinking*, as expected, is used as a two-place predicate specifying a relation between some animate being and some beverage. In (29b-c) the second argument is not specified. There is a difference between these two constructions, however, in that (29c) can only be interpreted in the pregnant sense of 'being a habitual consumer of alcoholic drinks': it comes close to ascribing a property to John, rather than describing an action in which he is involved. (29b), on the other hand, seems to be ambiguous between the sense of (29a), with a contextually retrievable second argument left unspecified, and the pregnant sense which we find in (29c). One way of capturing these differences is to assume that in one sense of the "absolutely" used predicate *drink* the second argument position, though present in the predicate frame, is not specified through term insertion, whereas in the pregnant sense the two-place predicate *drink* has been turned into a one-place predicate, ascribing a property to the remaining argument. Such a reduction of argument positions would be captured in a predicate formation rule of valency reduction.[10]

The difference between argument positions which have been left unspecified and those which have been removed through valency reduction is required in other cases as well. Compare the following constructions:

(30) a. *The door was slowly opened (by Peter).*
     b. *The door slowly opened (*by Peter).*

In the case of (30a), if the Agent is not specified, the construction is nevertheless interpreted as involving an Agent. In (30b), on the other hand, no Agent argument is understood, and no specified Agent can be added to the construction. We shall account for this difference by assuming that in (30a) the Agent may be left unspecified, whereas in (30b) the Agent position has been removed through valency reduction.

We retain from this discussion that when we find a predicate with n overt arguments, we cannot jump to the conclusion that it is an occurrence of an underlying n-place predicate: it may be an underlying $n+1$-place predicate, one argument position of which has been left unspecified either by virtue of the absolute use of the predicate or by virtue of the fact that its referent can be inferred on the basis of context and situation. Only when these two conditions do not obtain can it be concluded that the predicate is a genuine occurrence of an n-place predicate.

We return to the problems involved in determining the argument structure of predicates and distinguishing between argument and satellite positions in chapters 9 and 11.

---

10. These rules will be discussed in *TFG2*: chapter 1.

4.2.6. Selection restrictions

Let us again consider the predicate frame for *give*:

(31)   *give* [V] $(x_1: \text{<anim>})_{Ag} (x_2)_{Go} (x_3: \text{<anim>})_{Rec}$

In this predicate frame the first and the third argument positions carry the selection restriction <animate>. Note that the selection restriction itself can be considered as a one-place predicate: it designates a property which imposes a condition on the types of terms which may be inserted into the argument position. In relation to such selection restrictions, the following questions must be answered:

(i) Do we need selection restrictions at all? Can they indeed be regarded as specifying a linguistic property of predicate frames (as opposed to being a matter of "knowledge of the world" which should have no place in the linguistic description)?

(ii) What is the status of selection restrictions? Are they abstract predicates, or rather concrete predicates of the object language?

(iii) How do we interpret the condition imposed by a selection restriction? Do we allow selection restrictions to be violated, and if so, what is the effect of violating them?

Let us consider these questions one by one.

(i) *Do we need selection restrictions at all?*
The role of selection restrictions has been controversial ever since they were first proposed. Two positions on this matter can be distinguished, and these can be illustrated with the following example:

(32)   *John was eating a glass of beer.*

Both positions recognize that there is something strange about (32), but they differ on how this strangeness should be accounted for. Position I holds that the strangeness is a function of the linguistic properties of *eat* and *a glass of beer*, and that these properties must somehow be coded in the linguistic description. Position II says that the strangeness can be attributed to our knowledge of the world: we know that people do not normally eat beer, and that is why (32) is strange. Linguistically speaking, there is nothing wrong with (32).

I take position I, for the following reasons. Learning a language means at least learning the predicates of the language. But learning a predicate is not simply learning the combination of a form and a meaning: it means learning the predicate frame, which includes the combinatorial possibilities of the predicate. In part, these combinatorial possibilities are determined by formal factors, where they concern the number and the formal nature of the terms with which the predicate can occur. In part, however, the combinatorial possibilities of a predicate are determined by semantic factors, and this is a fact about the predicate rather than about the "world" to which we apply the predicate. This is especially clear in the case of predicates which can only combine with a very restricted class of arguments. Take a predicate such as *blond*. It is impossible to explain the most current usage of this predicate without mentioning 'hair' (as in fact any dictionary of English does). Suppose the meaning of this predicate were simply defined as 'light-coloured', or 'light-auburn-coloured'; then there would be nothing in my "knowledge of the world" which would predict that this predicate is restricted to terms which in some way involve 'hair'. The restriction must thus be a fact about the predicate, to be captured in the predicate frame.

For a second example, compare the following English and Dutch examples:

(33) a. *John   blew   his nose.*
     b. *Jan   snoot   zijn neus.*

At first sight English *blow* and Dutch *snuiten* are equivalent in meaning. In fact, however, *blow* has a far greater range of applications than *snuiten*, which is practically restricted to 'noses'. On the other hand, Dutch *blazen*, which is the closest translation equivalent to English *blow*, cannot be said of noses:

(34)   **Jan blies zijn neus.*

It seems correct to say, then, that it is a fact about *snuiten* that it is confined to taking "nosey" Goals.

For a third example, consider the following expression, as occurring, for example, in a mythical story:

(35)   *On the third day, following Zeus' instructions, Aphrodite donned a white pellarion.*

I have on purpose chosen the nonsense word *pellarion* to demonstrate that, if one knows the English predicate *don*, one is able to infer that the second argument of this predicate must indicate some kind of garment. This information cannot stem from one's knowledge of the world, since in this case no such knowledge (concerning *pellarion*) exists. The information is simply inferred from the fact that *don* takes only 'clothing' for its second argument. But this is precisely the kind of information which is coded in a selection restriction.

A further argument for the relevance of selection restrictions in linguistic description is of a rather different nature. It is a well-known fact that verbs of movement often undergo a process of "grammaticalization" through which they finally end up as aspectual auxiliaries. For a verb such as *go* this process could pass through the following phases:

(36) a. *John is going to the market.*
 b. *John is going to swim.*
 c. *John is going to be an important person.*
 d. *Prices are going to rise.*

First, we have a movement verb with animate Agent and concrete Direction; then, the Direction is getting more abstract, although still compatible with "movement"; in a third step, real "movement" cannot be involved any more: the dominant value of *go* now is the indication of "prospective" aspect;[11] in the last phase, finally, the first argument need not even be animate any more.

One important feature of this process is that the original movement predicate loses its own selection restrictions, and ends up as an auxiliary verb which, in a sense, inherits the selection restrictions of the predicate with which it is combined (in (36d), for example, the argument *prices* is not geared to *go*, but to *rise*). However, if we want to describe how a predicate loses its selection restrictions over a period of time, then obviously we must have the selection restrictions to start with.[12]

Finally, it may be argued that certain rules of predicate formation affect only the selection restrictions of a predicate frame.[13] If there were no selection restrictions in the predicate frame, then the effect of this kind of rule could not be properly described.

---

11. See chapter 9 for this notion.
12. For loss of selection restrictions as a feature of grammaticalization, see Lehmann (1982a); for applications of this idea to the development of modal verbs in English, Goossens (1987a, 1987b), and to aspectual verbs in Spanish, Olbertz (1989).
13. See Dik (1990) and *TFG2*: chapter 1.

94 *The nuclear predication*

(ii) *What is the status of the predicates figuring in selection restrictions?*
With respect to this question I take the position that, like all predicates in FG, selectional predicates must be predicates of the object language. This is based on the assumption that restrictions on the terms that can be selected by predicates will be made in terms of distinctions which are already made in the lexicon of the language. It embodies the empirical claim that, if a language has no predicate corresponding to English *clothing*, such a predicate will also fail to occur as a restriction on other predicates. Just as predicates in general are interpreted in a language-dependent way, so selectional predicates are also given such a language-dependent interpretation. However, since selection restrictions typically code the most general "categories" into which entities can be classified, the chances are high that they will have direct translation equivalents across languages. For example, I do not know of any language in which <human> and <animate> do not play some role in monitoring the selection of terms. Nor do I know of any language in which these properties cannot be expressed by some lexical item. Although the lexical items for "human" and "animate" necessarily differ across languages, they can thus be paired off as semantically equivalent from one language to another. Considering this equivalence we see that the assumption that selection restrictions are bound to the object language does not necessarily lead to "linguistic relativism" à la Sapir-Whorf.

(iii) *How do selection restrictions operate?*
I shall not interpret selection restrictions as prohibitions on term insertion if a given term does not conform to the selection restrictions imposed on some term position. In other words, the grammar should not forbid the production of such expressions as (32); such expressions do not only occur, but may even fulfil special communicative purposes in special styles. I will assume, however, that when such a construction is produced, it requires certain special strategies of interpretation. This can be achieved in the following way: when the compatibility condition on term insertion is not fulfilled, the result will be a predication which somewhere contains a clash between the selection restrictions and properties of the inserted term. This clash will be signalled in the underlying predication, and will trigger a special interpretation strategy which will try to make (metaphorical[14]) "sense" of the at first sight

---

14. When I say that trespassing against selection restrictions requires metaphorical interpretations, I do not mean to say that all metaphor is created in this way. See Steen (1985) for a wider discussion of metaphor.

contradictory information. Let us illustrate this with the predicate frame for *eat*:

(37)   *eat* [V] $(x_1: \text{<anim>})_{Ag} (x_2: \text{<food>})_{Go}$

Suppose now that the argument slots of this predicate frame are filled as in the following expression:

(38)   *Rust eats iron.*

We then have two "clashes": *rust* is not animate, and *iron* is not a kind of food. (38) will thus require special interpretation strategies for these incompatibilities to be resolved.

We can also say something about the way in which these special strategies may work. In the case of (38), two things could be done:

— retain the ordinary meaning of *eat*, and reinterpret *rust* as compatible with <animate>, and *iron* as compatible with <food>. For example, *rust* could be reinterpreted as 'Rust', a gigantic robot feeding on iron.

— retain the ordinary meanings of *rust* and *iron*, and reinterpret *eat* so as to be compatible with these ordinary meanings. Such reinterpretation could take the following course:

(39) i   'x eats y' normally means that x feeds himself with y;
    ii   in this feeding process, y is destroyed;
    iii what does rust to iron that is comparable to what x does to y when x eats y? Answer: rust corrodes iron;
    iv conclusion: *eat* must here be used as a vivid expression for 'corrode'.

It seems reasonable to ask of a linguistic description that it provide the basis for an understanding of such special interpretation strategies. And this is the case if selection restrictions are coded in predicate frames.

How can selection restrictions be formally treated if they are to achieve this purpose? Here, the following assumptions may be adopted:

(40) (a) the selection restriction is wiped out when the meaning of the inserted term is intrinsically characterized by the selectional predicate;
(b) the selection restriction is retained when the inserted term
(i) is intrinsically unmarked with respect to the selectional predicate in question;
(ii) is intrinsically characterized by some predicate which is incompatible with the selectional predicate.

In the case of (b)(i) the selectional predicate will act as a further specification of the required interpretation of the selected term; in the case of (b)(ii) the resulting "clash" will trigger the special interpretation strategies discussed above.

For a concrete example, consider the predicate *pretty*, which was discussed by Weinreich (1966: 429) in a similar connection. Let us assume that *pretty*, in one of its meanings, is restricted to <feminine> arguments:

(41)   *pretty* [A] (x_1: <fem>)$_\emptyset$

Let us further assume that the Types of *girl* and *man* are characterized as 'feminine' and 'masculine', respectively, whereas *child* is not semantically characterized for these features. Under these assumptions, the conventions (40a-b) above will have the following results:

(42) a.   *pretty* [A] (d1x_i: *girl* [N,fem]: <fem>)$_\emptyset$ →
         pretty [A] (d1x_i: *girl* [N,fem])$_\emptyset$
         'the girl is pretty'

    b.   *pretty* [A] (d1x_i: *child* [N]: <fem>)$_\emptyset$
         'the child is pretty'

    c.   *pretty* [A] (d1x_i: *man* [N,masc]: <fem>)$_\emptyset$
         'the man is pretty'

In (42a) the selection restriction may be wiped out because of its presence in the Type of *girl*. In (42b-c) it must be retained. In (42b) it informs us that *child* must get a 'feminine' interpretation. In (42c) there is a clash between the selection restriction <feminine> and the type feature 'masculine'. This will be a sign for special interpretation strategies to either reinterpret *man* in a way compatible with <feminine>, or *pretty* as being compatible with 'masculine'.

Weinreich proposed to account for such phenomena as these by a "transfer" of features from the predicate to the noun phrases with which it combines. In our analysis this is not necessary, thanks to the notion of the predicate frame: the selection restrictions can immediately be placed in the positions where they exert their influence: in the argument slots where the terms are to be inserted.

4.3. Meaning postulates and meaning definitions

Each basic predicate is listed in the lexicon in the form of a predicate frame in which its irreducible, unpredictable properties are defined. Obviously, the lexicon must also contain some kind of specification of the meaning of the predicate. We saw in 1.7.3. that FG wishes to avoid the use of a language-independent set of abstract semantic predicates. How, then, can the meanings of lexical predicates be specified if no such abstract vocabulary is used?

As a first step towards answering this question, we adopt the concept of "meaning postulate". This concept was first introduced by Carnap (1956) on the basis of the following considerations. Carnap compared such pairs as the following:

(43) a. *John is a bachelor.*
 b. *John is not married.*

When statement (43a) is true, he reasoned, it may be legitimately inferred that (43b) is also true. This inference is not warranted by the "logical form" of (43a), but rather by a semantic property of the predicate *bachelor*. In order to capture this property, Carnap proposed to adopt meaning postulates of the following form:

(44) $bachelor(x) \rightarrow not(married(x))$

If a logical system contains such a postulate, this will warrant the inference from (43a) to (43b). Note the following points about such meaning postulates.

— They relate one predicate to another predicate, or to a combination of predicates. The entailed predicate may itself be the antecedent of another meaning postulate. For example, 'married' might in turn be linked to 'having a spouse'.

— They are one-way implications: if we know that somebody is a bachelor, we may infer that he is not married, but if we know that somebody is not married, we may not infer that he/she is a bachelor (e.g., if the person is female, she might be a spinster).

Thus, a meaning postulate does not provide a definition of the meaning of the antecedent predicate; it does specify an aspect of that meaning. A full meaning definition would require that the meaning postulate forms a two-way implication (an equivalence). For example, the following might be an approximation to a meaning definition for (the relevant sense of) *bachelor*:

(45) $bachelor(x) \leftrightarrow unmarried\ man(x)$

For many basic predicates it is questionable whether such meaning definitions can be set up. Consider an example such as *geranium*. We all know that a geranium is a plant, and most of us recognize a geranium when we see one. But it is extremely difficult to formulate in words those properties which differentiate geraniums from all other plants. For this, we would need a definition of the form:

(46) $geranium(x) \leftrightarrow plant(x)\ \&\ ???(x)$

where "???" tells us precisely what properties a plant must have in order to qualify as a geranium and nothing else. It is questionable, I think, whether the knowledge represented by "???" is coded in verbal form at all. It might be that, associated with the predicate *geranium*, we have some kind of perceptual representation (a little "mental image") which allows us to discriminate geraniums from other plants. This would imply that the meaning of *geranium* cannot be fully specified in verbal form. Interestingly, certain dictionaries do provide little "pictures" with their definition of such words as these.[15]

For many other dictionary definitions it is questionable whether they add up to a full meaning definition. Consider the following example:

(47)   *robin*: small, red-breasted bird.

This paraphrase is correct as a meaning postulate, in as far as it warrants such inferences as the following:

---

15. Obviously, a botanist could give a full verbal definition of *geranium*; but that definition would not embody the kind of knowledge that allows the average natural language user to recognize a geranium.

(48)   John saw a robin yesterday.
         Therefore: John saw a bird yesterday.
                       It was relatively small.
                       It had a red breast.

But the following inference is not warranted:

(49)   John saw a small red-breasted bird yesterday.
         Therefore: John saw a robin yesterday.

We conclude that meaning postulates provide a partial specification of the meaning of a predicate. The more specific the meaning postulates are, the closer they approximate the full meaning of the predicate.

Let us now suppose that, for certain predicates, a full meaning definition is possible. It will then be clear that, given our assumptions, such a meaning definition will take the form of a two-way meaning postulate in which the predicate is associated with a full paraphrase in terms of other predicates of the language. In fact, this is not very different from what native speakers and current monolingual dictionaries do in trying to define the meaning of a word. For example, both native speakers and dictionaries are likely to define *bachelor*, in its most current usage,[16] as follows:

(50)   *A bachelor is an unmarried man.*

Note the following properties of this type of definition:
— the defining predicates *unmarried* and *man* are lexical items of English, just like the defined predicate *bachelor*;
— these defining predicates are themselves semantically complex. For example, *unmarried* can be further defined as 'not having a spouse', and *man* can be further defined as 'adult male person'.

We shall now assume that in those cases in which meaning definitions can be provided, these will take a form which closely corresponds to (50), adapted to the formal nature of predicate frames as conceived in FG. We shall refer to this kind of meaning analysis as "stepwise lexical definition".[17]

Before attempting to give a formal representation of (50), we have to take into account that the defining predicates *unmarried* and *man* do not have the

---

16. For the sake of the argument we disregard other meanings of *bachelor* here.
17. See Dik (1978b) for a more detailed motivation of this approach.

same status. As different authors have argued,[18] we can use the predicate *bachelor* to say, of a man, that he is unmarried, but not to say, of some unmarried person, that he/she is a man: in applying the predicate *bachelor*, we presuppose the predicate 'man', while asserting the predicate 'unmarried'. The following paraphrase would do more justice to this difference:

(51)   saying, of a man, that he is a bachelor is to say that he is unmarried; and saying, of a man, that he is unmarried is to say that he is a bachelor.

This brings us to the following form of meaning definition:

(52)   *bachelor* [N] $(x_i: <man [N]>)_\emptyset \leftrightarrow$ *unmarried* [A] $(x_i: man [N])$

Note that both the definiendum and the definiens here take the form of predicate frames; this is understandable, since predicates do not occur outside predicate frames according to FG. Note further that the predicate *man* acts as a selection restriction on (this meaning of) the predicate *bachelor*, and that both *unmarried* and *man* are themselves semantically complex predicates, i.e. will be specified by further meaning definitions or postulates. The definition in (52) warrants the following inferences:

(53) a.   *X is a bachelor.*
     b.   Therefore: *X is unmarried.*
     c.   *X is a man.*

However, (53b) is warranted by the assertion contained in *bachelor*, while (53c) is warranted by the presupposition associated with *bachelor*.

The idea of stepwise lexical definition may be illustrated with the following example. Let us assume the following definitions for the predicates *assassinate, murder, kill,* and *die*:

(54) a.   *assassinate*   murder in a treacherous way
     b.   *murder*   kill a human being intentionally
     c.   *kill*   cause an animate being to die
     d.   *die*   become dead

---

18. McCawley (1968: 268), Miller (1969), Fillmore (1971: 382).

Meaning postulates and meaning definitions 101

To the extent that these definitions are correct, we might also define *assassinate* as follows:

(55) *assassinate*   intentionally cause a human being to become dead, in a treacherous way

The idea of stepwise lexical definition is that (54a) is a better representation of the meaning of assassinate than (55), although (55) can be derived from the combined definitions in (54). The assumption is, in other words, that meaning definitions form a network between predicates, in such a way that each predicate is defined in terms of the "highest" available predicates which together provide a paraphrase of the definiendum. Each of the defining predicates will then be further defined, until we reach a set of predicates which cannot be further defined. A meaning definition, according to this "stepwise" concept, provides a "first order" paraphrase of the defined predicate.

The meaning definitions of the verbal predicates in (54) can now be more formally represented as follows:[19]

(56) a. *assassinate* [V] $(x_1: \text{<hum>})_{Ag} (x_2: \text{<hum>})_{Go} \leftrightarrow$
      murder [V] $(x_1)_{Ag} (x_2)_{Go} (x_3: \textit{treacherous} [A])_{Man}$

   b. *murder* [V] $(x_1: \text{<hum>})_{Ag} (x_2: \text{<hum>})_{Go} \leftrightarrow$
      kill [V] $(x_1)_{Ag} (x_2)_{Go} (x_3: \textit{intentional} [A])_{Man}$

   c. *kill* [V] $(x_1)_{Ag/Fo} (x_2: \text{<anim>})_{Go} \leftrightarrow$
      cause [V] $(x_1)_{Ag/Fo} (e_1: [\textit{die} [V] (x_2))_{Proc}])_{Go}$

   d. *die* [V] $(x_1: \text{<anim>})_{Proc} \leftrightarrow$
      come about [V] $(e_1: [\textit{dead} [A] (x_1)_\emptyset])_{Proc}$

Some features of these definitions are obviously tentative. Note that (56c) expresses that to kill an animate being is to cause a process e_1 in which that being dies; and (56d) expresses that to say that an animate being dies is to say that a process takes place through which it comes about that that being is dead.

Let us add the following notes to this conception of meaning definition:

(i) In contrast to what was assumed in Generative Semantics, these meaning

---

19. Man = Manner, Fo = Force, Proc = Processed (= the undergoer of a process); e_1 is an "event" or SoA variable.

definitions are not judged to play a direct role in the construction of predications. In constructing a predication with the predicate *assassinate*, for example, we do not first form some such expression as (55), which is then lexicalized into the verb *assassinate*. The predicate *assassinate* is immediately available in the lexicon for the construction of predications. Its meaning definition can be "unpacked" when necessary. It explains what meaning we attach to the predicate, and what inferences are warranted on the basis of the predicate.

(ii) Our view of stepwise lexical definition implies that after a number of definitions have been run through, we inevitably arrive at predicates which cannot be provided with a definition themselves. Otherwise, the whole procedure of defining meanings would be hopelessly circular. Often, this danger of circularity is advanced against the very idea of defining lexical items in terms of other lexical items. That counter-argument only holds, however, if it is assumed that all lexical items should be provided with a meaning definition, but not if it is assumed that in every language there is a set of lexical predicates the meaning of which cannot be defined in terms of the meanings of other predicates of the same language. These will be the semantically most basic predicates of the language. Note that this does not exclude the possibility that these predicates are connected to each other through meaning postulates of the one-way format of (44), nor that there may be other ways of characterizing such predicates (e.g. in terms of perceptual distinctions, or through ostensive means).

(iii) One property of the approach suggested here is that "defining meaning" is a language-internal affair, dealing with a network of implicational relations between the predicates of a language. One question which naturally arises is: how can we understand translation from one language to another, if such translation is not mediated through a set of language-independent semantic representations? The answer to this is that translation will have to be reconstructed in much the same way as is done in a bilingual dictionary. Such a dictionary establishes (partial) correspondences between the predicates of two distinct languages. Sometimes these correspondences are quite close, sometimes they are only approximations, and sometimes there are no correspondences at all. Typically, the position of some predicate in the network of semantic relations of the target language will not be precisely the same as in the source language network.[20] But this lack of correspondence

---

20. A system for precisely describing the possible differences between the lexical networks of two languages was developed by Van Leuven-Zwart (1984).

will come as no surprise to those who have experience in the matter of translation.

(iv) Since the defining expressions have the same formal structure as the defined expressions we can, in any underlying clause structure, replace the defined expression by the defining expression, thus arriving at a first-order paraphrase of the underlying structure. For the way in which this has been actually implemented in a computational version of FG, see Dik (1992).

4.4. Idioms

As noted before, predicates do not necessarily consist of words. They may consist of stems, but they may also consist of word combinations. The general rule is that any lexical expression which has unpredictable features either in a formal or a semantic respect will be stored in the lexicon in the form of a predicate frame. By "idiom" we shall understand any composite linguistic expression, the meaning of which cannot be compositionally derived from the meanings of its parts. Examples would be *kick the bucket* 'die', or *hit the sack* 'go to bed'. The most important problems concerning idioms are

— How can a unified meaning be assigned to a composite expression (which need not even form one constituent)?

— How can we account for the fact that idioms, although having a unified meaning, nevertheless undergo some (though not all) of the grammatical processes which are characteristic of the corresponding "free" expressions?[21]

For example, in the description of *kick the bucket* we must be able to assign the unified meaning 'die', while at the same time allowing sufficient freedom for the expression to occur in various tenses and aspects, as well as in nominalizations such as: *John's kicking the bucket*.

For these problems the notion of the predicate frame offers a rather natural solution. The idiom *kick the bucket*, for example, can have the following entry in the lexicon:

(57)   *kick* [V] (x_1: <anim>)$_{Proc}$ (*the bucket*)$_{[Go]}$
         ↔
         die [V] (x_1)$_{Proc}$

---

21. For discussion of these problems see Chafe (1968), Weinreich (1969) and Fraser (1970). The solution offered here is similar to that of Jackendoff (1975). For a fuller discussion of the treatment of idioms in FG, see Dik (1989b, 1992).

Note the following features of this lexical entry:

— *kick the bucket* is presented as one whole entry; but the advantage of the predicate frame is that *the bucket* can be placed in its proper argument position, which accounts for the fact that it does behave like a Goal-Object in surface structure;

— since *the bucket* is given as a "ready-made" expression, the term is "sealed off" in such a way that there is no chance for *kick a bucket* or *kick (the) buckets* to ever receive this particular reading;

— the first argument semantic function Processed characterizes the whole expression as designating a process rather than an action;

— the whole expression is semantically defined as 'die', which assigns the required unified meaning;

— *the bucket* is marked as what we might call "Pseudo-Goal"[22] [Go], a marking which signals that it is Goal-like in certain respects (e.g. with respect to placement rules), but lacks other properties typical of Goal constituents: for example, it cannot receive Subject function, since a passive version cannot get the idiomatic interpretation:

(58) a.　*John finally kicked the bucket.*　　　[literal / idiomatic]
　　 b.　*The bucket was finally kicked by John.* [only literal]

The precise "sealing off" of idioms in their lexical predicate frames in such a way that they can be input to just those grammatical processes which they can indeed undergo, and no others, is by no means a trivial matter, especially since idioms differ in their degrees of grammatical freedom (cf. Fraser 1970). But I hope it is clear that the predicate frame offers a powerful instrument for capturing both the formal and the semantic properties of idioms.

In the ProfGlot program (Dik 1992) this approach to idioms has been implemented in such a way that idioms can be correctly produced, parsed, and paraphrased in their literal as well as their idiomatic readings.

---

22. A term suggested by Tweehuysen (1988).

5. States of Affairs and semantic functions

5.0. Introduction

Nuclear predications consist of terms which designate entities in some world, and of predicates which designate properties of, or relations between such entities. The nuclear predication as a whole designates a set of States of Affairs (SoAs), each member of the set being defined by the particular property or relation designated by the predicate. The term "State of Affairs" is here used in the wide sense of "conception of something which can be the case in some world". This definition implies that an SoA is a conceptual entity, not something that can be located in extra-mental reality, or be said to exist in the real world.

SoAs can be divided into different types, according to their values for a number of semantic parameters. These parameters and their values together define a semantic cross-classification of SoAs. This cross-classification is relevant to both the semantic and the syntactic properties of the expressions involved. By "types" of SoA we mean such differences as between:

(1) a. *John saw a bird.* (Process, Experience)
　　b. *He shot at it.* (Action)
　　c. *The bird fell down.* (Process)
　　d. *It was dead.* (State)

The semantic functions which characterize the argument positions of a predicate frame have been devised in such a way as to correlate partially with the typology of SoAs. Thus, the type of SoA can partially be derived from the semantic function assigned to the first argument position of a predicate frame, in the sense that, for example, an Action type SoA is coded in a predicate frame with a first argument semantic function Agent, and conversely, a first argument function Agent signals an Action type SoA.

In this chapter, we first discuss the typology of SoAs,[1] and then the

---

1. There is an extensive literature on what is here called the typology of SoAs. Sometimes, the relevant distinctions are discussed under the label of "Aspect", sometimes under that of "Mode of Action" (Aktionsart). Most important for the distinctions made here are Lakoff (1966), Vendler (1967), Chafe (1970), Verkuyl

distribution of semantic functions over the argument positions of nuclear predicate frames.

5.1. States of Affairs, predicates, and "Modes of Action"

What is here called the typology of SoAs is sometimes discussed in terms of a typology of predicates. This is less appropriate, since many predicates can occur in predications which designate different types of SoAs. In such cases, the semantic nature of the whole predication is codetermined by the nature of the arguments and satellites with which the predicate combines. The SoA type is then a compositional function of the semantic properties of both predicate and terms. This compositional nature of the relevant distinctions was most clearly demonstrated by Verkuyl (1972). Setting up a typology of SoAs then raises the question of what properties of predicates and terms enter into the definition SoA types (Verkuyl 1972; De Groot 1985). From our present point of view, this problem is subordinate to the typology of SoAs as such.

A second, terminological matter concerns the use of such terms as "Aspect" or "Mode of Action" (Aktionsart) for the distinctions within the typology of SoAs. I will reserve the term "Aspect" for distinctions which are expressed by grammatical means (see chapter 9). By contrast, the distinctions made in the typology of SoAs concern the internal semantics of the predication. For such distinctions, the term "Mode of Action" will be used. This term will here be regarded as synonymous with "Type of SoA".

5.2. Semantic parameters for a typology of SoAs

The most important parameters for a semantic typology of SoAs are the following:

(1972), Comrie (1976), Lyons (1977), Dowty (1979), and Vet (1980). Within FG, relevant studies are Dik (1975b, 1978a), Pinkster (1983), Vester (1983), De Groot (1983b, 1984), and Brigden (1984). The present analysis is closest to Pinkster (1983) and Vester (1983), incorporating some modifications suggested in the other sources mentioned.

(2) ± Dynamic   [±dyn]
     ± Telic   [±tel]
     ± Momentaneous   [±mom]
     ± Control   [±con]
     ± Experience   [±exp]

These parameters, as well as some of their interactions, are discussed below.

5.2.1. ± Dynamic

A [-dyn] SoA is an SoA which does not involve any change, i.e., where the entities involved are presented as being or remaining the same at all points of the time interval during which the SoA obtains. We can use the general term *Situation* for such [-dyn] SoAs. The following predications describe Situations:

(3) a. *The substance was red.*
    b. *John was sitting in his father's chair.*

Suppose we want to claim that the substance was red for a whole day, then at whatever moment during that day the substance must have been red. And if John was sitting in his father's chair for an hour, then at any moment during that hour it must have been true that he was sitting in his father's chair.

[+dyn] SoAs, on the contrary, necessarily involve some kind of change, some kind of internal dynamism. This dynamism may consist in a recurrent pattern of changes all through the duration of the SoA, or in a change from some initial SoA into some different final SoA. [+dyn] SoAs may be called *Events* and are illustrated in (4):

(4) a. *The clock was ticking.*
    b. *The substance reddened.*
    c. *John opened the door.*

One criterion for distinguishing between [+dyn] and [-dyn] SoAs is that the former do, but the latter do not combine with satellites of Speed, as in:

(5) a. *The clock was ticking quickly.*
    b. *The substance reddened quickly.*
    c. *John opened the door quickly.*

(6) a. *The substance was red (*quickly).*
    b. *John was sitting in his father's chair (*quickly).*

This criterion requires some qualification, however, because of such constructions as:

(7) a. *Quickly, the whole substance was red.*
    b. *Quickly, John was sitting in his father's chair.*

In such constructions, however, the satellite of Speed does not specify the speed with which the SoA takes place, but the lapse of time before the moment at which the SoA is established. As we will see later on, *quickly* may thus either be a Level 1 satellite which specifies the internal constitution of the SoA, or a Level 2 satellite which serves to locate the SoA with respect to some reference point. The difference is reflected in both the position and the intonation contour of the satellite. Our criterion for [±dyn] should thus be formulated in terms of combinability with Level 1 satellites of Speed.

5.2.2. ± Telic

A [+tel] SoA is an SoA which reaches a natural terminal point[2] if it is fully achieved.

Compare the following expressions:

(8) a. *John was painting.*   [-tel]
    b. *John was painting a portrait.* [+tel]
    c. *John was painting portraits.* [-tel]

Note that one can go on painting or painting portraits indefinitely, but one cannot go on painting a portrait indefinitely. At least, the idea of painting a portrait is such that if the action is fully achieved, the product of the action, the portrait, is finished. It is clear that in the examples (8a-c) it is the nature of the

---

2. Compare Comrie (1976: 44) for this formulation. Vester (1983) uses [±change] for this feature, Vet (1980) uses [±transition], and Dowty (1979) speaks of "definite change" [+telic] and "indefinite change" [-telic]. I here follow Brigden (1984), and De Groot (1983b).

Goal term which determines the telicity. Telicity may also be determined by a Direction satellite, as in (9), or by the first argument of a one-place predicate (as in (10)):

(9) a. *John walked in the park.* [-tel]
 b. *John walked to the station.* [+tel]
(10) a. *Demonstrators were passing the station.* [-tel]
 b. *The demonstrators were passing the station.* [+tel]

Since (10b) presupposes a specified quantity[3] of demonstrators, it is clear that if the Action is finished, all the demonstrators will have passed the station. The same will be true "in reality" in the case of (10a) (because in practice demonstrations do not go on indefinitely), but since the term *demonstrators* does not designate a specified quantity, the predication as such does not linguistically signal the feature [+tel].

Several criteria can be used to determine the telicity of an SoA. [-tel] predications can take a Duration satellite of the form *for an hour*; [+tel] predications (if they are also [-momentaneous]) can take satellites of 'the time in which' of the form *in an hour*; but the converse does not hold:

(11) a. *John painted for an hour (*in an hour).* [-tel]
 b. *John painted the portrait in an hour (*for an hour).* [+tel]

A related test lies in the (im)possibility of embedding the predication under such expressions as 'It took X three hours to...':

(12) a. **It took John three hours to paint (portraits).* [-tel]
 b. *It took John three hours to paint a portrait.* [+tel]
(13) a. **It took John three hours to run in the forest.* [-tel]
 b. *It took John three hours to run the marathon.* [+tel]

A third test involves the semantic effect of adding a constituent such as *almost*:

(14) a. *John almost ran in the forest.* [-tel]
 b. *John almost ran the marathon.* [+tel]

---

3. This term is used by Verkuyl (1972).

These expressions differ in their possibilities of interpretation. (14a) can only mean that John was very close to running in the forest, but did not actually do it; (14b) can have the same interpretation, but also the additional interpretation that he did run, but stopped running just before finishing the marathon. The explanation of this difference is, that in [+tel] but not in [-tel] SoAs, *almost* can relate to the terminal point as well as to the initial point of the SoA.

A final test of telicity is based on a differential property of [±tel] SoAs which can most clearly be illustrated by the following schema:

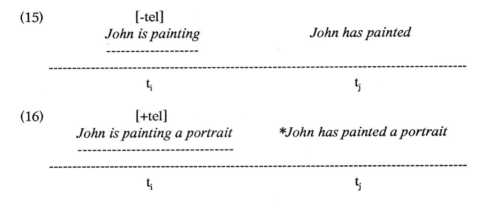

(15)   [-tel]
      John is painting   *John has painted*

      ----
                   t_i t_j

(16)   [+tel]
      John is painting a portrait   **John has painted a portrait*

      ----
                   t_i t_j

When it is truly said that, at some time interval t_i, a [-tel] SoA obtains, then it may be concluded at some later interval t_j, that this SoA has obtained. This is symbolized in (15). But when the original SoA was [+tel], as in (16), no such conclusion is warranted. For example, even if it is true that at some time interval t_i John was painting a portrait, we cannot with certainty conclude that it is true at some later interval t_j that John has painted a portrait. This is because the Perfect (*has painted*) presupposes that the SoA was fully achieved, whereas the Progressive (*is painting*), in the case of [+tel] SoAs, signals the non-achievement of the Action.[4] The same effect can be found in:

(17) a. *John was walking in the park yesterday.*
         Therefore, he has walked in the park.
     b. *John was walking to the station yesterday.*
         **Therefore, he has walked to the station.*

---

4. See Comrie (1976), Dowty (1979), Vester (1983) for this test.

If the conclusion from the Progressive to the Perfect is logically warranted, as in (17a), then the antecedent SoA is [-tel]; if not, as in (17b), then it is [-tel].

5.2.3. ± Momentaneous

Situations and [-tel] Events are conceived as having unlimited duration: they can go on forever. [+tel] Events have limited duration: they go on until the natural terminal point is reached. Within the category of [+tel] Events, we can distinguish between [+momentaneous] (or "punctual") and [-momentaneous] Events. [+mom] Events are conceived as having no duration: their beginning coincides with their terminal point; they occupy only one point in time. [-mom] Events, on the other hand, occupy a certain stretch of time, and have a distinct beginning and terminal point.

One test for the distinction between [±mom] Events is whether or not they can combine with aspectual verbs (see chapter 9) which signal the beginning, the continuation, or the end of the Event. If so, the Event is [-mom]:

(18) a. *John started / continued / finished painting the portrait.*
 b. **John started / continued / finished reaching the summit.*
(19) a. *The water started / continued / finished pouring down.*
 b. **The bomb started / continued / finished exploding.*

Note that in some cases [+mom] Events can be combined with aspectual verbs:

(20) a. *The climbers continued reaching the summit.*
 b. *The bombs finished exploding.*

But in such cases, the interpretation will have an "iterative" character: the predication is interpreted as signalling a series of [+mom] Events.

5.2.4. The interrelations between [dyn], [tel], and [mom]

The interrelations between the parameters [dyn], [tel], and [mom] can be described as in the following graph:

(21)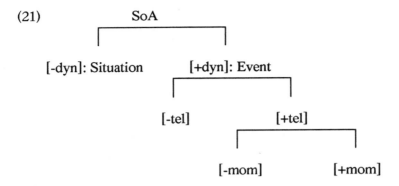

From (21) it is clear that Situations can never be [+tel], and that Situations and [-tel] Events can never be [+mom].[5] This is captured by the following redundancy rules:

(22) a. [±tel] → [+dyn]
     b. [±mom] → [+tel]

Thus, if the Type of a predication contains either [+tel] or [-tel], we may add the feature [+dyn]; when it contains either [+mom] or [-mom], we may add [+tel]. It follows that [±mom] redundantly implies [+tel] and [+dyn].

5.2.5. ± Control

Cutting across the distinctions made in (21) there is a fundamental distinction between [+controlled] and [-controlled] SoAs. An SoA is [+con] if its first argument has the power to determine whether or not the SoA will obtain. If so, the first argument entity is the controller of the SoA. The following are examples of [+con] and [-con] SoAs:

(23) a. *John opened the door.* [+con]
     b. *John was sitting in the garden.* [+con]
(24) a. *The substance was red.* [-con]
     b. *The tree fell down.* [-con]

---

5. See Pinkster (1983) and Vester (1983).

In the most usual interpretations of (23a-b) it is John who determines whether or not the SoA obtains. John could have decided not to open the door, or not to sit in the garden. John is the controller of these SoAs. In (24a), however, the substance can't help being red, and in (24b) the tree could not have decided not to fall. The substance / the tree are non-controlling participants in these SoAs.

The opposition between [+con] and [-con] SoAs is very important in relation to various rules of grammar. Consider the following examples:

— *orders and requests (directives)*
All expressions which designate an order or request from A to B require that that which is ordered / requested be in the control of B. Therefore, predications which occur in imperatives or in the complement of predicates such as *order, persuade, request*, etc. must designate [+con] SoAs. Compare:

(25) a. *John, come here!*   [+con]
     b. **John, fall asleep!*   [-con]
(26) a. *Bill ordered John to be polite.*   [+con]
     b. **Bill ordered John to be intelligent.*   [-con]

'Coming here' and 'being polite' are things which John may be presumed to control. 'Falling asleep' and 'being intelligent' are not. Note that interpretations may be imposed on the b-constructions, but only when some measure of control is attributed to SoAs which are normally out of control: for example, 'pretend to fall asleep / to be intelligent'.

— *promises (commissives)*
Expressions which designate a promise or some other commitment from A to B require that that which is promised be in the control of A:

(27) a. *John promised Bill to be polite.*   [+con]
     b. **John promised Bill to be intelligent.*   [-con]

— *satellites*
Certain satellites are sensitive to the [±con] character of the SoA which they modify; for example, Beneficiary and Instrument require [+con] SoAs:

(28) a. *John cut down the tree for my sake.*   [+con]
     b. **The tree fell down for my sake.*   [-con]
(29) a. *John cut down the tree with an axe.*   [+con]
     b. **The tree fell down with an axe.*   [-con]

Similar restrictions hold for other satellites. We return to this in chapter 9.

Each of the SoA types of diagram (21) has a [+con] and a [-con] subtype. The following terminology will be used for the resulting typology of SoAs:

Table 6. Typology of States of Affairs

general term	[+control]	[-control]
[-dyn] Situation	Position	State
[+dyn] Event	Action	Process
[-telic] Event	Activity	Dynamism
[+telic] Event	Accomplishment	Change

We shall not use special terms for [±mom] Events. When these features are relevant, they will be mentioned separately from the types Accomplishment and Change (compare Vet 1980: 68-69, Vester 1983: 36). Here are some further examples of the SoA types in Table 6:

(30) a. Position   *John kept his money in an old sock.*
     b. State   *John's money is in an old sock.*
     c. Activity   *John was reading a book.*
     d. Dynamism   *The clock was ticking.*
     e. Accomplishment   *John ran the marathon in three hours.*
     f. Change   *The apple fell from the tree.*

Note that Event = Action or Process, Action = Activity or Accomplishment, Process = Dynamism or Change, and Situation = Position or State. The possible combinations of [dyn], [tel], and [con] features can be read off from Table 7.

Table 7. Feature combinations for States of Affairs

Type of SoA	[dyn]	[con]	[tel]
Situation	—		
State	—	—	
Position	—	+	
Event	+		
Process	+	—	
Dynamism	+	—	—
Change	+	—	+
Action	+	+	
Activity	+	+	—
Accomplishment	+	+	+

5.2.5. ± Experience

By an Experience we understand an SoA which cannot obtain but through the sensory or mental faculties of some animate being. An Experience is an SoA in which some animate being perceives, feels, wants, conceives, or otherwise experiences something. Consider the following [+exp] examples:

(31) a.   [+exp] Position, [+exp][-dyn][+con]:
      John did not believe the story.
  b.   [+exp] State, [+exp][-dyn][-con]:
      John did not know the story.
  c.   [+exp] Accomplishment, [+exp][+dyn][+con][+tel]:
      John conceived a clever trick.
  d.   [+exp] Activity, [+exp][+dyn][+con][-tel]:
      John was thinking about his money problems.
  e.   [+exp] Change, [+exp][+dyn][-con][+tel]:
      John got an interesting idea.
  f.   [+exp] Dynamism, [+exp][+dyn][-con][-tel]:
      John dreamed about his girl friend.

116   *States of Affairs and semantic functions*

Each of the SoA types that we have distinguished in Tables 6 and 7 may occur in a [+exp] or [-exp] version, as shown by the English examples in (31). These examples do not differ in crucial ways from the corresponding [-exp] construction types. More generally, it often seems to be the case that languages model their [+exp] constructions on the pattern of the corresponding [-exp] constructions. This implies that the opposition [±exp] does not necessarily have a deep impact on the grammatical organization of natural languages.

This observation is reinforced by the fact that we do not find special coding devices for Experiencer arguments, for example in the form of a special case or a special adposition marking the Experiencer *John* in such constructions as displayed in (31). This in contrast to such semantic functions as Agent, Recipient, or Instrument, for which we usually do find some such coding device. For this reason I believe that "Experiencer" should not be recognized as a distinct semantic function on a par with the others mentioned.

There are languages, however, in which [+exp] predications do differ grammatically from [-exp] predications. In such languages it is typically the case that [+con][+exp] predications follow the pattern of the corresponding [-exp] predications, whereas [-con][+exp] predications have their own distinct construction type. In such languages we typically find such patterns as the following:

(32) a.   [-exp] Position: *John did not wait for his friend.*
     b.   [+exp] Position: *John did not believe the story.*
(33) a.   [-exp] State: *John did not sleep on the ground.*
     b.   [+exp] State: **John did not know the story.*
                             To John was not known the story.

Note that only the [+exp][-con] construction follows a pattern different from the corresponding [-exp] construction. For a concrete example, consider the following constructions from Kannada (Sridhar 1976a, 1976b):

(34) a.   *avaru   hadannu   kelidanu.*   [+exp][+con]
          he-nom   music-acc   heard
          'He listened to the music'
     b.   *avarige   hadu   kelisitu.*   [+exp][-con]
          he-dat   music-nom   heard
          'To him the music heard.' = 'He heard the music.'

(35) a. *avaru   ātmahatye   mūḍikoṇḍaru.*   [-exp][+con]
       he-nom   suicide   committed
       'He committed suicide'
   b. **avarige ātmahatye   āyitu.*   [-exp][-con]
       he-dat   suicide   happened
       'He experienced/underwent suicide'

(34a) is the normal construction for a controlled Position. The feature [+exp] does not trigger a special construction type in the [+con] condition. (34b), however describes the uncontrolled auditive perception of something, and does have a special construction type: the Experiencer appears in the dative, and the phenomenon experienced in the nominative. On the other hand, this special construction type is not allowed in those cases in which the SoA designated has the feature [-exp], whether controlled (35a) or not (35b).

In the dative Experiencer construction in Kannada the Experiencer usually precedes the nominative term in constituent order, contrary to what is otherwise the case when both a nominative and a dative cooccur in one clause. Thus, in order to be able to account for this construction type, we must in one way or another be able to identify it as [+exp] in underlying structure. We return to this below, in section 5.3.1.

5.3. Nuclear semantic functions

5.3.0. Introduction

In this section I discuss the distribution of semantic functions over the argument positions of basic nuclear predicate frames. Let us recall the points that are relevant to this discussion.

— Semantic functions specify the roles which entities play within the SoA designated by the predication.[6]

— Predicates can be verbal, adjectival, or nominal. We here restrict our attention to verbal predicate frames.

— Basic verbal predicate frames can be one-place, two-place, or three-place, designating properties, binary and ternary relations, respectively.

---

6. The relevance of semantic functions (termed "Deep Cases") to grammatical theory was first demonstrated by Fillmore (1968); most of the relevant semantic distinctions, however, already played a role in traditional grammar.

— A distinction is made between nuclear arguments and satellites. Semantic functions which usually attach to satellites may, with certain predicates, have the status of argument functions.
— The nuclear semantic functions of first arguments are devised in such a way as to partially reflect the typology of SoAs developed in 5.2.

5.3.1. First argument semantic functions

The first argument of a predicate frame is the only argument in one-place frames, and the most central argument in many-place frames.[7] First arguments can have the following semantic functions:

(36)   Agent: the entity controlling an Action
                    (=Activity or Accomplishment)
       Positioner: the entity controlling a Position
       Force: the non-controlling entity instigating a Process
                    (=Dynamism or Change)
       Processed: the entity that undergoes a Process
       Zero (∅):   the entity primarily involved in a State

These semantic functions can be exemplified by the following expressions:

(37) a. *John* (Ag) *was reading a book.*
     b. *John* (Po) *kept his money in an old sock.*
     c. *The earthquake* (Fo) *moved the rock.*
     d. *The rock* (Proc) *moved.*
     e. *The cup* (∅) *was on the table.*

Note that we distinguish two kinds of Processes: those which are presented as uninstigated, in which the first argument has the function Processed, and those which are presented as instigated, with a first argument function Force. Force function marks entities which are presented as instigators of Processes, without having control over these Processes. Forces cannot be equated with Agents, because there is no control; nor can they be equated with Instruments in the FG sense, since Instrument will be reserved for entities which are used

---

7. For the notion "first argument", see De Groot (1981b).

by some controller in performing an Action or maintaining a Position.[8]

As argued in section 5.2.5. we shall in certain cases want to mark a first argument as participating in an Experiencer predication. But we cannot only assign a putative function "Experiencer" to the first argument of [+exp] predications, since such predications necessarily also designate an Action, a Position, a Process, or a State. We saw also that it is typically only in [-con] predications that [+exp] makes any difference for the grammatical treatment. Furthermore, a semantic function "Experiencer" would not have the coding support (in the form of cases or adpositions) which is the usual outward manifestation of semantic functions.

For these various reasons I shall treat "Experiencer" as a "secondary" semantic function, a "footnote" to the other first argument functions. Since, as far as its formal expression is concerned, Experiencer is probably relevant only in the case of [-con] predications, and since Forces cannot be Experiencers, this view adds the following to our set of first argument functions:

(38)   ProcExp: the entity that experiences a [+exp] Process
        ZeroExp: the entity that experiences a [+exp] State

Our assumption is that in languages in which entities involved in [-con] Experiences display different grammatical behaviour from entities involved in other [-con] Processes or States, the additional Exp function triggers the relevant rules.

We can now define the notion "first argument" (A1) in terms of the semantic functions by which first arguments may be characterized:

(39)   A1 = {Ag, Po, Fo, Proc[Exp], Zero[Exp]}

When a rule of grammar is triggered by any first argument, no matter what its semantic function is, this rule can be formulated in terms of A1; when the semantic function of the first argument is relevant, this function will be mentioned in the rule. That there are rules which are to be formulated in terms of A1 is clear from the following examples: (i) in English, any A1 can be assigned the function Subject, regardless of semantic function; as Perlmutter (1981) has argued, specifying the semantic functions would require unduly

---

8. The function Force was introduced by Huddleston (1970).

complicated disjunctive statements. (ii) In Hungarian, the finite verb agrees with any first argument (De Groot 1981b). (iii) In Dholuo, any first argument can take a certain position in the clause (Okombo 1983).

In later chapters we will encounter other situations in which rules of grammar can best be formulated in terms of the notion "first argument". Likewise, there will be occasions on which we will refer to "second arguments" A2 and "third arguments" A3, whatever the semantic function of these arguments is.

5.3.2. Other nuclear semantic functions

The most usual combinations of semantic functions within basic nuclear predicate frames can be construed from schema (40) by means of the algorithm of (41):

(40) | [1] | [2a] | [2b] |
      |-----------------|------------|----------------|
      | Agent | Goal[Exp] | Recipient[Exp] |
      | Positioner | | Location |
      | Force | | Direction |
      | Processed[Exp] | | Source |
      | Zero[Exp] | | Reference |

(41) a. Nuclear predicate frames never contain more than one instance of a given semantic function.[9]
  b. In all predicate frames, A1 has one of the functions in [1];
  c. In two-place predicate frames, A2 has one of the functions in [2a] or [2b];
  d. In three-place predicate frames, A2 has the function in [2a], and A3 has one of the functions in [2b].
  e. [-dyn] SoAs are incompatible with semantic functions implying movement (Direction and Source).

The semantic functions for second (A2) and third (A3) argument positions can be described as follows:

---

9. This constraint was formulated in Fillmore's (1968) conception of Case Grammar.

(42) a. Goal: the entity affected or effected by the operation of some controller (Agent / Positioner) or Force.
b. Recipient: the entity into whose possession something is transferred.
c. Location: the place where something is located.
d. Direction: the entity towards which something moves / is moved.
e. Source: the entity from which something moves / is moved.
f. Reference: the second or third term of a relation with reference to which the relation is said to hold.[10]

The most important combinations of semantic functions for two- and three-place predicates, as defined by (40)-(41), may be illustrated by the following examples:

(43) a. Ag Go: *John* (Ag) *kissed Mary* (Go).
b. Ag GoExp: *John* (Ag) *scared Mary* (GoExp).
c. Ag Rec: *John* (Ag) *waved to the crowd* (Rec).
d. Ag RecExp: *John* (Ag) *apologized to Peter* (RecExp).
e. Ag Loc: *John* (Ag) *landed on Mars* (Loc).
f. Ag Dir: *John* (Ag) *drove to London* (Dir).
g. Ag So: *John* (Ag) *jumped from the table* (So).
(44) a. Po Go: *The enemy* (Po) *occupied the city* (Go).
b. Po GoExp: *John* (Po) *impressed Mary* (GoExp).
c. Po Rec: *John* (Po) *was grateful to Mary* (Rec).
d. Po Loc: *John* (Po) *lives in London* (Loc).
(45) a. Fo Go: *The storm* (Fo) *destroyed the harvest* (Go).
b. Fo GoExp: *The heat* (Fo) *suffocated John* (GoExp).
c. Fo Dir: *The rain* (Fo) *moved to the land* (Dir).
(46) a. Proc So: *The apple* (Proc) *fell from the tree* (So).
b. Proc Dir: *The tree* (Proc) *fell into the river* (Dir).
(47) a. Zero Loc: *The roof* (∅) *rests on six pillars* (Loc).
b. Zero Ref: *The boy* (∅) *resembles his father* (Ref).

---

10. For the function of Reference, see Mackenzie (1983).

122   *States of Affairs and semantic functions*

(48) a. Ag Go Rec: *John* (Ag) *gave the book* (Go) *to Mary* (Rec).
 b. Ag Go Loc: *John* (Ag) *placed the dustbin* (Go) *on the sidewalk* (Loc).
 c. Ag Go Dir: *John* (Ag) *brought the car* (Go) *to London* (Dir).
 d. Ag Go So: *John* (Ag) *took the book* (Go) *from the table* (So).
 e. Ag Go Ref: *John* (Ag) *taught the children* (Go) *mathematics* (Ref).
 f. Po Go Loc: *John* (Pos) *kept his money* (Go) *in a sock* (Loc).
 g. Fo Go Dir: *The wind* (Fo) *blew the leaves* (Go) *into the kitchen* (Dir).
 h. Fo Go So: *The wind* (Fo) *blew the papers* (Go) *from the table* (So).

None of the distinctions made here is definitive, nor is it clear which and how many nuclear semantic functions would suffice to capture the crosslinguistic inventory of semantic functions. In general we will try to find those semantic functions which are necessary and sufficient to capture both the semantics, the grammatical behaviour, and the formal expression of term structures in the nuclear predication.

The following notes may clarify some of the distinctions made above:
— Goal is used in the sense of Patient (as in Bloomfield 1933). In some other theories of semantic functions, Goal is used as equivalent to our Direction (and / or Recipient).
— We do not identify Goal and Processed. This means that in such a pair as:

(49) a. *John* (Ag) *moved the rock* (Go).
 b. *The rock* (Proc) *moved.*

the term *the rock* has two distinct semantic functions. This is contrary to what is done in Fillmore (1968), where both occurrences were labelled Objective, in Chafe (1970), where both were termed Patient, and in Jackendoff (1972) and other transformational grammarians, where the two occurrences are identified as Theme. Our reasons for not identifying these two functions are: (i) semantically, the status of 'the rock' does not appear to be the same in the two constructions: in (49a) it is said to be subjected to some outside operation; in (49b), no such outside operation is involved. (ii) our usage of Goal allows for a more specific definition of this function, as in (49a), restricting it to such instances in which an outside operation is involved. (iii) we shall use Goal and other semantic functions in our account of Subject and Object assignment. And these assignments require us to distinguish between the functions of *the rock* in (49a-b).

As a counterargument, one may point to those languages in which the two occurrences of *the rock* will be characterized in the same way (by the same case or adposition). However, such languages are either so-called "active" languages, in which all Agents (or Controllers) get one type of expression, and all non-Agents another. In such languages Goal and Processed naturally fall together as non-Agents. Or they are "ergative" languages, in which case marking is governed by the (in)transitivity of the predicate rather than by the semantic functions of the arguments.[11] In neither case is it necessary for Goal and Processed to be identified in one semantic function.

— A distinction must be made between a semantic function in the technical sense, and the possible semantic features which may be inferred from the meaning of the predicate as such. Consider the following examples:

(50) a. *John* (Proc) *received the money* (Go) *from Fred* (So).
 b. *John* (Ag) *used the money* (Go) *to bribe the policeman.*
 c. *John* (Proc) *reached the summit* (Ref).

In (50a), *John* is not the Recipient, although from the meaning of the verb it is clear that he receives the money. However, the predication describes him as being subject to a Process of 'receiving'. In (50b) *the money* does not have the semantic function Instrument, although from the meaning it is clear that it is used for certain purposes. In (50c) *the summit* is not a Direction, although from the meaning it is clear that it is something towards which John has moved. The point in all these cases is that semantic functions not only concern the content of the predication, but also the form into which this content has been moulded. We return to this point below.

— It is impossible to determine the semantic function of a term by only studying its lexical meaning. Compare:

(51) a. *The time* (∅) *seems to be suitable.*
 b. *The purpose* (∅) *is unclear to me.*
 c. *John did not accept the conditions* (Go).

The time in (51a) is a temporal expression, but it does not here have temporal semantic function, since it presents the entity to which a certain property is attributed. Likewise, *the purpose* in (51b) does not carry Purpose function, and

---

11. On ergative languages, see 11.6.2.

124   *States of Affairs and semantic functions*

the conditions in (51c) does not have the semantic function Condition.

— Note that we have not introduced Instrument as a nuclear argument. The reason for not treating Instrument as an argument function is that it can normally be left out without affecting the grammaticality or the semantics of the remaining predication (see 4.2.5. above, and chapter 9).

— Nor is Instrument assigned to the first argument in constructions such as:

(52)   *The key opened the door.*

as was done by Fillmore (1968). Fillmore's main argument for this analysis was the ungrammaticality of:

(53)   **The key opened the door with a screwdriver.*

This construction would then be ungrammatical for containing two occurrences of Instrument.

The key in (52) conforms to our definition of Force as a non-controlling entity presented as instigating some Process. Instrument will be defined more strictly as "entity used by a Controller in performing an Action or maintaining a Position". And the ungrammaticality of (53) follows from this definition: since *the key opened the door* does not designate an Action or Position it cannot be extended with an Instrument satellite.

5.4. Predication, State of Affairs, and "Reality"

We defined a SoA as the conception of something which can be the case in some world. We also saw that the constitution of a SoA is not only determined by what is said, but also by how what is said is moulded into the predicate frame. These various points boil down to the view that SoAs are not things which exist in reality, but are themselves interpretations or representations of reality. They present a certain codified "view" of reality rather than being part of reality themselves. Certain types of "real" events are so clear-cut that they in a sense "force" a certain interpretation / representation onto the language. For example, if it is to be expressed that a man hit a dog, any language is liable to do that by means of a two-place predicate 'hit' of which the man is the Agent, and the dog the Goal. There is little chance, for example, that the most unmarked expression for such an event would be something like:

(54)   *The dog drew beatings from the man.*

But other events in reality are less clear-cut, and may thus receive rather different interpretations and representations across different languages. For example, if it is to be expressed that John was very much afraid of the dog, languages may use rather different conceptualizations, such as:

(55) a. *John was very scared of the dog.*
 b. *John scared enormously because of the dog.*
 c. *John had great fear for the dog.*
 d. *Great fear came to John from the dog.*
 e. *There was great fear for John because of the dog.*
 f. *Great fear for the dog ate John.*
 g. *The dog scared John enormously.*
 h. *The dog made great fear in John.*

The reason for this variety of expressions is that a relation of 'fear' between two entities is something that can be viewed in many different ways. In our approach, that which is expressed in (55a-h) is not the same: the expressions manifest many different predications, expressing many different SoAs.

Likewise, such pairs as the following will not be said to be alternative expressions of the same underlying content, but alternative interpretations / representations of what might be the same constellation in reality:

(56) a. *The box contained five books.*
 b. *There were five books in the box.*
(57) a. *John filled water into the bottle.*
 b. *John filled the bottle with water.*
(58) a. *They encircled the city with a wall.*
 b. *They laid a wall around the city.*

What we typically find in the case of less clear-cut "realities" is a limited number of distinct alternative interpretations. For example, for the relation of 'teaching', as holding between a teacher, a set of pupils, and some subject taught, most languages have one or more of the following expression types:

(59) a. *John* (Ag) *teaches maths* (Go) *to the children* (Rec)
 b. *John* (Ag) *teaches the children* (Go) *maths* (Ref)
 c. *John* (Ag) *teaches the children* (Go) *with maths* (Instr)
 d. *John* (Ag) *teaches the children* (Go) *into maths* (Dir)

The expression properties of such predications are very difficult to understand if we assume, as is commonly done, that they are alternative expressions of the same underlying semantic structure. We can understand these differences if it is assumed that different languages have moulded the 'teaching' relation into different predicate frames, embodying different interpretations of this relation. As was demonstrated in Work Group FG (1981), these interpretations can be understood in terms of two main "models":

(60) THE GIVING MODEL:
 teach [V] $(teacher)_{Ag}$ $(maths)_{Go}$ $(children)_{Rec}$
(61) THE OPERATING MODEL:
 teach [V] $(teacher)_{Ag}$ $(children)_{Go}$ $(maths)_{Ref / Instr / Dir}$

In the Giving Model, the subject taught is conceptualized as a gift which is presented to the pupils; in the Operating Model, the teaching is conceptualized as a kind of operation on the pupils, with reference to, by means of, or "towards" the subject taught. It was found that on the assumption that there may be different predicate frames capturing the 'teaching' relation, the grammatical properties (both as regards coding and "behaviour") are much more easily accounted for than if it is assumed that there is one language-independent underlying content which is expressed in all these different forms.

The idea that the predicate frames of a language embody an interpretation rather than a direct mapping of "reality" contains an element of linguistic "relativism" which may raise the question of where we stand with respect to the Sapir-Whorf Hypothesis, according to which the grammatical organization of a language embodies the *Weltanschauung* or world view of its speakers. We believe that there is certainly an element of truth in this hypothesis, but that the relativism involved should be constrained in two respects:

(i) there are many aspects of "reality" which are so clear-cut that they receive much the same interpretation across different languages.

(ii) the interpretations embodied in the predicate frames of a language have sedimented into the linguistic system through centuries of historical development. There is, in many cases, little reason to suppose that present-day speakers, if they express themselves by means of the codified interpretations embodied in the predicate frames of their language, actually have the world view which these interpretations would suggest. After all, we speak of 'sunrise' while we all know very well that the sun does not rise, and of 'atoms' while we all know very well that atoms, unfortunately, can be split into smaller parts.

6. On the function and structure of terms

6.0. Introduction

Predications are formed through the insertion of term structures into the argument and satellite slots of predicate frames. By a term we understand any expression which can be used to refer to an entity or entities in some world. The entities that a term can be used to refer to are the potential referents of that term. The entities that a term is meant to refer to in a particular use are the intended referents of that term in that use.

This chapter discusses a number of aspects of the function and structure of terms, with the exception of a detailed treatment of term operators, which will follow separately in chapter 7. We first consider the nature of reference (6.1.); then the kind of structure ascribed to terms in FG (6.2.); just as we developed a typology of SoAs in the case of predicate frames, so we discuss a typology of entities in the case of terms (6.3.); we then show what types of restrictors can enter into term structures (6.4.); we consider how terms consisting of personal pronouns can be represented (6.5.); and finally we make some remarks on different ways in which term structures may be associated with predicate frames (6.6.).

6.1. The nature of reference

The predication may be understood in terms of the two basic acts of *referring* and *predicating* (cf. Searle 1969). Referring means pinpointing some entity about which something is to be predicated; predicating means assigning properties to, and establishing relations between such entities.

In accordance with our general view of verbal interaction, referring will here be interpreted as a pragmatic, cooperative action of a Speaker in a pattern of communication between Speaker and Addressee, according to the model:

(1)   S refers A to E by means of T

where T is some term, and E is some entity. In using a term, S intends to guide A to some entity about which he wishes to predicate something. The information provided in the term must be sufficient for A to be able to pick out the intended referent from the infinite class of possible referents virtually available in any communicative situation. In order to bring this about, S describes the intended referent by means of properties which successively narrow down the set of potential referents of the term used. In general, S need not give more, and may not give less descriptive information than is necessary for A to arrive at the intended identification. If S gives insufficient information, A may be unable to identify the intended referent; if S gives more information than is needed for identification, this may unnecessarily hold up and thus frustrate the further course of communicative interaction.[1]

The amount of descriptive information to be given in a term is thus dependent upon S's estimate of A's already existing capacities for identifying the intended referent, and these capacities depend on the current state of A's pragmatic information (see 1.3. above). If the intended referent is something about which S and A have been talking for some time, or relates to something which is immediately available in the situation, a minimum of descriptive information will suffice. If, on the other hand, the intended referent is quite new to the ongoing discourse, then S will have to provide more information in order for A to arrive at correct identification. Thus, depending on the setting, the same entity may be referred to by widely different terms:

(2) a. *Give* it *to me.*
 b. *Give me* the pen which I forgot at your place last week when we were doing our homework together.

As with any kind of linguistic act, S may fail to provide A with sufficient information for identification. In such cases, A may indicate this by asking for clarification, as in:

(3) S: *Please give me that pen.*
 A: *Which pen?*
 S: *The red one over there.*
 A: *Here you are.*

In such interactions as these, the cooperative nature of referring comes out clearly.[2]

---

1. The "maxim of quantity" (Grice 1975) is involved here.
2. For "referring" as an act of the speaker, see Brown—Yule (1983: 28).

6.1.1. Entities are mental constructs

I have defined terms as instruments for referring to entities in some world. By "world" I do not mean the "real world", but a mental world, a mental representation or model.[3] It is important to realize from the outset that entities (Es) are not "things in reality", but "things in the mind", just as SoAs have mental rather than real-world status. There are three main reasons why Es must be assigned mental status:

First, there are many things which we can refer to and talk about, but which do not exist in reality. Think of mythical, fictional, and hypothetical things, and of things which occur only in dreams or fantasies. Consider such examples as:

(4) a. *Last night I dreamed of ants as big as dogs. They fed on bananas.*
 b. *In the highlands of New Guinea there are ants as big as dogs. They feed on bananas.*
 c. *Suppose there were ants as big as dogs, feeding on bananas.*

In (4a) a dream world is described for which no real existence is claimed; (4b) pretends to be a description of reality, but it is unlikely that anyone will believe that reality to exist; (4c) creates a counterfactual world, the whole point of which is that it is taken not to exist. In each of these three cases, however, once the dog-sized ants have been introduced into the mental model, we can again refer to them and talk about their properties, no matter what existential status is assigned to them. What we refer to, then, is Es which have been mentally construed on the basis of the linguistic information provided. Reference, therefore, is independent of ontological commitment or existence in reality.

The second argument is that we can refer to "real" things only to the extent that we have some mental representation of them. For example, if I want to refer to the Colosseum in Rome, it must be the case either that my addressee already has some mental "picture" of the intended referent, or that I give sufficient information for him to be able to construe such a referent.

The third reason, connected with the second, is that we can refer to and efficiently talk about things in reality even in situations in which these things are nowhere to be perceived or otherwise directly experienced. Such reference can be effective only by virtue of the fact that we either possess or can

---

3. For the notion "mental model", compare Johnson-Laird (1983).

construe a mental representation in terms of which we can then monitor the further course of our communication.

There is a long-standing positivist idea in logic and philosophy according to which we can sensibly talk only about things which exist in reality. Quite contrary to that position, I take the view that it is one of the most beneficial features of our language that it enables us to create alternatives to reality through which we can evaluate that reality, plan our future actions, and ultimately also change the world.

6.1.2. Two ways of referring

Since Es are things that can be construed in the mind, we may distinguish two main usages of terms:

(5) (i) REFERENT CONSTRUCTION
S uses a term T in order to help A construe a referent E for T, and thus introduce E into his mental model.
(ii) REFERENT IDENTIFICATION
S uses a term T in order to help A identify a referent E which in some sense is already "available" to A.

Correspondingly, we can speak of "constructive" reference and "identifying" reference. *Constructive reference* is typically achieved through indefinite terms, *identifying reference* through definite terms, as in:

(6) *Yesterday in the park I saw* a black cat [construct a referent with the properties 'cat' and 'black']. *Today I saw* it / the cat / that cat *again* [retrieve the referent which you have just constructed].

The availability condition mentioned in (5)(ii) may be fulfilled in different ways:[4]

---

4. See Karttunen (1976) on the introduction of "discourse referents". Rijkhoff (1989) presents a detailed discussion of referent identification. For the notion of "inferrability", see Prince (1981), Hannay (1985a, 1985b), and 13.3.3. below.

(7)   SOURCES OF AVAILABILITY
    (a) E may be available in A's long-term pragmatic information.
    (b) E may be available in A's current pragmatic information because it has been introduced in the preceding discourse.
    (c) A may construe E on the basis of information which is perceptually available in the situation.
    (d) The identity of E may be inferred from information available in any of the sources (a)-(d).

For some examples of these different cases, consider:

(8) a. *It was a nice day. The sun was shining.*   [(7)(a)]
    b. *Last week I saw a cat. Today I saw it again.*   [(7)(b)]
    c. *Do you see the man with the green sweater?*   [(7)(c)]
    d. *I wanted to open the door but I could not find the key.*   [(7)(d)]

Summarizing, we can describe reference in terms of the following concepts:

(9) S refers A to E by means of T.
"Refer" = "help construe" when S does not assume E is available to A.
"Refer" = "help identify" if S assumes E is available to A.
E is available to A on the basis of: (a) long-term information, (b) contextual information, (c) perceptual (situational) information, (d) inferrability from (a)-(d).

It is to be noted that I restrict the function of reference to terms which act as arguments or satellites within the clause.[5] In using a term S either "sets up" a referent or helps A to retrieve a referent in order to predicate something about it. Predicates, predications, propositions, and clauses are not said to refer to entities of types f, e, X, and E, but rather to *designate* such entities. However, as a side-effect of using such expressions, mental representations are added to the pragmatic information or discourse model of A, which can later be referred to by means of anaphorical elements. Thus, if we were to apply the concept of "reference" at all in this connection, the function of designating comes close to what we have labelled "constructive reference". Anaphora will be discussed in *TFG2*: chapter 10.

---

5. Cf. the discussion in Keizer (1991).

132   *Function and structure of terms*

6.2. The structure of terms

The structure of (first-order) terms may be described by means of the following schema:

(10) $(\omega x_i: \varphi_1(x_i): \varphi_2(x_i): ... : \varphi_n(x_i))$ $[n \geq 1]$

in which x_i is the term variable, ranging over the set of potential referents of the term, ω stands for one or more term operators, and each $\varphi(x_i)$ is an "open predication in x_i", i.e., a one-open predication of which the open term position is occupied by x_i.[6] The colon ":" indicates that the information to the right gives a specification of, a restriction on, the possible values of x_i as it has been specified to the left. It can be read as "such that". To take a simple example, consider the following term:

(11) $(d1x_i: \textit{elephant} [N] (x_i)_\varnothing: \textit{old} [A] (x_i)_\varnothing)$
        'the old elephant'

in which "d" = definite, "1" = singular, and "$\varnothing$" = Zero semantic function. The whole term can be spelled out as follows:

(12)   'definite singular entity x_i
           such that the property "elephant" applies to x_i
           such that the property "old" applies to x_i'

Using the simplified notation introduced in 3.2.2. I will usually represent term structures such as (11) as follows:

(13) $(d1x_i: \textit{elephant} [N]: \textit{old} [A])$

Since (13) is a definite term, it can be interpreted as an invitation from S to A to identify a referent which is compatible with the information provided in the term, as paraphrased in (12). This can also be written in the form of an instruction:

---

6. For the notion "open predication", see 4.2. above.

(14)   Instruction from S to A:
— Identify a single entity x_i;
— Clue 1: x_i has the property 'elephant'
— Clue 2: x_i has the property 'old'

In this way, then, each of the open predications in x_i further restricts the "searching space" for A, and thus narrows down the set of potential referents of the term. For this reason, these open predications are called *restrictors*. As indicated in (11) and (13), restrictors are successively "stacked" onto each other through the relation ":", rather than being conjoined with each other. This is different from what is usually done in logic, where expressions of this type are analysed in terms of conjunctions of predicates, as in:

(15)   *old elephant*(x) ≡ *old*(x) & *elephant*(x)

This type of analysis implies that the set of entities to which *old elephant* can refer is regarded as the intersection of the set of entities denoted by *old* and the set of entities denoted by *elephant*. This view of term structure could be reformulated in the following instruction:

(16)   Instruction from S to A:
— Take the set {O} of old things.
— Take the set {E} of elephants.
— Now identify the single element in the intersection of {O} and {E}.

There is evidence that this type of analysis is not adequate for terms as they are used in natural languages. Dahl (1971) presented the following arguments against it.

If an expression such as *pregnant women* were to be analysed in terms of the intersection of two sets, the following paraphrases should represent its meaning equally well:

(17) a.   *persons who are female and pregnant*
     b.   *persons who are pregnant and female*

In fact, however, (17b) is redundant in a way in which (17a), and the expression *pregnant women*, are not. Further, compare the following expressions:

(18) a. *Maoist Marxist*
　　b. *Marxist Maoist*
(19) a. *Buddhist Japanese*
　　b. *Japanese Buddhist*

(18b) is again semantically redundant, while (18a) is not. And (19a-b) would be assigned the same meaning in the conjunctive analysis, while in fact, although they may finally apply to the same set of persons, they are not identical in sense: (19a) designates a subset of the set of Japanese, singled out on the basis of religion; (19b) designates a subset of the set of Buddhists, singled out on the basis of nationality.

From such facts as these Dahl concludes that in Modifier-Head constructions of the kind discussed here, the information given in the Head is "logically prior" to the information contained in the Modifier. And he suggests that "... the normal way of defining a set in natural language is to choose a universe and a defining property which singles out a set within that universe."[7] (1971: 2). Indeed, we can represent what is transmitted in (19a) as follows:

(20)　　Instruction from S to A:
　　　　— Take the set {J} of Japanese.
　　　　— Now single out the subset from {J} whose members have the property B.

This analysis, then, not only takes into account the nature of the final set of entities referred to, but also the dynamic way in which this set is construed; and this is relevant to the semantics of this type of term.

The difference between the logical analysis and the FG analysis of term structure can be illustrated as follows:

---

7. There is some psycholinguistic evidence, too, that the information in the Head is psychologically prior to the information in the Modifier (Clark—Clark 1977: 474).

(21)   Logical analysis:
       Designation of both   (a) *Buddhist Japanese*
                              (b) *Japanese Buddhists*

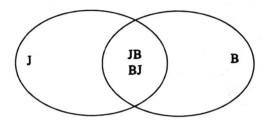

(22)   FG analysis:
       (a) *Buddhist Japanese*   (b) *Japanese Buddhist*

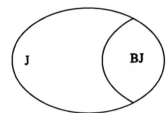 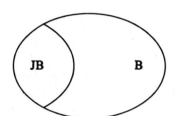

We see in (22) that, although the final extension of the two terms is the same, the way in which that extension is reached is different. The FG claim is that this constructional difference is relevant to the semantics of the term.[8] The general FG term format is meant to reflect this. Thus, (19a-b) will get different term structures:

(23) a. *Buddhist Japanese*:   (x_i: *Japanese*: *Buddhist*)
     b. *Japanese Buddhist*:   (x_i: *Buddhist*: *Japanese*)

Note that this does not mean that restrictors cannot be conjoined with one another. Conjunction is quite appropriate for such terms as:

---

8. Thus, in a very real sense, "die Art des Gegebenseins" (Frege 1892) co-determines the semantics of the expression.

(24)   *men who are old and wise*
        (x_i: *man*: *old and wise*)

In fact, certain ambiguities can be resolved by means of the difference between conjunction and stacking of restrictors:

(25) a. *beautiful old houses*
         'old houses which are beautiful'
         (x_i: *house*: *old*: *beautiful*)
   b. *beautiful, old houses*
         'houses which are old and beautiful'
         (x_i: *house*: *beautiful, old*)

We return to the various types of restrictors and their expression in 6.4.

6.3. A typology of entities

Just as we needed a typology of SoAs to understand a number of things about the semantics and the formal expression of predicate frames, so we need a typology of entities to understand certain semantic and formal properties of terms. In the first place we must distinguish different "orders" of entities, partially corresponding to the types of entities designated by the different layers of underlying clause structure (6.3.1.); secondly, various distinctions must be made among first-order entities.

6.3.1. Different orders of entities

Prototypically, terms refer to entities such as 'John', 'a letter', and 'the library', which can be conceived of as existing in space. These have also been called "first-order entities", and they have been represented by means of the variable "x". This terminology has been inspired by distinctions made by Lyons (1977). Lyons distinguishes first-order entities from "second-order entities" (our States of Affairs) and "third-order entities" (our Possible Facts). Expanding on this terminology we can make the distinctions presented in Table 8 (cf. Keizer 1991).

Table 8. Types of entities as referred to by terms

ORDER	TYPE	VARIABLE
0	Property / Relation	f
1	Spatial entity	x
2	State of Affairs	e
3	Possible Fact	X
4	Speech Act	E

Examples of the term types listed in Table 8 are the following:

(26) a. *John admired* Peter's intelligence.
(reference made to a zero-order Property "f" (intelligence) of Peter's)
b. *John admired* Peter.
(reference made to a first-order Spatial Entity "x" (Peter))
c. *John saw* Peter open the safe.
(reference made to a second-order State of Affairs "e" of Peter opening the safe)
d. *John believed* that Peter had opened the safe.
(reference made to the third-order Possible Fact "X" that Peter had opened the safe)
e. *John tried to answer* Peter's question why he had not called earlier.
(reference made to a fourth-order Speech Act "E" of Peter's)

Terms which are used to refer to second-, third-, and fourth-order entities will be discussed in *TFG2*: chapters 5-7. Reference to zero-order entities is discussed in 6.3.3. below. Elsewhere in this work, when no information to the contrary is given, "term" will be used for prototypical first-order terms.

6.3.2. Different types of first-order entities

We saw in 5.2. that predications can be divided into different types according to the different kinds of States of Affairs they can designate. To the extent that the type of State of Affairs a predicate can designate is coded in the lexical predicate frame, the term *Aktionsart* ('mode of action') is often used for the relevant distinctions. In chapter 9 we shall say that mode of action is lexically coded "aspectuality" pertaining to the predicate. We reserve the term Aspect for grammatically coded aspectual distinctions. The aspectual distinctions relevant to predicates concern dynamic and perspectival properties relevant to the temporal dimension.

As Rijkhoff (1988, 1990, 1991, 1992) has argued, similar things can be said about terms and nominal predicates, but now concerning the way in which the intended referent is represented in relation to the spatial dimension. Thus, we can divide terms into distinct types according to the types of (first-order) entities they can be used to refer to. The relevant distinctions are often coded as lexical properties intrinsic to nouns. Such nominal aspectual distinctions might be called "modes of being"; they can be captured in the Type of the nominal predicate frame. To the extent that such distinctions are coded by grammatical means, we can speak of Nominal Aspect operators.

In the present section I consider the distinctions which seem to be essential to nominal aspectuality (in other words, to a typology of entities) in general. In doing so, I integrate some of Rijkhoff's results into my earlier analysis of entity types. In 7.3. I consider to what extent grammatical operators of Nominal Aspect can be distinguished, and what this implies for the underlying structure of terms. There, we shall also see that the term operator ω can be divided into several hierarchically ordered subtypes of term operators.[9]

6.3.2.1. The insufficiency of set theory. So far we have talked about first-order entities as if all of them were discrete individuals which can be collected in sets. We talked about subsets of such sets, intersections of sets, etc. But set theory is not sufficient to capture the first-order entities designated by the different types of natural language terms.

Set theory is construed on the basis of the primitive relation:

(27) $a \in A$ 'a is a member of A'

---

9. Interesting work on this subject has been done by Seiler and associates under the label of "Apprehension" (= the manner in which objects are "grasped" or conceptualized in languages). See Seiler—Lehmann eds. (1982). Craig ed. (1986) also contains a number of studies relevant to the typology of entities. See Dik (1987d) for some more detailed discussion. The notion "nominal aspect" was introduced by Rijkhoff (1988, 1991).

Any set thus consists of members, which can be counted. Sets have a "cardinal number": the number of members in the set. Set theory, however, is not immediately applicable to terms involving mass nouns:

(28)   *There was Ø water / some water / much water in the pool.*

Water does not obviously designate a set of distinguishable and countable members. There are two possible ways out of this problem: (i) assume that mass terms nevertheless designate sets; they must then have members of some kind; (ii) assume that mass terms do not designate sets; there must then be something other than sets to account for the properties of some referent types.

I here follow Bunt (1985) along the second route. In Bunt's theory, masses are distinguished from sets, but both are unified in a higher concept of "ensemble", according to the following schema:

(29)

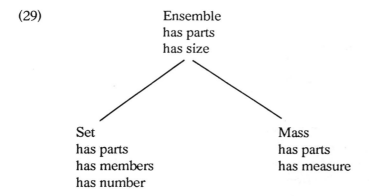

Ensemble
has parts
has size

Set
has parts
has members
has number

Mass
has parts
has measure

Ensembles are either sets or masses; sets have members which can be counted by the number, masses have measures. Since masses have no members, the relation 'is a member of' cannot be the primitive relation of ensemble theory. Therefore, ensemble theory is developed by Bunt on the basis of the primitive relation:

(30) $A \subseteq B$ 'A is part of B'

This primitive relation can then be used to define the notions 'intersection', 'union', and 'difference' for ensembles. The notion 'is a member of', particular to sets, then has to be defined in a derivative way.

When an entity as designated by a term has Set status its cardinal number may be anything from zero upwards; a set with zero number is an empty set;

a set with just one member is an *individual*;[10] a set with more than one member may be called a *collection*.

6.3.2.2. Types of entities. It is interesting that the different types of entities mentioned above can be distinguished in terms of the single dimension of counting. We can ask whether or not the entity can be counted, and if so, how many members it has. In this way we can distinguish the following entity types:

Table 9. Different types of entities

Entity Type	Count
Ensemble	neutral
Mass	—
Set	≥ 0
Individual	1
Collection	>1

An ensemble is neutral as between a set or a mass. Therefore, it is neither clearly countable nor non-countable (see 6.3.2.3. below). A mass cannot be counted (though it can be measured). A set can be counted; its number of members can be anything from zero upwards. An individual can be counted; its number is 1. A collection can also be counted, and its number is more than one.

Note that any non-empty set, including individuals and collections, will consist of entities, which may be of any of the entity types. Masses, however, can only consist of submasses. This recursively defines such E types as the following:

---

10. Note that with Brown (1985) I treat individuals as singleton sets. In Dik (1987d) I have presented some linguistic arguments for the correctness of this view.

(31)   Individual   Mass   Set
                       Mass of Masses   Set of Masses
                                           Set of Sets
                                           Set of Individuals
                                           Set of Collections
                                           Set of Sets of Masses
                                           etc.

First-order terms can now be divided into different types, depending on the kind of E they can be used to refer to:

(32)   Mass term   *some water, much gold, ...*
         Individual term   *John, this boy, ...*
         Collection term   *these boys, this family, ...*

We can also divide *nouns* into different types according to the typology of Es. A problem here is that most nouns can be used to refer to different types of E:

(33) a. *I saw* a chicken *in the garden.*   (Individual)
     b. *I saw three* chickens *in the garden.*   (Collection)
     c. *We had* chicken *for dinner.*   (Mass)
(34) a. John *was at the party too.*   (Individual)
     b. *There were three* Johns *at the party.*   (Collection)
     c. *There was too much* John *at the party.*   (Mass)

For this reason Bunt (1985) argues that we should not speak of "mass nouns", but of "mass occurrences" of nouns, etc. The nouns as such are neutral as to E type. A problem for this view is that there are clear differences in markedness between the different occurrences. For example, (34b-c) are clearly marked usages of a proper noun which is "normally" used as in (34a). In (33) we have the intuition that *chicken* as used in (33c) is a derived usage: an individual chicken is not an individuated mass; but chicken for dinner may well be called a "massified" individual. For this reason, I believe it is more adequate to divide nouns into subcategories on the basis of their unmarked usages, and then assume that they can be "converted" into other subcategories by a process of "subcategorial conversion". Following this line, we could distinguish the subcategories of nominals in Table 10. Between these basic subcategories we can define such forms of subcategorial conversion as the following:

(35) a. [N,prop] → [N,count]   *There were three* Johns *at the party.*
b. [N,count] → [N,mass]   *There is too much* chair *in this room.*
c. [N,mass] → [N,count]   *I would like three* butters *please.*
      (e.g. 'three slices with butter')
d. [N,coll] → [N,mass]   *There was too much* family *in the room.*

Within the framework of FG, subcategorial conversion may be regarded as a form of predicate formation with clear semantic and formal effects, the latter consisting in (im)possibility of pluralization and combinability with different sets of term operators (see 7.4.2.1. below). It would be interesting to know if there are languages which also express this type of conversion through morphological markers on the noun.

Table 10. Different types of nominal predicates

Type of Nominal	Designates		Example
	Singular	Plural	
Proper Noun [N,prop]	Ind	—	John
Count Noun [N,count]	Ind	Coll of Ind	chair
Mass Noun [N,mass]	Mass	—	butter
Collective Noun [N,coll]	Coll	Coll of Coll	family

6.3.2.3. *Ensemble nouns and set nouns.* We saw in Table 10 that there are types of nominals corresponding to the E types of Individual, Mass, and Collection. The question now arises: do we also have reason in natural languages to distinguish the categories of *ensemble noun* and *set noun*? Such reasons can indeed be found.

(i) *Ensemble nouns*
Ensemble nouns would be nominal predicates which can be used to refer to ensembles without forcing the question whether these are sets or masses, thus leaving open the question of whether or not they can be counted.

There is reason to apply this notion in the case of so-called "classifier languages", more particularly in languages which have so-called "sortal classifiers".[11] Sortal classifiers come in two types, as illustrated in:

(36) a. *three* animal *elephant* 'three elephants'
 b. *three* flat *blanket* 'three blankets'
(37) a. *three* dog *dog* 'three dogs'
 b. *three* stone *stone* 'three stones'

In (36) the classifier specifies a superordinate category (a hyperonym) with respect to the head noun: an elephant is a kind of animal; a blanket is a kind of flat thing. In (37) the classifier repeats, but apparently has a different function the head noun. Sortal classifiers typically have the following recurrent properties (cf. Allan 1977):

— Although the head noun can appear without classifier, the classifier must occur when the number of entities is specified. Thus, we typically find the following pattern:

(38) a. *John saw elephant in the jungle.*
 'John saw (one / more) elephant in the jungle.'
 b. **John saw three elephant in the jungle.*
 c. *John saw three animal elephant in the jungle.*

— In the structure of the term, numeral and classifier are never separated from each other by the head noun:

(39) *three animal elephant* **three elephant animal*
      animal three elephant **animal elephant three*
      elephant three animal *elephant animal three*

This property signals that there is an intimate connection between numeral and classifier. In a sense, the presence of the classifier makes it possible for the numeral to occur.
 — It is exceptional for the head noun to be marked for plural in the classifier construction. Classifiers occur only in languages in which plural marking is either absent or at most optional.

---

11. Classifiers may be divided into "mensural classifiers", which indicate "a measure of x", and "sortal classifiers", which indicate "a unit type of x" (Lyons 1977). We here restrict our attention to sortal classifiers. Mensural classifiers will be discussed in chapter 7. Compare Dik (1987d) for some further discussion.

— Classifier languages typically have a limited number of classifiers (say, between 10 and 40), which together classify all the classifiable nouns. The restriction "classifiable" is necessary, since probably all classifier languages also have nouns which do not take classifiers.

— In many classifier languages the classifiers can also have anaphorical function, as in:

(40)   *John saw three animal elephant, but I not saw animal.*
       'John saw three elephants, but I didn't see them.'

It is clear from these various properties that the classifier modifies the aspectuality of the head noun in such a way that it can be used to refer to sets consisting of individual entities. Greenberg (1978) aptly called the classifiers "unit counters": they specify units in terms of which the referent of the head noun can be counted. It will be clear from this that the head noun itself cannot be categorized as a count noun: it cannot, by itself, be used to refer to a set. When it is used without classifier, it carries no suggestion of individuation or number. What, then, is the referential nature of the head noun in classifier languages?

It is sometimes suggested that such head nouns by themselves are mass nouns: a noun such as *elephant* in (36a) would designate something like 'elephant-stuff', and the addition of the classifier would be a form of mass-to-count conversion. Several authors (e.g. Serzisko 1982, Kölver 1982) have argued, however, that even in classifier languages there are reasons for distinguishing "real" mass nouns from other nouns. For example, we find differences such as those between *water* and *banana* in:

(41)   WATER (mass noun)
       three bucket water   'three buckets of water'
       **three liquid water*   'three waters'
(42)   BANANA (non-mass noun)
       three basket banana   'three baskets of banana'
       three fruit banana   'three bananas'

The difference is that, in languages of this type, *water* can only be specified by a "mensural classifier" (see note 11), and cannot be individuated through a sortal classifier, in contrast to *banana*. Therefore, if *water* is a mass noun, then *banana* cannot be a mass noun in such languages. What, then, is the status of *banana*-like nouns?

I believe that our typology of Es allows us to answer this question in an interesting way through the following hypothesis:

(43)   Nouns that take sortal classifiers are ensemble nouns, which can be used to refer to ensembles, and are neutral with respect to the set/mass distinction, as well as with respect to individuation and quantification.

If this hypothesis is correct, we can describe the relevant typological parameter as follows: in non-classifier languages, when forming a referring expression, we are forced to make a choice as to whether the referent is to be described as a set or a mass. In classifier languages, however, this choice is not forced upon us. We can describe the referent as an ensemble, leaving unresolved the question whether the intended referent is individuated or not. If we wish to be more precise, however, we can optionally turn the ensemble noun into a format which unequivocally designates either a set or a mass, through forms of subcategorial conversion (or specification) which crucially rely on classifiers.

(ii) *Set nouns*
Set nouns (Rijkhoff 1991, 1992) are nouns which are used to refer to countable entities, but leave completely unresolved the question of how many entities reference is made to. Rijkhoff found that in many languages there is reason to distinguish a category of set nouns. Such nouns do not force a choice between a singular and a plural form (as count nouns do), but can be used as such for indicating one or more entities of the relevant type. If the cardinal number is to be indicated, this can be done by means of a numeral. Such languages often have an optional "collective" marker, which signals collectivity rather than plurality (e.g. *coll tree* = 'forest' rather than 'trees'); and they may have an optional "individuating" marker which signals that an individual entity of the relevant type is intended. We thus get patterns such as:

(44) a.   *I saw elephant.*
          'I saw one or more elephants'
     b.   *I saw three elephant.*
          'I saw three elephants'
     c.   *I saw coll elephant.*
          'I saw a herd of elephants'
     d.   *I saw indiv elephant.*
          'I saw an individual elephant'

6.3.3. Referring to properties and relations[12]

A simple predication such as (45a) can be represented as in (45b):

(45) a. *John is intelligent.*
   b. Pres e_i: (f_i: *intelligent* [A] (f_i)) (d1x_i: *John* [N])$_\emptyset$

In using (45a) I refer to the entity x_i specified as 'John', and I assign to him the property f_i specified as 'intelligent'. In this predication I do not refer to this property. I can, however, also refer to this property and assign another property to it, as in:

(46) a. *John's intelligence is remarkable.*
   b. Pres e_j: (f_j: *remarkable* (f_j)) [A]
         (d1f_i: *intelligence* [N]: {(d1x_i: *John* [N])$_{Poss}$})$_\emptyset$
      'The intelligence that John possesses is remarkable'

Intelligence is a nominal predicate which designates a property rather than an individual. *John's intelligence* is a term which is used to refer to a property. *Remarkable* is here used as a predicate which assigns a property to a property.
   Similar constructions (Keizer 1991) are:

(47) a. *John's love for Mary is intense.*
   b. *The colour of her eyes is beautiful.*
   c. *Modesty is a virtue.*

We can now compare (46) with such constructions as the following:

(48)   *John is remarkably intelligent.*

In this construction, again, I refer to John, assigning to him the property of being 'remarkably intelligent'. *Remarkably*, however, specifies a property of

---

   12. The issues discussed in this section have been clarified by Keizer (1991, 1992) and Hengeveld (1992).

John's intelligence rather than of John. It can be seen as a satellite to *intelligent*, specifying the Degree to which this property applies to John. *Remarkably intelligent* can thus be analysed as a complex predicate along the following lines:

(49) $(f_i: intelligent\ (remarkable)_{Degree})\ (John)_\varnothing$
'John has the property of being intelligent to a remarkable degree'

Terms such as *John's intelligence, John's love for Mary, the colour of her eyes* can thus be analysed as instruments for referring to properties and relations, or zero-order entities. These entities can be placed "below" first-order entities, since the latter presuppose the former: first-order entities can be described in terms of properties and relations, but not the other way around. Nevertheless, terms are prototypically used to refer to first-order entities. In some sense, these appear to be the "best referents". Reference to the more basic zero-order entities is typically made by means of complex or derived nominal predicates.

6.4. Types of restrictors

We will now further explicate the notion of restrictor and show what types of restrictors are to be distinguished in underlying term structure, and how they can be expressed in linguistic expressions.

6.4.1. Some properties of underlying term structure

Note first of all that the notion of restrictor can only be used to capture restrictive as opposed to non-restrictive modifiers. Thus, (50a) contains an underlying restrictor, while (50b) contains a non-restrictive (appositive) modifier of some sort:

(50) a. *The students who take Spanish go to Spain for a summer course.*
     b. *The students, who take Spanish, go to Spain for a summer course.*

In (50a) the relative clause restricts the set of students to those who take Spanish. No such restriction is involved in (50b): all the students are supposed to take Spanish, and therefore all of them go to Spain. The non-restrictive relative clause gives additional information on the set of students, without restricting is to a subset. An analysis of non-restrictive modifiers will be suggested in *TFG2*: chapter 2.

Secondly, it follows from the definition of "restrictor" that individuals cannot be restricted. This is correct, witness:

(51) a. **John who I met last year suddenly appeared today.*
 b. *John, who I met last year, suddenly appeared today.*
 c. *The John who I met last year suddenly appeared today.*

(51a) shows that a term referring to an individual cannot be restricted. (51b) has a non-restrictive modifier; such a modifier gives additional information concerning the referent, without restricting it. In (51c) *John* has been converted into a count noun, witness the article and the meaning of the construction, which presupposes that more than one John is involved.

So far, most of our examples of restrictors have been based on one-place predicates (as in (11)). Indeed, all one-place predicate frames stored in the lexicon (or derived through predicate formation) are immediately available as restrictors: they are by definition "open predications in x_i" (see 4.2. above). However, the class of potential restrictors is much wider (in fact, virtually infinite), because any predication, no matter how complicated, may be used as a restrictor, as long as one of its term positions is left free for the term variable x_i. Any predication with one open position in x_i can in fact be interpreted as specifying a property of x_i, which can then be used to restrict the ensemble of potential referents of the term. Consider such examples as:

(52) the property of x_i such that
 — x_i is an elephant,
 — x_i lives in the zoo,
 — John once saw x_i when he was six years old,
 — Mary believes Peter to be afraid of x_i,
 etc. etc.

When a predication has *n* term positions, it can be turned into an open predication in x_i by filling *n*-1 of these positions with terms, and specifying the remaining position with x_i. Since the terms inserted into the other positions may have any degree of complexity, and thus again contain restrictors of any type, the process of term formation is recursive through the restrictors, and thus specifies a virtually infinite set of possible term structures.

The question of whether an open predication in x_i can be used as a restrictor in a given term structure is dependent on two factors: predicability[13] and expressibility. A restrictor is predicable of an entity if the property specified by the restrictor is the kind of property which can be meaningfully assigned to that entity. In the case of term structures, "entity" should be understood as: "entity as so far defined by the term under construction". Consider a simple example:

(53)   *the pregnant man*

In construing this term, there will be a point where the term-under-construction has the following form:

(54)   (d1x_i: *man* [N]: ...

At this point, the following predicate frame may be considered as a potential further restrictor:

(55)   *pregnant* [A] (x_1: <fem>)$_\emptyset$

This predicate frame is selectionally restricted to <feminine> arguments. The structure built up in (54) contains the predicate *man*, which is incompatible with <feminine>. Thus, (55) is not predicable of the entity as defined so far. With respect to this situation we can follow the same strategy as with selection restrictions in general (see 4.2.6.): there is no prohibition against forming such terms as (53), but if they are formed the incompatibility of the second restrictor with the first will be explicitly coded, a coding which will invoke special interpretation strategies meant to assign some kind of metaphorical interpretation to the resulting combination. The mechanism used here will be the same as that for a construction such as:

(56)   *This man is pregnant.*

---

13. For the notion of "predicability" see Sommers (1965); for the application of this notion within the framework of FG, see Hengeveld (1990). Hengeveld rightly distinguishes between ontological predicability ("what kinds of things can have what properties?") and linguistic predicability ("what kinds of things can be meaningfully said about what kinds of other things, given the semantic conventions of a language?"). We are here concerned with linguistic predicability.

That is, either *man* will be interpreted as being compatible with *pregnant*, or conversely (see the discussion in 4.2.6. above).

The issue of predicability is complicated by the fact that it is the full series of restrictors placed on a term as construed so far which determines the predicability of the next restrictor in the series. In other words, it is not only the head noun of a term which determines predicability. Consider the following example:

(57)   *the pregnant male professor*
       (d1x_i: *professor* [N]: *male* [A]: *pregnant* [A])

The predicate *pregnant* is predicable of professors, but not of male professors. Thus, the predicate *male* is here the crucial factor responsible for the incompatibility. This may be taken as a further argument for the idea that in the construction of terms restrictors are successively stacked onto each other independently of the actual surface order in which they will finally appear in linguistic expressions.

As for the requirement of "expressibility", consider the following examples:

(58) a.   *I saw John with a girl in New York.*
     b.   *I saw John with x_i in New York.*
     c.   *the girl with whom I saw John in New York*
(59) a.   *I saw John and a girl in New York.*
     b.   *I saw John and x_i in New York.*
     c.   **the girl and who I saw John in New York*

An open predication such as (58b) can be used as a restrictor as in (58c). On the other hand, the open predication (59b), which can be formed just as easily and does not seem to be that different from (59b), cannot be used as a restrictor in term construction, since it cannot lead to a well-formed term: it is not expressible (in English). To put it somewhat differently: the conjuncts of a coordinate structure A and B are not "accessible" to relativization (in English). This Coordinate Structure Constraint, along with many other such constraints, was first formulated by Ross (1967).

We will thus have to prevent the construction of terms such as (59c). This can in principle be done in two ways: (a) form the underlying term structure, but block its expression, or (b) take measures such that the underlying term structure cannot be formed in the first place. Since (a) involves a form of filtering which FG wishes to avoid (see 1.7.2. above), we will prefer method (b), which means that we have to impose conditions on the formation of underlying term structures in such a way that they can only be formed if they can also be expressed in the language in question. This problem will be discussed at greater length in *TFG2*: chapter 16.

6.4.2. Different surface forms of restrictors

Restrictors can be expressed in different forms in the surface structure of terms. The most basic distinction is that between the Head of a term and the Modifiers of the Head. Which restrictor will function as the Head need not be coded in underlying term structure, since it can be defined by general rule: the first restrictor in underlying term structure will become the Head of the term phrase. In many languages only nominal predicates can fill the Head position in a term (in fact, this is a defining property of nominal predicates, see 8.1.). Languages use different strategies for solving the problem which arises when there is no explicit nominal predicate in the first restrictor position. For example, English inserts the dummy nominal *one*, while Dutch simply leaves the Head position empty:

(60) a. *the blue one*
    b. *de blauwe Ø*
(61) a. *that one with the red tie*
    b. *die Ø met de rode das*

All restrictors which do not qualify for Head status will be expressed as Modifiers. These take different forms, depending on the properties of the restrictor in underlying term structure. Consider the following types:

(62) (A) ATTRIBUTIVE PHRASES
      — unmodified nominal: the paper *box*
      — nominal + case / adposition: John's *box* / the chair *in the garden*
      — adjectival: the blue *box*
      — participial: the hard-working *man*
   (B) ATTRIBUTIVE CLAUSES (= relative clauses):
            the box which is made of paper
            the box which is John's / *the chair* that is in the garden
            the box which is blue
            the man *who is working hard*

In general, restrictors which can be expressed in attributive phrases (type (A)) can also be paraphrased in the form of relative clauses (type (B)), but the converse does not necessarily hold. The relative clause thus offers wider possibilities of restrictor expression than the attributive phrase.

The various types of attributive phrases are further discussed in chapter 8, where we introduce non-verbal predicates. Relative clauses are treated in *TFG2*: chapters 2-4.

6.5. The representation of personal pronouns[14]

Term positions may be filled with personal pronouns, as in:

(63) a. *I saw him.*
     b. *They saw us.*

Pronominal terms have a number of special properties, which distinguish them from other terms:

— pronominal terms have a minimum of descriptive value: they come close to being simple "pointers" to, or deictic indicators of their referents.

— they form a closed class within the full class of possible terms of a language.

— they can be described in terms of a few basic distinctions, which always involve the participant features [+S] (speaker, first person), [+A] (addressee, second person), and [-S, -A] (non-participant, third person), and which may further include Number (singular, dual, trial, plural), Gender (masculine, feminine, neuter), and Politeness ([±polite], or degrees of politeness).

— in languages which have case distinctions they will be typically marked for case.

— they can typically be used only as terms, not in predicative function. Examples such as:

(64)   *Mary is clearly the* he *in the family.*

form the marked exception to this rule.

We can account for these different properties by means of the following

---

14. In this section and the following, I largely follow the much more detailed discussion in De Groot—Limburg (1986).

assumptions:
— Pronouns are basic terms, i.e. terms which are listed as "ready-mades" in the term compartment of the lexicon (see Figure 3 in 3.2.2.).
— We can give them an abstract representation in which the different features mentioned above are interpreted as a kind of "abstract predicates" over the term variable. For example:

(65)   +Subject   -Subject
   a. (d1x_i: [+S,-A])   *I*   *me*
   b. (d1x_i: [-S,+A])   *you*   *you*
   c. (d1x_i: [-S,-A, +M])   *he*   *him*
   d. (dmx_i: [+S,...])   *we*   *us*
   e. (dmx_i: [-S,-A])   *they*   *them*

Note that the second person plural form *we / us* is characterized as having the operator "m" (plural) and as including at least the Speaker. In languages which have a ±inclusive distinction in the first person non-singular, we can use the combinations [+S,+A,...] (inclusive) and [+S,-A,...] (exclusive).

— Since we need both the abstract analysis and the actual forms in the lexicon (since the latter cannot be productively derived), we may well assume that all the information in schema (65) is somehow contained in the lexicon, so that, in generating linguistic expressions, we know that (65a) is to be expressed as *I* when in Subject function, and as *me* in non-Subject function, and, in parsing linguistic expressions, we can identify a form such as *me* as the non-Subject form of term (65a).

— That we need the information coded in the abstract representation is clear, for example, when we try to formulate rules for capturing agreement between a predicate and its Subject. Take the very simple example *he runs*. The expression rules must know that the form *run-s* rather than *run* must be formed when the Subject is a singular "third person" entity. In terms of the abstract analyses in (65), we can now simply formulate the relevant rule by saying that the present tense finite verb gets the ending *-s* when the Subject is singular ("1") and does not contain any of the features [+S], [+A].

Where this is appropriate we will abbreviate "first person" [+S,-A] to "p1", "second person" [-S,+A] to "p2", and "third person" [-S,-A] to "p3".

6.6. Types of relations between terms and predicate

We have so far said that predications are formed through the insertion of term structures into the term slots of predicate frames. This is certainly true for the simplest cases. But for certain languages we need a somewhat more complicated method for associating term structures with predicates.

In order to see this, let us start by comparing the following patterns in French and Latin:

(66)   FRENCH   LATIN
     a.   *nous chantons*   **nos cantamus*   'we sing'
     b.   **chantons*   *cantamus*   'we sing'
     c.   *nous chantons*   *nos cantamus*   'WE sing'

In Latin, the form *cantamus* by itself, without pronominal element, suffices to express the full predication 'we sing'. A pronominal argument is added only when Focus is assigned to the subject. In French, on the other hand, the pronominal argument is required to express the full predication 'we sing'.[15] Focus is expressed by extra stress on that argument, or (preferably) by special Focus constructions such as:

(67)   *C'est nous qui chantons.*
          'It is us who sing'

The French construction *nous chantons* can be described in terms of a relation of agreement between subject and predicate. The underlying structure can be represented as:

(68)   Pres e: *chant-* [V] (dmx_i: [+S,...])$_{\text{AgSubj}}$

and the rule of agreement (see 15.3.) will state that the verb is to take the ending *-ons* if the Subject argument has the features "m, +S,...". Now, if we start from the assumption that French somehow represents the unmarked case, we could describe the Latin form *cantamus* in the same way, starting from an underlying structure of the form:

---

15. Note that *chantons* by itself can mean 'let us sing'; but that is not relevant here.

(69)   Pres e: *cant*- [V] (dmx$_i$: [+S,...])$_{AgSubj}$

On this structure a rule of agreement could apply which would finally lead to the addition of the ending *-amus*; then, we could stipulate that the argument term will be expressed as ∅, unless it has received Focus function, in which case it will come out as *nos*. We could say that Latin differs from French in that it does not require the pronoun to be overtly expressed, and call Latin a "Pro-Drop" language, as against French, which would then be a "non-Pro-Drop language".

That such an approach is not correct emerges when we compare what happens with third person arguments in Latin and French:

(70)   FRENCH   LATIN
  a.   *chante*   *cantat*   'he / she / it sings'
  b.   *il chante*   ---   'he sings'
  c.   IL *chante*   *ille cantat*   'HE sings'
  d.   *le garçon chante* *puer cantat*   'the boy sings'

The point is that *cantat* in a sense already contains the expression of an argument term, but that this argument term is more general than any pronoun that could be added to it: the form *cantat* only signals "third person singular" (i.e. "1,-S,-A"), whereas any overt pronoun necessarily requires the specification of Gender as masculine, feminine, or neuter. One could try to account for this by means of the agreement rule, by starting from an underlying structure of the form:

(71)   Pres e: *cant*- [V] (d1x$_i$: [-S,-A,+M])$_{AgSubj}$

and then stipulating that the verb will take the form *cantat* through agreement with the Subject argument with respect to the features "1,-S,-A", whereas the pronominal argument will remain unexpressed. But this suggests that *cantat* is three-ways ambiguous between masculine, feminine, and neuter, whereas in fact the form simply signals "third person singular", without specification of Gender. A better paraphrase for *puer cantat* would thus be: 'the boy sings-p3'. This paraphrase brings out the fact that the form *cantat* in itself already signals 'third person singular sings', to which the overt subject *puer* gives a kind of further specification.

We must conclude, it seems, that the relation between the subject term and the predicate is rather different in French than it is in Latin. In French, the relation can be described in terms of an agreement rule: the subject term is required, and the verb adjusts to it in person and number. In Latin, we will rather speak of "crossreference": the information about person and number is coded in the verbal form as such, and it is coded again in the overt subject term, if present. If this overt subject term is pronominal, it must have Focus; if it is nominal (and thus third person), it provides a further specification to the person-number information coded in the verb. The overt subject term is in a kind of "appositional" relation to the person-number information coded in the verb. For this reason, we can also speak of an appositional language.[16]

Once we have recognized the appositional relation of crossreference, we see that it can be found in many languages, and that its occurrence is not restricted to the relation between Subject and predicate. We find crossreferential relations in the following circumstances:

(i) between the predicate and one or more argument terms. For example, we find languages with such constructions as:

(72) a. *The man he-slept.*   Ag
     b. *The man he-it-caught the tiger.*   Ag Go
     c. *The man he-it-him-give the boy the book.*   Ag Go Rec
     d. *The man he-it-for him-cook the boy the soup.*   Ag Go Ben
     e. *The man he-it-with-it-cut the meat the knife.*   Ag Go Instr

The following is an actual example from Abkhaz (Hewitt 1979: 104), a language with a great variety of crossreferential relations coded on the verb:

(73)   *wəy à-wayº   à-hºəzba a-kº'ət'ə (∅)-à+le-y-šə-yt'.*
         that the-man   the-knife   the-chicken   it-it+with-he-kill
         'That man killed the chicken with the knife.'

The examples in (72) suggest that the types of semantic functions crossreferenced in the verb might be sensitive to the Semantic Function Hierarchy (see 10.4.2. below). Further typological research will be needed to

---

16. See De Groot—Limburg (1986). The idea of an "appositional" relationship was already formulated by Boas (1911) in relation to Chinook and related languages. More recently, Nichols (1986) and Van Valin (1985) have argued for a distinction between "Head marking" and "Dependent marking". The idea is that in some languages the person/number information is basically coded on the noun phrase (the dependent), in other languages on the verb (the head). For a similar analysis of "agreement" in Bantu languages, see Bresnan—Mchombo (1987).

establish whether this is the case.

(ii) the second type of crossreference is that between possessor and possessed in constructions such as:

(74)	*The man his-dog died.*

(iii) the third type is found between adpositions and the term which they govern. Here we find such constructions as:

(75) a.	*The man was sitting on-it the chair.*
 b.	*The man was sitting the chair its-on.*

It is probable that (75a) originates in an earlier construction with a "right-dislocated" or "Tail" term (see 13.2.),[17] whereas (75b) derives historically from a stage in which the adposition was a full noun:

(76) a.	*The man was sitting the chair its-top.* = 'on top of'
 b.	*The man was sitting the hut its-front.* = 'in front of'

If that is true, then the "adpositional" type (b) of crossreference reduces (at least historically) to type (ii), the relation between possessor and possessed.[18]

De Groot—Limburg (1986) have worked out a cyclical historical scenario in which appositional structures figure as one of the stages that a language may run through. This scenario can be briefly illustrated as follows:

(77)			'The woman sings'	'She sings'
	Stage 1.	*The woman, she sing.*	*She sing.*
	Stage 2.	*The woman she-sing.*	*She-sing.*
	Stage 3.	*The woman she-sing.*	*She she-sing.*
	Stage 4.	*The woman sing.*	*She sing.*
	Stage 5.	Return to Stage 1.

In Stage 1 we have a language without agreement, but with a strong tendency to use so-called "left-dislocated" (or "Theme") constructions such as *The woman, she sing*. In Stage 2, the Theme has been integrated into the clause (through markedness shift), and the pronominal element has become a

---

17. See 13.2. for the notions of "Tail" and "Theme".
18. See Hyman (1975b) for this kind of development.

redundant marker on the verb. However, *she-sing* can still be independently used. Stage 2 therefore represents the appositional stage. In Stage 3, the pronominal element on the verb has lost its independent semantic value: it has developed into a pure agreement marker which cannot stand on its own without nominal or pronominal argument. In Stage 4, finally, this agreement marker has disappeared, and the process can start anew at Stage 1.[19]

---

19. See Givón (1976) for this type of development from independent pronoun, through clitic, to agreement marker.

7. Term operators

7.0. Introduction

FG makes a rather sharp distinction between lexical (or content) elements and grammatical (or form) elements in the structure of linguistic expressions. Lexical elements are captured by the basic predicates listed in the lexicon. Grammatical elements reflect the various operators and functions which at different levels can be applied to underlying structures; together, these operators and functions define the grammatical framework within which lexical predicates can be combined into the structures underlying linguistic expressions. In this chapter we shall be concerned with *term operators*, the various elements which can occupy the position of ω in the general schema:

(1) $(\omega x_i: \varphi_1(x_i): \varphi_2(x_i): ... : \varphi_n(x_i))$

I start out with some general remarks about types of operators distinguished in FG, and about how operators differ from predicates (7.1.). Following Rijkhoff (1990, 1992) I then make a distinction between Qualifying, Quantifying, and Localizing term operators (7.2.). These three types of operators are discussed separately in the order: Qualifying operators (operators pertaining to the type of entity that can be referred to by the term, 7.3.), Quantifying operators (quantifiers, numerators, ordinators, genericity, 7.4.), and Localizing operators (demonstratives, (in)definiteness, (non-)specificity, 7.5.).

7.1. Operators in FG

Depending on their domain of operation, we have so far recognized the following types of operators:

(2) a. ω : term operators
 b. π_1 : predicate operators
 c. π_2 : predication operators
 d. π_3 : proposition operators
 e. π_4 : illocutionary operators

160   *Term operators*

Some properties which distinguish operators[1] from predicates are the following:

— operators are grammatically rather than lexically expressed. By grammatical expression I mean expression through items belonging to closed paradigms, manifesting themselves in the inflectional modifications of lexical predicates, and / or in "form words" such as articles, quantifiers, auxiliary verbs, etc.

— operators typically capture a limited number of crucial distinctions in some semantic domain, as illustrated in Table 11.[2]

Table 11. Distinctions in operator systems

Domain	Distinctions
Number	singular — dual — plural
Tense	past — present — future
Polarity	positive — negative
Aspect-1	imperfective — perfective
Aspect-2	prospective — perfect
Mood	possible — necessary
Illocution	declarative — interrogative — imperative

In each of these domains, many more possible distinctions can be made by lexical means. For example, on the temporal axis a virtually infinite number of temporal intervals can be lexically designated (for example, by temporal satellites). But in most languages, a limited number of rough distinctions have

---

1. The notion "operator" stems from algebra and formal logic. In predicate logic, for example, quantifiers are treated as operators, modal logics use modal operators, and tense logics tense operators. An early example of systematic usage of operators in linguistic theory is Seuren (1969). More recently, Foley—Van Valin (1984) have contributed to the typology and the hierarchical structuring of operators in natural languages. The idea of distinguishing between predicate, predication, and proposition operators within FG stems from Hengeveld (1989).

2. Each of these distinctions, here given by way of examples, will be more extensively discussed in later sections of this book.

as it were sedimented into the grammatical system. These distinctions are not identical across languages, but they seem to be drawn from limited sets of possible distinctions which are especially liable to grammatical expression.

— operators have scope, i.e. they extend their influence over a certain section of the underlying clause or term structure, depending on the level of structure on which they operate. Illocutionary operators have wider scope than proposition operators, these have wider scope than predication operators, and these again have wider scope than predicate operators. Operators may have certain influences on all the elements which fall in their scope, including lower-level operators (see Hengeveld 1989). Term operators extend their influence over the whole term on which they operate. This can be illustrated with the following simple example:

(3)   *the three grey elephants*
        (d3x_i: *elephant* [N]: *grey* [A])

In this term the predicates *elephant* and *grey* attribute properties to each of the entities intended to be referred to by the term. But "definite" (d) and "three" rather define properties of the whole set referred to. Therefore, the proper paraphrase is not 'entities such that they are definite, three, elephant, grey', but rather 'definite three entities such that they are elephant, such that they are grey'.

7.2. Semantic domains of term operators

Term operators can be subdivided according to the level or layer of term structure at which they apply, which in turn determines the semantic domains to which they pertain, and the scope relations that exist between them. Rijkhoff (1990, 1992) argues that term operators can be divided over three semantic domains: Quality, Quantity, and Localization.[3] *Qualifying term operators*, in the languages that have them, provide a specification of the type of entity that the term is used to refer to, in terms of distinctions which we have made in the "Typology of Entities" discussed in 6.3. above. *Quantifying*

---

3. These correspond to three of the fundamental "categories" of Aristotle (*Categories* 4): the ποιόν 'how it is', the ποσόν 'how much / many it is', and the ποῦ 'where it is'.

term operators tell us about the size of the ensemble of entities that reference is made to (measure or amount in the case of masses, number in the case of sets). *Localizing term operators* indicate the position of the referent ensemble in relation to spatial coordinates and to other entities which are presumed to already have a position in the pragmatic information or discourse model of the Speaker and the Addressee.

Rijkhoff also points out that there are certain similarities between these semantic domains and those covered by π-operators in the underlying structure of the clause. Consider a construction such as:

(4)   John used to be reading a book *whenever I visited him.*

The part of (4) in roman type expresses that in the Past (Localization) it was habitually (Quantity) the case that John was in the process (Quality) of reading a book. In the underlying clause structure, we divide these elements over different levels as in (5):

(5)   Past Hab e: [Progr *read* [V] (*John*)(*a book*)]

Thus, "Progr" is analysed as a π_1 predicate operator telling us about the internal dynamics of the SoA, while "Past" and "Hab" are analysed as π_2 predication operators which serve to localize the SoA in terms of spatial, temporal, and cognitive parameters. As Rijkhoff points out, however, the notion of "Localization" is not appropriate for such distinctions as 'habitually', 'frequently', 'repeatedly', etc., which will be analysed as forms of "Quantificational Aspect" in chapter 9. What these elements do, rather, is quantify the number of SoAs involved, just as term operators of Quantity quantify the number of entities referred to. Since Quantity operators of this kind are typically in the scope of localizing operators such as Past, this might even occasion us to recognize a separate layer of quantification in underlying clause structure, in between the Qualifying layer 1 and the Localizing layer 2. I will discuss some implications of this proposal in chapter 9. For more detailed argumentation I refer to Rijkhoff (1992).

We can provisionally capture the parallelism between clause structure and term structure with respect to these different semantic domains by distinguishing three types of term operators and using the following types of representation for underlying clause and term structures:

(6) a. UNDERLYING CLAUSE STRUCTURE
π_2-Loc π_2-Quant e: [π_1-Qual pred [V / A] (args)]
b. UNDERLYING TERM STRUCTURE
ω_2-Loc ω_2-Quant x: [ω_1-Qual pred [N] (args)]

I the following sections I discuss the different manifestations of the three types of term operators represented in (6b).

7.3. Qualifying term operators

In 6.3.2. we saw that terms may differ in the way in which they conceptualize or represent the entities referred to. The relevant distinctions were assigned to the domain of nominal aspectuality. Distinctions of nominal aspectuality are commonly incorporated in the lexical meanings of nouns, which thus not only capture the basic property of the entity referred to, but also information on its "mode of being". To the extent that distinctions of nominal aspectuality can be expressed by grammatical means, we shall say that the relevant grammatical elements express Qualifying term operators ω_i indicating different forms of nominal Aspect.

7.3.1. Modes of being

In 6.3.2., Table 9, we saw that the most important distinctions relevant to nominal aspectuality are defined in terms of the status of the entity in relation to the operation of counting. We also saw that there is reason to distinguish noun types in terms of these different entity types:

(7) a. *Ensemble nouns* [N,ens]
The entity is represented as neutral between mass and set, and (therefore) also as undetermined with respect to measure or number.
b. *Mass nouns* [N,mass]
The entity is represented as a mass which can be measured, but not counted.
c. *Set nouns* [N,set]
The entity is represented as a set, but no information is provided about the cardinal number of the set.

d. *Proper nouns* [N,prop]
   The entity is represented as an individual.
e. *Count nouns* [N,count]
   The noun must either be used in the singular and then represents the entity as an individual, or in the plural, in which case the entity is represented as a collection.
f. *Collective nouns* [N,coll]
   The entity is represented as a collection.

Some of these noun types can be specified or converted by grammatical means so as to designate more specific types of entity. Languages which have ensemble nouns typically have grammatical means through which the entity referred to can be specified as being either a mass or a set, and languages which have set nouns often have grammatical means through which the entity referred to can be specified as being either an individual or a collection.

7.3.2. Sortal classifiers

We saw in 6.3.2.3. above that in languages which have classifiers, the noun may be interpreted as an ensemble noun, which is neutral as to the distinctions set / mass and singular / plural. Classifiers may be of the sortal or mensural type. Here I will restrict myself to sortal classifiers. Mensural classifiers will be discussed in 7.4.1.

It can be demonstrated that sortal classifiers should be treated as operators rather than as restrictors. The following argument supports this claim. We saw in 6.3.2.3. that we find so-called "repetitive" constructions of the form:

(8) a. *three dog dog*   'three dogs'
    b. *three stone stone* 'three stones'

If we analysed the sortal classifiers in these examples as restrictors, we would get such representations as:

(9)   (i 3 x_i: *dog*: *dog*)

Such a representation would be redundant, but (8a) is not redundant, since the nominal predicate *dog* and the classifier *dog* have different functions: the nominal predicate specifies a property of the intended referent; the classifier individuates that referent, so that it can be counted. This difference could be captured by analysing sortal classifiers as Qualifying term operators, as in:

(10)   (i 3 x_i: Dog [*dog* [N,ens]])
         'three Dog-units of dog' = 'three dogs'

In this structure it is indicated that the lexical noun *dog* is an ensemble noun, which can be specified by the Qualifying term operator *Dog* in such a way that the resulting combination can now be counted.

The interpretation of classifiers as operators finds support in the fact that sortal classifiers, in the languages which have them, always form a finite set, even though this set may have up to several dozens of members.

7.3.3. Collectivizing and individualizing operators

Rijkhoff (1991) gives the following criteria for whether a language has set nouns:

(11) a.   the noun may be used to refer to one or more individuals
     b.   there are no classifiers
     c.   there is a collectivizing and possibly also an individuating nominal aspect marker
     d.   when a numeral is used, the collectivizing aspect marker is not used.

One language interpreted along these lines is Oromo, as described in Stroomer (1987). The basic Oromo noun gives no information on number. But there are optional collectivizing suffixes which can be used to refer to 'a counted or countable group of items'; these suffixes are not used with numerals. On the other hand there are optional individuating suffixes of limited distribution (only productive in ethnonyms) which signal 'a (male or female) individual out of a group'. For example:

(12) a.   basic form: *sangaa*   'ox, oxen'
     b.   collective form: *sangoollee*   'group, herd of oxen'
(13) a.   basic form: *sidama*   'Ethiopian(s)'
        individuating form:
     b.   masc.   *sidamtica*   'Ethiopian man'
     c.   fem.   *sidamtittii*   'Ethiopian woman'

According to Rijkhoff's analysis, these suffixes can be seen as the expression of Qualifying term operators Coll (collectivizing) and Ind (individuating) such that we can represent them, for example, as in (14) and (15):

(14) a. (.. x_i: *sangaa* [N,set])   *sangaa*
     b. (.. x_i: Coll [*sangaa* [N,set]])   *sangoollee*
(15) a. (.. x_i: *sidama* [N,set])   *sidama*
     b. (.. x_i: Ind_m [*sidama* [N,set]])   *sidamtica*
     c. (.. x_i: Ind_f [*sidama* [N,set]])   *sidamtittii*

As is clear from these examples, the operations effected by Qualifying term operators come very close to (nominal) predicate formation rules. It is even questionable whether the two can be distinguished in this domain. The same is true for Qualifying predicate operators: aspectual modifications of the nuclear verb also typically lie on the borderline between predicate formation and grammatical inflection.

7.4. Quantifying term operators

Quantifying term operators in one way or another indicate the size of the ensemble that the term is used to refer to. Under this heading I discuss *mensural classifiers* (7.4.1.), *quantifiers* and *numerators* (7.4.2.), *generic* and *non-generic reference* (7.4.3.), and *ordinators* (7.4.4.).

7.4.1. Mensural classifiers

Apart from the sortal classifiers discussed in 7.3.2., there are languages with mensural classifiers, as we saw in 6.3.2.3. In these languages, too, the nouns to which these classifiers are applied may be interpreted as ensemble nouns, which are neutral as to the distinctions set / mass and singular / plural. Suppose that in such a language we have an ensemble noun *tobacco*. We may now expect that the referent of that noun may be specified in different ways:

(16) a.   *three bag tobacco*   'three bags of tobacco'
     b.   *three pound tobacco*   'three pounds of tobacco'

The elements *bag* and *pound* in (16) in the first place designate a quantity in terms of which 'tobacco' can be measured. Secondarily, they also classify the head noun referent into different types of entity, inasmuch as different measuring units are used for different head nouns:

(17) a. *a pound of tobacco*
 b. *a litre of wine*
 c. *a slice of bread*
 d. *a yard of thread*

With Lyons (1977) we may call these measuring units "mensural classifiers", as distinct from the "sortal classifiers" discussed in 7.3.2., which specify units (not quantities) in terms of which the referent of the head noun can be counted. Note that all languages have mensural classifiers of some sort, whereas sortal classifiers are restricted to true "classifier languages".

The status of mensural classifiers in underlying term structure is not immediately clear. Note, however, that with a term such as *three pounds of tobacco* we do not talk about three entities called 'pounds', which happen to consist of tobacco; rather, we talk about a certain quantity of tobacco. This would point to term operator status for the mensural classifier:

(18)   (i 3 pound x_i: *tobacco* [N,ens])

In such a representation it is (correctly) expressed that *three pounds* quantifies over that which is designated by *tobacco*, rather than that *three* quantifies over *pounds of tobacco*. As such, the mensural classifier forms part of the quantifying expression, whereas sortal classifiers form part of the quantified expression.

The different status of these two types of classifier comes out most clearly in languages in which the two occur, as argued in Craig (1992), who gives the following example from Kanjobal (Zavala 1989:282):

(19)   *Ox-ep   koxtal   ixim   ixim*
         three-NbCL.INAN sack   CL   corn
         'three sacks of corn'

In this example there is a fused numeral classifier (*-ep*) suffixed to the numeral, then a mensural classifier (*koxtal*), then a sortal classifier (*ixim*) which occurs in a repetitive construction with the head noun *ixim* 'corn'.[4] The positions of these classifiers seem to indicate that there is a closer connection between the head noun and the sortal classifier than there is between the head noun and the mensural classifier.

7.4.2. Quantifiers and Numerators

Quantifiers are term operators which inform us in one way or another about the size of the intended referent ensemble. In treating quantifiers as *term* operators we take a course which is different from the usual treatment in logic. Consider the usual logical analysis of a universally quantified expression:

(20) a. *All humans are mortal.*
 b. $(\forall x)(human(x) \rightarrow mortal(x))$

According to this analysis, the logical form differs in two crucial ways from its linguistic expression: (i) in the linguistic expression the quantifier is part of the subject term, while in the logical form it is represented as a propositional operator; (ii) in the logical form, the two properties 'human' and 'mortal' are related through an implication, which is not overtly expressed in the linguistic form.

If (20b) is the logical form of (20a), two questions arise: (a) why should there be such a big difference between logical form and linguistic form? (b) why do we not find languages in which the presumed logical form is more faithfully mapped onto the linguistic expression, as in:

(21) *For all things, if human then mortal.*

---

4. It should be noted that Craig (1992) further argues that it would be better to subdivide the types of classifier under discussion into *noun classifiers* such as the first occurrence of *ixim* in (20) and *numeral classifiers* such as *koxtal* in (20). Numeral classifiers necessarily cooccur with a numeral, whereas noun classifiers do not. She furthermore shows that numeral classifiers do not necessarily express mensural concepts, but may be of the sortal type as well. The data presented seem to indicate that the reverse is not the case. See Craig (1992) for further discussion.

In fact, however, languages generally organize universal quantification in the form of (20a), where the quantifier is part of the subject term, and the equivalent of 'mortal' is applied to that term as a predicate.

For these reasons, we assume that the predication underlying (20a) is much closer to its linguistic expression, and can be represented as:

(22)   *mortal* [A] (all x_i: *human* [N])$_\emptyset$

This predication can be interpreted as saying that the property 'mortal' can be assigned to every member of the set of human beings.

If this approach is correct, we need a theory of quantification which can do justice to the fact that quantifying expressions in natural languages typically pattern as term operators rather than as predicate, predication, or proposition operators. Such a theory was proposed in Brown (1985), and the main points of this theory will be summarized below. As Brown suggests, this approach to quantification may have major consequences for any form of logic that wishes to do justice to the syntactic and semantic organization of natural languages.

7.4.2.1. General principles of term quantification. On the basis of Brown (1985) we can give the following sketch of linguistic quantification. Note first of all that quantification presupposes multiplicity or divisibility. This means that quantification operates on ensembles, where these are either sets or masses. Sets have members which can be counted. We can talk about the number of members in a set. This can be analysed in terms of a cardinal number function "c", which assigns to each set an integer indicating the number of its members:

(23) $c(X) = n$ 'set X has n members'

Masses have no members. They cannot be counted, only measured. This can be expressed in a measure function "m" which assigns a certain measure to a mass:[5]

(24) $m(X) = n$ 'mass X has measure n'

---

5. For the notion "measure function" see also Bartsch—Vennemann (1972).

As we saw before, certain properties which sets and masses have in common can be formulated in terms of the superordinate notion of ensemble. Compare:

(25) *I have more marbles than you.*
      = 'the number of my marbles is greater than the number of your marbles.'
(26) *I have more wine than you.*
      = 'the quantity of my wine is greater than the quantity of your wine.'

Note that the same quantifier *more ... than* can be used to quantify over sets and masses. Both cases can be captured by the following paraphrase:

(27) 'the size of the ensemble of my marbles / wine is greater than the size of the ensemble of your marbles / wine.'

In order to express this, we can introduce a size function "s" over ensembles, such that:

(28) $s(X) = n$ 'ensemble X has size n'

It will be evident then that the size of X is either the cardinal of X or the measure of X, depending on the nature of the ensemble X:

(29) $s(X) = c(X)$ or $m(X)$

Therefore, $s(X)$ can also be written $c/m(X)$ (Brown 1985). The relation expressed in (25)-(26) can now be analysed as:

(30) $s(X_i) > s(X_j)$, or: $c/m(X_i) > c/m(X_j)$

where X_i and X_j stand for the two ensembles compared.

Some types of quantifiers, then, can be defined in terms of the size of ensembles; some must be restricted to the cardinal of sets, or the measure of masses. For example, *many* is restricted to sets, *much* to masses.[6]

---

6. Languages may differ in the distribution of their quantifiers over these types. For example, Dutch *veel* can be used to translate *many* as well as *much*, and can thus be regarded as an ensemble quantifier.

7.4.2.2. *Referent ensemble, Domain ensemble, and Universal ensemble.* In discussing quantification it is useful to distinguish three types of ensemble (Brown 1985):

(31) a. the Referent Ensemble R: R is the ensemble that is being referred to in a given usage of a term.
  b. the Domain Ensemble D: D is the ensemble from which R is taken as a sub-ensemble.
  c. the Universal Ensemble U: U is the ensemble containing all the entities that have the properties specified in the term.

Consider the following example:

(32) *John is a great lover of* books [R=D=U]. *Yesterday he bought* five books [R⊂D=U] *in a second-hand shop, and today he has already read* three of them [R⊂D⊂U].

The term *books* is a generic term, used to refer to books in general, or to any arbitrary book [R=U]; *five books*, as an indefinite term, is used to create an arbitrary subset of books "cut out" from the domain set established by U [R⊂D=U]; *three of them* then "cuts out" a subset from the domain set established by the term *five books* [R⊂D⊂U].

As is the case in this example, the last ensemble referred to usually serves as the domain set for the next ensemble to be referred to. This means that we need only one D, which may or may not coincide with U, or with a previously introduced R. It will be evident that the following relations hold between U, D, and R, and between their sizes, cardinals, and measures:

(33) a. $R \subseteq D \subseteq U$
  b. $s(R) \leq s(D) \leq s(U)$, and therefore: $c/m(R) \leq c/m(D) \leq c/m(U)$

Thus, R (the ensemble currently referred to), which is usually smaller than D (the domain ensemble from which R is "cut out"), may also coincide with D. Why this is so will be clarified below, in 7.4.2.4.

7.4.2.3. *A typology of quantifiers.* As Brown (1985) has shown, quantifiers may be divided into different types, along the dimensions of:
  (i) Absolute/Relative. Absolute quantifiers define the size of an ensemble in absolute terms; relative quantifiers do not inform us about the absolute size,

but compare the size to some explicit standard of comparison, or to some implicit standard (a tacitly assumed "norm").

(ii) Proportional/Non-Proportional. Proportional quantifiers inform us about the size of an ensemble R in relation to the size of a super-ensemble D, from which R is "cut out"; non-proportional quantifiers restrict their quantification to a single ensemble R. Since quantifiers can independently be ±absolute and ±proportional, these two dimensions define four basic types of quantifiers which we shall now consider one by one.

(A) *Absolute non-proportional*
For sets, absolute non-proportional quantifiers may be called *numerators*. They are expressed by the number expressions of natural languages:

(34)   *fifteen boys*   (i 15 x_i: *boy* [N])   : c(R) = 15

For masses there are no absolute quantifiers. One might think that absolute quantification of masses is involved in such expressions as:

(35) a.   *three glasses of wine*
     b.   *three litres of wine*

In fact, however, the mass predicate has in these cases first been converted into a count expression through the mensural classifiers *glass* and *litre*, resulting in a set, which can be quantified over like any other set (cf. 7.4.1. above).

(B) *Relative non-proportional*
For sets, such quantifiers as *many, few, some* have the status of relative non-proportional quantifiers:[7]

(36)   *I saw* many / some / few *birds.*

Each of these quantifiers presupposes some implicit norm with which the number of members of the set is compared. This norm cannot be absolutely fixed and is co-determined by extralinguistic properties of, and expectations about the referent set. In this respect relative quantifiers are similar to relative

---

7. For masses the corresponding quantifiers are *much, some,* and *little*.

adjectives such as *big / small, heavy / light, high / low*, etc. We may thus write:

(37)   *many birds*   (i many x_i: *bird* [N])   : $c(R) >$ norm[*many*]

Determining the norm is a complex matter which we shall not further discuss here.

(C) *Absolute proportional*
Proportional quantifiers in general define the size of R with respect to some contextually defined domain ensemble D. The clearest examples are provided by partitive constructions:

(38) a.   *three   of   the   five boys*
     b.   *three   of   the   boys*

In each of these constructions a set D of boys is presupposed, and R is said to consist of three members from D.[8] Note that D must be described as definite, R as indefinite:

(39) a.   **three of five boys*
     b.   **the three of the five boys*

That D must be described as definite is understandable, since it is taken as a point of departure for "cutting out" R. Therefore, D must be available to A. That R must be indefinite can be understood as follows: proportional quantification is specifically used to "cut out" a new referent ensemble R from an already available ensemble D. Once R has been established, D can be "forgotten". Consider the following examples:

(40) a.   *Yesterday on my way home I met five boys. Three of them were rather drunk. These started bullying me ...*
     b.   *Yesterday on my way home I met five boys. Three of them were rather drunk.* *These three of them *started bullying me ...*

---

8. The presupposed character of D is in some languages iconically expressed by placing the D-term in initial position in a kind of Theme-function: *Those five apples, I have eaten two (of them)*. See Li—Thompson (1976) for an example from Mandarin Chinese. Cf. 13.2. below for the pragmatic function "Theme".

Brown (1985) has suggested that proportional quantifiers can be represented as complex quantifiers of the form n_1/n_2, where n_1 indicates the size of R, and n_2 the size of D. Given this convention, we can write:

(41) *three of the five boys*
      (i 3 / d 5 x_i: *boy* [N])   : c(R) = 3 < c(D) = 5

As we saw in 7.4.2.2., R cannot exceed D in size. This would again be incompatible with the fact that R is "cut out" from D:

(42) **Six of the five boys were drunk.*

Where R is a proper subensemble of D, the construction can be referred to as *partitive*. The complex quantifier in (41) may be called a partitive quantifier.

The size of D may be left unspecified, as in (40b). In such a case, we can analyse as follows:

(43) *three of the boys*
      (i 3 / d n x_i: *boy* [N])   : c(R) = 3 < c(D) = n

For masses, again, there are no absolute proportional quantifiers.

(D) *Relative proportional*
Relative proportional quantifiers for sets and masses are illustrated by such examples as:

(44) a. many / few / some *of the (ten) birds*
     b. much / little / some *of the water*

(44a) can be represented and defined according to the following patterns:

(45) a. (i many / d 10 x_i: *bird* [N]) : c(R) > norm[many] < c(D) = 10
     b. (i many / d n x_i: *bird* [N]) : c(R) > norm[many] < c(D) = n

Note that the norm for *many* (and for the other quantifiers) must be relativized with respect to the size of D: *many of the twenty birds* indicates a higher number of birds than *many of the ten birds*.

In general, relative quantifiers are rated with respect to a norm which is defined in terms of the size of the ensemble from which R is "cut out". This norm, however, may be codetermined by other types of norms, such as a norm of "expectancy" or a norm of "functionality". Consider a case such as:

(46) *You haven't peeled many of the potatoes.*
= 'not many in respect to the total number'
(norm derived from size of superset);
= 'not as many as I had expected you to peel'
(norm of expectancy);
= 'not as many as we need for the mashed potatoes'
(norm of functionality).

The norm for *many* is not the same as the norm for *few*, as appears from the following examples:

(47) a. *Not many of the arrows hit the target, only few of them did.*
b. *The target was neither hit by many, nor by few of the arrows.*

If there were a norm N such that *few* was 'below N' and *many* 'above N', then (47a) should be tautologous, and (47b) contradictory. But this is clearly not the case. Therefore, *few* and *many* must be analysed as contraries rather than contradictories, according to the following schema:

(48) ø ----- *few* ------#---------- *not few* -------------------- n
ø --------- *not many* ----------#--------- *many* -------- n

7.4.2.4. Universal quantification. We speak of universal quantification for terms in which it is expressed that the size of R equals the size of D, where D may or may not coincide with U:[9]

(49) a. *All humans are mortal.* $c(R)=c(D)=c(U)$
b. *Every human is mortal.* $c(R)=c(D)=c(U)$
(50) a. *All the students have gone.* $c(R)=c(D)$
b. *Every student has gone.* $c(R)=c(D)$
(51) a. *All of the students have gone.* $c(R)=c(D)$
b. *Every one of the students has gone.* $c(R)=c(D)$
(52) a. *All of the ten students have gone.* $c(R)=c(D)=10$
b. *Every one of the ten students has gone.* $c(R)=c(D)=10$

---

9. Brown (1985) speaks of exhaustive quantifiers.

All universally quantified terms behave as definite terms: since the ensemble referred to R is said to coincide with D, which is necessarily "available", R inherits the identifiability of D. We can thus give an analysis such as the following:

(53)   *all of the ten students*
        (d all / d 10 x_i: *student* [N])   : c(R)=c(D)=10

By presenting universal quantifiers in this way as a limiting case of partitive quantification, we do justice to both the semantic and the syntactic properties of universally quantified terms. Compare:

(54) a.   *nine of the ten students*
     b.   **ten of the ten students*
     c.   *all of the ten students*

Thus, *all of the ten* in a sense fills the gap of *ten of the ten*. Note that *all* can quantify over sets and masses (is an ensemble quantifier), and takes count nouns in the plural, whereas *every* and *each* can only quantify over sets, and take singular count nouns.[10]

7.4.3. Genericity

Both definite and indefinite terms may either be used to indicate an individual referent, or to refer generically to a whole class or category of referents. The latter usage may be called *generic*. Generic terms express that the size of R equals the size of U. Consider:

(55) a.   *I saw* the dog *in the garden.*   [-generic]   c(R)=c(D)=1
     b.   The dog *is man's best friend.*   [+generic]   c(R)=c(U)

---

10. For some more subtle differences between these different types of universal quantifier, see Vendler (1967). For their counterparts in Dutch, Dik (1975a). See Brown (1985) for further aspects of quantification not discussed here. Brown distinguishes a further class of "rational" quantifiers (as in *half of the students*) and makes some remarks about "quantifier modifiers" such as *exactly, almost, around,* etc.

(56) a. *I saw a dog in the garden.*   [-generic]   c(R)=1
      b. *A dog is very faithful.*   [+generic]   c(R)=c(U)

Generic reference is incompatible with cutting out any subensemble from the relevant ensemble U. Therefore, generic terms cannot contain numerals, nor can they have a partitive structure.

Generic reference is close to universal quantification, if that quantification pertains to a D which equals U:

(57) a. *Dogs are faithful.*   c(R)=c(U)
      b. *All dogs are faithful.*   c(R)=c(U)
      c. ≠ *All the dogs are faithful.*   c(R)=c(D)≠c(U)

Therefore, generic reference cannot be identified with universal quantification, since the latter can be applied to any ensemble D, while genericity necessarily pertains to U.

We may take non-generic reference as the default usage of terms, and use an operator "g" for generic terms. We could then differentiate the generic and non-generic usage of *the dog* as follows:

(58) a.   (d 1 x_i: *dog* [N])   (-generic)
      b.   (d 1 g x_i: *dog* [N])   (+generic)

It is clear that the [±generic] opposition is semantically very important. There is an enormous distance between the two possible readings of a sentence like:

(59)   *The dog is a nuisance.*   (+generic or -generic)

It seems clear, then, that the distinction must be coded in underlying term structure in some such way as is done in (58b).

Genericity is hardly ever expressed directly in specific generic forms. The following points are worth mentioning in this respect:

— the generic term operator typically does not have an expression of its own, but is expressed in the same way as non-generic terms;

— generic terms may be expressed as definite or indefinite, and as singular or plural:

(60) a.   *A dog is very faithful.*
      b.   *The dog is very faithful.*
      c.   *Dogs are very faithful.*

— the expression possibilities for generic terms may differ from one language to another (cf. Croft 1990: 4-6). In French, for example, one uses definite plural terms where English uses indefinite plurals:

(61) a. *Dogs are very faithful.*
 d. *Les chiens sont très fidèles.*

— there may be differences between generic terms with definite or indefinite expression: such definite and indefinite generic terms are not always substitutable for one another (Smith 1975, Lyons 1977). For example:

(62) a. *The dodo is extinct.*
 b. **A dodo is extinct.*

— there may be ordering differences according to whether a term has ±generic reference, as in Dutch:[11]

(63) a. *Een hond   blaft.*   [+generic]
       a   dog   barks
       'A dog barks.'
 b. *Er   blaft   een hond.* [-generic]
       there   barks   a   dog
       'There is a dog barking.'

7.4.4. Ordinators

By "ordinators" we understand such elements as *first, second, third, ..., last*. These elements presuppose that the intended referent belongs to a linearly ordered series of similar entities, and they indicate the position of the intended referent in that sequence. For example:

(64) *It is* the third house on your left hand.

presupposes that there is a series of houses on your left hand, and that the intended house is number 3 in the series.

---

11. Cf. Philippaki-Warburton (1985) for ordering phenomena in Modern Greek which are judged to be dependent on the specific / generic opposition.

Ordinators can be productively formed from numerators, and they often behave like adjectives. Nevertheless, there are various reasons to regard them as term operators rather than as restrictors.

First, ordinators serve to locate the intended referent in the superordinate series rather than to specify independent properties of the intended referent. Consider:

(65)   *Aldrin was the second man on the moon.*
Therefore, Aldrin was a man.
Therefore, Aldrin was on the moon.
*Therefore, Aldrin was second.

It makes no sense to say that Aldrin was 'second' in any independent sense: *second* locates Aldrin in a presupposed series of 'men on the moon'.

In the second place, ordinators can take a numeral in their scope, as in:

(66)   *the first two problems*

This implies that if *two* expresses a quantifying term operator (which must be the case, since it specifies a property of the whole referent set R), *first* must represent a term operator as well.

Therefore, writing "n°" for the n-th ordinator, we can use such representations as:

(67)   (d 1° 2 x_i: *problem* [N])   *the first two problems*

In the case of ordinators we can make the same four-way distinction as we made for quantifiers:

(68) (A)   Absolute non-proportional
the third problem
(B)   Relative non-proportional
the next problem
(C)   Absolute proportional
the third of the ten problems
(D)   Relative proportional
the next of the ten problems

Relative ordinators such as *next, following, preceding*, etc. specify the position of R within the sequence D in relation to some other member of the sequence. We can thus arrive at the following analysis:

(69) *the next of the ten problems*
 (d next° 1 / d 10 x_i: *problem* [N])
 presuppositions: — D is a sequence of ten problems
  — a problem x_j has been specified as taking position n in the sequence.
 instruction: the intended referent is at n + 1 in D.

7.5. Localizing term operators

Localizing term operators serve to characterize the intended referent in terms of the position it takes in cognitive space. Cognitive space may be a reflection of "real" spatial relationships, or it may concern more abstract relationships between the intended referent and parameters of pragmatic information, including its relation to other entities which are already available in the discourse model.

7.5.1. Demonstratives

Demonstrative elements most clearly localize the intended referent with respect to spatial or other kinds of orientational parameters. Consider the opposition between constructions such as:

(70) a. *I want* these *three red books.*
 b. *I want* those *three red books.*

In both cases S refers A to a set of three entities, each having the properties 'book' and 'red'. In both cases the term used is definite (i.e. A is invited to identify rather than to construe a referent), although this is not coded in separate definite articles. The demonstratives are intrinsically definite, and this is not a particular property of English *this* and *that*, but a general property of demonstrative systems.

The demonstratives can be interpreted as hints for where to search for the intended referents. These hints are relative in two senses: they crucially depend on the "deictic centre" of the communicative event, consisting of {S, A, l_0, t_0} (cf. 2.4.3. above); and they never provide "absolute", but always "relative" relationships to the deictic centre. Thus, we might describe the impact of the demonstratives in (70) as follows:

(71) a.   'Identify three red books and do so by searching in an area relatively close to the deictic centre'
    b.   'Identify three red books and do so by searching in an area relatively far from the deictic centre'

Let us indicate the value of *these*, as specified in (71a), by "proximate" (prox), and that of *those*, as specified in (71b), by "remote" (rem). We can then represent the two terms as follows:

(72) a.   (d prox 3 x_i: *book* [N]: *red* [A])
    b.   (d rem 3 x_i: *book* [N]: *red* [A])

It does indeed seem appropriate to treat demonstratives by means of term operators, since they apply to the whole ensemble of intended referents rather than to the individual parts of the ensemble, and since they belong to closed grammatical systems rather than to "open" patterns of lexical items.

In 2.4.3. we defined the "deictic centre" as the central point of "pragmatic space", where "space" was interpreted in an abstract, cognitive sense of the term. We can now say, in general, that demonstratives locate intended referents on vectors or in subareas of pragmatic space, taken in this same cognitive sense. We tend to think of demonstratives in the first place as defining "relative distances in physical space", and indeed, in many cases such spatial orientation appears to be their basic value. On the more abstract, cognitive interpretation of "pragmatic space", however, we may expect that demonstratives may also signal more abstract "searching instructions". And this is indeed the case. In the first place, demonstratives with basic spatial value may often be used to provide more abstract directions; secondly, certain languages have demonstrative distinctions which cannot be described in terms of spatial relations, although they can still be interpreted as providing orientations in the more abstract dimensions of pragmatic space.

Languages differ considerably in the number of distinct demonstratives, and in the kinds of distinctions signalled by these elements. Demonstrative systems range from a minimum of two to a maximum of well over twenty distinct demonstratives. The most important semantic and pragmatic dimensions designated by demonstratives across languages may be described as follows:

(A) Relative distance from S, from A, or from [S & A]:
'Search for the referent in an area relatively close to / remote from me, you, us.'
(B) Relative degrees of distance (a further specification of (A)):
'Search for the referent in an area relatively close / moderately close / moderately remote / very remote from me, you, us.'
(C) Orientation in the vertical plane:
'Search for the referent in the area above / below / level with me, you, us.'
(D) Position relative to the bodily orientation of S or A:
'Search in the area in front of / behind / left of / right of me, you.'
(E) Position with respect to landmarks which have special importance in pragmatic space:
'Search in the area this side of / that side of / in front of / behind X, where X = river, mountain, sea, ...'
(F) Visibility:
'Search among items which are visible / invisible to me, you, us.'
(G) Contextual distance:
'Search among items mentioned recently / earlier / later in the ongoing discourse.'
(H) Temporal distance:
'Search among items which still / no longer exist.'

All of these parameters except (G) and (H) concern different aspects of (primarily) spatial orientation. When demonstrative elements get temporal values this can be understood through such metaphorical extensions as the following:

(73) a. close, visible, tangible, present, alive   →   now
     b. remote, invisible, no longer there, dead   →   long ago

The parameters (A)-(H) combine in different ways, giving rise to a wide variety of possible demonstrative systems. Consider one example of a moderately complex demonstrative system, from Lillooet (Salish), as described in Van Eijk (1985: 198):

Table 12. The twelve demonstratives in Lillooet

		VISIBLE			INVISIBLE	
	'this'	'that'	'that' (farther)	'this'	'that'	'that' (farther)
singular	c?a	ti?	t?u	kʷ?a	ni?	kʷu?
plural	?izá	?iz'	?izú	kʷɬa	nəɬ	kʷɬ
	'these'	'those'	'those' (farther)	'these'	'those'	'those' (farther)

This system can be described in terms of the interaction of two localizing parameters: relative distance (in three degrees) and visibility, and the quantifying parameter of number.

7.5.2. Definiteness and indefiniteness

One extension of demonstrative orientation, as described in (G) above, is orientation with respect to contextual parameters: mentioned recently / earlier in the ongoing discourse. Such orientation is mediated via the "discourse model" which S and A have built up, and which is part of their pragmatic information. When the orientational parameter only concerns the question whether or not the intended referent is presumed to be already available in A's pragmatic information, we speak of *definite* vs. *indefinite* term operators.

The difference between definite and indefinite terms can be symbolized by means of the term operators "d" and "i", as we have done in many examples in the preceding chapters. Thus, we write:

(74) a. (d 1 x_i: *man* [N])   the man
    b. (i 1 x_i: *man* [N])   a man
    c. (d m x_i: *man* [N])   the men
    d. (i m x_i: *man* [N])   men

The difference between definite and indefinite terms can be defined in terms of the theory of reference outlined in 6.1.2. above. This theory can be summarized as follows:

S refers A to E by means of T. We speak of *constructive reference* when S helps A construe a referent through T, and of *identifying reference* when S helps A to identify a referent which is in some way supposed to be already "available" to A. A referent may be presumed to be available to A on the basis of (a) long-term pragmatic information, (b) short-term (contextual) information, (c) perceptual information, (d) inferences drawn on the basis of information from (a)-(d).

Definite terms are typically used to establish identifying reference, indefinite terms to establish constructive reference. Thus:

(75) a. By means of a definite term S invites A to identify a referent which S presumes is available to A.
 b. By means of an indefinite term S invites A to construe a referent conforming to the properties specified in the term.

It follows from these characterizations that indefinite terms will typically be used to introduce referents into the discourse, whereas definite terms will typically be used for referring back to a referent which has already been established in the discourse. The great majority of usages of definite and indefinite terms can be understood on the basis of this distinction. Consider such examples as:[12]

(76) a. *Yesterday I met* an old friend of mine (construe referent x_i). He (identify x_i, which is now available through contextual information) *did not even recognize me!*
 b. *I was greatly impressed by* the Empire State Building.
    (referent presumed to be available through long-term information).
 c. *Do you see* the man with the yellow sweater?
    (referent presumed to be available through perceptual information).
 d. *I like the car but I do not like* the colour.
    (referent presumed to be available through inference).

There are three features often associated with definite terms which require some discussion here. These are the features of *existential commitment*,

---

12. Compare the theory of "discourse referents" proposed in Karttunen (1976), and the studies of Strawson (1971) on "identifying reference". Strawson describes the usage of definite terms by means of a principle of "Presumption of Knowledge". See also Rijkhoff (1989).

uniqueness, and *inclusiveness*. Russell (1905) analysed definite descriptions in terms of the notions "existential commitment" and "uniqueness". Thus, he gave the following paraphrase for the famous expression *The present king of France is bald*:

(77) a. *There is (presently) a king of France* (existence);
 b. *There is one and only one king of France* (uniqueness);
 c. *That king of France is bald.*

From our point of view, the notion of existential commitment is clearly mistaken if "existence in the real world" is meant. Existential commitment should be reanalysed as "presumed availability in the pragmatic information of A"; referents do not exist in the real world: they are mental constructs which may or may not correspond to things in reality (see 6.1.1. above).

The feature of uniqueness is relevant if it is reanalysed in terms of unique identifiability in the mental model currently under consideration. No definite description guarantees unique reference all by itself: even for a proper name there are usually different potential referents. Uniqueness of reference results from the interaction between the definite term used and the mental model as built up in the interaction between S and A. This uniqueness feature can be considered as an "implicature"[13] of "identifiability". Consider an example such as:

(78) *Give me the red ball.*

In interpreting the term *the red ball* A may reason as follows: S instructs me to identify an entity x_i with the properties 'ball' and 'red' such that the entity is available to me; if there were several entities having these properties in the situation under consideration, I would be unable to identify which particular entity x_i S wants me to identify; in that case, the intended entity would not be "available" to me; presumably, then, there is only one (relevant) entity with the properties 'ball' and 'red' in the situation under consideration.

Another feature which has been taken to be characteristic of definite terms is "inclusiveness of reference" (Hawkins 1978). Compare:

(79) a. *Please remove the books from the table.*
 b. *Please remove some books from the table.*

---

13. In the sense of Grice (1975).

It seems clear that (79a) can be interpreted only on the assumption that all the books are intended to be cleared from the table; by contrast, (79b) strongly suggests that only a subset of the books must be cleared from the table. I believe that, again, this feature of inclusive reference can be interpreted as an implicature of identifiability. *The books* in (79a) presents the intended set of referents as being identifiable and available to A. Now suppose that there are ten books on the table, and S wants only some of these, say five books, to be removed by A. Since there are many possible subsets of five out of ten, the intended subset would then not be available to A. The only way in which *the books* refers to a set of books available to A is if all the books on the table are meant to be included in the referent. On the other hand, if an indefinite term is used in similar circumstances, as in (79b), it will be clear to A that, since the intended set of books is not presented as "available" to him, it cannot be the case that the whole set of books is intended by S; and since A gets the instruction to "construe a referent", he may conclude that it is up to him to determine which subset of books is to be removed.

As for the formal expression of the operators d and i there is a frequent, but not a necessary correspondence with definite and indefinite articles or affixes. That this correspondence is far from complete even in English appears from the following facts:

— indefinite plural terms take no indefinite article.
— personal pronouns take no definite article, although both grammatically and pragmatically they behave as definite terms.
— proper names normally have no definite article, although again they have all the properties of definite terms.

In the case of pronouns and proper nouns, we can say that they have intrinsic definiteness. For example, personal pronouns (at least for first and second person) have no indefinite counterparts. This is understandable, since they are used to refer to the participants in the speech situation, which may be presumed to be "available" and thus identifiable in any circumstance. Similarly, proper nouns will normally be used only when S has reason to believe that A is able to identify the entity referred to. In both pronouns and proper names, therefore, the opposition definite / indefinite is "neutralized" in favour of definiteness, and since something which is always X need not be marked for X, the definite article is not necessary.[14]

---

14. The absence of definite articles or affixes with proper names is a widespread, but not a universal feature of natural languages: we do find languages (e.g. Ancient Greek) in which even proper names carry the definite article.

Even in the case of intrinsically definite terms, however, definiteness must be marked in underlying structure, as in:

(80) a.   (d 1 x_i: [+S])   *I*
     b.   (d 1 x_i: *John* [N])   *John*

This is necessary, since intrinsically definite terms pattern with other definite terms with respect to rules which are sensitive to definiteness. For example, in a context such as:

(81)   *There was / were T in the house this morning.*

the position of T can be taken by indefinite terms, but not by most definite terms:

(82) a.   *There was / were* a man / men *in the house this morning.*
     b.   **There was / were* the man / the men *in the house this morning.*

Likewise, we cannot get proper names and personal pronouns in the position of T:

(83) a.   **There was* John / he *in the house this morning.*

It is clear that these facts cannot be accounted for in terms of "presence or absence of the (in)definite article". It can be captured in terms of "(in)definiteness" if it is assumed that not only terms marked by the definite article, but also proper names and pronouns possess the feature of definiteness. Our operator "d" captures this feature.

In other languages, we may find other kinds of expression devices for ±definite: affixal expression, as in the Scandinavian languages; coding of definiteness on the adjective rather than the noun, as in Serbo-Croatian (see 15.1.3.); a special type of verbal agreement for definite terms, as in Hungarian (De Groot 1981b); or systematic differences in constituent order correlating with ±definite, as in Latin. Typological adequacy is served, therefore, if we use a uniform operator in underlying term structure, and leave the specification of the particular form to the expression rules of the language involved.

In general, it is too simplistic to think that a certain grammatical operator can be relevant to a language only if it finds direct expression in a separate formal element. The "exponency" of such an operator may be indirect, or fused with the expression of other operators. The criterion for deciding whether a grammatical operator is relevant to a language rather lies in the question of whether there are rules and principles in the grammar which are most adequately captured by mentioning that operator. Only when this is not the case anywhere in the grammar of a language is the conclusion warranted that the operator in question is irrelevant to the language.

7.5.3. Specificity[15]

Definite vs. indefinite reference was defined in terms of presumed identifiability of the intended referent by the Addressee. As far as the status of the intended referent in S's pragmatic information is concerned, this still leaves open two distinct possibilities:

(84) a. *specific* (+s) reference: S has a particular intended referent in mind and invites A to either identify the corresponding referent in his own pragmatic information, or construe a corresponding referent.
  b. *non-specific* (-s) reference: S has no particular referent in mind; any referent answering to the description will be appropriate.

The opposition between ±specific reference interacts with ±definite reference, as can be seen in the following examples:

(85) a. *Yesterday John Smith was murdered. The murderer* (+s) *was caught on the spot.*
  b. *Yesterday John Smith was murdered. The murderer* (±s) *must be insane.*

In (85a) the reference of *the murderer* must be specific: S can only claim that the murderer has been caught if he has a particular individual, say Peter Brown, in mind. In (85b) S may also have a particular individual in mind; but it is also possible for (85b) to be used if nobody, let alone S or A, is presumed to know who the murderer is. The definiteness of *the murderer* is in that case

---

15. Brown (1985) and Vester (1985, 1987) suggested including the ±specific opposition in underlying term structure in the form of term operators. Compare Orlandini (1983) and Pinkster (1988: 147). See Dik, Dik, et al. (1989) for more detailed discussion of this problem.

warranted by the presumed inference: if a person has been murdered, it follows that there must have been a murderer, even though the identity of that murderer may be unknown. This usage of definite terms has been called "attributive" by Donnellan (1971). It may be interpreted as non-specific definite reference.

Indefinite terms can likewise be used in two different ways. Consider:

(86) a. *Yesterday I met* a Norwegian (+s).
   b. *Mary wants to marry* a Norwegian (±s).

In (86a) S must have a particular person, say Olav, in mind. In (86b) there are two possibilities. Either S has a particular individual in mind, or what he means to convey is that any individual answering to the description of the term will be a suitable candidate for marrying Mary. This usage of indefinite terms may be interpreted as non-specific indefinite reference.

A problem with the opposition between ±specific is that it is not usually coded in the form of the terms in question: *the murderer* in (85b) and *a Norwegian* in (86b) do not give away their +s or -s character through some kind of formal difference. This is not only true of English: it is not easy to find languages in which there are special articles or affixes which unambiguously express the values ±specific. This raises the question of whether the differences involved are indeed relevant to the grammar of languages, or rather arise only in the pragmatic interpretation of otherwise undifferentiated terms.

If the opposition is not coded in the form of terms, it can only be accepted as a grammatically relevant distinction if there are grammatical rules and principles which in one way or another are sensitive to the opposition. This brings us to the different phenomena which may be sensitive to the ±specific opposition in different languages. We do indeed find a variety of phenomena in different languages which can be most easily described in terms of this opposition:

— Some languages have different indefinite pronouns corresponding to the ±specific distinction:

(87)

	+SPECIFIC	-SPECIFIC
Latin[16]	*quidam*	*aliquis*
Russian[17]	*kogo-to*	*kogo-nibud'*
English	*someone*	*someone/anyone*

— There are differences in paraphrase potential; for example, on its specific, but not on its non-specific reading, (86b) can be paraphrased as:

(88) a. *Mary wants to marry a certain / a particular Norwegian.*
    b. *There is a Norwegian that Mary wants to marry.*

— In languages such as Latin (Vester 1985, 1987) and French (Kampers-Manhe 1985), the choice of indicative vs. subjunctive in relative clauses correlates with ±specific reference:

(89) a. *Je cherche une fille qui sait le latin* [+spec]
       I seek a girl who knows.IND the Latin
   b. *Je cherche une fille qui sache le latin* [-spec]
       I seek a girl who knows.SBJ the Latin
     'I'm looking for a girl who knows Latin'

For the description of the semantics of predicates the opposition is relevant as well:

— There are cooccurrence restrictions:

(90) a. *John saw a dog.*   [only +specific]
    b. *John wanted a dog.*   [+specific or -specific]

— The possibilities of coherently continuing the discourse are different (Karttunen 1976):

(91) a. *John wants a dog. It is black.*   [+specific]
    b. *John wants a dog. It must be black.*   [-specific]

---

16. Lyons (1977), Vester (1987). However, there appear to be counterexamples to this claim (Machtelt Bolkestein, pers. comm.).
17. Dahl (1970).

Localizing term operators 191

It seems that in any language a number of phenomena can be found which can best be handled in terms of the ±specific opposition. The opposition is also of obvious importance to semantics, and to the logical inferences that can be drawn from a proposition depending on whether it gets a specific or a non-specific reading.

The specificity opposition can be captured by means of term operators +s and -s, which may interact with the operators d and i. We may take specific reference as the unmarked, default case which need not be especially signalled, and thus make the following distinctions:

(92) a. definite specific term:
 (d 1 x_i: *murderer* [N]) *the particular murderer*
 b. definite -specific term:
 (d -s 1 x_i: *murderer* [N]) *the murderer, whoever it is*
(93) a. indefinite specific term:
 (i 1 x_i: *murderer* [N]) *a particular murderer*
 b. indefinite -specific term:
 (i -s 1 x_i: *murderer* [N]) *a murderer, whoever it is*

Those grammatical and semantic phenomena which are sensitive to the specific or non-specific character of a term can now be captured by reference to the presence or absence of the -s operator.

8. Non-verbal predicates

8.0. Introduction[1]

So far, we have been mainly concerned with verbal predicates. In probably all languages, however, there are also non-verbal constituents which can be used in predicative function. If, for the moment, we disregard the copular verb, the following constructions contain such non-verbal predicates:

(1) a. *John (is)* intelligent. [adjective]
    b. *John (is)* president. ["bare" nominal]
    c. *John (is)* a nice boy. [indefinite term]
    d. *John (is)* the winner. [definite term]
    e. *John (is)* in the garden. [adpositional phrase]

After a discussion of categorial differences between predicates (8.1.), this chapter concentrates on the treatment of non-verbal predicates in FG. First, we consider adjectival predicates (8.2.) and introduce the principle of *copula support*, i.e. the introduction of the copula in constructions with non-verbal predicates (8.3.). We then treat nominal predicates (8.4.), adpositional predicates (8.5.), possessive predicates (8.6.), and locative and existential constructions, which will be considered as special kinds of non-verbal predications (8.7.). In 8.8. we consider the role of the argument type in non-verbal predications.

8.1. Categorial differences between predicates

In introducing the notion of *predicate* we have distinguished the main categories V(erbal), N(ominal), and A(djectival). The question arises how we define these categories. This question has been debated since antiquity. In the traditional approach these categories are defined in terms of the types of things which they designate. But such a semantic approach does not yield a viable

---

1. For a more extensive treatment of the construction types dealt with here, see Hengeveld (1992).

solution, since what is designated by a V in one language may well be designated by an A or an N in other languages. And even within one language it is often not clear on semantic grounds why one thing should be expressed by a verb, while a quite similar thing is described by a noun.

The structuralist alternative was to define the categories primarily in terms of formal morphosyntactic properties. This approach is all right as far as it goes, but it is difficult to generalize across languages, since the defining morphosyntactic properties may be quite different from one language to another. For example, morphological criteria do not take us very far in languages without morphology.

I believe it is profitable to take a functional view of the categories, and define them in terms of the prototypical functions they fulfil in the construction of predications. We will say that we find the three categories V, N, and A in their prototypical functions in such a construction as:

(2) *The old man died.*
  die [V] $(d1x_i$: man [N]: old [A]$)_{Proc}$

In this construction *die* fulfils the "predicative" function: it is the main predicate of the predication; *man* has the function of "head of the term": it is the first restrictor in the term structure; and *old* has "attributive" function: it is a non-first restrictor in the structure of the term.

Using these notions, the three categories of predicates can be defined as follows:

(3) a. A Verbal predicate (V) is a predicate which is primarily used in predicative function.
  b. A Nominal predicate (N) is a predicate which is primarily used as head of a term.
  c. An Adjectival predicate (A) is a predicate which is primarily used in attributive function.

Note that we need the hedge "primarily". This is because most categories, as we shall see below, can also be put to secondary or derived uses, which coincide with the primary uses of the other categories. In such cases, however, there is usually some formal indication of the derived character of the predicate.

The definitions given in (3) may be assumed to be universally valid across languages, since the three main defining functions "predicative", "head of a term", and "attributive" may be assumed to be relevant to the grammar of any language. This does not mean, however, that all languages necessarily distinguish the three distinct categories V, N, and A. Suppose we have a language in which all the "adjectives", as defined in (3c), can also occur in predicative use, without any formal difference, so that we systematically find pairs such as:

(4) a. *The wall whites.* 'The wall is white.'
    b. *the white wall* 'the white wall'

In such a language there would be no category which is primarily used in attributive function, and thus the distinction between V and A would not be relevant: there would be one category of predicates, say VA, which covers the ground which is covered by V and A in other languages. Such a situation may obtain, for instance, in Bahasa Indonesia, where it is very difficult to find any criterion distinguishing between V and A (cf. Sie Ing Djiang 1988). It has even been claimed that there are languages with one undifferentiated category of predicates, without any distinction between V, N, and A. Different authors claim that this situation obtains in the Salish languages (Kuipers 1968, Kinkade 1983). It is certainly true that a predicate in these languages can just as easily be put to "predicative", "head", or "attributive" uses. Consider, for example, the predicate *nk'yap* 'coyote' in Lillooet (Van Eijk 1981, 1985):[2]

(5) a. *ƚ'ak   ti   nk'yáp-a*
       go   the   coyote
       'The coyote goes.'
    b. *nk'yap   ti   ƚ'ák-a*
       coyote   the   go
       'That which goes is a coyote'
    c. *nk'yap   száyten*
       coyote   things
       'coyote doings'

Although the differences between V, N, and A do not seem to be syntactically relevant in these languages, there are nevertheless certain morphological criteria for distinguishing at least N and VA predicates (Van Eijk 1985, Van Eijk—Hess 1986): N, but not VA predicates take possessive markers, and VA,

---

2. *ƚ'* stands for a glottalized lateral plosive. Note that the ending *-a* goes with the article *ti*.

196 Non-verbal predicates

but not N predicates can be characterized for various aspectual distinctions. This means that the first language with no distinctions between V, N, and A whatsoever, has yet to be found.

In languages which do distinguish separate categories of V, N, and A predicates, these categories can usually be converted into each other in different ways. The relevant relations can be represented as in Figure 4.

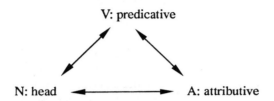

Figure 4. Possible derivative relations between predicate categories

Each of the arrows in Figure 4 indicates some derived use of the given predicate type. These derived uses are normally quite clearly marked in the form of the predicate. Consider the situation in English:

— V can be put to attributive function through relativization or participle formation (to be treated in *TFG2*: chapters 1 and 3).

(6) a. *the man* who died *in the accident*
    b. *the* dying *man*

— V in head function requires nominalization (see *TFG2*: chapter 1):

(7) a. *the* killing *of the tiger*
    b. *the frequent* mowing *of the lawn*

— A in predicative function usually requires a copular verb (treated in this chapter):

(8) a. *The man* is old.
    b. *The stuff* stayed red.

— A in head function requires nominalization of A:

(9)   *great* kindness, *a beautiful* blue

— N in predicate function usually requires "term predicate formation" (discussed in 8.4. below):

(10) a. *John* is a soldier.
     b. *John* is my best friend.

— some Ns may be put to attributive use without modification; others require derivation of an adjectival predicate:

(11)   a paper *box,* a kite-like *flying object*

Although the different secondary uses of V, N, and A may have different manifestations in different languages, the general picture given in Figure 4 may be assumed to be in some way or other relevant to most languages.

8.2. Adjectival predicates

In many languages adjectives can be put to predicative use without any further support, in constructions of the form:

(12)   *John intelligent.*
         'John is intelligent'

It is often assumed that such constructions have some kind of underlying copular verb, which is deleted in the derivation of the final linguistic expression. Within the framework of FG such an assumption is unwarranted and unnecessary. It is unwarranted because in FG we try to avoid deletion operations wherever this is possible (see 1.7.1.) and because, more generally, it is no advantage for a theory if it has to postulate underlying elements which do not appear at the surface. The assumption is unnecessary since, in FG, a construction such as (12) can be immediately formed from the predicate frame of the adjectival predicate *intelligent*, which is found in the lexicon. The structure of (12) will thus be as follows:

(13)   *intelligent* [A] (d1x_i: *John* [N])$_\varnothing$

This structure can be directly mapped onto (12), without any intervening verbal element. Clearly, then, there are adjectival predications alongside verbal ones.

8.3. Copula support

In many languages, of course, the expression of a predication such as (13) requires a copular verb corresponding to English *be*. This copular verb can then be used to code the distinctions for Tense, Aspect, and Mood otherwise reserved for verbal predicates, resulting in e.g.:

(14) a. *John* is *intelligent.*
 b. *John* was *intelligent.*
 c. *John* may be *intelligent.*

In languages which do have such copular verbs, it is usually only in certain conditions that the copula appears. Even in English there are several construction types which may be interpreted as adjectival predications without copula:

(15) a. *Mmmm, very intelligent, that man!*
 b. *John intelligent? Good heavens, no!*
 c. *Peter considers John intelligent.*

Ferguson (1971: 147) suggests that copular verbs tend to be absent:
— in main rather than in subordinate clauses;
— in non-emphatic rather than in emphatic constructions;
— in timeless or unmarked present tense rather than in other tenses;
— with third person rather than with first or second person subjects;
— with adjectival rather than with nominal predicates.

An example of the conditioning force of both tense and person is Hungarian, where the copula is absent in the third person present tense, but present elsewhere (cf. Kiefer 1968):

(16) a. *Péter   barna.*
     Peter   brown
     'Peter is brown'
 b. *Péter   barna   volt.*
     Peter   brown   was
     'Peter was brown'
 c. *Péter   barna   lesz.*
     Peter   brown   will-be
     'Peter will be brown'

In accordance with the general principles of FG we should like to have a description in which the copula only figures in underlying structure if it also appears in the actual linguistic expression. This can be achieved if we assume that the copula is introduced in those conditions in which it appears, rather than being deleted in those conditions in which it does not occur. The expression rule which has this effect will be called the rule of "copula support" (compare the rule of *do*-support in English grammar). The term "support" suggests that the copula serves to carry those operators of Tense, Aspect, and Mood which require a verbal form if they are to be expressed.

In its most general form the rule of copula support can be formulated according to the following schema:

(17)   COPULA SUPPORT
       input: π predicate [Type] $(x_1)(x_2)...(x_n)$
       conditions: π = ...
                     Type = ...
                     [other conditions]
       output: π copula [V] predicate [Type] $(x_1)(x_2)...(x_n)$

Thus, a copular verb is introduced, depending on the presence of certain π-operators, given a certain Type or category of the predicate, and under certain further conditions (e.g. p3 rather than p1/p2 subject). As a first approximation[3] to copula support in English, we can formulate the following rule:

(18)   COPULA SUPPORT IN ENGLISH: *BE*-SUPPORT
       input: π predicate [Type] $(x_1)(x_2)...(x_n)$
       conditions: π = any specified π-operator
                     Type $\neq$ V
       output: π *be* [V] predicate [Type] $(x_1)(x_2)...(x_n)$

When applied to a predication of the form (19a), this rule will produce (19b), which will finally be mapped onto (19c):[4]

---

3. In Dik (1983a) I have shown how the rule can be generalized so as to take care of all occurrences of *be* in English.

4. The underlying predications in this chapter present only those elements which are relevant to the present discussion.

(19) a. Past e_i: *intelligent* [A] (d1x_i: *John* [N])$_\varnothing$
    b. Past e_i: *be* [V] *intelligent* [A] (d1x_i: *John* [N])$_\varnothing$
    c. *John was intelligent.*

Consider now the case in which an adjectival predicate appears as a restrictor within a term structure:

(20)   (d1x_i: *boy* [N]: *intelligent* [A])

This term structure can be expressed in two ways:

(21) a. *the intelligent boy*
    b. *the boy who is intelligent*

Rule (18) was formulated on the assumption that in the case of (21a) the adjectival restrictor in (20) is not provided with a π-operator: the restrictor is completely unspecified with respect to Tense, Aspect, etc. In the case of (21b), however, the assumption is that the restrictor is provided with a specified π-operator and that, for this reason, rule (18) will introduce *be*. It must thus be assumed that the term structure underlying (21b) is not (20), but rather:

(22)   (d1x_i: *boy* [N]: [Pres e_i: *intelligent* [A]])

where the operator Pres will trigger *be*-support.

Note that there is a correlation between specification of π-operators and relativization: if the operator is specified, the restrictor must be relativized; if there is relativization, the operator must be specified.[5]

Had we started from underlying structures with a copula in cases such as (21), then obviously a rule of copula deletion would have had to be applied in all constructions with a simple attributive adjective such as (21a). As noted in 1.7.1. above, this type of description is to be avoided in FG. The rule of copula support will introduce the copula only where it is needed in the expression.

A natural question concerning copula support is: how are we to deal with a language like Spanish, which has two copular verbs, *ser* and *estar*, which, in certain constructions, are in direct contrast with each other? It would seem impossible to maintain that these copular verbs are simple support verbs. As Hengeveld (1986) has demonstrated, however, the Spanish facts can be

---

5. This correlation will be further discussed in *TFG2*: 2.2.

accounted for if we assume two distinct copula support rules for introducing *ser* and *estar*, such that these rules are triggered by different parameters. The reasoning is as follows. In certain conditions *ser* is obligatory, in others *estar*:

(23) a. *Un perro   es/*está un animal.*
         a   dog   is   a   animal
         'A dog is an animal'
     b. *El vaso   *es/está roto.*
         the vase   is   broken
         'The vase is broken'

In constructions with locative predicates we may find either *ser* or *estar*, but here the choice is dependent on the nature of the subject term: if the subject indicates a first-order entity, *estar* is obligatory; if it indicates an event, *ser* must be used (cf. also 8.8.):

(24) a. *La reunión es en la sala 315.*
         the meeting is in the room 315
         'The meeting is in room 315.'
     b. *La mesa   está en la sala.*
         the table is   in the room
         'The table is in the room.'

There is only one condition in which true minimal pairs with *ser* and *estar* can be formed. This is with a certain class of adjectival predicates, where *ser* signals that a permanent, intrinsic property is involved, whereas *estar* implies that the state in question is contingent and temporary:

(25) a. *Antonia es guapa.*
         Antonia is pretty
         'Antonia is (by nature) pretty.'
     b. *Antonia está guapa.*
         Antonia is pretty
         'Antonia looks pretty (now).'

Hengeveld compares this semantic difference with the aspectual difference between ±Progressive in verbal predicates:

(26) a. Juan   canta.
         John   sings
         'John sings.'
    b.   Juan   está cantando.
         John   is   singing
         'John is singing.'

We may now suppose that the difference between (25a-b) is identical to that between (26a-b). Just as Antonia is said to be temporarily in the state of prettiness in (25b), so John may be said to be temporarily in the act of singing in (26b). We may thus assume that the underlying structures of (25a-b) differ in the following way:

(27) a. Pres e: *guap-* [A] (*Antonia*)$_\varnothing$
    b.   Pres e: Progr *guap-* [A] (*Antonia*)$_\varnothing$

We can then say that the presence of Progr triggers *estar*-support in both verbal and adjectival predications, whereas the absence of Progr in adjectival predications triggers *ser*-support. In this way, two distinct rules can be set up for *ser*-support and *estar*-support, so that the two copular verbs are correctly introduced in the appropriate conditions.

8.4. Nominal predicates

Consider a construction such as:

(28)   *John is president.*

Such a construction can be handled in precisely the same way as constructions with an adjectival predicate: the nominal predicate *president* is immediately applied to the term *John*, and the rule of copula support (18) will introduce the copular verb *be*. In English, such direct predicative use of nominal predicates is rather limited. In Dutch, for example, it is more extensive. There is a whole class of nominals (roughly, designations of functions, professions and political or religious denominations) which can be used directly in predicative function:

(29)   Jan   is   schilder/directeur/communist.
         John   is   painter/director/communist
         'John is a painter / a director / a communist'

The underlying structure takes the form of (30), to which copula support will be applied in the relevant conditions:

(30)   *schilder* [N] / *directeur* [N] / *communist* [N] (d1x_i: *Jan* [N])$_\varnothing$

Just as in English, a nominal predicate can also take an indefinite article:

(31)   *Jan is een schilder / een directeur / een communist.*

Thus, Dutch has an opposition between (29) and (31) which is absent in English. This opposition is semantically relevant (Kraak—Klooster 1968: 143-149), though the semantic differences are rather subtle. Roughly, (29) gives an objective account of Jan's profession / function / ideology, while (31) presents a more subjective assessment of his qualities. This difference comes out in such constructions as:

(32)   *Ik   vind   jou net een communist / *communist.*
         I   find   you just a   communist / communist
        'To my mind, you are just like a communist.'

The nominals in (29) can be treated as "bare" predicates, immediately used in predicative function, while those provided with the indefinite article must rather be considered as indefinite *terms*, which have been turned into predicates. One reason for this distinction is that the nominal predicates in (29) can be used in the singular, even where the subject is plural:

(33)   *Jan   en   Piet   zijn communist.*
         John   and   Peter   are communist
        'John and Peter are communists.'

A second reason is that bare nominal predicates can in no way be modified or restricted:

(34)   **Jan   is   ouderwetse   communist.*
         John   is   old-fashioned communist
        'John is an old-fashioned communist.'

whereas predicates with the indefinite article can take any kind of modification possible for indefinite terms in general:

(35)   Jan   is   een   ouderwetse   communist,   die   toch
       John   is   an   old-fashioned communist,   who   yet
       probeert mee   te   doen   met   de   laatste mode.
       tries   along to   do   with   the   latest   fashion
       'John is an old-fashioned communist, who nevertheless tries to keep up with the latest fashion.'

For this construction type, then, we need a way to turn an indefinite term into a derived predicate. For example, in construing the underlying structure of (36a), we must first build the term (36b), and then apply this term as a predicate to *Jan*, as in (36c):

(36) a. *Jan is een communist.*
     b. (i1x_j: *communist* [N])
     c. Pres e: {(i1x_j: *communist* [N])} (d1x_i: *Jan* [N])$_\emptyset$

Note that the basic predicate *communist* is first incorporated into a term, and then that term is turned into a predicate. We shall call such a predicate a *term-predicate*. Note that both in Dutch and in English (but not necessarily in other languages), copula support will have to apply to (36c) to introduce the copular verb. This can be done by suitably parametrizing the rule of copula support: in fact, stipulating that the predicate should be non-V, as is done in (18), will have the desired result.

Semantically, we can understand this type of structure in terms of the notion of "class-inclusion". Remember that we interpret individuals as singleton sets. In (36a) it is predicated of the singleton set consisting of 'Jan' that it is a subset of the set designated by *een communist*.[6]

Once we have taken the step of recognizing that indefinite terms can act as predicates, we immediately see that definite terms, as well, can function as such. Compare:

(37) a. *John is a painter I met in Paris.*
     b. *John is the painter I met in Paris.*

Rather than saying that John is included in the set of 'painters I met in Paris', (37b) identifies the entity designated by *John* as no one else than the entity

---

6. Note that when individuals are interpreted as singleton sets, the difference between "class-membership" and "class-inclusion" is neutralized.

designated by *the painter I met in Paris*. We see that the difference between "class-inclusion" and "identification" resides in the choice of the indefinite vs. the definite article in the term-predicate.

Our analysis as developed so far implies that any term, whether definite or indefinite, can be turned into a one-place predicate over another term. This can be captured by means of a general rule of Term-predicate Formation:

(38)   TERM-PREDICATE FORMATION
        input: any term (t)
        output: {(t)} $(x_1)_\emptyset$

This rule, when applied to the term (39a), yields the term-predicate (39b), the argument position of which can be filled in as usual, yielding (39c), the underlying structure of (39d):

(39) a. ($d1x_i$: *winner* [N])
     b. {($d1x_i$: *winner* [N])} $(x_1)_\emptyset$
     c. Past e: {($d1x_i$: *winner* [N])} ($d1x_j$: *Peter* [N])$_\emptyset$
     d. *Peter was the winner.*

If the term-predicate is an indefinite term, the resulting construction signals class-inclusion; with a definite term-predicate, it signals identification. The semantic relations expressed by non-verbal predications as discussed so far can thus be defined in terms of the types of predicate which they contain, as in Table 13.

Table 13. Semantic relations in non-verbal predications

TYPE OF PREDICATE	SEMANTIC RELATION
adjectival / bare nominal	Property Assignment
indefinite term	Class Inclusion
definite term	Identification

The different semantic relations in Table 13 are often described as if they were due to the alleged multiple ambiguity of the copular verb 'be': one then distinguishes "property-assigning *be*", "class-inclusion *be*", "identifying *be*", etc. According to our analysis, this is incorrect: the copula has nothing to do

206 *Non-verbal predicates*

with the different semantic relations. This is clear from languages in which we find constructions such as:

(40) a. *John — intelligent / president.*   Property Assignment
     b. *John — a painter.*   Class Inclusion
     c. *John — the winner.*   Identification

in which precisely the same semantic relations are expressed without a copular verb. The semantic differences must thus reside in the type of predicate applied rather than in the copula, which is a semantically innocent supportive element with no deep conceptual or philosophical significance.[7]

8.5. Adpositional predicates

Adpositional phrases can also function as predicates. Consider the following constructions:

(41) a. *The chair is* in the garden.
     b. *the chair* in the garden

In (41b) the prepositional phrase *in the garden* is used in attributive function, as a restrictor on the possible values of x_i: 'the entity x_i such that "chair" of x_i such that "in the garden" of x_i'. Thus, *in the garden* must be interpreted as a predicate over the term variable. In (41a) this same predicate is used in predicative function.

The term structure underlying *in the garden* is as follows:

(42) $(d1x_i: garden\ [N])_{Loc}$

We can thus achieve the desired result by allowing terms provided with a semantic function such as Loc in (42) to be input to the rule of Term-predicate Formation. This can be done by a slight modification of this rule, as follows:

---

7. This is a rather interesting conclusion in view of the importance which has been assigned to the verb *be* throughout Western philosophy.

(43) TERM-PREDICATE FORMATION
input: any term $(t)_{[sf]}$
where [sf] indicates an optional semantic function
output: $\{(t)_{[sf]}\} (x_1)_\varnothing$

This rule now allows us to construe the following underlying structures for (41a-b):

(44) a. Pres e: $\{(d1x_i: garden\ [N])_{Loc}\} (d1x_j: chair\ [N])_\varnothing$
 b. $(d1x_i: chair\ [N]: \{(d1x_j: garden\ [N])_{Loc}\})_\varnothing$

The generalization expressed in rule (43) is that terms characterized by a semantic function may be turned into predicates over other terms.[8] This predicts that in languages in which such terms are expressed in some case form (without adposition), we will find such case-marked terms in predicative function. This prediction is borne out in a language such as Latin in which, for example, nominal terms in the genitive can be used as predicates of "quality" in both predicative and attributive function:

(45) a. *Dumnorix fuit magnae auctoritatis.*
 Dumnorix was great-gen authority-gen
 'Dumnorix was (a man) of great authority'
 b. *vir magnae auctoritatis*
 man-nom great-gen authority-gen
 'a man of great authority'

Another confirmation of the idea that terms provided with a semantic function may be turned into predicates is the fact that what is expressed by adpositional predicates in some conditions may be expressed by adjectival predicates in other conditions. Thus, the Dutch adjective *houten* 'wooden' can only be used attributively; the corresponding adpositional predicate *van hout* 'of wood' can be used both attributively and predicatively:

---

8. It has been objected to this treatment of adpositional predicates that it requires us to have terms provided with semantic functions available even outside the predicate frames in which they normally occur. See Mackenzie (1983), who also formulates an alternative to the analysis presented here. I do believe, however, that our analysis is both empirically necessary and formally feasible.

208   Non-verbal predicates

(46) a. *een houten stoel*   *een stoel van hout*
         a   wooden chair   a   chair of   wood
         'a wooden chair'   'a chair of wood'
    b.   **De stoel   is   houten.*   *De stoel   is   van hout.*
         the chair   is   wooden   the chair   is   of   wood
         'The chair is wooden.'   'The chair is of wood.'

The same phenomenon may occur across languages: what in one language is expressed by an adjective such as *strong*, may in another language require adpositional expression: *with strength*.

8.6. Possessive predicates

Once we have admitted rule (43) to the grammar, we can exploit this rule to account for a number of further construction types. Many languages, for example, have possessive constructions in which the Possessor appears in predicative or attributive function in the form of a case-marked or adpositional term, as in English and Dutch:

(47)   *This house is John's.*   *John's house*
(48) a. **Dit   huis   is   Jans.*   *Jans   huis*
         this   house   is   John's   John's   house
         'This house is John's.'   'John's house'
    b.   *Dit huis   is   van Jan.*   *het huis   van Jan*
         this house is   of   John   the house   of   John
         'This house is John's'   'John's house'

These constructions can be described by means of rule (43) if we allow a semantic function Poss ('Possessor') to be assigned to terms which can then be input to rule (43). This will yield the following structures underlying (47):

(49) a. Pres e: {(d1x_i: *John* [N])$_{Poss}$} (dprox1x_j: *house* [N])$_\emptyset$
    b.   (d1x_i: *house* [N]: {(d1x_j: *John* [N])$_{Poss}$})

The notion "possessive predicate" introduced in this manner accounts for the parallelism with other types of predicate created through rule (43); this notion is reinforced by the fact that in certain languages (in certain conditions) possessive predicates may take adjectival form, as in Latin:

(50) Domus   mea   est.   domus   mea
      house   my-adj is   house   my-adj
      'The house is mine'   'my house'

I do not mean to claim, however, that the notion "possessive predicate" can be used to account for ALL possessive constructions. First of all, this notion is quite inapplicable to constructions with verbs of 'having', as in:

(51) John has a beautiful house.

Secondly, many languages have possessive constructions of some such form as:

(52) There is a beautiful house to John.

Such constructions cannot be adequately described by means of possessive predicates. Rather, they have much in common with existential constructions, to which we turn in the next section.[9]

8.7. Locative and existential constructions

8.7.1. Initial analysis

In many languages there are intricate relationships between locative and existential constructions (cf. Lyons 1967, 1968, Clark 1978). Existential constructions, especially, provide difficulties for grammatical interpretation. In Dik (1980: 108-110) the following approach to these construction types was suggested. First, compare the following two Dutch constructions:

(53) a. De   hond   loopt   in   de   tuin.
         the   dog   walks   in   the garden
         'The dog is walking in the garden.'
     b. Er   loopt   een   hond in   de   tuin.
         there walks   a   dog in   the garden
         'There is a dog walking in the garden.'

---

9. Detailed studies are available on the possessive constructions of Latin (Bolkestein 1983), Hungarian (De Groot 1983a) and French (Vet 1983).

210   Non-verbal predicates

These two constructions differ rather markedly in constituent order, and (53b) has an initial "dummy" adverb *er* which is absent in (53a). The SoAs described in the two constructions, however, are quite similar: in both constructions the Activity of 'walking in the garden' is predicated of a 'dog'-entity. The main difference at the level of the underlying predication is that (53a) contains the definite specific term *de hond*, and (53b) the indefinite specific term *een hond*. The underlying predications for (53a-b) can thus be quite similar:

(54) a. Pres e: [*lopen* [V] (d1x_i: *hond* [N])$_{Ag}$] (d1x_j: *tuin* [N])$_{Loc}$
     b. Pres e: [*lopen* [V] (i1x_i: *hond* [N])$_{Ag}$] (d1x_j: *tuin* [N])$_{Loc}$

That the difference between "definite specific" and "indefinite specific" is crucial to the expression of these predications becomes apparent when we compare (53a-b) with:

(55) a. **Er   loopt   de hond   in de tuin.*
         there   walks   the dog   in the garden
         'There is the dog walking in the garden.'
     b. *Een hond   loopt   in de tuin.*
         a dog   walks   in the garden
         'A dog walks in the garden.'

Thus, the expression form (55a) cannot be used when the first argument is definite; and although (55b) is a grammatical sentence, it is difficult to interpret it otherwise than by assigning a generic interpretation to *een hond*. The differences in outward expression between (53a-b) may thus be captured by different placement rules, which are sensitive to the differences in term operators between (54a-b), and carry a definite term such as *de hond* in (54a) to clause-initial position, and an indefinite specific term such as *een hond* in (54b) to the basic subject position, which in Dutch is post-verbal. In that case, the initial position will be marked by the dummy *er* 'there'.

In the light of this analysis, we now compare the following pair:

(56) a. *De hond   is   in de tuin.*
         the dog   is   in the garden
         'The dog is in the garden.'
     b. *Er   is   een hond   in de tuin.*
         there is   a   dog   in the garden
         'There is a dog in the garden.'

Locative and existential constructions 211

We find similar differences as between the pair (53a-b). If these differences are taken care of in the same way, i.e. through the differential placement of the terms *de hond* and *een hond*, corresponding to the underlying differences in term operators, then again the underlying structures may be otherwise the same. From the analysis of adpositional predicates presented in 8.5. it follows that (56a) can have underlying structure (57a); (56b) can correspondingly be analysed as (57b):

(57) a. Pres e: {(d1x_i: *tuin* [N])$_{Loc}$} (d1x_j: *hond* [N])$_\emptyset$
 b. Pres e: {(d1x_i: *tuin* [N])$_{Loc}$} (i1x_j: *hond* [N])$_\emptyset$

In both these constructions there is a locative predicate which will trigger the Dutch rule of copula support. The placement rules will again take care of the different orderings of (56a-b). (56a) is a locative construction; (56b) may be called an "existential-locative" construction. Our analysis implies that the existential-locative construction may result from the application of a locative predicate to an indefinite specific argument term.

From this point we can take our argument one step further by comparing the following constructions:

(58) a. *There are black swans in Africa.*
 b. *There are black swans.*

(58a) is an existential-locative, to be analysed along the lines of (57b). (58b) is a purely "existential" construction. But note that it differs from (58a) only in the absence of the phrase *in Africa*, which was analysed as the predicate of that construction. And indeed the existential construction can be interpreted as stating that there are black swans 'somewhere', i.e. that they are located in some world without any further specification of the nature or the whereabouts of that world. This is in accordance with the philosophical adage that "to say that something exists is to say that it is located somewhere" (Lyons 1967).

On the basis of such considerations as these, we may arrive at the conclusion that existential constructions can be analysed as containing an unspecified locative predicate which is applied to an indefinite specific argument. This could be represented as follows:

(59) Pres e: {($\emptyset$)$_{Loc}$} (imx_i: *swan* [N]: *black* [A])$_\emptyset$

This analysis, though a bit strange at first sight, has a number of properties to commend itself: it accounts for the parallelism between (58a) and (58b) and, if the notion "unspecified location" is taken in a sufficiently abstract sense, it correctly captures the relation between existence and abstract location. Furthermore, the presence of the non-verbal predicate will automatically trigger copula support, and the presence of the element *there* in both (58a) and (58b) can be described in a uniform way. One consequence of the analysis is that the existential character of (58b) does not reside in the presence of yet another verb *be* ("existential *be*"), but rather in the presence of an unspecified locative predicate, which will trigger *be* as an automatic consequence of the rule of *be*-support. It is indeed true that many languages use some kind of copula in the existential construction; other languages have a special existential verb or particle, which can be interpreted as a direct expression of the empty locative predicate.

However, it cannot be maintained that such differences as those between (58a-b) are ONLY a function of the difference between ±definite term operators. This will be clarified in the next section.

8.7.2. The role of pragmatic functions

It is often assumed, as we have done in the preceding section, that such constructions as are introduced with *er* in Dutch (or with *there* in English) are subject to a so-called "definiteness restriction", according to which they cannot contain definite arguments. Hannay (1985b: 108-112), however, shows that this restriction is only a tendency, and that there is a variety of communicative conditions in which definite terms may appear in English *there*-constructions.[10] For example, the following sequence would be quite acceptable:

(60) A: *What problems are we going to meet in trying to get into the house?*
    B: *Well, first of all there is the dog in the garden...*

Such a construction as (60B) has certain special pragmatic features: it suggests that what B says is the first item in a "list" of problems which might be encountered upon entering the house. Such pragmatic markedness is typical of *there*-constructions with definite arguments.

---

10. The same point was made in Rando—Napoli (1978). The problem is not restricted to English: similar examples can be found in Dutch.

What (60B) shows is that under given circumstances we may have oppositions such as those between:

(61) a. *The dog is in the garden.*
     b. *There is the dog in the garden.*

These oppositions demonstrate that the parameter ±definite is insufficient for triggering the expression differences between such constructions. The underlying predications must thus differ from each other in ways which go beyond the ±definite character of the first argument.

I here follow Hannay's solution to this problem.[11] This solution is based on the following points: (i) the difference between (61a) and (61b) is located in a difference in pragmatic function relevant to the argument term *the dog*; (ii) the argument term in the *there*-construction is said to have the pragmatic function "Presentative", which is defined as follows (Hannay 1985b: 171): "A term with presentative function refers to an entity which the speaker by means of the associated predication wishes to explicitly introduce into the world of discourse."; (iii) this pragmatic function is then used to trigger those rules which carry the argument term to its non-initial position, and introduce the dummy element *there*. In 13.3. below I shall use the term New Topic for this "presentative function", in order to stress its position in the strategies for introducing, maintaining, and renewing "discourse topics". In contrast, the argument term *the dog* in a construction such as (61a) will typically have the pragmatic function of Given Topic, signalling that we use it to refer again to a topic which has already been introduced into the discourse.

In terms of this approach we can reconsider the relationship between such constructions as:

(62) a. *The dog is in the garden.*
     b. *There is a dog in the garden.*

These constructions can now be assigned the following underlying structures:

(63) a. Pres e: {*(the garden)*$_{Loc}$} (d1x_i: *dog* [N])$_{\emptyset SubjGivTop}$
     b. Pres e: {*(the garden)*$_{Loc}$} (i1x_i: *dog* [N])$_{\emptyset SubjNewTop}$

---

11. This solution is similar to that advocated by Hetzron (1975) in a crosslinguistic study of "presentative" constructions. See 13.3.1. for further discussion.

214 *Non-verbal predicates*

We can then take the difference between GivTop and NewTop function to be primarily responsible for the differences in formal expression between (61a) and (61b). This difference is still there when the argument term in (63b) carries the term operator "definite". In that case, the output will be (61b).

A New Topic is typically not yet considered to be "available" to A. Therefore, the argument term in constructions of type (63b) will typically be indefinite. However, we now see that "New Topic" and "available" (definite) do not necessarily exclude each other. And indeed, it may well be the case that S wishes to introduce an entity into the discourse which he nevertheless considers to be "available" to A in one of the senses distinguished in 7.5.2. The effect should then be something like: 'I am now introducing an entity which, though new to this turn in the discourse, is well-known to you'. This might take the form of a "reminder" to A, and this is indeed the typical communicative value which constructions such as (61b) would appear to have.

8.8. Differences in argument type

We have so far classified non-verbal predications in terms of different types of non-verbal predicates, each of which creates a different kind of semantic relation. Extending Table 13 we can summarize the relevant differences as in Table 14.

Table 14. Semantic relations in non-verbal predications (2)

TYPE OF PREDICATE	SEMANTIC RELATION
adjectival / bare nominal	Property Assignment
indefinite term	Class Inclusion
definite term	Identification
possessor term	Possession
locative term	Location / Existence
unspecified locative term	Existence

A further classification of non-verbal predications can be achieved if we also distinguish the various argument types which may occur in such predications, in particular with respect to the difference between first-, second-, third-, and fourth-order entities. This has been demonstrated by Hengeveld (1990), of which the following is a brief summary, with the addition of zero-order terms (cf. Keizer 1991). Recall from 3.1. that we distinguish the entity types listed in Table 15.

Table 15. Different orders of entities

Variable	Entity type	Order
E_i	speech act	4
X_i	possible fact	3
e_i	state of affairs	2
x_i	1st-order entity	1
f_i	property/relation	0

The relevance of these distinctions for non-verbal predications can be seen from such facts as the following. Compare:

(64) a. *The colour was remarkable.* (order 0)
   b. *The table was remarkable.* (order 1)
   c. *The meeting was remarkable.* (order 2)
(65) a. **The colour was in room 14.* (order 0)
   b. *The table was in room 14.* (order 1 → Location)
   c. *The meeting was in room 14.* (order 2 → Occurrence)
(66) a. **The colour was at five o'clock.* (order 0)
   b. **The table was at five o'clock.* (order 1)
   c. *The meeting was at five o'clock.* (order 2)

The colour indicates a zero-order entity, *the table* a first-order entity, and *the meeting* a second-order entity (an Event). Certain non-verbal predicates, such as *remarkable*, can be applied to any order of entities. Locational predicates can only be applied to first and second-order entities, but with rather different semantic effects. Only second-order entities can be located in time, as is clear from (66). Note that an apparent first-order noun can be used to indicate a second-order entity, as in:

(67)   *The Round Table is at five o'clock in room 14.*

The difference in type between the argument terms of (64)-(66) can be symbolized in the following way:

(68) a.   (d 1 f_i: *colour* [N])
    b.   (d 1 x_i: *table* [N])
    c.   (d 1 e_i: *meeting* [N])

and the differences in term variable can now be used to account for the differences of (64)-(66).

A second respect in which the "order" of entities is relevant for non-verbal predications was presented in Hannay (1985b). Hannay showed that in English a distinction must be made between "Entity existentials" and "State of Affairs existentials"; the former introduce a first-order entity, the latter a second-order entity into the discourse:

(69) a.   *There's a man outside.* (order 1)
    b.   *There's a man being beaten up outside.* (order 2)

Hannay convincingly argued that constructions of type (69b) can be analysed in terms of an unspecified locative predicate being applied to an embedded predication which refers to the SoA of 'a man being beaten up'. Again, in terms of the typology in Table 15, the SoA argument of this construction type will carry an e-type rather than an x-type variable. Thus, the underlying structure of (69b) will have roughly the following form:[12]

(70)   Pres e_i: {$(\emptyset)_{Loc}$} (e_j: [*beat-up* (x)(*a man*)])$_{\emptyset NewTop}$

Hengeveld (1990) shows that there are also non-verbal predications which can be analysed as having propositional (third-order) and speech act (fourth order) arguments, each time with characteristic effects on the semantic relation expressed by the non-verbal predication. I refer to Hengeveld's study for further detail on this matter.

---

12. Such embedded predications will be more fully discussed in *TFG2*: chapters 5-7.

9. Nuclear, core, and extended predication

9.0. Introduction

So far we have been mainly concerned with the inner structure of the nuclear predication, formed from the basic predicate frames stored in the lexicon, or from the derived predicate frames which form the output of the predicate formation component. As we saw in 3.1., however, the nuclear predication can be extended by several layers of elements, until finally we reach the fully specified underlying structure of the clause. In this chapter we shall be concerned with the two innermost layers of extension, by which the nuclear predication is turned into a *core predication* (Level 1), and the core predication into an *extended predication* (Level 2). The extensions are effected by operators, satellites, and higher-order variables. The operators are indicated by π_1, π_2, π_3, π_4, the satellites by σ_1, σ_2, σ_3, and σ_4. In this chapter we restrict our attention to operators and satellites of Levels 1 and 2. The difference between operators and satellites is that operators are used to capture those distinctions which get grammatical expression, while satellites represent modifications which get lexical expression. The higher-order variables relevant in this chapter are variables for states of affairs (SoA), symbolized by e_i, e_j, e_k, etc.

The abstract structure of nuclear, core, and extended predication can be represented as follows:

(1) $[\pi_2 \, e_i:$ $[\pi_1$ [pred(arg)] $\sigma_1] \, \sigma_2]$
                               [-----------]
                              nuclear predication
                 [-------------------------------]
                           core predication
     [---]
                          extended predication

Thus, the nuclear predication is extended to a core predication by predicate operators π_1 and satellites σ_1, and the core predication is turned into an extended predication through the SoA variable e_i, the predication operators π_2, and satellites σ_2.

The structure of this chapter follows the layout represented in (1). We first consider how the nuclear predication is turned into a core predication (9.1.); in this connection we first discuss the nature of π_1 operators (9.1.1.), and then devote a separate subsection to aspectual distinctions, finding reasons to divide these over Levels 1 and 2 (9.1.2.); then, we discuss the nature of σ_1 satellites (9.1.3.). In section 9.2. we discuss how the core predication is turned into an extended predication, through SoA variables (9.2.1.), operators π_2 (9.2.2.), and satellites σ_2 (9.2.3.). It is to be noted throughout that satellites are always optional. We may thus well have an extended predication in which both σ_1 and σ_2 are left unspecified. The π-operators are obligatory in the sense that if a language has a distinctive π-opposition at any level, then the construction of any clause at least involves a choice between activating or not activating the π-operator.[1]

9.1. From nuclear to core predication

The transition from nuclear predication to core predication is effected by predicate operators π_1 and satellites σ_1. The common semantic property of these elements is that they specify additional features pertaining to the quality of the SoA designated by the predication: they add features which enter into the constitution of the SoA; in other words, the SoA designated by the core predication will in some respect be different from the SoA designated by the nuclear predication, if π_1 and/or σ_1 elements have been specified. This distinguishes π_1/σ_1 from π_2/σ_2 elements: the latter leave the internal constitution of the SoA intact, but either quantify it or locate it with respect to spatial, temporal, and "objective" cognitive dimensions.

As we saw in 7.2. above there are certain parallelisms between the structure of terms and the structure of predications, which we have provisionally represented as in:

(2) a. UNDERLYING CLAUSE STRUCTURE
π_2-Loc π_2-Quant e: [π_1-Qual pred [V/A] (args)]
b. UNDERLYING TERM STRUCTURE
ω_2-Loc ω_2-Quant x: [ω_1-Qual pred [N] (args)]

---

1. Throughout this chapter frequent use is made of ideas which have been put forward by Vet (1986) and Hengeveld (1989). For the layering of satellites, see Dik, Hengeveld, Vester, and Vet (1989).

Thus, predicate operators π_1 could also be called Qualifying operators, while the predication operators π_2 can be divided over Quantifying and Localizing operators. Concerning the relation between Quantification and Localization of SoAs Rijkhoff (1990, 1992) has argued that the former typically fall inside the scope of the latter, as indicated in (2a). Consider the following example:

(3)   *In 1980* John visited Copenhagen *twice*.

The satellite *twice* multiplies the SoA of John's visiting Copenhagen by two. The satellite *in 1980* localizes these two visits in one year: it is the quantified set of SoA occurrences which is affected by the localizing satellite. Rijkhoff concludes from this that there might be reasons to set up a separate layer for Quantification in the underlying structure of the clause. That I do not fully adopt this proposal here is because I believe more research should be done on the interaction between Quantification and Localization of SoAs before such a separate layer can be properly established.

9.1.1. Predicate operators

Predicate operators π_1 capture the grammatical means through which additional features of the nature or quality of the SoA are specified. At this innermost extension layer, it is often difficult to decide whether a certain elaboration of the predicate is a matter of predicate formation, or of the influence of some grammatical operator π_1. The same is true for Qualifying term operators, as we saw in 7.3.3. above. Nevertheless, some criteria can be formulated for deciding this issue.

First of all, a predicate operator must qualify the SoA as expressed in the nuclear predication; it cannot create a different type of SoA. In particular, it cannot effect any change in the valency of the nuclear predicate frame. For example, many languages have rules for deriving transitive predicates from intransitive ones (transitivizing or causativizing rules). Compare:

(4)   *The paper was white.*
        white (*paper*)
(5) a. *The liquid whitened the paper.*
        whiten (*liquid*) (*paper*)
    b. *The liquid made the paper white.*
        make white (*liquid*) (*paper*)

220 *Nuclear, core, and extended predication*

The predicate *white* is one-place, *whiten* and *make white* are two-place. The rule affects the valency of the input predicate, and must therefore be a matter of predicate formation rather than predicate operators.

From this it also follows that a predicate operator cannot change the categorial status of the input predicate. Compare:

(6) a. *The paper was white.*
    b. *The paper whitened.*

White is an adjective, *whiten* a verb. Even though the rule deriving *whiten* from *white* does not affect the valency of the input predicate, it does change the category from adjective to verb, and this is more than a modification of the input SoA. Correspondingly, this predicate formation rule exemplifies an operation which can be applied to adjectival predicates rather than an operation on nuclear SoAs.

By contrast, a language may have a predicate operator with the value Inchoative or Ingressive. Such an operator will in principle be applicable to any kind of nuclear predication, with such results as the following:

(7) a. Ingr *white (paper)*   'The paper became white'
    b. Ingr *sit (John)*   'John sat down'
    c. Ingr *walk (John)*   'John started walking'

Such a generally applicable rule will be a matter of predicate inflection rather than derivation: it is something we can do with a predicate frame once we have it, rather than a matter of deriving one predicate frame from another.

We can thus characterize predicate operators in the following way:

(8) π_1 operators
     — are not expressed by lexical, but by grammatical means;
     — provide additional qualification of the nuclear SoA;
     — do not change the categorial status or the valency of the nuclear predication to which they apply;
     — are part of the inflectional rather than the derivational system of the language.

We mentioned Ingressive as a candidate for π_1 status. The English Progressive is another such candidate, as is the distinction between Perfective and Imperfective aspect, in languages in which this distinction has the status of a regular, inflectional process. In general, then, Qualifying predicate operators pertain to the domain of verbal aspectuality. Not all aspectual distinctions have this status, however. We therefore have to consider the whole domain of aspectuality, in order to sort out to which level of underlying clause structure different aspectual distinctions can be assigned.

9.1.2. Aspectuality

When we consider how the term "aspect" is used in the literature, we find that a number of different semantic distinctions are covered by this term, and that it is not altogether clear what the common denominator of these distinctions could be. We shall therefore use the pretheoretical term "aspectuality" to cover all these distinctions, and reserve the term *Aspect* for those aspectuality distinctions which are grammatically rather than lexically expressed. Under the general label of aspectuality, the following subareas may be distinguished:[2]

(i) *The type of SoA* as designated by the predicate frame. This subarea is also called "Aktionsart" (Mode of action), and we have captured it in our typology of SoAs (see 5.2.). It falls outside our more restricted usage of the term Aspect, since it is not a matter of grammatical, but of intrinsic lexical coding.

(ii) *Perfectivity / Imperfectivity*. This type of aspectuality hinges on the question of whether the SoA is presented from an outside point of view, as one complete, indivisible whole (Perfective), or from an inside point of view, as being non-complete or in progress (Imperfective).

(iii) *Phasal aspectuality* distinctions serve to specify the phase of development of the SoA, in terms of beginning - continuation - end of the SoA. We may here distinguish such values as Ingressive, Progressive, Continuous, and Egressive Aspect. They concern the inner dynamics of the SoA.

(iv) *Perspectival aspectuality* distinctions relate the occurrence of the SoA to an outside temporal reference point. Do we look ahead at the SoA, are we on the brink of entering the SoA, do we have the SoA just after us, or do we look back upon the SoA from an ulterior point in time. We can here distinguish such values as Prospective, Immediate Prospective, Recent Perfect, and Perfect Aspect.[3]

---

2. Compare Maslov (1978) for a similar subdivision of areas of aspectuality.
3. Note that Perfective Aspect ≠ Perfect Aspect. Cf. Comrie (1976).

(v) *Quantificational aspectuality* distinctions express different forms of quantification over sets of occurrences of SoAs. Here we find such values as Iterative, Habitual, and Frequentative Aspect.

Since Perspectival and Quantificational Aspect distinctions leave the inner structure of the SoA intact, we consider them to belong to the level of π_2 predication operators. These will be discussed in 9.2.2. below. We here concentrate on the Perfective/Imperfective opposition and the Phasal Aspect distinctions which serve to qualify the nature of the nuclear SoA.

9.1.2.1. Perfective and Imperfective. In trying to capture the semantics of the Perfective/Imperfective opposition, different authors use such terms as the following:

(9) PERFECTIVE   IMPERFECTIVE
    the nuclear state of affairs is presented as:
    complete   non-complete
    bounded   non-bounded
    closed   open
    indivisible   divisible
    from external viewpoint   from internal viewpoint

Some of the more enlightening metaphors used to characterize the opposition are the following:

— Isačenko (1962): Compare the SoA to a parade. In the Imperfective, the parade is presented as if from the point of view of a person marching along in it: we are in the middle of the parade, unable to oversee the beginning, the end, and the full length of the parade. In the Perfective, on the other hand, the parade is presented as if from the point of view of a spectator who, from some elevated vantage point, can oversee the entire extension of the parade.[4]

— Comrie (1976: 34, 18): The Perfective presents the SoA as a single unanalysable whole, with beginning, middle, and end rolled into one. The Imperfective looks at the SoA from an internal point of view, and crucially involves the internal structure of the SoA. The Perfective presents the SoA like a "blob", a three-dimensional object which, regardless of its internal complexity, is now considered as a single unit with clearly circumscribed limits.

---

4. See Ten Cate (1985: 104-105).

The opposition thus depends on different ways of conceptualizing the SoA, with the crucial parameter of whether the internal dynamics of the SoA is (Imperfective) or is not (Perfective) taken into account. Since this crucial factor involves the internal dynamics of the SoA, it seems appropriate to consider the opposition, in languages where it is grammatically expressed, as a matter of π_1 articulation. One such language is Hungarian (De Groot 1986), in which we find regular oppositions such as between:

(10) a. *olvastam az újság-ot.*
         read-I   the paper-acc
         Impf *olvas* [V] (d1x_i: [+S])$_{Ag}$ (d1x_j: *újság* [N])$_{Go}$
         'I was reading the paper.'
     b. *el-olvastam az újság-ot.*
         Pf-read-I   the paper-acc
         Pf *olvas* [V] (d1x_i: [+S])$_{Ag}$ (d1x_j: *újság* [N])$_{Go}$
         'I read the paper.' (from beginning to end)

An important criterion for determining the relevance of the Pf / Impf distinction lies in such constructions as:[5]

(11) a. *While I was reading the paper, John entered.*
     b. *I was reading the paper when John entered.*

In both constructions, John's entering is described as an intrusion into my reading the paper. Since the Perfective makes the SoA immune to such intrusions, the phrase *was reading* can only be expressed by the Imperfective form of the verb in the relevant languages. We thus expect that in Hungarian (10a) can, but (10b) cannot be used in contexts such as (11a-b). This is indeed the case.

The Imperfective can be assumed to have a unified semantic content which can be described in such terms as "non-complete, non-bounded, divisible, open". This semantic content can, in actual usage, get several more specific interpretations, such as "progressive" (SoA presented as ongoing), "habitual" (recurrent by virtue of habit), "iterative" (occurring repeatedly), and "continuous" (occurring continuously, without interruption or endpoint). We shall assume that these different interpretations of the Imperfective must be distinguished from the distinct grammatical aspect values Progressive,

---

5. See Comrie (1976: 3), De Groot (1984, 1986).

Habitual, Iterative, Continuous, which may get separate expression in other languages (and sometimes even in languages which do have the Pf / Impf opposition). Thus, the English Progressive, though it expresses one facet of what may be covered by the Imperfective of other languages, is not itself to be equated with Imperfective Aspect. We shall consider the English Progressive as one type of "Phasal Aspect", to be discussed in 9.1.2.2. below.

If it is true that Pf / Impf belong to the innermost layer of π operators and operate immediately on the nuclear predication, then we may expect interactions between these operators and the type of SoA designated by the predicate frame. Such interactions do indeed occur, and they often take the following form: when one of the operators is at first sight incompatible with the SoA type of the predicate frame, its application is not blocked, but a special interpretation is "forced out", so to speak, which restores compatibility. Consider the following example:

(12)　　Imperfective x [+telic] =　　a. 'conative'
　　　　　　　　　　　　　　　　　　　b. 'iterative / distributive'

Explanation: a [+telic] SoA has a natural endpoint; Impf signals 'incomplete, unbounded'. This apparent incompatibility can be solved in the following ways: (a) the SoA was attempted, but not finished (conative), (b) several entities achieved the SoA at the same time (distributive) or successively (iterative). In languages which do have the Perfective / Imperfective opposition, we may thus find such examples as:

(13)　　Impf *run* (*the athletes*) (*the marathon*)
　　　 =　(i) 'The athletes tried to run the marathon.'
　　　　　(ii) 'The athletes ran the marathon several times.'
　　　　　(iii) 'Each of the athletes ran the marathon.'

Another example of such interaction would be:

(14)　　Perfective x [-dynamic] =　　'ingressive'

Explanation: Perfective signals that the SoA is complete, bounded; but a [-dynamic] SoA (a Situation = a Position or State) has no natural limits. The Pf now imposes a boundary on the Situation, in this case signalling its beginning. We might thus find such constructions as:

(15)   Pf *sit* (*the men*) (*around the table*)
        = 'The men sat down around the table.'

9.1.2.2. Phasal Aspect distinctions. By *Phasal Aspect* I understand those aspectual distinctions which bear on the developmental phase of the SoA, in terms of beginning — continuation — end of the SoA. The different Phasal Aspect values can be symbolized as in Figure 5:

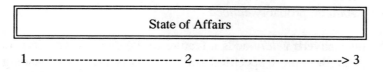

1 -------------------------------- 2 --------------------------------> 3

Figure 5. Developmental stages of a State of Affairs

The SoA begins at 1, continues through 2, and ends at 3. Aspectual distinctions relevant to this internal development of the SoA would be:

(16) a.   Ingressive   'John started crying'
     b.   Progressive   'John was crying'
     c.   Continuous   'John continued crying'
     d.   Egressive   'John stopped crying'

Phasal Aspects thus have a temporal component, but this component is relevant to the internal development of the SoA rather than locating the SoA on the temporal axis.

Perfectivity / Imperfectivity and Phasal Aspects primarily concern the internal dynamics of the SoA. They may be called "internal aspects", as opposed to the "external aspects" which concern different types of quantification over SoAs (Quantificational Aspect) or the relevance of the SoA to an external temporal reference point (Perspectival Aspect). I assume that the internal aspects can be captured by predicate operators π_1, while external aspects concern predication operators π_2. External aspects, as well as their interactions with internal aspects, will be discussed in 9.2.2. below.

9.1.3. Level 1 satellites

Level 1 satellites (σ_1) represent the lexical means through which additional features can be specified of the SoA as defined in the nuclear predication. Let us first consider the question of how σ_1 satellites can be distinguished from higher-level satellites on the one hand, and nuclear arguments on the other. The general criterion for σ_1 status is whether the SoA as specified by the nuclear predication is somehow different with the satellite than it is without. For example, compare:

(17) a. *Annette danced.*
 b. *Annette danced* wildly.
 c. *Annette* probably *danced.*

The Manner adverb *wildly* adds a feature to the dancing activity: 'dancing wildly' is another, more specified kind of activity than just 'dancing'. The adverb *probably*, on the other hand, does not modify the kind of SoA that we talk about: it comments on this SoA in terms of the Speaker's estimate of its likelihood. The difference between the two adverbs comes out in a number of behavioural properties. One of these is the position they take in the most unmarked structure of the clause, as evidenced in (17). Another is that they can easily be combined in one clause, without interfering with each other's semantics, as in:

(18)   *Annette* probably *danced* wildly.

Further, note the differences between:

(19) a. *Annette danced* in a wild manner.
 b. *Annette danced* *in a probable manner.
(20) a. *Annette di*n't *dance* wildly.
 b. *Annette* probably *di*dn't *dance.*

(19a-b) show that *wildly*, but not *probably*, specifies the manner of Annette's dancing. (20a-b) show that the negation takes *wildly* in its scope, whereas *probably* takes the negation in its scope. These are some of the differences which distinguish σ_1 satellites from higher-level satellites (in chapter 12 we will see that *probably* is a Level 3 satellite).

At the other end, the question may arise why σ_1 satellites are to be distinguished from arguments: if they enter into the definition of the SoA, why not integrate them into the predicate frame from which the nuclear predication is construed? There are several arguments for why this would not be appropriate:

— Satellites are always optional additions to the SoA. When the satellite is

not specified, we do not feel that something is missing which should be reconstrued on the basis of context and situation.
— It is strange to regard satellites as terms in the relationship designated by the predicate. Consider an example such as:

(21)   Peter cautiously removed the lid from the jar.

It would be very strange indeed to say that *remove* specifies a four-place relation between (Peter), (the lid), (the jar), and (caution). Rather, *cautiously* specifies the way in which the three-place relation *remove* was established between (Peter), (the lid) and (the jar). An appropriate representation for (21) is thus something of the form:

(22)   [remove (Peter) (the lid) (from the jar)] (cautiously)

in which the square brackets enclose that which is further specified by the Manner adverb *cautiously*.
— The possibilities of adding a certain satellite to a nuclear predication are determined by features of the nuclear predication as a whole rather than by the predicate. For example, the Manner satellite *cautiously* can be added to any nuclear predication with the feature [+control], i.e., to any Action or Position (cf. 5.2.5.).
— Each nuclear predication can be modified by a large number of different satellites. If these satellites were to be separately specified for each predicate, this would lead to an enormous redundancy in the lexicon, especially since, as we saw above, the possibilities for adding satellites to nuclear predications can much more simply be defined in terms of semantic properties of the nuclear predication as a whole.
On the other hand it should be noted that certain σ_1 satellites are in a sense already "implied" by the nuclear predication. Consider again example (23). If we have a nuclear predication such as:

(23)   Peter removed the lid from the jar.

it is *implied* that he did it in a certain manner. Adding, denying, or questioning the relevance of this manner makes no sense:

(24) a.   *Peter removed the lid from the jar in a manner.
     b.   *Peter removed the lid from the jar, but not in a manner.
     c.   *Did Peter remove the lid from the jar in a manner, or didn't he?

In general, if we have a nuclear SoA with the features [+control] and / or [+dynamic], it is immediately understood that the SoA took place in some manner. This can also be seen from the acceptability of:

(25)   Peter removed the lid from the jar. The manner *in which he did it was rather cautious.*

Once we have specified some Action, we may go on talking about the manner in which the Action was performed without first specifying that it was performed in a manner. We could say that the manner is implied or "hidden" in the Action. This could be accounted for by the following rule:

(26)   Given a nuclear predication with the features [+con] and/or [+dyn], add a slot $(x_i)_{Manner}$; this Manner slot will not be expressed, unless it is further filled in with some more specific information.

Thus, given the nuclear predication (27a), rule (26) authorizes the extension to (27b); the open Manner slot will not be expressed, unless it is filled with further information, as in (27c):

(27) a.   [*remove* [V,+con,+dyn] (*Peter*) (*the lid*) (*the jar*)]
     b.   [*remove* [V,+con,+dyn] (*Peter*) (*the lid*) (*the jar*)] $(x_i)_{Man}$
     c.   [*remove* [V,+con,+dyn] (*Peter*) (*the lid*) (*the jar*)]
          $(x_j: cautious(x_j))_{Man}$
          Peter cautiously removed the lid from the jar.

There are also grammatical criteria for distinguishing arguments from satellites. Compare:

(28) a.   **Peter removed the lid, and he did it from the jar.*
     b.   **Peter removed from the jar, and he did it the lid.*
     c.   *Peter removed the lid from the jar, and he did it cautiously / with a screwdriver / for Mary / in a minute / quickly.*

This test shows that satellites can, but arguments cannot be detached from what is expressed in the nuclear predication.

Let us now turn to the question of what types of σ_1 satellite must be distinguished. We provisionally recognize four main types of σ_1, and discuss some properties of each of these:

(i) additional participants involved in, or associated with the SoA: Beneficiary, Company.

(ii) specifications of the manner in which or the means by which the SoA is effected: Instrument, Manner, Speed, Quality.

(iii) spatial orientations of the SoA: Direction, Source, Path.

(i) *Additional participants*
Beneficiary (Ben) is the person or institution for whose benefit (sometimes: against whose interest) the SoA is effected:

(29) a. *John bought some flowers* for Mary.
 b. *The police set a trap* for John. [= against John]

The expression for Ben is in many languages identical to, or a variant of, that for the Recipient (e.g. dative case, or a shared adposition).

Ben requires a [+control] SoA (a Position or an Action) in the nuclear predication (cf. 5.2.5. above). If the SoA is at first sight [-con], a [+con] interpretation is imposed on it in the presence of Ben:

(30) *Mary was beautiful for Steve.*
   = 'Mary made herself / took care to be beautiful'

Company (Com) specifies an entity together with whom the SoA is effected:

(31) a. *John went to Paris* with Mary.
 b. *The roof came down* with the walls.

Com in many languages (as in English) has the same expression as Instrument, but can be distinguished from it by the following tests:

(32) *John went to Paris* with Mary.
   Therefore: John and Mary *went to Paris.*
(33) *John cut the meat* with a knife.
   Therefore: *John and a knife *cut the meat.*

The paraphrase relation in (32) explains why in many languages there is a close relationship between Com and conjunction of terms.[6]

---

6. See *TFG2*: chapter 9.

(ii) *Means and manner*
Instrument (Instr) specifies the tool with which some Action is carried out or a Position maintained. It thus requires a [+con] SoA in the nuclear predication (cf. 5.3.2. above). Instr allows for paraphrases with *use* and equivalent verbs:

(34) a.   *John cut the meat* with a knife.
     b.   *John* used a knife *to cut the meat.*

This does not mean that *a knife* has the function Instr in (34b): semantic functions cannot be determined solely on semantic grounds, but also require us to consider the behaviour and the formal expression of the term in question (cf. 5.3.2.). *A knife* in (34b) has both the behaviour and the formal expression of a Goal term.

Manner satellites indicate the way in which an Action is carried out, a Position is maintained, or a Process takes place:

(35) a.   *John drove the car* recklessly.
     b.   *John* quietly *stayed in his hotel.*
     c.   *The tree fell down* silently.

If a constituent can both be the answer to a question with *how?*, and be paraphrased by 'in a ... way / manner', it has the status of a Manner satellite. Manner satellites interact with the typology of SoAs in the following way (Dik 1975b):
 — Manner satellites are hardly compatible with [-con][-dyn] SoAs (i.e. States).
 — Some require [+con] SoAs (e.g. *recklessly*).
 — Some require [+dyn] SoAs (e.g. *rhythmically*).
 — Some require [+con][+dyn] SoAs, i.e. Actions (e.g. *energetically*).
 — Some are compatible with [+con] or [+dyn] SoAs (e.g. *peacefully*).
A further refinement of Manner satellites is required into Controller-oriented, Goal-oriented, and SoA-oriented ones:

(36) a.   *John answered* eagerly.
          [John was eager in answering: Controller-oriented]
     b.   *John writes* illegibly.
          [what he writes is illegible: Goal-oriented]
     c.   *Annette dances* beautifully.
          [her dancing is beautiful: SoA-oriented]

Speed satellites indicate the amount of Action / Process run through per unit of time; they require [+dyn] SoAs:

(37)   *John answered the question* quickly.
        [did the answering in a short time]

Quality satellites designate the role / function / authority by virtue of which an Action is carried out, or a Position maintained; they require [+con] SoAs:

(38) a. *John accompanied Mary* as her lawyer.
     b. *John stayed in the country* as an exile.

(iii) *Spatial orientation*
Source, *Path*, and *Direction* designate the point of origin, the route, and the terminal point of a movement:

(39)   Source ------------------> Direction
                    Path

(40)   *John drove* from Amsterdam (Source) to Rotterdam (Direction) along the highway (Path).

Several refinements of these spatial orientation functions are required. For example, Direction may be distinguished into movement TOWARDS some point (in the direction of that point, without suggestion that the point is actually reached) and TO a point (with the suggestion that it is reached). Both Direction and Source may be distinguished according to the position of the item in question in relation to the terminus / origin that the movement is oriented to:[7]

(41) a. *John drove* to *Amsterdam,* into *Amsterdam.*
     b. *John jumped* onto *the table.*
(42) a. *John came* from *the house,* out of *the house.*
     b. *John jumped* off *the table.*

---

7. Certain languages have separate case distinctions for expressing such subdistinctions: for example, "allative" (towards, to), "illative" (into), "sublative" (onto), "ablative" (from), "elative" (from out of).

Path may be further subdistinguished according to such differences as:

(43)   *John drove* along *the highway,* through *the tunnel,* past *Leyden.*

For more extensive discussion of σ_1 satellites and the criteria which can be used to identify them, see Dik, Hengeveld, Vester, and Vet (1989).

9.2. From core to extended predication

Consider again the representation in (1). We see there that the core predication can be elaborated to yield an extended predication through the addition of an SoA variable e_i, predication operators π_2, and Level 2 satellites σ_2. We now discuss these three items one by one.

9.2.1. Variables for states of affairs

Compare the following constructions:

(44) a.   *John saw the tiger.*
     b.   *John saw the killing of the tiger.*

In both constructions it is expressed that John saw some entity, but the entities are rather different: a tiger is an animal, a thing, a physical object (a *first-order* entity, Lyons 1977); the killing of a tiger is an SoA, an Event, an Action, an Achievement (a *second-order* entity). Linguistic expressions may be ambiguous between designating first-order or second-order entities:

(45)   *John saw the painting of a monk.*
       a.   the painting = a physical object
       b.   the painting = the activity of either a monk painting something, or of a monk being painted.

If we want to be able to disambiguate (45), we will somehow have to make a distinction between first-order and second-order entities. One way of achieving this is to use different variables for these different entity types. For example, we can write:

(46) a.   John saw x_i, where x_i = the painting of a monk.
   b.   John saw e_i, where e_i = the painting of a monk.

The variable e_i now symbolizes an SoA, whereas x_i symbolizes a first-order entity. The idea of using different variables for entities of different orders was introduced into those types of logic which came to be known as "typed logics". An early application of this idea to natural language analysis is Reichenbach (1947). The "e" variable stands for "event", but note that States and Positions also need this type of variable. In our terminology, "e" will be interpreted as symbolizing SoAs of any type, as distinguished in 5.2. above. It is clear that e-variables may be used in the analysis of embedded predications, as in:

(47)   *John saw the painting of a monk.*
   Past e_i: *see* [V] (*John*) (d1e_j: [*paint* [V] (*a monk*)$_{Ag}$ ($\emptyset$)$_{Go}$])

This underlying structure represents the case in which John witnessed a monk (Agent) paint something. The SoA which John saw is symbolized by e_j, and e_j is specified by the embedded predication placed between [...]. The whole clause, however, also designates an SoA, namely the SoA e_i of John seeing the SoA e_j. The operator Past may now be seen as operating on the whole predication, locating the SoA e_i at some time interval preceding the moment of speaking t_0.

There are several arguments for using these SoA variables in the underlying structure of the clause. One argument lies in the resolution of such ambiguities as exemplified by (45). Another argument is the fact that nominals which usually designate first-order entities may sometimes be used for specifying SoAs. We saw an example of this in 8.8., where it was suggested that *Round Table* should be analysed as an SoA noun in order to explain its behaviour in non-verbal predications. There are other arguments for this kind of analysis. Consider:

(48)   *John began X at five o'clock.*

One constraint on X in (48) is that it should indicate some Action of John's, as in:

(49) a.   *John began* to do his homework *at five o'clock.*
   b.   *John began* to prepare his speech *at five o'clock.*

However, we can also find simple nouns in the position of X:

(50) a. *John began* his homework *at five o'clock.*
    b. *John began* his speech *at five o'clock.*

Nevertheless, the SoA constraint is not cancelled in this usage: we understand (50a) as saying that John began doing something with his homework, and (50b) as saying that John began doing something with his speech at five o'clock. *His homework* and *his speech* are abbreviated descriptions of Actions of John's, rather than designations of first-order things. This can be captured in representations of the following form:

(51)   *began (John)* (e_i: [...*(his homework)*...])

in which it is correctly expressed that *his homework* is here a specification of an SoA e_i, i.e. some Action of John's, which has to be completed from the context.

For a second example, consider (52a): *after* requires some SoA, as in (52b); but in (52c) the noun *bridge*, normally designating a first-order entity, takes the position of X, but this does not cancel the SoA interpretation: the noun is taken as an abbreviated expression of some SoA connected with 'the bridge':

(52) a. *You will see the house after X.*
    b. *You will see the house after you have passed the bridge.*
    c. *You will see the house after the bridge.*

The SoA variables thus allow us to take care of nominal predicates which either designate or are used to designate SoAs.

Another type of argument for SoA variables is based on the possibility of anaphorical reference to that which is expressed in a whole clause (which may be a subordinate clause, but also the main clause):

(53) a. *John kissed Mary, but Peter didn't see* it (=John's kissing Mary).
    b. *John kissed Mary, and* that (= John's kissing Mary) *was not the first time.*

In general, the treatment of anaphora in FG is such that the anaphorical element will contain a variable identical to the antecedent, marked by the anaphorical operator A (cf. *TFG2*: chapter 10):

(54)   John (x_i) asked Peter to help him (Ax_i).

This means that for the anaphorical elements *it* and *that* in (53a-b) we should like to have a variable available for anaphorical reference. That variable must represent the whole SoA designated by the clause *John kissed Mary*. This can be the variable e_i if we accept the following analysis:

(55)   Past e_i: [*kiss* [V] (*John*) (*Mary*)]

This variable can then later be referred to by (Ae_i), and thus the anaphorical relationship can be correctly established.

Vet (1986) has a further argument which, however, I will not adopt here. The idea is that the satellite *in the garden* in a construction such as:

(56)   *John kissed Mary in the garden.*

can be represented as a "restrictor" predicate over the SoA variable:

(57)   Past e_i: [*kiss* [V] (*John*) (*Mary*)](e_i): {(*in the garden*)}(e_i)

The structure of the predication, on that interpretation, follows the schema of the term phrase as discussed in 6.2. above. And it is correctly expressed that *in the garden* restricts the SoA 'John's kissing Mary' to a specified location.

I do agree that locative and temporal satellites *can* function as predicates over SoAs, as in:

(58) a.   *John kissed Mary, and* that was in the garden.
     b.   *John kissed Mary, and* that was three years ago.

But I find it more difficult to see a simple predication such as (56) as a kind of referential expression which can be restricted in precisely the same way as a term phrase. The primary function of the predication is not to refer, but to predicate something, and thus create some SoA, which once it has been created, can then be referred to. This is the reason why I prefer a representation of the following form:

(59)   Past e_i: [*kiss* [V] (*John*) (*Mary*)] (*the garden*)$_{Loc}$

in which it is correctly expressed that *in the garden* on the one hand modifies the whole nuclear predication *John kissed Mary*, while on the other hand co-specifying the parameters of e_i.

9.2.2. Predication operators

Predication operators π_2 represent the grammatical means through which the SoA designated by the core predication can be quantified, and located with respect to temporal, spatial, and cognitive parameters. We can thus distinguish Quantifying and Localizing predication operators, as indicated in 9.1. above. Quantification can be achieved by various (quantificational) aspect operators (9.2.2.1.), Localization through operators for Tense, Perspectival Aspect, Objective Mood, and Polarity (positive / negative) (9.2.2.2.). Although in principle one might conceive of grammatical operators serving to locate the SoA on spatial dimensions (e.g. 'SoA happened close to / far away from the deictic centre') there do not seem to be languages that have such *grammatical* distinctions. Obviously, such distinctions can be expressed by lexical means (through σ_2 satellites).

9.2.2.1. Quantifying predication operators. Quantificational aspect operators quantify (in different ways) over sets of SoAs, without entering into the definition of the SoAs themselves. Quantificational Aspect distinctions deal primarily with the Frequency with which the SoA is said to occur:

(60)   The SoA occurs:
    — just a single time   : Semelfactive Aspect
    — several times   : Iterative Aspect
    — many times   : Frequentative Aspect
    — several times, with different participants   : Distributive Aspect

Secondly, we may assign Habitual Aspect to the domain of quantificational aspect. Habitual Aspect signals that the SoA (potentially) recurs due to a habitual propensity of the participant involved. An example of a construction with Habitual Aspect is:

(61)   *John used to be reading a book whenever I entered his office.*

This construction also shows that a predicate operator such as Progressive occurs inside the scope of the Habitual:

(62)   Past Hab e_i: Progr *read* [V] (*John*) (*a book*)

The operator Progr tells us what phase the SoA of John's book reading was in; the operator Hab multiplies the number of occurrences of this SoA; and the operator Past locates this quantified set of qualified book reading occurrences in the interval preceding the moment of speaking.

9.2.2.2. Localizing predication operators.

9.2.2.2.1. Tense[8]. Parallel to the distinction between "Aspectuality" and "Aspect", we may distinguish "Temporality" and "Tense". Temporality distinctions serve to locate the SoA, as designated by the predication, at some interval along the time axis. Temporality may be grammatically coded in Tense operators, or expressed by lexical means. Temporal satellites are the most important of these lexical means.

Although languages differ in the degree of articulation of their Tense operators, the most important potential distinctions can be laid out in a rather simple way, in terms of the following diagram:

(63)   1   2 3 4   5
     --------......---------------------......--------
                         t_r

In this diagram, the horizontal line symbolizes the temporal dimension, t_r stands for a reference point on that dimension, and 1-5 indicate positions of SoAs relative to t_r. Tense operators serve to locate the SoA on the time axis in relation to some t_r. Where t_r coincides with the moment of speaking t_0, we speak of *Absolute Tense*. Where t_r is distinct from t_0, we speak of *Relative Tense*. As to the possible relations between the SoA and t_r, the following parameters may be relevant:

(i) the SoA is anterior to, simultaneous with, or posterior to t_r;
(ii) the SoA is relatively close to, or relatively far removed from t_r.

The following tree summarizes the most important Tense operator distinctions as found across languages in terms of these parameters. The numbers refer to the SoA positions in (63):

---

8. This section is largely based on Comrie (1985).

238 *Nuclear, core, and extended predication*

(64)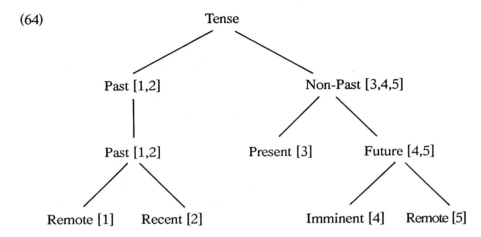

This tree should be read in the following way:
  — a language may stop at the top level, and have no Tense distinctions at all.
  — if it does have a Tense operator opposition, Past vs. Non-Past is the most current first option. Exceptionally, a first split is made between Future [4,5] and Non-Future [1,2,3] (cf. Comrie 1985: 49, where Hua is mentioned as one example of this).
  — a next potential split is that between Present and Future within Non-Past.
  — further articulations will concern the relative distance from t_r. On this parameter, some languages may even have more than two degrees of remoteness.

9.2.2.2.2. Perspectival Aspect. Perspectival Aspect distinctions concern the way in which the SoA is viewed upon from an external point in time. When we look forward to the SoA, it is presented *prospectively*: this is Prospective Aspect. When we look backwards to the SoA, it is presented *retrospectively*: this is commonly called Perfect Aspect. At first sight there is little difference between Future Tense and Prospective Aspect, or between Past Tense and Perfect Aspect. The differences can be illustrated with such examples as the following:

(65) a. *One day, stocks will rise again.* [Future Tense]
      b. *Stocks are going to rise again.* [Prospective Aspect]
(66) a. *In 1959 I lived in New York.* [Past Tense]
      b. *Since 1959 I have lived in New York.* [Perfect Aspect]

(65a) is a simple statement about what will happen in the future. (65b), on the other hand, is a prediction about what is going to happen in the future on the basis of what information the speaker has now: 'the indications which I have now allow me to predict that stocks will rise in the future'.

(66a) simply locates my living in New York in the past. (66b), however, can only be used correctly if, at the moment of speaking, I am still living in New York: the Perfect links the past to the present; it tells me something about the past which is still relevant at reference time.

More generally, Perspectival Aspect distinctions can be described in terms of the following schema:

(67)   What can be said on the basis of information available at some reference point t_i about the occurrence of some SoA at some interval t_j?

The different values that t_i can take in relation to t_j can be laid out as in Figure 6.

Figure 6. Perspectives on a State of Affairs

The different possible Perspectival Aspect distinctions can be defined in relation to the reference points in Figure 6.

(68)   1   Prospective   'John is going to cry.'
        2   Immediate Prospective   'John is about to cry.'
        3   Recent Perfect   'John has just cried.'
        4   Perfect   'John has cried.'

Perspectival Aspects thus have a temporal component, but their semantics is more complex than just locating the SoA on the temporal axis. For example, if an expression such as *John has cried* has its pure aspectual value, then its meaning can be described as containing the following elements:

(69) (a) John cried at some t_j before t_i;
     (b) This crying is (in some way) still relevant at t_i.

The Perfect will thus be used to describe past SoAs, the occurrence of which is still relevant for the situation which obtains at t_i. This is what is often called the "current relevance" of the Perfect.

Let us add the following remarks to this discussion of Perspectival Aspect:
— Perspectival Aspect distinctions are liable to undergo a process of semantic simplification. This process can take two forms, which can be illustrated with (69): either the (b) element may disappear, so that the original Perfect develops into a simple Past Tense; or the (a) element may disappear, so that the original Perfect turns into a simple stative Present.[9]

— As Perspectival Aspects turn into Tenses, new Perspectival Aspects may be created, which are often based on certain metaphorical models (in the sense of Claudi—Heine 1985), in which the relation between some participant and an SoA is often expressed in terms of location or movement. Such metaphors may also involve the SoA-internal Phasal Aspects:

(70) | ASPECT | LOCATIVE METAPHOR | MOVEMENT METAPHOR |
| --- | --- | --- |
| Prospective | X before SoA | X moves towards SoA |
| Imm. Prosp. | X on brink of SoA | X approaches SoA |
| Ingressive | X at entrance of SoA | X enters SoA |
| Progressive | X inside SoA | X passes through SoA |
| Egressive | X at exit of SoA | X leaves SoA |
| Rec. Perfect | X just after SoA | X just comes from SoA |
| Perfect | X after SoA | X comes from SoA |

— Perspectival Aspects can take Phasal Aspects in their scope:

(71)   *John has been crying.*
Pres Perf e_i: Progr *cry* [V] (*John*)
'John has been in the process of crying in the past, and this is still relevant at the present moment'

Some languages express this kind of constellation by a compounding of the locative metaphor. Consider the Welsh construction (Awbery 1976):

(72) | Mae | Ifor wedi | bod | yn | darllen | llyfr. |
| --- | --- | --- | --- | --- | --- |
| is | Ifor after | being | in | reading | book |

'Ifor has been reading the book.'

---

9. See Dik (1987c) for discussion of this historical process and references to the relevant literature.

At this point it is useful to recall that those distinctions which are termed "aspectual" in the literature have been argued to pertain to rather different semantic domains, and correspondingly to different layers of the underlying clause structure:

(i)   Aspect-1 = mode of action, encoded in the nuclear predicate frame.
(ii) Aspect-2 = various distinctions in respect to the internal dynamics of the SoA, coded in Qualifying predicate operators π_1 ((Im)Perfectivity, Phasal Aspect).
(iii) Aspect-3 = Quantificational Aspect, captured in Quantifying predication operators π_2.
(iv) Aspect-4 = Perspectival Aspect, coded in Localizing predication operators π_2.

In fact, these various types of "aspect" are so different that their true significance can only be ascertained when some such distinction as that between (i)-(iv) is made.

9.2.2.2.3. Objective mood and Polarity.[10] Just as in the case of aspectuality, the phenomena which are discussed in the literature under the labels of "mood" and "modality" do not constitute a unified semantic domain which could be given a single cover-definition. Therefore we first distinguish a number of modality types, which we then assign to different parts of the structure of the clause and, correspondingly, to different parts of the grammar. We shall reserve the term Mood for those modality distinctions which are grammatically expressed (cf. Aspectuality vs. Aspect, Temporality vs. Tense). Following Hengeveld, we can lay out and define the various subareas of modality in the following way:

— Level 1: *Inherent modality* distinctions define relations between a participant and the realization of the SoA in which he is involved. These distinctions may consist in the ability or the willingness of a participant to do the SoA (*can, be able to* / *want, be willing to*), or in the question whether the participant is obliged (*must, have to*) or permitted (*may, be allowed to*) to do the SoA. Inherent modalities are not expressed by grammatical means, and belong to the internal structure of the predication. They are mainly mentioned

---

10. In this section I follow Hengeveld (1987, 1988, 1989), who himself was inspired by Lyons (1977), Foley—Van Valin (1984), and Chung—Timberlake (1985). Compare also Bolkestein (1980) and Goossens (1985, 1987a).

under Modality because the predicates used to express these SoA inherent features often develop into more strictly "modal" expressions over time.

— Level 2: *Objective modality* distinctions express the speaker's evaluation of the likelihood of occurrence (the "actuality") of the SoA. We can usually be rather certain of the actuality of that which we see happen before our very eyes. But we often talk about SoAs that do not have this *prima facie* tangibility. In such cases, objective modality distinctions allow us to express what we think of the chances of occurrence of the SoA in terms of what we know about SoAs in general. Objective modality can be divided into two subareas: (i) *Epistemic objective modality*, in which the speaker evaluates the actuality of the SoA in terms of his knowledge of SoAs in general; (ii) *Deontic objective modality*, in which the actuality of the SoA is evaluated in terms of a system of moral, legal, or social norms. These two subareas yield the following two scales of potential distinctions:

(73) EPISTEMIC OBJECTIVE MODALITIES
Certain-Probable-Possible-Improbable-Impossible
(74) DEONTIC OBJECTIVE MODALITIES
Obligatory-Acceptable-Permissible-Unacceptable-Forbidden

Polarity distinctions (Positive: 'it is the case that SoA', and Negative: 'it is not the case that SoA') may be regarded as the logical extremes of Epistemic objective modality: they signal that the speaker is certain about the actuality or non-actuality of the SoA.[11]

As Hengeveld argues, Objective modality distinctions operate on the predication, and thus belong to Level 2. To the extent that they are coded in grammatical Mood operators, they belong to the set of π_2 operators.

— Level 3: To this level belong those modal distinctions which signal the speaker's personal commitment to the truth of the proposition. Through *Subjective modalities*, the speaker may take personal responsibility for the content of the proposition, and signals how certain he is about its truth: whether he personally finds it certain, likely, possible, or unlikely that what he says is true. Through *Evidential modalities* the speaker expresses his assessment of the quality of the proposition in terms of how he has obtained it: has he inferred it from certain outside evidence (*Inferential*), from personal experience (*Experiential*), or heard it from someone else (*Quotative, Reportative*)? Since these modalities relate to the speaker's attitude towards the content

---

11. In *TFG2*: chapter 8 a more differentiated view of Polarity is developed.

of the proposition, they belong to the propositional level (Level 3), and to the extent that they are grammatically expressed, they have the status of π_3 operators. We return to these Level 3 distinctions in section 12.2.2.

9.2.3. Level 2 satellites

Level 2 satellites (σ_2) represent the *lexical* means through which the SoA designated by the core predication can be located with respect to spatial, temporal, and cognitive dimensions. Most of the distinctions which have been discussed as potentially expressible by π_2 operators can in principle also be expressed in the form of σ_2 satellites. Consider such theoretical examples as:

(75) a. *John* Past-*see Peter.*
     b. *John see Peter* in the past.
(76) a. *John* Freq-*meet Peter.*
     b. *John meet Peter* frequently.
(77) a. *John* Hab-*drink beer.*
     b. *John drink beer* habitually.

We restrict ourselves here to briefly exemplifying the most important types of σ_2 satellites:

Location: the place at which a certain SoA takes / took place:

(78)   *John met Peter* on the platform.

Time (at which, from which, until which):

(79) a. *John met Peter* at five o'clock.
     b. *John walked in the park* from after lunch until three o'clock.

Circumstance: an SoA presented as obtaining concurrently with the SoA expressed in the core predication:

(80) a. *Mary was smoking a cigarette,* while John was washing the car.
     b. No more matters arising, *the meeting was closed.*
     c. Lighting a cigarette, *John left the building.*

We see that Circumstance satellites take the form of predications embedded within the main predication. This subject will be extensively discussed in *TFG2*: chapter 7.

Result: an SoA presented as being established as a consequence of the SoA presented in the core predication:

(81)   *All the shops were closed,* so that we had nothing to eat.

Purpose satellites provide a motivation for the occurrence of a (necessarily [+control]) SoA-1 by specifying a future SoA-2 that the controller wishes to achieve through SoA-1. For example:

(82)   *John ran to the station* in order to catch the train.

Note that the purpose is necessarily ascribed to the controller: it was John who wanted to catch the train, and therefore he ran to the station.

Reason satellites provide a motivation for why an SoA (again, necessarily [+control]) took place in terms of a causal ground ascribed to the controller.[12] Such a Reason may consist in a close paraphrase of a Purpose:

(83)   *John ran to the station* because he wanted to catch the train.

The difference with respect to (82) is, that the Reason satellite in (83) describes John's wish to achieve the future SoA rather than that future SoA as such. The Reason may also consist in some preceding SoA:

(84)   *John ran to the station* because he had been late the day before.

Cause[13] satellites provide a motivation which is not ascribed to any of the participants in the SoA, but which is advanced by the speaker as an explanation for the occurrence of the SoA. The SoA may in this case be of any type:

---

12. For this sense of "Reason" one might also use "Motive" (cf. Pinkster 1988a).

13. Note that English *because* can be used for both Reasons and Causes. Other languages use different subordinators (e.g. Dutch *omdat* [Reason] vs. *doordat* [Cause]).

(85)   *The car slipped* because the street was wet.

Satellites of Reason and Purpose may not only modify the SoA designated by the predication (e_i), but also the speech act as a whole (E_i). In that case they function as σ_4 or "illocutionary" satellites. This usage will be discussed in 12.3.3. below.

10. Perspectivizing the State of Affairs: Subject and Object assignment

10.0. Introduction

In many languages the SoA designated by a predication can be presented from different perspectives or "vantage points", as in:

(1) a. *John gave the book to Peter.*
    b. *The book was given to Peter by John.*
    c. *Peter was given the book by John.*

Each of these constructions expresses the same SoA: an action of John's giving the book to Peter. Accordingly, they may be assumed to have the same form at the underlying level. In some sense, to be made more precise below, (1a) presents the SoA from the point of view of 'John', (1b) presents it from the point of view of 'the book', and (1c) presents it from the point of view of 'Peter'. Thus, (1a-c) serve to present the same SoA from different perspectives. The relations between an active sentence such as (1a) and its possible passive alternatives are traditionally described in terms of the notion "subject": *John* is the subject of (1a), *the book* the subject of (1b), and *Peter* the subject of (1c). We shall retain this terminology, and describe differences in perspective in terms of the functions Subject and Object. Both on theoretical and on empirical-typological grounds, however, we shall come to a reinterpretation of these functions, such that our final usage of these notions will be markedly different from the ways in which they have been used traditionally.

The structure of this chapter is as follows. First, we signal some differences between our usage of Subject / Object and the usage of traditional grammar and some more recent linguistic theories (10.1.); then we present the FG theory of Subj/Obj assignment in general terms (10.2.), and demonstrate that these functions cannot be reduced to semantic functions, nor to pragmatic functions, nor to combinations of semantic and pragmatic functions. In languages in which Subj/Obj are relevant, these functions define a level of organization distinct from the levels of semantic and pragmatic functions (10.3.). In 10.4. we treat the problem of the "accessibility" to Subj/Obj assignment: which terms can be assigned Subj/Obj under which conditions, how do languages differ in this respect, and what general principles underlie the variation across languages? 10.4.1. presents some criteria for deciding whether Subj and / or Obj are relevant to a language at all, and concludes that there are languages without Obj assignment, and even languages without Obj *and* Subj assignment. In languages which do have these assignments, however, accessibility appears to be systematically determined by a number of factors which can be formulated across languages. 10.4.2. discusses the Semantic Function Hierarchy (SFH), which was proposed in Dik (1978a) as the factor determining accessibility to Subj/Obj. In chapter 11 we will see that this theory requires reinterpretation, adjustment, and extension in the light of the present version of Functional Grammar, as well as on the basis of a number of empirical phenomena which find no direct explanation through the SFH hypothesis.

10.1. Some differences with other approaches

Consider again examples (1a-c). In the traditional approach to the passive, it was often suggested that only (1b), in which the Goal or "Patient" has become the subject, was an example of the true "passive"; constructions such as (1c), in which the subject corresponds to a Recipient in the corresponding active construction, and all other cases in which some non-Patient appeared as the subject, were considered secondary or derivative "pseudo-passives". Typological data show, however, that the passivization possibilities found in English only represent the initial segment of a whole range of virtual Subject assignment possibilities. In fact, there is hardly a term type within the core predication (including σ_1 satellites), which cannot acquire Subject status in some language. Thus, Subject assignment is potentially a much more extensive phenomenon than would appear from the better-known Indo-European languages.

Likewise, the "voices" that the verb takes in active vs. passive constructions were traditionally described in terms of a binary active-passive opposition. However, languages which have more extensive Subject assignment possibilities may also have more than two voices, each of these voices corresponding to one or more term types which may be "passivized" in that voice. Some examples of this will be provided below.

In our approach we will give a unified account of Subject and Object assignment. The latter will be used to capture such oppositions as between:

(2) a. *John* (AgSubj) *gave the book* (GoObj) *to Peter* (Rec).
    b. *John* (AgSubj) *gave Peter* (RecObj) *the book* (Go).

Differences with other approaches

We shall interpret Obj assignment as defining a secondary "vantage point", once the primary vantage point has been fixed through Subj assignment. Traditional grammar used the notion "indirect object" both for *to Peter* in (2a) and for *Peter* in (2b), and was then usually at a loss to determine the differences between (2a) and (2b). Transformational Grammar initially described the relation between (2a-b) in terms of a rule of "Dative movement" which, however, had no direct or obvious connection with the rule of passivization.

Both traditional grammar and early Transformational Grammar described the active-passive relation in transformational terms, in the form of recipes for building a passive structure out of an initial active one. In our approach, in accordance with the constraints imposed on FG as discussed in 1.6.1. above, we shall see the active and the corresponding passive construction(s) as alternative realizations of the same underlying predication.

Transformational Grammar presents such rules as "Passive" or "Dative" as purely formal rules, without bothering about what work such rules do in the functioning of a language. By contrast, we shall want to give a unified *functional* account of such oppositions.

One theory which has greatly contributed to a proper understanding of the typology of Subj/Obj assignment is the theory of Relational Grammar (cf. e.g. Perlmutter (1980), Perlmutter ed. (1983), Perlmutter—Rosen ed. (1984)). The central idea of Relational Grammar is that there is a limited number of grammatical relations (Subject [SU], Direct Object [DO], Indirect Object [IO]), such that one term can bear more than one such relation at different levels or "strata" of the structure underlying the clause. This can be briefly illustrated by a simplified account of the analysis of a clause such as (3a), which would get a structure as represented in (3b):

(3) a. *Peter was given the book by John.*
    b.
	give	John	book	Peter
stratum 1	pred	SU	DO	IO
stratum 2	pred	SU	chômeur	DO
stratum 3	pred	chômeur	chômeur	SU

The idea is that *Peter*, which has the IO relation at the deepest stratum 1, is "promoted" to DO relation at the second stratum, which promotion, by general convention, leads to a "demotion" of the original DO to the status of *chômeur* (= jobless); then, the DO *Peter* is further promoted to SU relation, this time demoting the original SU to chômeur status. In describing the various properties of such constituents as *Peter* in (3a), reference can then be made to the grammatical relations at each of the strata. For example, if *Peter* has certain IO-like properties, this can be captured in terms of the fact that it is IO at the deepest stratum. Relational Grammar formulated a number of rules and principles defining admissible promotions and demotions along the "relational hierarchy", and the various consequences such relational shifts could have for the further organization of clause structure. Although occasional reference is made to semantic and pragmatic functions in the Relational Grammar literature, these functional levels do not play an essential role in the theory of clause structure as briefly outlined above.

In contrast to the Relational Grammar approach, we assume that a term will normally[1] have only a single Subj/Obj function alongside its underlying semantic function and the possible overlay of a pragmatic function. This implies, for example, that the term *Peter* in (3a) will have the functions Recipient and Subject, and will in no way pass through an Object stage before it can be promoted to Subject status. It has been argued in the Relational Grammar literature that the "multistratal" approach is superior to the FG analysis.[2] But although some of the Relational Grammar criticisms have led to a better formulation of some aspects of the FG analysis, I do not believe it has been demonstrated convincingly that the overall adequacy of our theory of Subj/Obj assignment lags behind that of Relational Grammar; on the contrary, I believe it is a distinct advantage of the FG approach that we can distinguish Subjects and Objects in terms of the underlying semantic functions to which they have been assigned. For example, some of the semantic properties of *Peter* in (3a) can be understood in terms of the underlying semantic function Recipient, while other properties of this constituent can be understood in terms of the "perspectivizing" function Subject.

10.2. The FG interpretation of Subject and Object

The predicate frame on which a predication is formed specifies a certain "basic perspective" on the SoA which it designates. The basic perspective runs from the first argument A^1 to A^2, and on to A^3, if present. Consider the situation in which some Y moves in a certain direction, and X comes after Y in the same direction:

---

1. Except in the case of "Raising" constructions: see 11.5.
2. See Perlmutter (1981, 1982), W.D. Davies (1981).

(4)   X >-------------> Y >------------->

This situation may be described as either (5a) or (5b):

(5) a.   X follows Y.
    b.   Y precedes X.

In (5a) situation (4) is presented from the point of view of X, in (5b) from the point of view of Y. This difference in perspective is in this case coded in the basic predicates *follow* and *precede*, which are each other's "converses". Not all predicates have such converse lexical counterparts. Suppose we have a situation of the following kind:

(5)   John ------earn------> the money

and that we want to describe this situation from the point of view of the money. There is then no lexical predicate f_i such that 'The money f_i John' could be used to achieve this aim. Instead, in languages which allow this, we can use a passive construction:

(6)   The money was earned by John.

We could represent this structure in the following way:

(7)   John ----- earn -----> the money [*]

where [*] is a "pointer" which indicates the entity from whose perspective we present the SoA. We shall now interpret the Subj function as just such a pointer. We can then say that Subj assignment allows for alternative specifications of the "perspective", the "vantage point" from which the SoA is to be presented.

The relevant differences can be compared to different photographs taken of one and the same event. For example, if the event consists of a fight between policemen and demonstrators, one picture might represent the event from the point of view of the demonstrators, another might represent it from the point of view of the policemen. And these two pictures may "tell a different story", even though the event pictured is one and the same. A similar difference is here claimed to hold between active-passive pairs such as:

(8) a. *The police removed the demonstrators from the platform.*
    b. *The demonstrators were removed from the platform by the police.*

(8a) presents the SoA from the point of view of the police, in accordance with the basic perspective of the predicate frame of *remove*, whereas (8b) presents the same SoA from the point of view of the demonstrators, thus reversing the basic perspective of the underlying predicate frame.

There may be different reasons why one should want to present an SoA from a different point of view than is determined by the underlying predicate frame. Among such reasons the following may be mentioned:

— The Speaker "empathizes" or identifies himself more with the second argument entity than with the first argument entity.[3] This factor might lead to a preference for (8b) over (8a): in (8a) the Speaker places himself in the role of the Agent in describing the event; in (8b) he places himself in the role of the demonstrators.

— The second argument represents a Given Topic, and will thus be definite, whereas the first argument is a New Topic, and thus usually indefinite. We may then find a preference for (9b) over (9a):

(9) a. *A man hit the dog.*
    b. *The dog was hit by a man.*

— The first argument entity is not (sufficiently) known or identifiable, or it is unimportant, or S consciously wishes to leave it unidentified. Most languages do not allow an active construction with unspecified first argument in such conditions. The passive is then a useful alternative:

(10) a. *bite* [V] (???)$_{Ag}$ *(the man)*$_{Go}$
     b. *Some creature bit the man.*
     c. **Bit the man.*
     d. *The man was bitten.*

— There is a rule of grammar (e.g. relativization)[4] which is restricted to

---

3. For the factor of "empathy", see Kuno (1976), Kuno—Kaburaki (1977), and section 2.4.3. above.

4. Such a constraint is operative in many Malayo-Polynesian languages. See Keenan (1972b), Keenan—Comrie (1977). Such languages are typically also rich in passivization possibilities.

Subjects. Thus, we may have a language in which (11b) is ungrammatical. Passivization may then be a strategy to "feed" the rule of relativization, as in (11c):

(11) a. *the dog that bit the man*
  b. **the man that the dog bit*
  c. *the man who was bitten by the dog*

— There may be politeness conventions which prevent a direct address of the Addressee, and lead to preferred passive expression of imperatives, as in:

(12) a. *(You) read this book!*
  b. *This book is to be read (by you).*

For three-place predicates, there may be similar factors leading to a preference for inverting the order of presentation of second and third argument. Consider the possible formulations of an act of 'giving': such acts seem to pose a built-in conflict for verbal expression: on the one hand, there is a certain natural, "iconic" conception in which the gift "moves" from the giver to the receiver; on the other hand, the giver and the receiver, as animate entities, are intrinsically more prominent than the gift (unless the gift is also animate, which is uncommon). If a choice is made for iconicity, we will get a predicate frame such as (13a); if the choice is in favour of prominence, the result will be a predicate frame such as (13b):

(13) a. *give (the man) (the book) (to the boy)*
  b. *present (the man) (the boy) (with the book)*[5]

Languages may also opt, however, for a basic predicate frame such as (13a), and then allow the perspective to be modified through Object assignment, as in (14b):

(14) a. The man (AgSubj) *gave the book* (GoObj) *to the boy* (Rec).
  b. The man (AgSubj) *gave the boy* (RecObj) *the book* (Go).

Such a language, in a sense, has the best of both worlds: the basic orientation

---

5. Compare the discussion of alternative "models" for verbs of teaching in 5.4. above.

of the predicate frame iconically represents the conception of the act of giving; but Object assignment allows this orientation to be modified in favour of the relative prominence of one of the non-Agent participants.[6] Again, as in the case of Subj assignment, there may be various reasons for assigning Object to the Recipient, thus giving it a more prominent position than it has in the basic orientation of the predicate frame.

A full theory of "perspective" will have to take into account the following potentially relevant factors: (i) the basic perspective of the predicate frame; (ii) the possible influence of predicate formation rules; (iii) modulations of perspective effected by Subj/Obj assignment; (iv) the influence of pragmatic function assignment. Thus, Subj/Obj represent one of a number of levels which may contribute to the organization of the content in the clause. As we will see later on, this Subj/Obj level is not universally present in all languages.[7]

10.3. Subject / Object vs. semantic and pragmatic functions

It will be clear that the perspectivizing functions Subj/Obj cannot be reduced to semantic functions. For the whole point of Subj and Obj is that they may be assigned to terms with DIFFERENT semantic functions, thus reorganizing the basic orientation inherent in the predicate frame.

Since Subj and Obj are assigned to terms with semantic functions, we have the advantage that at any time we can retrieve the semantic functions underlying these functions. Thus, we have AgSubj, GoSubj, RecSubj, BenSubj in (15a-d):

(15) a. *John* (AgSubj) *bought the book.*
 b. *The book* (GoSubj) *was bought by John.*
 c. *Peter* (RecSubj) *was given the book by John.*
 d. *Peter* (BenSubj) *was bought the book by John.*

The common behaviour of the initial terms in (15a-d) (initial position,

---

6. Note that one language may have several of these strategies side by side.
7. Subj assignment plays at most a marginal role in Serbo-Croatian (Dik—Gvozdanović 1981, Gvozdanović 1981, but compare Kučanda 1984) and Hungarian (De Groot 1981b). See also Okombo (1983) on Dholuo, and Dik (1980: chapter 6) on the problem in general.

nominative case (in pronouns), agreement on the verb) can now be described in terms of the Subj function; their differences can be understood in terms of the underlying semantic functions. Note that terms which have NOT been assigned Subj or Obj will usually be expressed through a characteristic case form or adposition. This expression is "masked" or neutralized by the Subj/Obj functions. This is the case in English (with the Goal, which has no overt expression, as a notable exception):

(16)   Ag : *by John*   AgSubj : ∅ *John*
       Go : ∅ *John*   GoSubj : ∅ *John*   GoObj : ∅ *John*
       Rec : *to John*   RecSubj : ∅ *John*   RecObj : ∅ *John*
       Ben : *for John*   BenSubj : ∅ *John*   BenObj : ∅ *John*

More complicated is the question about the relationship between Subj/Obj function and pragmatic functions, specifically Topic. We define the Subj as specifying the vantage point from which the SoA is presented in the predication, and the (Given) Topic as that entity about which the clause predicates something in the given setting. Subj has to do with the presentation of the SoA, Topic with the contextual embedding of the information transmitted by the clause. The two notions, though distinct, have a strong tendency to correlate, in the sense that the Given Topic will usually also be the Subj, and the Subj will usually also be the Given Topic of a given construction. Itagaki—Prideaux (1983) demonstrated the special link between Subject and Given Topic in the following way: they presented listeners with a story in which two participants (say, a farmer and his donkey) appeared in about equally prominent roles. Then, they let them retell the story as either 'a story about a farmer', or 'a story about a donkey'. They found that the participant that was in this way established as the main Discourse Topic appeared significantly more often in Subj function. Similar effects were obtained for the Obj function in Smyth—Prideaux—Hogan (1979). Related to this is the fact that in certain languages (in particular, the Philippine languages), Subj function can only be assigned to definite (or at least specific) terms. Clearly, the Given Topic will usually be definite, and the close association between Subj and definiteness can thus be understood as being mediated through the Given Topic function.[8]

---

8. For the interdependence between Subj/Obj and Given Topic, see also the discussion in Bolkestein (1985), Bolkestein—Risselada (1985), and De Vries (1983, 1985). See also 13.3.2. below.

Several authors have interpreted these facts as indicating that Subj and Obj are primarily pragmatic notions. Sometimes the Subject is characterized as the "grammaticalized topic" (e.g. by Comrie 1981, Givón 1979, 1984). From our point of view, however, there are several reasons for not following this course, and for regarding Subj and Given Topic as two distinct notions which, however, display a strong tendency to coincide in the same term.

First, the correlation between Subj and Given Topic is not complete: the Given Topic may well be a non-Subj, and the Subj may be a non-Given Topic, as in the following examples:

(17) A: *Who* (Subj-Focus) *removed the demonstrators?*
      B: *The police* (Subj-Focus) *did.*
(18) A: *What happened to the demonstrators?*
      B: *Well, the police* (Subj) *removed them* (Obj-GivTop) *from the platform.*

Second, in languages which do not have the particular type of "passive" and "dative" constructions which we describe in terms of Subj and Obj assignment, the Given Topic function may be just as relevant as in languages which do have such constructions. This suggests that Subj/Obj determine an additional level of SoA organization, which languages may possess over and above the modulations determined by the pragmatic functions.

Third, languages which have extensive Subj assignment possibilities by which terms can be brought into prominence (for example, the Philippine languages),[9] typically have a second, additional, and more pragmatically determined process of "foregrounding" terms. The term foregrounded by this process may, but need not be identical to the term which has received Subj function. This can be seen, for example, in Maranao, as described in McKaughan (1962, 1969). If we start from a theoretical initial structure such as (19a), in which each term is marked for its underlying semantic function,

---

9. Note that we assume throughout this chapter that the relevant phenomena in Philippine languages can be adequately described in terms of Subject assignment. This is a point of controversy, as can be seen from the discussions in Schachter (1976, 1977), Van der Auwera (1981), and Foley—Van Valin (1984). In Dik (1978a: 5.4.4.) I have argued that the notion Subject in its FG interpretation can and even must be used in describing the relevant constructions. See also Bell (1983), where it is argued that the relevant terms in Cebuano can be treated as Subjects ("final" subjects in the terminology of Relational Grammar).

Subj function will be assigned either to the Agent (as in (19b)) or to the Goal (as in (19c)). The particular Subj assignment is signalled by the marker *so* in front of the Subj term, and by the voice of the verb, which correlates with differences in Subj assignment:[10]

(19) a. [*sombali'*   *o*   *mama'*   *sa*   *karabao.*]
         butcher   Ag   man   Go   carabao
     b. *som-om-bali'*   *so*   *mama'*   *sa*   *karabao.*
         butcher   Subj   man   Go   carabao
         'The man butchered the carabao'
     c. *sombali'-in*   *o*   *mama'*   *so*   *karabao.*
         butcher   Ag   man   Subj   carabao
         'The carabao was butchered by the man'

The process of pragmatic foregrounding may now select one term, place it in initial, preverbal position, marked (again) by *so*, and by a final particle *na*. The term thus selected may be the Subj, as in (20a), but also a non-Subj, as in (20b):

(20) a. *so*   *kokoman na*   *kataoan*   *o*   *mama'*
         law   know   Ag   man
         'The law, it is known by the man'
     b. *so*   *mama'*   *na*   *kataoan*   *ian*   *so*   *kokoman*
         man   know   by-him   Subj   law
         'The man, the law is known by him'

Note that in the second case the postverbal Agent position is marked by a pronoun crossreferencing the Agent.

It seems clear, then, that Maranao has two distinct processes for lending special "prominence" to a term. The first process, which is restricted to the more central terms of the predication, is of the kind which we will describe through Subj assignment. The second process, which may also apply to more peripheral terms, may be described in terms of alternative assignments of pragmatic functions.

---

10. Note that Subj assignment has no immediate effect on constituent order.

10.4. Accessibility to Subj/Obj assignment

Consider the following constructions in English:

(21) a. *John* (AgSubj) *gave the book* (GoObj) *to Peter* (Rec) *in the library* (Loc).
   b. *The book* (GoSubj) *was given by John* (Ag) *to Peter* (Rec) *in the library* (Loc).
   c. *Peter* (RecSubj) *was given the book* (Go) *by John* (Ag) *in the library* (Loc).
   d. **The library* (LocSubj) *was given the book* (Go) *[in] by John* (Ag) *to Peter* (Rec).
(22) a. *John* (AgSubj) *gave the book* (GoObj) *to Peter* (Rec) *in the library* (Loc).
   b. *John* (AgSubj) *gave Peter* (RecObj) *the book* (Go) *in the library* (Loc).
   c. **John* (AgSubj) *gave the library* (LocObj) *the book* (Go) *[in] to Peter* (Rec).

We see in (21) that Subj can be assigned to Ag, Go, and Rec, but not to Loc; we shall say that Ag, Go, and Rec are, but Loc is not "accessible" to Subj assignment. (22) shows that Go and Rec are, but Loc is not accessible to Obj assignment. In this section we shall see that languages differ in the accessibility of their terms to Subj/Obj assignment, but also that the variation across languages is not arbitrary, and can be described in terms of general principles. In order to be able to determine accessibility to Subj/Obj, we obviously need criteria for determining when these functions are relevant to the grammar of a language. The discussion of such criteria in 10.4.1. will lead us to the conclusion that many languages lack distinctive Obj assignment, and a considerable number of languages also lack distinctive Subj assignment (in the latter type of languages, no terms are accessible to either Subj or Obj assignment). The general principles mentioned above, then, should be interpreted in the following way: languages may lack Obj, or Subj/Obj assignment, but if they have Subj/Obj assignment possibilities, these possibilities can be described in terms of general principles.

10.4.1. Criteria for the relevance of Subject and Object

Subject function, in our interpretation, is relevant to a language if and only if that language has a regular opposition between active and corresponding passive constructions. A necessary property of "passive" constructions is that they are alternative expressions of a predication which can also be expressed in the active. For example, the valency of the predicate in the passive must be the same as in the active. Compare, in this respect, the following constructions of English:

(23) a. *John opened the door.*
 b. *The door was opened by John.*
 c. *The door was opened.*
(24) a. *The door opened.*
 b. **The door opened by John.*

(23b) is clearly an alternative expression of that which can also be expressed by (23a). This is less clear in (23c), since there is no overt Agent. In that construction, however, an Agent can always be added without changing the meaning or affecting the grammaticality; and if no Agent is expressed, it is at least "understood". For these reasons, (23b-c) can be interpreted as "passive" counterparts to (23a).

Now consider (24a), which seems close to a passive and is often described as such. As (24b) shows, however, there is no room for an Agent phrase in this construction, and on closer inspection we find a meaning difference, as well, between (23c) and (24a): the latter does not presuppose any identifiable Agent; the door may well have opened "by itself", without the involvement of any Agent or Force. Therefore, (24a) will not be considered as a passive counterpart to (23a). Rather, *open* in (24a) will be considered as an intransitive predicate, which may have been formed through valency reducing predicate formation:[11] there simply is no Agent slot in the underlying predicate frame.

Alternative expression of the same SoA is a necessary condition for recognizing an active-passive opposition. But it is not a sufficient condition. Compare:

(25) a. *John cannot open this door.*
 b. *This door John cannot open.*

---

11. See *TFG2*: chapter 1.

(25a-b) are clearly alternative expressions of the same SoA. But we would not want to call (25b) a "passive" counterpart to (25a). (25a-b) only differ in constituent order and intonation. Such differences can be described by means of alternative placement rules, triggered by different assignments of pragmatic functions to constituents of otherwise identical underlying predications.

The extra condition needed for distinguishing true "passives" from mere alternative orderings such as (25a-b) is the following: in a passive construction, some non-first argument must have acquired the coding and behavioural[12] properties which characterize the first argument in the active construction. The relevant coding properties in English are the following:
— occurrence in positions reserved for subjects;
— no prepositional marking;
— nominative, if pronominal (*he / she* vs. *him / her*);
— agreement in person and number with the finite verb.

By "behavioural properties" we mean the types of roles a constituent can play with respect to grammatical rules and processes. Across languages we find a number of grammatical processes which may typically be sensitive to the Subj function. Consider the following examples:

(i) *Reflexive control*
In certain languages only Subjects can control reflexives. In such languages we find the following grammaticality patterns:

(26) a. *The man looked at himself.*
  b. **The man reconciled the boy$_i$ with himself$_i$.*
  c. **John wanted Mary$_i$'s money to be spent by herself$_i$.*

As a result, in most languages the Subject itself cannot be reflexivized:

(27) **Himself was looked at by Peter.*

(ii) *Relativization*
In certain languages only Subject terms can be relativized.[13] In such languages we find the following pattern:

---

12. The distinction between coding properties and behavioural properties is due to Keenan (1976b).
13. See Keenan—Comrie (1977).

(28) a. *I saw the man who killed the chicken.*
 b. **I saw the chicken that the man killed.*
 c. *I saw the chicken that was killed by the man.*

(iii) *Infinitival complements*
In many languages only the Subject may be left unspecified in infinitival complements:

(29) a. *John$_i$ wanted $\emptyset_i$ to kiss Mary.*
 b. **John$_i$ wanted Mary to kiss $\emptyset_i$.*
 c. *John$_i$ wanted $\emptyset_i$ to be kissed by Mary.*

In some languages the antecedent (*John* in (29a-c)) must also be Subject.

(iv) *Participial constructions*
In many languages participial constructions can only be formed around a Subject:

(30) a. *$\emptyset_i$ seeing nobody, John$_i$ left the hotel.*
 b. **Nobody seeing $\emptyset_i$, John$_i$ left the hotel.*
 c. *$\emptyset_i$ seen by nobody, John$_i$ left the hotel.*

(v) *Raising*[14]
In many languages, only Subjects of subordinate clauses can be raised:

(31) a. *John believed* Peter *to have seen the show.*
 b. **John believed* the show *Peter to have seen.*
 c. *John believed* the show *to have been seen by Peter.*

All such cases of Subject-dependency of grammatical processes may provide arguments for recognizing distinctive Subj assignment in the language involved.
 We may thus conclude that Subj assignment may be assumed to be relevant in a language if that language has "passive" constructions with the following properties:
 (i) the construction provides an alternative way of expressing the same SoA as the corresponding "active" construction;

---

14. See section 11.5. below on the treatment of Raising phenomena in FG.

(ii) it contains a non-first argument which has a number of coding properties in common with the first argument of the corresponding active construction, and

(iii) has a number of behavioural properties in common with the first argument of the active construction.

Similar criteria apply in the case of Object assignment: identity of SoA, and coding / behavioural properties in common, this time with the second argument of the active construction. Compare in this respect the following pairs from English and German:

(32) a. *The boy gave the flowers to the girl.*
 b. *The boy gave the girl the flowers.*
(33) a. *Der Junge gab die Blumen dem Mädchen.*
 b. *Der Junge gab dem Mädchen die Blumen.*

In (32b) the Recipient differs in two ways from that in (32a): in position and in absence vs. presence of preposition. In the German pair (33) there is only a positional difference: the Recipient appears in the dative case in both constructions. The German pair can be accounted for in terms of alternative placement rules. But such a treatment would not capture the coding difference between (32a) and (32b). In English, but not in German, we expect further behavioural similarities between the Recipient-Object in (32b) and the Goal-Object in (32a). Therefore, we assume that only in (32a-b) do we need the Object function, whereas (33a-b) can be accounted for by alternative placement rules, possibly triggered by differences in pragmatic function.

10.4.2. The Semantic Function Hierarchy

We saw in 10.1. above that it would be a mistake to think that the only true passive is that construction in which the underlying "Patient" becomes the Subject. Some languages have a much wider range of Subj assignment possibilities. Let us consider some examples from one of these languages, Kapampangan, as described in Mirikitani (1972). In Kapampangan Subj can be assigned to Ag, Ø, Go, Rec, Ben, Instr, and Loc terms. The assignment of Subj to a term with one of these functions has the following formal consequences:

— the term is marked by a special Subj marker, "masking" the normal expression of the underlying semantic function. In the examples below, this marker is *ing*.

— the verb takes different voices corresponding to the particular semantic function to which Subj has been assigned.
— there is a crossreferencing pronominal element, marking person and number of the Agent and the Subject. These crossreferencing pronouns are unanalysable "portmanteau" forms. Now consider the following examples, all based on the verbal predicate *sulat* 'write':[15]

(34) a. s-um-ulat   ya   ng   poesia ing   lalaki   para
       act-write   he   Go   poem   Subj boy   for
       king   babai.
                    girl
       'The boy (AgSubj) will write a poem for the girl.'
    b. i-sulat   ne   ning   lalaki ing   poesia.
       pass₁-write   he-it   Ag   boy   Subj   poem
       'The poem (GoSubj) will be written by the boy.'
    c. sulat-anan   ne   ng   poesia ning   lalaki   ing
       pass₂-write   he-her Go   poem   Ag   boy   Subj
       mestra.
       teacher
       'The teacher (RecSubj) will be written a poem by the boy'
    d. pan-yulat   ne   ng poesia   ning lalaki   ing   pen.
       pass₃-write   he-it Go poem   Ag boy   Subj   pen
       'The pen (InstrSubj) will be written the poem with by the boy.'
    e. pi-sulat-an   ne   ng   poesia ning   lalaki   ing
       pass₄-write   he-it   Go   poem   Ag   boy   Subj
       blackboard.
       blackboard
       'The blackboard (LocSubj) will be written the poem on by the boy.'

Note how all the terms which have not been assigned Subj have their own semantic function marker, and how the form of the verb co-varies with the form of Subj assignment. We can thus say that the semantic function of the Subj is at least partially recoverable from the form of the verb. We have to add "partially", since in most of the relevant languages several semantic functions,

---

15. Note that, depending on the verb considered, there are may be idiosyncratic restrictions as to the applicability of Subject assignment to arguments with various semantic functions. Thus, the verb meaning 'to write' in (34) does not allow Subject assignment to Beneficiaries, whereas the verb meaning 'to clean' does.

when assigned Subj, "share" the same voice of the verb.

Just as Subj assignment is not restricted to Agents and Goals, so Object assignment is not restricted to Goals and Recipients. Even in English there is a marginal possibility of assigning Obj to the Beneficiary, so that we find the following pattern:

(35) a. *John* (AgSubj) *gave the book* (GoObj) *to Peter* (Rec).
 b. *John* (AgSubj) *gave Peter* (RecObj) *the book* (Go).
(36) a. *John* (AgSubj) *bought the book* (GoObj) *for Peter* (Ben).
 b. *John* (AgSubj) *bought Peter* (BenObj) *the book* (Go).

It might be thought that Obj assignment is something quite different from Subj assignment, since there is no marking on the verb for different Obj assignments. In other languages, however, we do find such verb marking: in such languages we can say that the verb takes different "Object voices", corresponding to the particular semantic function to which Obj has been assigned. Consider the following examples from Bahasa Indonesia:[16]

(37) a. saya   mem-bawa   surat   itu   kepada   Ali.
        I   act-bring   letter   this   to   Ali
   'I (AgSubj) bring this letter (GoObj) to Ali (Rec).'
 b. saya   mem-bawa-kan   Ali   surat   itu.
    I   act-bring-kan   Ali   letter   this
   'I (AgSubj) bring Ali (RecObj) this letter (Go).'
(38) a. mereka   men-dapat suatu   pekerjaan   untuk   anak-ku.
        they   act-find a   job   for   child-my
   'They (AgSubj) found a job (GoObj) for my child (Ben).'
 b. mereka   men-dapat-kan   anak-ku   suatu   pekerjaan.
    they   act-find-kan   child-my   a   job
   'They (AgSubj) found my child (BenObj) a job (Go)'

Note that the ending *-kan* is attached to the verb if Obj is assigned to Rec or Ben. Similar Object-sensitive verb marking is found in the Bantu languages. Traditionally this is referred to as the "applicative form" of the verb. In a number of Bantu languages, not only Rec and Ben, but also Instr and sometimes even Loc can receive Obj function. Consider the following example of

---

16. See Chung (1976), where it is also shown that the terms labelled Object here have similar coding and behavioral properties.

InstrObj from Luganda (Keenan 1972a):

(39) a. *John   yatt-a   enkonko   n'enkiso.*
     John   killed   chicken   with knife
  b. *John   yatt-is-a   enkiso   enkonko.*
     John   killed-with   knife   chicken
     'John (AgSubj) killed-with the knife (InstrObj) the chicken (Go)'

Note the typical differences between (39a) (Instr in final position with preposition, no marking of the verb) and (39b) (Instr without preposition in "Object" position, verb marked for Object voice). In Swahili, too, we find the possibility of assigning Obj to Instr, but only in a restricted construction type of the following form (a kind of "infinitival relative"; cf. Ashton 1947):

(40)   *Nataka   kisu   cha ku-kat-i-a   nyama.*
           I-want   knife   for Inf-cut-appl-ind   meat
           'I want a knife for to-cut-with meat.'

Possibilities for Obj assignment to Loc will be considered in section 11.3. below.[17]

The different examples of Subj and Obj assignment possibilities give us the feeling that these possibilities are far from randomly spread across languages, and that there is a "pattern" in the variation found. In Dik (1978a) it was suggested that this pattern could be described in terms of a hierarchy of semantic functions, which was formulated as follows:[18]

---

17. Detailed discussions on Obj assignment possibilities in Bantu languages can be found in Trithart (1975) [on Chicewa], Kisseberth—Abasheikh (1977) [on Chimwi:ni], Gary—Keenan (1977) and Dryer (1983) [on Kinyarwanda], and Duranti (1977) [on Nyakisa].

18. The idea that Subj/Obj assignment possibilities can be formulated in terms of some sort of hierarchy has been advanced by different authors, in somewhat different terms. Fillmore (1968: 33) first formulated the view that Subj and Obj formation are in some way sensitive to a hierarchy of case relations, but restricted his attention mainly to English. A similar view was advanced by Jackendoff (1972). Johnson (1974, 1977) postulated a language-independent hierarchy of Subj and Obj formation within the framework of Relational Grammar. Compare also Trithart (1975) and Keenan (1975, 1976b). In the Relational Grammar approach, however, no use is made of semantic functions.

(41) SEMANTIC FUNCTION HIERARCHY (SFH)

	Ag	>	Go	>	Rec	>	Ben	>	Instr	>	Loc	>	Temp
Subj	+	>	+	>	+	>	+	>	+	>	+	>	+
Obj			+	>	+	>	+	>	+	>	+	>	+

The idea is that as we proceed through the SFH from the more "central" to the more "peripheral" semantic functions, Subj and Obj assignment become more and more "difficult", and the resulting constructions become more and more "marked". Intuitively, we can understand that presenting a certain SoA from the point of view of the Instrument used in it requires a more radical restructuring of the basic orientation coded in the predicate frame than presenting it from the point of view of the Goal. This can also be ascertained by studying the examples from Kapampangan given in (34), which have been ordered according to the SFH, and the examples of Obj assignment to Instr given in (39) and (40). That there is a strong element of truth in the SFH can be seen from Table 16,[19] in which I have tabulated the Subj/Obj assignment possibilities of a number of languages according to the SFH.[20]

The quite regular pattern displayed in Table 16 does indeed suggest that the SFH has the properties of a typological hierarchy with respect to accessibility to Subj/Obj assignment. Recall the various concomitant features of such hierarchies as discussed in section 2.3. above:

(i) *possible language systems*: the SFH predicts which combinations of Subj and Obj assignments may be expected to occur in a language. For example, we do not expect a language in which Subj can be assigned to Rec, Instr, and Loc, but not to other semantic functions.

---

19. Specification of sources: [1]= Clayre (1973), [2]= Johnson (1977), [2*]= Van de Walle (1990), [3]= Kuno (1973), [4]= Robins (1968), [5]= Manley (1972), [6]= McKaughan (1962), [7]= Keenan (1972a), [8]= Keenan (1972b), [9]= Keenan (1976a), [10]= Lee (1964), [11]= Naylor (1975), [12]= Schachter (1976), [13]= Mirikitani (1972), [14]= Bell (1974), [15]= Bell (1983), [16]= Chung (1976), [17]= Kisseberth—Abasheikh (1977), [18]= Ashton (1947), [19]= Vitale (1981), [20]= Gary—Keenan (1977), [21]= Dryer (1983).

20. Note that the SFH is not complete: certain languages have possibilities (e.g. Obj assignment to Direction terms) which should be fitted into the SFH. However, the available data are not sufficient to determine the exact place of such semantic functions.

Table 16. Subj/Obj assignment possibilities across languages

LANGUAGE	SFH							SOURCES
	Ag	Go	Rec	Ben	Instr	Loc	Temp	
SUBJECT ASSIGNMENT								
Dutch	+	+						
Melanau	+	+						[1]
English	+	+	+					
Japanese	+	+	+					[2,3]
Sanskrit[21]	+	+	[+]					[2,2*]
Sundanese	+	+	+	+				[4]
Sre	+	+	+	?	+			[5]
Maranao	+	+	+	+	+			[6]
Malagasy	+	+	+	+	+	+		[7,8,9]
Maguindanao	+	+	?	+	+	+		[10]
Tagalog	+	+	+	+	+	+		[11,12]
Kapampangan	+	+	+	+	+	+		[13]
Kalagan	+	+	+	+	+	+		[8]
Cebuano	+	+	+	+	+	+	+	[2,14,15]
OBJECT ASSIGNMENT								
Dutch		+	+	±				
English		+	+	+				
Bahasa Ind.		+	+	+				[16]
Sundanese		+	+	+				[4]
Luganda		+	?	+	+			[7]
Chimwi:ni		+	+	+	+			[17]
Swahili		+	+	+	+			[18,19]
Kinyarwanda		+	+	+	+	+		[20,21]

---

21. Subj assignment to Rec in Sanskrit is quite restricted; cf. Van de Walle (1990).

(ii) *continuity*: Table 16 shows that languages generally possess a continuous initial subsegment of the SFH as being accessible to Subj/Obj assignment.[22]

(iii) *cut-off point*: Subj/Obj assignment possibilities can thus be described in terms of a particular cut-off point in the SFH.

(iv) *language change*: Table 16 predicts, for example, that if a language has its cut-off point for Subj assignment after Ben, then it may change by extending Subj assignment to Instr, or narrowing it down to Rec.

(v) *linguistic insecurity*: Table 16 predicts linguistic insecurity around the cut-off point: since the last assignment before the cut-off point may be in a state of flux, some speakers may accept, while others may reject the construction in question. An example of this is Subj assignment to Ben in English, as in:

(42)   *Peter* (BenSubj) *was bought a beer by John.*

Similar phenomena may be found in other languages.

(vi) *dialectal differences*: such differences may also follow dialectal boundaries: one dialect may have, another may lack construction (42).

(vii) *frequency of occurrence*: we expect the frequency of the relevant constructions to decrease as we proceed through the hierarchy, not only across languages (typological frequency), but also within languages (text frequency). There is evidence that this prediction is indeed borne out by the facts of at least certain languages. Thus, Naylor (1975) presents frequency data on "passives" in Tagalog. These data lead to the following sequence:

(43)   Ag > Go > Rec > Ben > Loc > Instr

It should be added that AgSubj and GoSubj constructions make up the great majority of Tagalog constructions as they occur in actual texts. InstrSubj constructions are very infrequent, and even judged ungrammatical by certain speakers. Note that (43) almost completely agrees with the SFH, except for the position of Loc. We return to Subj/Obj assignment to Loc in the next chapter.

Although, as we have shown in this section, the SFH certainly has explanatory power with respect to the distribution of accessibility to Subject and Object assignment across languages, we shall see in the next chapter that

---

22. See Johnson (1977) for a formulation of the continuity property in terms of his particular version of the Subj/Obj hierarchy.

this theory requires some reconsideration in the light of our present version of Functional Grammar, and in relation to certain empirical phenomena which it leaves unexplained.

11. Reconsidering the Semantic Function Hierarchy; Raising; Ergativity.

11.0. Introduction

The SFH leaves a number of phenomena concerning Subj/Obj assignment unexplained, and it needs further refinement for both theoretical and empirical reasons. In this chapter we consider a number of problems, the solution of which may bring us to a better understanding of Subj/Obj-related phenomena. First of all, we reconsider the SFH in relation to the "layered" analysis of the clause as developed in this book (11.1.). It turns out that it is especially Subj/Obj assignment to Loc and Temp that needs closer inspection. This closer scrutiny brings us to the hypothesis that in principle only arguments and σ_1 satellites are accessible to Subj/Obj assignment (11.2.). In 11.3. it is argued that in certain cases Subj/Obj assignment may require reference to the notions "first argument" and "second argument" in addition to semantic function. In 11.4. we then sketch a more refined view of accessibility to Subj/Obj assignment, a view in which a variety of factors rather than just a one-dimensional hierarchy is held responsible for accessibility differences. This approach also sheds some new light on so-called "Raising phenomena", which are discussed in 11.5. Finally, 11.6. gives a brief restatement of the idea that a markedness shift operating on passives may lead to languages with "ergative" properties.

11.1. Subj/Obj assignment and the layering of the clause

In the preceding chapters we have acted on the following assumptions:

— Of the terms in the underlying clause structure, only arguments and Level-1 (σ_1) satellites contribute to the specification of the quality of the SoA designated by the predication. Level-2 (σ_2) satellites leave the internal constitution of the SoA intact, quantifying the SoA as a whole and locating it with respect to spatial, temporal, and cognitive dimensions.

— Subj and Obj serve to impose alternative "perspectives" on the SoA: they lead to presentations of the same SoA from the point of view of different participants.

From these assumptions it follows that we expect Subj/Obj assignment to be restricted to arguments and σ_1 satellites, since only these enter into the definition of the quality of the SoA. We do not expect these assignments to apply to σ_2 or higher-level satellites, since these concern the framework in which the SoA is placed rather than being part of the SoA themselves. Nevertheless, the SFH as given in 10.4.2. listed examples of Subj/Obj assignment to Loc and Temp. The question now arises whether these are true examples of σ_2 satellites. Let us consider this question in more detail.

11.2. Subj/Obj assignment to Loc and Temp

The evidence for Subj assignment to Temp is very slight indeed. It is reported for two Philippine languages, Kalagan (Keenan 1972b) and Cebuano (Bell 1983). Keenan gives no examples. Bell (1983: 146) gives the following example from Cebuano:[1]

(1) a. *Mogikan ang   barko   sa   alas   sayis.*
       act-leave Subj   ship   at   clock   six
       'The ship will leave at six o'clock.'
    b. *Igikan   sa   barko   ang   alas   sayis.*
       ins-leave by   ship   Subj   clock   six
       'Six o'clock will be left by the ship.'

Bell adds, however, that constructions of type (1b) are quite rare, except in relative constructions. In Cebuano (as in Kalagan) only Subjects can be relativized. Thus, the only way of expressing something like 'The time *at which the ship will leave*' is through embedding a construction of type (1b). It may thus be assumed that it is this constraint on relativization which has occasioned Subj assignment to exceptionally go beyond its natural limits.

The evidence for Subj/Obj assignment to Loc is much more extensive. Thus, Subj assignment to Loc is reported for Maguindanao, Tagalog, Kapampangan, Kalagan, and Cebuano (all Philippine languages); for Malagasy (which also belongs to the Malayo-Polynesian languages); and Subj and Obj assignment to Loc is reported for Luganda, Chimwi:ni, Swahili, and Kinyarwanda (all Bantu languages).

Note, however, that Loc does not necessarily have the status of a Level-2 satellite, which simply locates the whole SoA in some spatial domain. Loc can

---

1. Note that the verb takes the "instrumental" voice when Subj is assigned to Temp. This is also reported for Kalagan.

also have argument status (see 4.2.5. above) and, depending on the way the notion Loc is used, it might also cover one or more of the "inner" local satellites of Source, Path, or Direction, which were assigned σ_1 status in 9.1.3. Could it be, then, that it is especially these "inner" locatives which can be assigned Subj function? That there may be something to this idea can be seen even in English. Compare the following pair:

(2) a. *John was writing on the terrace.*
     (i) 'John inscribed something on the terrace'
     (ii) 'John was writing something while he was on the terrace'
   b. *The terrace was written on by John.*
     = only (i).

In the (i) interpretation of (2a), *the terrace* can be considered as an argument of the predicate *write on*, or at least as a σ_1 satellite closely associated with the predicate; in the (ii) interpretation it is a σ_2 satellite. Only in the former case can Subj be assigned to it, witness the unambiguous character of (2b). Something similar is involved in the following pair (Quirk et al. 1972: 804):

(3) a. *This problem was very carefully gone into by the engineers.*
   b. **The tunnel was very carefully gone into by the engineers.*

Again, it appears that Subj assignment is possible only when the term in question is close to being an argument of the nuclear predicate.

There are similar indications in this direction for the languages mentioned above. Thus, in her description of Kapampangan Mirikitani (1972) makes a distinction between "Terminus Locative", defined as 'the case designating the place towards or from which an activity is directed' (= Source + Direction), and "General Locative", comparable to our σ_2 locative satellite. It is the Terminus Locative, not the General Locative, which may receive Subj function. For example, in the Kapampangan equivalents of:

(4) a. *I will go* to school.   (Terminus Loc)
   b. *I will read* in school.   (General Loc)

it is only the Terminus Locative in (4a) which can be assigned Subj. Examples of predicates which take a Terminus Loc are 'write on something', 'cook in something', and 'go, walk to some place'. Reconsider example (34e) in chapter 10. We may be certain, given the above information, that in that construction the 'blackboard' is the place on which the poem is inscribed.

Though we have not been able to check this for all the Philippine languages mentioned above, it is probable that the situation in these languages is similar. For example, Bell (1983: 209) notes that Loc in Cebuano includes Source and Direction, and the only example she gives of a locative subject is again 'cook something in a pot', where the Loc term is obviously closely associated with the predicate.

As for the Bantu languages, many of the examples in which Subj or Obj is assigned to Loc again concern "inner Locatives" which either have the status of arguments of the predicate, or of σ_1 satellites. Gary—Keenan (1977: 114) provide a direct parallel to (2) in Kinyarwanda. Compare:

(5) a. *Yohani   y-a-andits-e   ku   meza   n-ikaramu.*
       John   he-past-write-asp on   table   with-pen
       'John wrote on the table with the pen.'
    b. *Yohani   y-a-andits-e-ho   ameza   n-ikaramu.*
       John   he-past-write-asp-on   table   with-pen
       'John wrote-on the table with the pen.'

(5a) has the same ambiguity as (2a); but (5b) can only be interpreted as saying that John inscribed something on the table with the pen. Many of the examples from Kinyarwanda given in Gary—Keenan (1976), Dryer (1983), and Perlmutter—Postal (1983) likewise concern "inner" locatives, as in 'throw something into the water', 'send someone to school', 'sit on a chair'. The same is true for the examples given from Chimwi:ni in Kisseberth—Abasheikh (1976): 'spill water on something', 'bring, send, write something to somebody'. The only counterexamples to the idea that only "inner" locatives can be assigned Subj/Obj function are the Kinyarwanda variants of:

(6) a. *John killed a hyena in the forest.* (Gary—Keenan 1976: 110)
    b. *The man showed the girl the food in the school.* (Dryer 1983: 135)

On the basis of this evidence, though admittedly incomplete, I believe there is good reason to formulate the following hypotheses:

(H1) In languages in which Subj/Obj can be assigned to Loc and Temp, this is in principle restricted to Loc and Temp arguments and σ_1 satellites.

(H2) In the exceptional cases in which σ_2 satellites can receive Subj/Obj function, this is under the external pressure of some rule (such as Relativization) which is restricted to Subj and / or Obj terms.

To the extent that these hypotheses are correct they can be interpreted as evidence that the SoA, and thus the core predication, is the natural domain for defining alternative perspectives through Subj/Obj assignment.

11.3. First and second argument as targets for Subj

We have so far assumed that Agent takes the first position in the SFH, and that Subj is assigned to Agent in the active construction. This raises two questions: (i) why should Subj be assigned to Agent at all, if this assignment merely reconfirms the basic perspective already coded in the predicate frame? (ii) how about the other semantic functions (Positioner, Force, Processed, Zero) which may characterize first arguments?

As for question (i), our theory of the perspectivizing function of Subj assignment would indeed lead us to assume that Subj need only be assigned when the perspective is defined from the point of view of a non-first argument; if not, the vantage point would by "default" fall on the first argument, by virtue of the basic perspective of the predicate frame. Nevertheless, there are various reasons to assume that, if a language has alternative Subj assignment at all, Subj is normally also assigned to the first argument in the active construction. These reasons are the following:

— In languages which have a wide range of "passives" (such as the Philippine languages) it is typically the case that one term must be selected as Subj, even if this should be the first argument.

— Such languages often have an overtly marked "active voice" of the verb, which can be described as being due to Subj assignment to the first argument.

— In Subj-assigning languages, first arguments in active constructions typically share the characteristic "Subj properties" with respect to coding and behaviour. Consider English: the present tense finite verb agrees with a third person singular Subj, including first argument Subjects. It is easier to formulate this rule if Subj is assigned to first arguments as well.

— If we do this, we can formulate the general principle that any term will carry its characteristic semantic function marker (case or adposition) if it has not been assigned Subj or Obj.

— There may be situations in which it is useful to be able to differentiate between assigning and not assigning Subj to a first argument. Compare:

(7) a. *John* (AgSubj) *signed the contract.*
    b. *the signing of the contract by John* (Ag).

In the context of the nominalization (7b) Subj assignment will not be applied, and thus the Agent will carry its characteristic marker.

As for question (ii) it has been pointed out (e.g. by Perlmutter 1981) that we need to be able to generalize across "first arguments" in general (not just Agents), since all first arguments usually (though not necessarily) behave in the same way under Subj assignment. This can be taken care of by replacing Agent in the SFH by "First Argument" (A^1), which was defined in 5.3.1. above in terms of its possible semantic functions:

(8) A^1 = {Agent, Positioner, Force, Processed, Zero}

The notion A^1 is also needed for another purpose, as shown in De Groot (1981b): a language such as Hungarian, in which there is no productive passive, and therefore no reason to assume distinctive Subj assignment, may nevertheless have agreement between "First Argument" and verb. The notion A^1 can in such languages be used to trigger the agreement rule, without resorting to the notion Subject. Using Subject in such a language is less adequate, since Subj could then only be assigned to A^1, and would therefore add no differential value with respect to the information already coded in the underlying predicate frame. From our point of view we shall accept distinctive Subj assignment only if there is at least an opposition between A^1-Subj and Go-Subj.

There is evidence that in certain languages the notion "Second Argument" (A^2), as well, is relevant to Subj assignment. This was suggested by Mulder (1988) on the basis of data from Ancient Greek. Very briefly stated, the evidence is as follows. Most two-place verbs in Ancient Greek have a second argument in the accusative, and all these verbs can be passivized. Presumably, an accusative second argument has Goal function. There is a class of two-place verbs, however, which take non-accusative second arguments. For example, the verb *boetho* 'help' takes a second argument in the dative. Such non-accusative second arguments typically behave like Goal arguments in some respects (in particular, they can often be passivized), but differently from Goal in certain other respects. The dilemma is now as follows: if we assume that the dative second argument has Goal function, we cannot account for the differences from ordinary accusative second arguments; if we assume that it has Recipient function (which might in this case be semantically appropriate),[2] we face the problem that Recipients in general are not passivizable in Ancient Greek. What we would want to say, then, is that Subj assignment is possible to semantic functions other than Goal if these are carried by second arguments. But this would mean that the notion A_2 would have to be integrated into the SFH, for example in the following way (Mulder 1988):[3]

(9) A^1 > A^2 > Rec > Ben ...
         Ag   Go
         Pos   Rec
         Fo   Ben
         Proc   Instr
         φ   etc.

This assumption does not run against the spirit of the FG theory of Subj/Obj assignment: the basic idea of this theory is that Subj/Obj assignment is easier, the closer a term is to the centre of the predication. And A^2 terms are obviously "more central" than A^3 terms.

What these facts show, however, is that accessibility to Subj/Obj cannot be one-dimensionally defined in terms of semantic functions. We need a pluridimensional, "multi-factor" approach, in which different parameter values may contribute to the relative accessibility of a term to Subj/Obj assignment.[4]

11.4. A multi-factor approach to Subj/Obj assignment

An approach to Subj/Obj assignment which takes the different contributing factors into account could be formulated in the following points:
 — Subj/Obj assignment is a means of modifying the basic perspective on the SoA as coded in the predicate frame.
 — Subj assignment serves to upgrade a non-first argument or σ_1 satellite to represent the primary vantage point from which the SoA is presented.
 — Obj assignment serves to upgrade a third argument or σ_1 satellite to represent the secondary vantage point through which the SoA is presented.

---

2. It is difficult, however, to give a semantic explanation for all cases of non-accusative marking. Cf. Pinkster (1988b) on the analogous problem in Latin.
    3. The problem remains that not ALL non-accusative second arguments accept Subj assignment.
    4. Compare Allan (1987), Siewierska (1988, chapter 2).

— Obj assignment operates on structures in which Subj has been fixed on the first argument. Accordingly, we do not expect Obj assignment to be distinctive in languages which have no Subj assignment possibilities. Subj assignment without Obj assignment, however, is quite possible.

— Subj/Obj assignment concerns alternative presentations of SoAs. We thus expect Subj/Obj assignment to be restricted to the domain of the core predication. In principle, only argument and σ_1 satellite terms qualify for these assignments.

— For the few known exceptions to this domain principle (cases, in other words, in which Subj/Obj assignment to σ_2 satellites is possible), we assume the influence of some factor which goes beyond the original functionality of Subj/Obj assignment, for example, a constraint on relativization such that σ_2 satellites can only be relativized if Subj has been assigned to them. This implies, of course, that we should find this type of Subj assignment above all in those particular constructions which trigger them.

— Since Subj/Obj assignment serves to create alternative presentations of the same SoA, the difference between the relevant constructions may not be such as to affect the identity of the SoAs expressed.

— A mere difference in constituent order and / or intonation is not sufficient to accept the relevance of Subj/Obj assignment: such a difference can be accounted for by alternative placements, triggered by different pragmatic function distributions. There must be additional formal differences between the relevant construction pairs, differences consisting in some choice from among (i) special case or adpositional marking of Subj/Obj, (ii) special positions for Subj/Obj, (iii) differential "voices" of the verb corresponding to choice of Subj/Obj, (iv) agreement or cross-referential relations between Subj/Obj and the predicate.

— Languages vary from no Subj/Obj assignment at all to maximal exploitation of these strategies. The intermediate possibilities display the orderly progression of a typological hierarchy, which can be defined in terms of accessibility of term types to Subj / Obj assignment.

Accessibility is determined by a number of factors, among which the following appear to be the most important:

— All argument positions are more accessible than all σ_1 satellite positions.

— Among the argument positions, A^1 is more accessible than A^2, and A^2 is more accessible than A^3, *ceteris paribus*.

— The chance that Subj/Obj will be assigned to a term is further influenced by the following priorities:
- (i) definite > other specific > non-specific.
- (ii) 1 / 2 person > 3 person.
- (iii) singular number > plural number.
- (iv) human > other animate > inanimate.
- (v) concrete entities > abstract entities.
- (vi) first-order entities > higher-order entities.
- (vii) terms from same predication > terms from subordinate predication.

In some languages these priorities[5] may take the form of absolute constraints on the non-preferred options. For example, there are languages in which Subj may only be assigned to definite terms. It may be assumed, however, that in more liberal languages this factor will nevertheless create a difference in the frequency with which the alternative constructions are used.[6]

Note that most features of the SFH, as originally formulated, can be derived from the various factors listed above. For example, the order Ag > Go > Rec follows the priority from A^1 through A^2 to A^3 (unless Rec attaches to a second argument, as we saw above for Ancient Greek); Rec precedes Ben because Rec is an argument, Ben a satellite function. Ben precedes Instr, because Ben is (usually) human, Instr (usually) inanimate. Ben and Instr precede Loc, since they are more concrete, more "detachable" than Loc. The concreteness factor also explains why (as far as we know) there is no language in which Subj/Obj may be assigned to Manner satellites.

Various other facts and tendencies can be understood in terms of the factors listed above. For example, compare:

(10) a. *John offered a book to Peter.*
 b. *John sent a letter to the president.*
(11) a. *John offered his secretary to Peter.*
 b. *John sent a messenger to the president.*

---

5. Compare section 2.4. above. Itagaki—Prideaux (1985) present experimental evidence for a significant effect on Subj selection of a hierarchy Animate > Inanimate Concrete > Abstract, holding at least for high-frequency nouns. They suggest that part of the SFH may be explained as the resultant of such, more elementary, properties.

6. See section 2.3. above on the relation between cross-linguistic (typological) frequency and intra-linguistic frequency of occurrence.

In (10) we expect a rather strong tendency to assign Obj to Rec, since Rec is animate and Go is inanimate. In (11) this tendency should be less strong, since Go is animate as well. In several languages we find evidence that such differences do indeed exist. For another example of the animacy effect, compare:

(12) a. *John bought Peter a book.*
    b. *??John bought the library a book.*

An inanimate Ben, such as *the library* in (12b), is less accessible to Obj assignment.

Some of the other factors will be further discussed in the next two sections, on Raising and Markedness shift.

11.5. Raising phenomena

Compare the following constructions:

(13)   *John believed that Bill had made the mistake.*
(14) a.   ?That Bill had made the mistake *was believed by John.*
    b.   It *was believed by John* that Bill had made the mistake.
(15) a.   *John believed* Bill *to have made the mistake.*
    b.   Bill *was believed to have made the mistake by John.*
(16) a.   *John believed* the mistake *to have been made by Bill.*
    b.   The mistake *was believed by John to have been made by Bill.*

In (13) Obj has been assigned to the embedded clause *that Bill had made the mistake*. Assigning Subj to this embedded clause is possible, but rather awkward, as is clear from (14a); the construction can be improved by the alternative constituent order of (14b), for reasons which will be discussed in chapters 16 / 17. In (15a-b) the Subj of the embedded clause, *Bill*, appears as if it were the Obj or the Subj of the matrix verb *believe*. And in (16a-b) we see that the same thing can be done with *the mistake*, the GoSubj of the embedded clause (that it is GoSubj is clear from the passive form of the embedded verb).

Since it is as if the subject of the embedded clause has been "raised" into the matrix clause, the relevant rule is referred to as "Subject Raising". Within our theory of Subj/Obj assignment, we shall interpret these phenomena as due to exceptional assignment of Subj/Obj at the level of the matrix predication to the Subj of the embedded clause, rather than to the embedded clause as a whole (see Dik 1979 for discussion of how this can be implemented).

The question we have to face here is: why should such exceptional Subj/Obj assignment take place? We believe this question can be answered by considering the balance of the positive and negative factors which favour and disfavour the assignment of Subj/Obj to the embedded clause as a whole, or to the embedded Subj of that clause:

(17)		Emb Clause	Emb Subj
	definite	-	+
	human	-	+
	concrete	-	+
	1st-order entity	-	+
	argument of matrix	+	-

We see that there are a number of factors favouring Subj assignment to the embedded Subj *Bill* rather than to the embedded clause *that Bill had made a mistake*. This balance need not be decisive: it is not only the number of factors involved, but also the weight attached to these factors which determines what strategy will be followed. In many languages, the factor "matrix vs. embedded term" is apparently so strong that no Raising is allowed at all. Nevertheless, the balance of factors in (17) makes us understand why Raising can occur: it is due to the preference for "tracing a path" from John to Bill to what Bill has done, rather than from John to the more abstract entity consisting in 'what Bill has done'.[7]

11.6. Markedness shift

In section 2.5.3. above we introduced the notion of "markedness shift", through which originally marked constructions develop into new unmarked constructions, and thus push the originally unmarked constructions out of work. There is evidence that the constructions resulting from Subj/Obj assignment are liable to undergo such a process of markedness shift. We shall first discuss the Obj assignment case, and then the case involving Subj assignment.

---

7. Further properties of Raising and related phenomena will be discussed in *TFG2*: chapter 15.

11.6.1. Markedness shift and Obj assignment

We saw in 10.4.1. above that a necessary condition for the recognition of distinctive Obj-assignment in a language is the existence of an opposition such as that between:

(18) a. *John gave the book* (GoObj) *to Peter* (Rec).
   b. *John gave Peter* (RecObj) *the book* (Go).

Let us now consider the Bantu languages in this regard. In some of these, we find exactly the same kind of opposition as between (18a-b). Compare the following example from Chicewa (Trithart 1975: 619):

(19) a. *John   a-na-pats-a   nthochi kwa mai   ache.*
         John   he-past-give-ind   banana   to mother his
         'John gave the bananas to his mother.'
   b. *John   a-na-pats-a   mai   ache   nthochi.*
         John   he-past-give-ind   mother   his   banana
         'John gave his mother the bananas.'

Note, however, that Obj assignment to Rec in (19b) does not require the characteristic marking of the verb by the "applicative" suffix. This suffix generally does appear in Bantu languages when Ben or later semantic functions are assigned Object function.

In many other Bantu languages, however, constructions containing a Rec or a Ben can only be expressed as in (19b), without the corresponding counterpart (19a). This is the case, for example, in Standard Swahili (Vitale 1981), Chimwi:ni (Kisseberth—Abasheikh 1976) and Kinyarwanda (Gary—Keenan 1977, Dryer 1983). In these languages it is often the case that a construction with a BenObj, even though there is no alternative, does have the special "applicative" marking on the verb which is otherwise a symptom of productive Obj assignment to Ben. Compare the following Swahili examples:

(20) a. *Hamisi   a-li-pik-a   chakula.*
         Hamisi   he-past-cook-ind   food
         'Hamisi cooked food.'
   b. *Hamisi   a-li-m-pik-i-a   Juma   chakula.*
         Hamisi   he-past-him-cook-appl-ind   Juma   food
         'Hamisi cooked Juma (Ben) some food.'

Note that the verb in (20b) has the applicative verb suffix -*i*-, which shows that a Ben is involved; at the same time, the cross-referential prefix -*m*- shows that *Juma*, the Ben, is at the same time the Obj. In comparison to pairs such as (18), this situation could be described by saying that in a configuration such as:

(21)   pred   Ag   Go   Ben

Obj is obligatorily assigned to Ben, with all the consequences which go with optional Obj assignment to Ben in other languages.

In three-place predicates with Rec, however, we often find constructions which are in all respects similar to (18b), except that the verb shows no trace of any special "Obj voice". Compare Swahili:

(22)   *Hamisi   a-li-m-p-a   Juma   zawadi.*
        Hamisi   he-past-him-give-ind   Juma   present
        'Hamisi gave Juma (Rec) a present.'

It is clear that here a notion of obligatory Obj assignment would be out of place, since there is nothing which indicates that (22) is derived from an underlying structure similar to that of (18a).

How are we to understand these facts? We shall try to do so in terms of the following scenario: remember that we argued earlier that there is a certain built-in dilemma involved in three-place predicates of 'giving' and the like, in that there is a kind of natural orientation Giver > Gift > Receiver, but on the other hand a natural ranking Giver > Receiver > Gift. Some languages choose for a basic predicate frame such as (23a), others for (23b), and others again for (23b) plus the alternative perspective effected by Obj assignment in (23c):

(23) a.   X presents Y with Z.
     b.   X gives Z to Y.
     c.   X gives-α Y Z.

where α is some marker signalling the marked assignment of Obj to Rec. From what we saw in 11.4., however, we may expect strong pressures to lend priority to Rec (Y) over Go (Z), since the former is typically human, singular, and definite, whereas the latter is usually inanimate, may have any number, and may well be indefinite. It might thus be expected that (23c) may be used more often than not, and lose much of its marked character in the process. At a certain point, (23c) would be much more frequent than (23b), and would even become the "normal" way of expressing this kind of content. At that point (23b) may go out of usage completely, as predicted by the theory of markedness shift as sketched in 2.5.3. In this particular case the effect of markedness shift may be represented as follows:

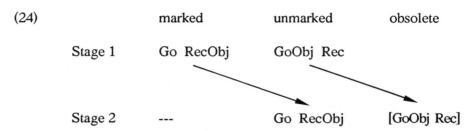

(24)   marked   unmarked   obsolete

Stage 1   Go RecObj   GoObj Rec

Stage 2   ---   Go RecObj   [GoObj Rec]

Stage 3 might then see the introduction of a new marked construction type.

When the original opposition has been lost, as in Stage 2, the special marker $-\alpha$ of (23b) loses its functionality: there is no other verb form to which it stands in opposition. We might then expect this element to get integrated into the verbal predicate, or to be dropped. In both cases there would be no further reason to regard the relevant construction as derived in any way. In fact, we have no reason to analyse Swahili *-p-* 'give' as anything else than a basic predicate which, however, has the Receiver in second, and the Gift in third argument position, just like the predicate *present* in (23a). And since Obj is assigned to the second argument (witness the prefix *-m-*) without any further consequence to verb morphology, we may assume that this second argument has basic Go rather than Rec function. Thus, the final outcome of the markedness shift process would bring us back to basic predicates of the form of (23a).

11.6.2. Markedness shift and Subj assignment: ergativity

A similar historical scenario, this time involving markedness shift with respect to Subj assignment, may help us understand the nature of so-called "ergative" languages. Ergative languages are opposed to "accusative" languages. The difference between these language types lies in the treatment of the central arguments of intransitive (one-place) and transitive (many-place) predications, especially (though not exclusively) with respect to case marking. Accusative languages use one case (the *nominative*) for the subjects of intransitive and transitive predicates, and another (the *accusative*) for the objects of transitive predicates; ergative languages use one case (the *absolutive*) for intransitive subjects and transitive objects, and another (the *ergative*) for transitive subjects. The difference can be symbolized as follows:

(25)   Accusative   Ergative
     intr.   nom *walk*   abs *walk*
     trans.   nom *eat* acc   erg *eat* abs

The nominative is typically the most neutral, "unmarked" case in accusative languages; it may, for example, get zero expression, as against some kind of overt expression for the accusative. It is also typically the "citation form" of the noun (the form used when the noun is mentioned in isolation). In ergative languages, the absolutive is in this sense the most unmarked case, and the ergative is typically overtly marked. The accusative-ergative distinction is not restricted to case marking. It may also be reflected in agreement and cross-reference patterns, and may have behavioural consequences as well. For example, in certain ergative languages grammatical processes may be sensitive to "absolutive terms", so that we get patterns such as:

(26) a. *John wanted ∅ [abs] to swim.*
         'John wanted to swim.'
     b. *John wanted Peter [erg] to help ∅ [abs].*
         'John wanted Peter to help (him).'

This, however, is not a general property of ergative languages. There are quite a few such languages in which the relevant rules must be formulated in terms of the notion Subj (or "first argument"), generalizing across the intransitive absolutive and the transitive ergative term.

In many ergative languages, the transitive "ergative" construction has a number of similarities with a passive construction:

— the ergative case is often identical to an "instrumental" or "agentive" case which in closely related languages is used (*inter alia*) for coding the Agent in a passive construction.

— the verb in the ergative construction may have morphological features which are characteristic of the passive voice in closely related languages.

— in the transitive construction, there may be agreement between the absolutive term and the verb rather than between the ergative term and the verb.

— in certain ergative languages, it is the ergative term rather than the absolutive term which can be omitted. Consider the following example from Tongan (Keenan 1976b):

(27) a. na'e   tamate'i 'e   Tevita   'a   Koliate.
       past   kill   erg David   abs Goliath
       'David killed Goliath.'
    b. na'e   tamate'i 'a   Koliate
       past   kill   abs Goliath
       'Somebody / something killed Goliath'
       'Goliath was killed'

These various properties have led to the assumption that the ergative construction might be understood as due to a reinterpretation of an earlier passive construction.⁸

From our point of view, the processes involved can be interpreted as follows. Let us start with an accusative language which can form passives from transitive constructions. We will then find the following construction types:

(28) TYPE I. ACCUSATIVE LANGUAGE WITH MARKED PASSIVE
                Active [unmarked]   Passive [marked]
     intr.   V AgSubj[nom]   -----
     trans.   V AgSubj[nom] GoObj[acc]   Vpass GoSubj[nom] Ag[ag]

where [ag] indicates the expression of the Agent phrase in the passive. Let us now suppose that markedness shift applies to the passive construction: this construction is used more and more, becomes the dominant expression for transitive predications, and finally puts the original unmarked active construction out of work. We will then arrive at the following situation:

(29) TYPE II. ACCUSATIVE LANGUAGE WITH UNMARKED PASSIVE
                Active [unmarked]   Passive [unmarked]
     intr.   V AgSubj[nom]   -----
     trans.   -----   Vpass GoSubj[nom] Ag[ag]

However, since the opposition between active and passive has disappeared, Type II might also be called "ergative". It will then be an ergative language

---

8. The idea that there is a close association between ergative and passive is at least as old as Schuchardt (1895). It was revived more recently by Hohepa (1969) and Hale (1970). Further discussion can be found in Chung (1978), Comrie (1978), Dik (1978a, 1980), Chung—Seiter (1980), Estival—Myhill (1988).

in which the terms marked [nom], which could now also be called [abs], will behave in the same way with respect to Subj-sensitive grammatical processes. This language type, though documented, is rare,[9] and this can be understood if we see this language type as a temporary, intermediate stage liable to further reinterpretation. It has the peculiarity of giving priority to the Goal over the Agent (or first argument) in the transitive construction, and it has originally passive morphology on the verb which no longer stands in opposition to an active form of the verb. This may lead to the following further changes: the passive morphology is either lost or reinterpreted as a marker of transitivity, and the unmarked passive construction is reinterpreted as an active one, with a concomitant shift of Subj and Obj function. It is essential to assume, however, that the case marking is retained under the reinterpretation. This will then result in the following language type:

(30) TYPE III. ERGATIVE WITHOUT PASSIVE
	Active	Passive
intr.	V AgSubj[abs]	-----
trans.	V[tr] AgSubj[erg] GoObj[abs]	-----

Type III represents the most usual sort of "ergative" language. The case marking is ergative, but the behavioural properties of terms can be described in terms of Subj, generalizing over the absolutive term in the intransitive and the ergative term in the transitive condition, and in terms of Obj.

In Type III languages, the case marking correlates neither with the semantic, nor with the syntactic functions: Subjects are marked by abs or erg, and both Agents and Goals may be marked by abs, in both cases depending on transitivity. We may thus expect a further adaptation of case marking to correspond with Subj/Obj articulation; and we may expect the introduction of some new kind of passive construction. The conjunction of these two processes will bring us back full circle to Type I.

There is much evidence that some such scenario as this underlies the rise of ergative organization in the Polynesian, the Australian, and the Indo-Iranian languages.[10] The whole process, of course, raises the question of why markedness shift should, in certain conditions, apply to passives in the first

---

9. From our point of view Dyirbal, as described in Dixon (1972), would be one of the few clear examples of this language type.

10. See note 8 for references. For Indo-Iranian, see for example Matthews (1953) and Payne (1980).

place. The precise reasons for this are not altogether clear. But there is evidence from different languages that under certain conditions a passive construction may become the preferred, or even the only possible expression of a transitive predication. Thus, it is reported in Schachter (1976: 511) that certain Tagalog main clause predications can only be expressed through assigning Subj to the Goal rather than the Agent. For example:

(31) a. *Tinakot   ng   lalaki   ang   bata.*
        frighten-pass Ag   man   Subj   child
        'The child was frightened by the man.'
    b. **Tumakot   ang   lalaki   ng   bata.*
        frighten-act   Subj man   Go   child
        'The man frightened the child.'

Some of the factors inducing this kind of preference may be understood from the following example:

(32) a. *The movie impressed me.*
    b. *I was impressed by the movie.*

The English predicate *impress* defines a basic perspective which runs counter to the "natural" priorities of participants in terms of animacy. We may thus expect a tendency to use (32b) much more frequently than (32a); this could easily lead to a situation in which (32b) became the unmarked expression for this type of relationship. And such "local" markedness shift might then generalize to other groups of passive constructions, which by themselves are less liable to overexploitation. The precise routes of such shifts from marked to unmarked through the entire active-passive opposition remain to be explored.

Although markedness shift applied to passives accounts for a considerable number of ergative languages in different language families, it is not necessarily the only scenario through which ergativity might arise. Another route might be through demarking of nominalized constructions. Suppose we have a language in which it becomes fashionable to use such constructions as the following:

(33)   A: *What irritated you?*
        B: *It was the laughing* of John (Ag)
        B: *It was the killing* of the duck (Go) *by John* (Ag)

Markedness shift

Note that here we have a kind of ergative patterning in which *of* marks the Agent of the intransitive predicate *laugh* and also the Goal of the transitive predicate *kill*; whereas *by* marks the Agent of transitive *kill*. There is independent evidence that:

— terms are typically marked in this way in the context of nominalizations (cf. *TFG2*: chapter 7);

— languages may have Focus constructions of the type exemplified in (33B); and

— Focus constructions may themselves undergo a process of markedness shift, through which they end up as the normal, unmarked expression type of the predication (cf. *TFG2*: chapter 14).

If these various factors were to coincide, they might lead to an ergative expression for unmarked main clauses which would, in this case, not betray traces of a passive origin, but of an earlier nominalized and focused character.

This ends our discussion of the mechanisms of Subj/Obj assignment, and at the same time our treatment of the nuclear, the core, and the extended predication. In the next chapter, we consider the higher layers of organization of underlying clause structure.

12. Predication, proposition, clause

12.0. Introduction

So far we have been concerned with the internal structure of the (extended) predication and its semantic designation, the (located) State of Affairs. In this chapter we discuss the higher layers of underlying clause structure. We show how the extended predication can be built into a *proposition*, designating a "Possible Fact", and how the proposition can be built into a clause, designating an *illocutionary act*. Let us first recall the overall structure and representation of the clause, from the inner nucleus defined by the prediate frame up to the highest level of the underlying clause structure:

(1)   nuclear predication = [pred [type] (args)]

The *nuclear predication* consists of the predicate, its type, and its argument terms, as defined in the (basic or derived) predicate frame.

(2)   core predication = [π_1 [nuclear predication] σ_1]

The *core predication* consists of the nuclear predication, extended by predicate operators π_1 and Level-1 satellites σ_1. These elements have in common that they specify additional features of the internal constitution (the quality) of the SoA designated by the predication.

(3)   extended predication = [π_2 e_i: [core predication] σ_2]

The *extended predication* contains an SoA variable e_i, which is specified by the core predication, predication operators π_2, and Level-2 satellites σ_2. Level-2 operators and satellites serve to quantify over the SoA designated by the core predication, and to locate it with respect to spatial, temporal, and cognitive parameters.

(4)   proposition = [π_3 X_i: [extended predication] σ_3]

The *proposition* consists of a propositional content variable X_i, symbolizing a possible fact PF, specified by the extended predication, propositional (or:

"attitudinal") operators π_3, and Level-3 satellites σ_3. These Level-3 elements serve to specify the speaker's evaluation of and commitment to the PF defined by the proposition.

(5) clause = [π_4 E_i: [proposition] σ_4]

The *clause* consists of an illocutionary act variable E_i, symbolizing the speech act expressed by the clause, specified by the proposition, illocutionary operators π_4, and illocutionary (Level-4) satellites σ_4. Level-4 elements serve to specify (or modify) the illocutionary force with which the proposition is presented.

The structure of this chapter is as follows: in 12.1. we consider the differences between SoAs and PFs, and the reasons why they should be considered as belonging to different levels of analysis. In 12.2. we discuss the way in which the extended predication can be built into a propositional frame. 12.2.1. motivates the propositional content variable X_i; 12.2.2. discusses the proposition operators π_3, and 12.2.3. the propositional satellites σ_3. In 12.3 we consider how the proposition can be built into an illocutionary frame. 12.3.1. motivates the illocutionary variable E_i; 12.3.2. treats the illocutionary operators π_4, and 12.3.3. the illocutionary satellites σ_4.

12.1. States of Affairs and Possible Facts

Vendler (1967) argued on linguistic grounds that a distinction should be made between "events" (our SoAs) and "facts" (our PFs). SoAs are second-order entities which can be said to occur, begin, last, and end; they can be perceived: watched, heard, felt, etc.; and they can be said to be sudden, gradual, violent, etc. PFs are third-order entities which can be said to be believed, known, or thought; they can be reason for surprise or doubt; they can be mentioned, denied, and remembered; and they can be said to be true or false in relation to the occurrence of some SoA in some world.

Some of the linguistic arguments for this distinction are the following. Compare:

(6) a. *John's death surprised me.*
    b. *John's having died surprised me.*
(7) a. *John's death occurred at noon.*
    b. **John's having died occurred at noon.*

We see that the expression *John's death* can occur either in an SoA context, as in (7a), or in a PF context, as in (6a). But expressions such as *John's having died* are only appropriate in PF contexts. This can also be seen in:

(8) a. *The fact of John's having died surprised me.*
    b. **The event of John's having died surprised me.*

For another such difference, consider the following pair:

(9) a. *John deplored Peter's driving the car recklessly.*
    = John deplored the fact that Peter drove the car recklessly.
    b. *John deplored Peter's reckless driving of the car.*
    = John deplored the reckless way in which Peter drove the car.

In (9a) we have a more verbal type of nominalization, appropriate for representing PFs; the more nominal type of nominalization in (9b) is appropriate for representing SoAs. This creates the following ambiguity:

(10) *John deplored Peter's driving.*
    = (a) the fact that Peter drove.
    = (b) the way in which Peter drove.

When we mix SoAs and PFs, this leads to strange or unacceptable results:

(11) a. *John believed what Peter said.*
    b. *?John believed what Peter saw.*
(12) a. *John believed, but Peter questioned her being in London.*
    b. **John believed, but Peter saw her being in London.*

These various differences require us to make a distinction between expressions designating SoAs and expressions designating PFs. We therefore distinguish between the predication as designating SoAs, and the proposition as designating PFs. In the course of this chapter more arguments for such a distinction will be given.[1]

---

[1] The idea of making a principled distinction between SoA- and PF-designating expressions within the model of FG was advanced in Hengeveld (1989). A number of arguments for this distinction presented in this chapter are due to that paper.

We use the term "Possible Fact" rather than just "Fact" for the designation of PF-designating expressions, because it is possible to use these expressions in a context in which it is denied that they represent facts, or in which it is presupposed that they have no factual status:

(13) a. *It is not a fact / true that the Germans collapsed completely.*
b. *If the Germans had collapsed completely (which would have surprised me), ...*

Clearly, if it can be denied of X_i that it is a fact, then X_i cannot intrinsically designate a fact. It can, however, designate a potential or possible fact which may or may not be evaluated as having the status of a true fact.

12.2. From predication to proposition

We defined the proposition in (4) as consisting of an extended predication embedded within a frame consisting of a propositional content variable X_i, proposition operators π_3, and satellites σ_3. We now consider these three types of element one by one.

12.2.1. The propositional content variable

Compare the following cases of anaphorical reference:

(14) a. *John saw that Mary was pregnant, but Peter didn't see it / *so.*
b. *John thought that Mary was pregnant, but Peter didn't think so / *it.*

We can refer to 'what John saw' by means of *it*. According to our way of treating anaphora, if 'what John saw' is represented by the SoA variable e_i, then *it* can be represented in underlying clause structure by (Ae_i), where A is the anaphorical operator (see *TFG2*: chapter 10). (14b) shows that we can also refer anaphorically to 'what John thought'. This is (in this case) done by *so* rather than by *it*, another indication that 'what we see' and 'what we think' are different types of things. If 'what John thought' is represented by the propositional content variable X_i, then *so* in (14b) can be represented by (AX_i). For a second example, consider:

(15)   *John didn't believe what Peter said.*

We may assume that *what Peter said* is a headless relative clause. For such a clause, we need a term variable symbolizing the intended referent. This cannot be a first- or second-order entity (x_i or e_i). It must be the sort of thing that John can be said to believe, i.e. a third-order entity of type X_i. We can thus analyse *what Peter said* as:[2]

(16) $(X_i: [say [V] (Peter)_{Ag} (X_i)_{Go}])$

These examples show that, given our assumptions about grammatical processes such as anaphorical reference and relativization, it is not only useful but even mandatory that we should have propositional content variables as distinct from SoA variables.

12.2.2. Proposition operators

Proposition operators capture the grammatical means through which S can specify his attitude towards the propositional content.[3] This attitude may concern S's personal assessment of, or his personal commitment to the propositional content X_i, or it may give an indication of the kind of evidence that S has to warrant the correctness of the propositional content. The following semantic distinctions seem to be the most important in the field of these propositional modalities:

---

2. In giving such structural fragments as (16) I leave out details which are not relevant to the point under discussion.
3. Compare 9.2.2.2.3. above, Chung—Timberlake (1985) and Hengeveld (1989).

(17)   *Subjective*: the source of S's evaluation is
— Personal opinion: it is S's personal opinion that X_i is certain / probable / possible;
— Volition: it is S's wish / hope that X_i is / will be realized.
Evidential: the source of S's proposition is
— Experience: S concludes that X_i on the basis of previous personal experience ("experiential");
— Inference: S infers X_i on the basis of available evidence ("inferential");
— Hearsay: S signals that he has heard X_i from someone else ("quotative", "reportative").

Note that certainty, probability, and possibility can also refer to distinctions of Objective modality, which we assigned to the π_2 level in section 9.2.2.3. above. The difference is that in the case of objective modality the assessment is presented as being independent of S's personal opinion, whereas in subjective modality the claim is expressly restricted to S's personal opinion. One reason for making this distinction is that Objective and Subjective modalities can be combined, as in:

(18)   *It is certainly possible that John is ill.*
'In my opinion it is certain that it is (objectively) possible that John is ill'

More generally, in languages which distinguish Objective and Subjective / Evidential Moods in the verb, these can typically be combined in such a way that the Subjective / Evidential Mood takes the Objective Mood distinction in its scope. Hengeveld (1989) gives the following Turkish form as an example:

(19)   *Gel-me-meli-ymiş-siniz.*
come-neg-necess-infer-2pl
'It seems (inferential) you ought (objective deontic) not to come'

12.2.3. Attitudinal satellites[4]

Attitudinal satellites (σ_3) are the lexical means by which S can express his attitude towards the propositional content. Satellites of this type can be used to express by lexical means those distinctions which have been mentioned in the preceding section. Consider such examples as the following:

(20) a. In my opinion, *we should do it.*
       (Subjective, Opinion)
   b. Hopefully, *you will succeed.*
       (Subjective, Volition)
   c. In my experience, *such questions are seldom solved.*
       (Experiential)
   d. Apparently, *John has failed.*
       (Inferential)
   e. Allegedly, *John was guilty of perjury.*
       (Quotative, Reportative)

Apart from expressing such modal distinctions as these, σ_3 satellites can also express personal evaluations of that which is contained in the proposition. Consider the following examples:

(21) a. Wisely, *John didn't answer the question.*
   b. Fortunately, *we found him immediately.*
   c. Understandably, *no patriot wants to fall into disrepute.*

Note that these satellites can be paraphrased in the form of a description of the personal opinion of S:

---

4. The term reflects Greenbaum's (1969) notion "attitudinal disjunct". Some of the examples below are also from this work. Greenbaum used the term "disjunct" (as against "adjunct") to suggest the "lack of integration" of these elements in the structure of the clause. He divided them up into *attitudinal* disjuncts and *style* disjuncts. The latter will return in 12.3.3. below as "illocutionary satellites". See also Pinkster (1972, 1988a) on the differences between adjuncts and disjuncts in Latin.

(22) a. *I think it was wise of John not to answer the question.*
b. *I think it is fortunate that we found him immediately.*
c. *I find it understandable that no patriot wants to fall into disrepute.*

Note that in English the same adverb *wisely* can be used as a Manner satellite (σ_1) and as an Attitudinal satellite (σ_3). The differences between these can be read off from the placement of the adverb and the intonation pattern with which the construction is provided:

(23) a. Wisely, *John answered the question.*
b. *John,* wisely, *answered the question.*
c. *John answered the question,* wisely.
(24) a. ??Wisely *John answered the question.*
b. ?*John* wisely *answered the question.*
c. *John answered the question* wisely.

Although these differences are not absolute, the Manner satellite clearly prefers a non-initial position, whereas the Attitudinal satellite has a preference for initial position. Furthermore, the Manner satellite is intonationally integrated in the predication, whereas the Attitudinal satellite is usually marked off from the rest by prosodic inflections which suggest that it is less integrated with the rest. This corresponds, in iconic fashion, to the different roles these satellites play in the fabric of the clause.

In German and Dutch we find formal differences between the adverbs, corresponding to their roles as σ_1 or σ_3 satellites:[5]

(25) a. Klugerweise *beantwortete Hans die Frage.* [=(23)]
b. *Hans beantwortete die Frage* klug. [=(24)]
(26) a. Wijselijk *beantwoordde Jan de vraag.* [=(23)]
b. *Jan beantwoordde de vraag* wijs. [=(24)]

We have analysed negation (negative polarity) as a predication operator of level π_2. If we are correct that attitudinal satellites are of level 3, while Manner satellites are of level 1, we would expect the following scope relations:

(27) σ_3 [neg [... σ_1 ...]]

---

5. For the German data, see Bartsch (1972, 1976).

and this is, indeed, exactly what we find. Compare:

(28) a. *Wisely, John didn't answer the question.*
    = 'It was wise of John not to answer the question'
   b. *John didn't answer the question wisely.*
    = 'It was not in a wise manner that John answered the question'

The fact that we cannot give wide scope to neg in (28a), nor to *wisely* in (28b), follows immediately from the layered structure of the clause in (27).

12.3. From proposition to clause

As Austin (1962) and Searle (1969) have convincingly argued, we do not communicate by displaying propositions, but by performing speech acts, interpretable as instructions from S to A to perform certain mental actions with respect to the content of the proposition. The following clauses, for example, contain the same proposition, integrated into different speech act or illocutionary frames:

(29) a. *John forgot to warn Peter.*   (Statement)
   b. *Did John forget to warn Peter?*   (Question)

At the highest level of underlying clause structure, therefore, we need a way to show that a full clause consists of some illocutionary force indicating device, and a proposition to which this device is applied. We achieve this by articulating the clause structure in the way indicated in (5) above. In this structure, E_i is the illocutionary variable symbolizing the intended speech act. This variable can be specified by illocutionary operators π_4 and illocutionary satellites σ_4. Extending the terminology used for different "orders" of entities, we can say that speech acts represent "fourth-order entities".

12.3.1. The illocutionary variable

Consider the following example:

(30)   A: *I think you are a crook.*
         B: That *is preposterous!*

The anaphoric element *that* is ambiguous in its reference: (30b) may be paraphrased in two different ways:

(31) a. *It is preposterous of you to think that I am a crook.*
    b. *It is preposterous of you to say that you think I am a crook.*

On the second interpretation, *that* refers anaphorically to the whole speech act (30A). We thus need a variable for that speech act. This is provided by E_i, so that we can use (AE_i) as the representation underlying *that* on this interpretation. For another example, consider:

(32)   *John said that Peter failed the test,* which *was rather remarkable.*

Again, the reference of *which* is equivocal: it may refer to the content 'that Peter failed the test' (X_i), or to the fact that John said it (E_i). Clearly, the difference in variable can be used to capture this ambiguity.

12.3.2. Illocutionary operators

There have been four tendencies in the Austin-Searle development of speech act theory which have led to analyses which are less than fully adequate in a linguistic sense:
   — The tendency to set up typologies of speech acts without bothering too much about the ways in which these speech acts are grammatically coded in natural languages. We should rather want to have an approach in which we start out from the most universally made sentence type distinctions.
   — The tendency to describe the conditions for the correct use of speech act expressions predominantly from the point of view of the Speaker. We should prefer an analysis in which the communicative relation between S and A is taken into account.
   — The tendency to take the so-called "explicit" performative (as in (33a)) as a model for the analysis of the "implicit" performative in (33b):

(33) a. *I order you to go away.*
    b. *Go away!*

In natural language communication, however, we normally speak in implicit performatives. Explicit constructions of type (33a) are the exception rather than the rule, and typically have special pragmatic significance.

— The tendency to take the final interpretation of an utterance as the "primary" illocutionary force of that utterance. Thus, when a statement such as:

(34)   *The window is open.*

is used with the intention and effect of a request, it is assigned the primary illocutionary force "Request", and only secondarily treated as a declarative. We shall prefer an analysis in which the illocutionary force AS CODED IN THE LINGUISTIC EXPRESSION is given more importance.

The FG alternative interpretation of illocutionary acts will be more extensively discussed in *TFG2*: chapter 11. It can be briefly summarized as follows:

(i) We start by making a basic distinction between:

(35) a.   The illocutionary intention of S [Ill_S]
     b.   The illocution-as-coded-in-the-expression [Ill_E];
     c.   The illocutionary interpretation of A [Ill_A].

The ultimate goal of successful communication is of course that $Ill_A = Ill_S$. But just as there may, in general, be a difference between S-intention, E-content, and A-interpretation (see 1.3.4. above), so it may well be the case that Ill_E is not identical to Ill_S / Ill_A. For example, there is nothing in (34) which marks it linguistically as conveying a request. Therefore, assigning a request value to (34) is a matter of pragmatic interpretation rather than of linguistic content.

(ii) We start our analysis of Ill_E by considering the most pervasive sentence type distinctions made across languages. In all languages we find special sentence types classifiable as Declaratives, Interrogatives, and Imperatives, and in most languages we find a special sentence type for Exclamatives. Accordingly, we regard these illocutionary values as the *basic illocutions* distinguished in natural languages.

(iii) We interpret these basic illocutions as instructions from S to A to effect certain changes in A's pragmatic information (see 1.3.2. above). Roughly, these interpretations can take the following form:

(36) a. Decl: S instructs A to add the propositional content to his pragmatic information.
b. Int: S instructs A to provide him with the verbal information as specified in the proposition.
c. Imp: S instructs A to perform the controlled SoA as specified in the proposition.
d. Excl: S instructs A to add to his pragmatic information that S finds the propositional content surprising, unexpected, or otherwise worthy of notice.

(iv) We treat the basic illocutions as illocutionary operators of type π_4.[6] We thus assign the following underlying clause structure to (34):

(37)   Decl E_i: [*the window is open*]

(v) We assume that the basic illocution of an expression can be "converted" into other illocutionary values. This process of *illocutionary conversion* can take different forms:
— *pragmatic* conversion: the conversion is effected at the level of intention and interpretation, and has no reflection on the linguistic properties of the expression (not even on its prosodic properties). This type of conversion will not be handled in the linguistic description, but in a wider, pragmatic theory of verbal interaction.
— *lexical* conversion, in which the illocution is specified in some explicit performative verb or other lexical expression. Thus, the step from (38a) to (38b) is seen as a form of lexical conversion:

(38) a. *Will you marry me?*
b. *I ask / request you to marry me.*

— *grammatical* conversion, when the language has certain grammatical means for changing the basic illocution of an expression into some derived illocutionary value. For one example of grammatical conversion, compare:

---

6. The idea of integrating illocutionary operators into the FG analysis of clause structure was advanced, in slightly different ways, in De Jong (1981), Peres (1984), and Moutaouakil (1986).

(39) a. *She is a nice girl.* (Decl)
 b. *She is a nice girl, isn't she?* (Decl > Int)

The "tag" in (39b) serves to convert a basic Decl into a derived Int. Note that it would not be appropriate to label (39b) as just Int, because there is a clear difference in form, as well as in content, between:

(40) a. *She is a nice girl, isn't she?* (Decl > Int)
 b. *Is she a nice girl?* (Int)

We could interpret the tag in (40a) as an operator which modifies Decl and yields Int:

(41)   Tag [Decl] > Int

One way of representing the full structure of (40a) would be as follows:

(42)   [Tag [Decl] > Int] E_i: [*she is a nice girl*]

Further elaboration of this theory of illocutionary force will involve:
 — establishing the set of basic illocutionary operators as coded in the sentence types of natural languages;
 — establishing the types of illocutionary conversion that can be effected by grammatical means;
 — establishing the grammatical means which can be used to effect such conversion.
These points will be discussed in more detail in *TFG2*: chapter 11.

One particular type of grammatically coded illocutionary conversion which languages may possess is systematic ways of "weakening" (mitigating) or "reinforcing" the impact of the basic illocutionary operators.[7] It is typical of such strategies that they are generally applicable across all sentence types, as in the following examples of illocutionary reinforcement in Spanish (Haverkate 1979):

---

7. See Haverkate (1979) on Spanish, and Hengeveld (1989) for more examples.

(43) a. ¡Que   no   me   gusta   nada   esa película!
        that   not me   please   nothing   that movie
        'I don't like that movie at all!'
    b. ¡Que   no   te   marches   mañana!
        that   not you[refl]   leave-2sg   tomorrow
        'Don't you leave tomorrow!'
    c. ¡Que   si   vienes   mañana!
        that   if   come-2sg   tomorrow
        'Are you coming tomorrow???'

The reinforcing feature can be treated as an illocutionary modifier operating on the basic illocutionary operator and strengthening its pragmatic effect (in ways which may depend on the context, see Hengeveld (1989)).

We may conclude that π_4 operators may have a rich internal structure. The typological properties of this structure remain to be investigated in detail.

12.3.3. Illocutionary satellites

Illocutionary satellites (σ_4) represent the lexical means through which the illocutionary value of the clause can be specified or modified. Consider the following example:

(44)   Frankly, *he isn't very intelligent.*

It is clear that *frankly* does not have the status of a Manner satellite to the SoA. Rather, it provides comment from S on his manner of saying what he does say in uttering (44): it can thus be interpreted as an illocutionary satellite operating at Level 4.[8] That this is correct can be seen from such paraphrases as the following (Greenbaum 1969: 82):

(45) a. *I am speaking frankly when I say that ...*
    b. *If I may speak frankly, I would say that ...*

---

8. Greenbaum (1969) introduced the term "style disjunct" for this type of modifier. See note 4 above. Many of the examples in this section are from Greenbaum's work.

Frankly is part of a whole family of expressions which can be used in this function:

(46)   *in (all) frankness, to be frank, to speak frankly, frankly speaking, put frankly, if I can speak frankly,* etc.

All these expressions have in common that they comment on the manner in which S says what he says. There are also illocutionary satellites which comment on the Reason, Condition, or Purpose of the speech act:[9]

(47) a.   Since you are interested, *John is a Catholic.*
b.   *John has left*, in case you haven't heard.
c.   Just so I'll be able to tell my mother when she asks, *what is this stuff we're smoking?*

Illocutionary satellites such as those exemplified above are among the strongest arguments in favour of the so-called "performative analysis" (Ross 1970), according to which an implicit performative such as (48a) should be derived from an explicit underlying structure (48b) through deletion of the performative super-structure:

(48) a.   *Prices slumped.*
b.   *I tell you that [prices slumped].*

The argument is that *frankly* in (44) is indistinguishable from a Manner adverb; such adverbs usually modify some action verb; and the performative analysis provides just such an action verb (the performative verb) for the Manner adverb to modify:

(49) a.   Frankly, *prices slumped.*
b.   *I tell you* frankly *that prices slumped.*

Even those who otherwise reject the performative analysis sometimes accept it in cases like these (this position is taken, for example, by Boër—Lycan

---

9. See Boër—Lycan (1980), from which these examples are borrowed. Pinkster (1988a) speaks of "pseudo-causes", "pseudo-conditions", etc. Compare Bolkestein (1991) on the differences between causal satellites of type σ_2 and σ_4 in Latin, and Rijksbaron (1976) on similar phenomena in Classical Greek.

(1980)). For us, this is impossible for theoretical reasons: first, FG does not allow for the kind of deletion operations needed to convert (49b) into (49a) (see 1.7.1. above). Second, we argued above that the implicit performative (49a) is the basic expression type to be accounted for, and that (49b) should be regarded as an expansion of (49a), rather than (49a) as a reduction of (49b).

However, there are also empirical problems with accepting the performative analysis in order to find a proper "niche" for illocutionary satellites. As several authors have shown, there are illocutionary satellites which can NOT occur in the corresponding explicit performatives:[10]

(50) a. In brief, *we've had it.*
    b. **I tell you* in brief *that we've had it.*
(51) a. To put it paradoxically, *losers may turn out to be winners.*
    b. **I hereby tell you* to put it paradoxically *that losers may turn out to be winners.*

For these illocutionary satellites, then, we need another, presumably more direct source than the explicit performative underlying structure. But if we need that more direct source for these cases, we might just as well use it for the other examples, for which the performative analysis seems at first sight to provide an elegant solution. For us, this more direct source is the σ_4 satellite slot, operating at the illocutionary level. We thus arrive at an underlying structure of the following form:

(52)   Frankly, *he is stupid.*
           Decl E_i: [*he is stupid*] $(x_i: frank \, [A] \, (x_i))_{Man}$]

Note that *frankly* is here analysed as a Manner satellite which occupies the σ_4 rather than the σ_1 slot: the internal structure is the same, but the level is different. We can, in fact, get combinations of σ_1 and σ_4 satellites within one and the same overall construction:

(53)   Frankly, *John answered the question* frankly.
           Decl E_i: [Past e_i: [*John answer the question* $(frankly)_1$]] $(frankly)_2$

---

10. Greenbaum (1969: chapter 4), Lyons (1977: 783); cf. also Levinson (1983: 255-257).

in which $(frankly)_1$ operates within the core predication, specifying the SoA designated by the nuclear predication, whereas $(frankly)_2$ operates on the illocutionary level, specifying the nature of the illocutionary act E_i.

This analysis also accounts for the question of why a Manner adverb such as *frankly* can be associated with the illocutionary level. Normally, such a Manner adverb must be associated with an Action SoA; more specifically, it requires an Action of speaking or otherwise formulating a thought. But "Decl E_i" does symbolize such an Action of speaking, namely the illocutionary act itself. Thus, even without using the performative analysis, we account for the particular selection restrictions which illocutionary satellites are sensitive to in terms of the speech act variable E_i and the basic illocutionary operators applied to it.

If the same satellite may operate at different levels, as in (53), and if the occurrence of such a satellite is insufficiently differentiated in formal expression, we may expect ambiguities. Such cases do indeed occur, as in the following example in which there is ambiguity between σ_2 and σ_4 status of the satellite in roman typeface (Boër—Lycan 1980):

(54) Since you asked, *I've decided to tell you my secret name.*
     (i) 'The reason that I've decided to tell you my secret name is that you asked for it'
     (ii) 'The reason that I tell you that I've decided to tell you my secret name is that you asked about it'

It will be clear that this ambiguity will be resolved in underlying clause structure when the two readings of (54) are analysed according to the model of (53), with *since you asked* as a Reason satellite on the σ_2 level in the one case, and on the σ_4 level in the other.

For further discussion of the illocutionary layer of underlying clause structure, I refer to *TFG2*: chapter 11.

13. Pragmatic functions

13.0. Introduction

Consider an example of underlying clause structure as developed so far:

(1) a. *The duckling was killed by this farmer.*
  b. Decl E_i: X_i: Past e_i: *kill* [V]
    (d 1 prox x_i: *farmer* [N])$_{Ag}$ (d 1 x_j: *duckling* [N])$_{GoSubj}$

Although the underlying structure (1b) can be realized as (1a), it could also lead to a number of alternative expressions, differing from each other in intonation and / or constituent ordering, as in the following examples:[1]

(2) a. *The DUCKling was killed by this farmer.*
  b. *The duckling was KILLed by this farmer.*
  c. *The duckling was killed by THIS farmer.*
  d. *The duckling was killed by this FARMer.*
(3) a. *The duckling was killed by this farmer.*
  b. *By this farmer the duckling was killed.*

These various alternative expressions of structure (1b) cannot simply be described as optional alternatives: in certain contexts, one of them will be appropriate, while another may be inappropriate. Compare:

(4)   A: *Who killed the duckling?*
    B: *The duckling was killed by this FARMer.*
    B: **The DUCKling was killed by this farmer.*

Suppose we provide a language-producing device with only the underlying structure (1b). That device might then be able to produce the various alternative realizations in (2) and (3), but it will be unable to choose the correct alternative in a context such as (4A), since it has no means of

---

1. I provisionally indicate the peak of the prosodic contour by writing the relevant syllable in small capitals. In chapter 18 we return to the question of how to analyse prosodic contours within FG.

310 *Pragmatic functions*

differentiating between the alternatives, and adapting them to the context at hand. In other words, it lacks information essential to the contextual embedding of the expression. The device would thus lack pragmatic adequacy.

We will now assume that the relevant differences can be captured by different assignments of *pragmatic functions* to the constituents of the underlying clause structure. By pragmatic functions (as relevant within the structure of the clause) we understand functions which specify the informational status of the constituents in relation to the wider communicative setting in which they are used. The main parameters along which (clause-internal) pragmatic functions can be distinguished are "topicality" (= characterizing "the things we talk about") and "focality" (= characterizing the most important or salient parts of what we say about the topical things). When a language gives special distinctive treatment to some topical or focal element, we assign to it one of the pragmatic functions subsumed under Topic and Focus. In this chapter we discuss the various distinctions which must be made in the area of topicality and focality.

In 13.1. we make a distinction between clause-external and clause-internal pragmatic functions. We then restrict our attention to the clause-internal ones. 13.2. makes some general remarks on the nature of clause-internal pragmatic functions. 13.3. treats the notions Topic and topicality, and discusses the strategies languages may have for introducing, maintaining, and (if necessary) "reviving" topical elements. 13.4. deals with Focus and focality. In this section we consider the role of Focus in question-answer pairs, different subtypes of Focus, and different types of elements which may be in the scope of Focus. Then, we look at the grammatical organization of Focus in two languages.

13.1. Extra-clausal and intra-clausal pragmatic functions

Any natural language text may be exhaustively divided up into clauses and "extra-clausal constituents" (ECCs).[2] ECCs are not part of the clause proper, but more loosely associated with it in ways which can most adequately be described in terms of pragmatic functionality. Consider some examples of ECCs, together with a rough indication of their pragmatic functions:

---

2. In spoken conversation speakers often produce fragments of clauses rather than full clauses (cf. Brown—Yule 1983). I assume that a difference can be made between "clause fragment" and ECC. ECCs will be more extensively discussed in *TFG2*: chapter 17.

(5) a. Well [Initiator], *what about some dinner?*
 b. Ladies and gentlemen [Address], *shall we start the game?*
 c. As for the students [Theme], *they won't be invited.*
 d. *I'm afraid,* Peter [Address], *that you are going a bit too fast.*
 e. *John was,* so they say [Modal parenthesis], *a bright student.*
 f. *It's rather hot in here,* isn't it? [Tag, Illocutionary Modifier]
 g. *He's a nice chap,* your brother. [Tail, Clarification]

ECCs have the following general properties:
— They may precede, interrupt, or follow the clause proper;
— They are typically "bracketed off" from the clause by pause-like inflections in the intonation pattern;
— They are not sensitive to the clause-internal grammatical rules, though they may entertain relations of coreference, parallelism (e.g. same case marking), or antithesis (e.g. negative Tag with positive clause) with the clause they are associated with.
— They are not essential to the integrity of the internal structure of the clause: when they are left out, the remaining clause structure is complete and grammatical.

As is evident from the examples in (5), ECCs may serve a variety of pragmatic functions. In general, these functions concern (i) the "management" of the interaction, (ii) "comments" on the content of the clause proper, and (iii) the organization of the content of the expression, in relation to the context in which it occurs. In *TFG2*: chapter 17 we give a fuller discussion of the various types of ECCs. Here, we concentrate on the pragmatic organization of the content of the clause proper. In other words, we restrict our attention to pragmatic functions to be assigned to constituents which operate within the limits of the clause.

13.2. Clause-internal pragmatic functions

Clause-internal pragmatic functions concern the informational status of constituents of the clause in relation to the wider communicative setting in which they are used; "communicative setting" can be understood in terms of the Speaker's estimate of the Addressee's pragmatic information at the moment of speaking. The pragmatic information P_X of a person X was defined in 1.3.2. above as consisting of the full body of knowledge, beliefs, feelings, and preconceptions of X at the moment of speaking. Pragmatic information was subdivided into *general, situational,* and *contextual* information. It was argued that S organizes his linguistic expressions in accordance with $(P_A)_S$, his estimate of A's pragmatic information at the moment of speaking. S's aim will in general be to cause A to effect some change in P_A, and in order to achieve this, S will typically start from some piece of information that A presumably already possesses, and then go on to build some information onto this, which he thinks is new to A and may thus lead to a modification of P_A. A linguistic expression will thus usually contain some *given* information and some *new* information. Both "given" and "new" should be interpreted as being mediated through S's estimate of P_A; given information is thus information which is contained in $(P_A)_S$, new information is information not contained in $(P_A)_S$. It may be that S's estimate is not fully correct, i.e. does not fully correspond to the actual structure of P_A. This may cause certain hitches in the communication process. But it is $(P_A)_S$ rather than P_A which determines the way in which S pragmatically organizes his expressions.

Partially corresponding to the given / new distinction, we may distinguish the dimensions of *topicality* and *focality*. Topicality concerns the status of those entities "about" which information is to be provided or requested in the discourse. The topicality dimension concerns the participants in the event structure of the discourse, the "players" in the play staged in the communicative interaction. Focality attaches to those pieces of information which are the most important or salient with respect to the modifications which S wishes to effect in P_A, and with respect to the further development of the discourse. The focality dimension concerns the "action" of the play.

These two dimensions of discourse organization have a certain area of overlap, in that certain topical elements may at the same time be focal to the communication. This is the case in two main circumstances. First, when a new participant is introduced into the discourse (a New Topic in the terminology to be developed below), this is part of topicality management in that it concerns the entities about which the Speaker wishes to say something. At the same time, the "entering on the stage" of this new entity may be the main point of the utterance in question. Thus, new (focal) information may be topical, as in:

(6) *All of a sudden we saw A GIGANTIC SHARK.*

On the other hand, given topical information may at the same time be focal, as when some contrast is established between two or more already established topics:

(7)   (A and B have been talking about John and Peter for some time)
        A: *Do you have any further news about John and Peter?*
        B: *Well, JOHN seems to be all right, but PETER is really in deep trouble.*

In many languages certain topical elements are singled out for special treatment in the expression of the clause. Such elements will receive the pragmatic function of Topic, to be distinguished below into different sub-functions. Likewise, if such special treatment is given to focal elements, these will be assigned the pragmatic function of Focus, again to be divided into different sub-functions below.

By "special treatment" I mean one or more of the following features, when these refer to the topical or focal status of the constituents concerned:
(i) the constituent gets a special form;
(ii) it gets a special marker signalling its pragmatic status;
(iii) it gets a special position in the linear order of the clause;
(iv) it gets a special prosodic contour;
(v) it otherwise leads to the selection of a special construction type.

Note especially the importance of prosodic properties: constituents may receive special treatment in terms of prosody even when we do not see this in a written representation of the clause in question. The impact of pragmatic functions on the prosodic contour of the clause will be discussed in chapter 18.

It may be assumed that the dimensions of topicality and focality are relevant in some way to the organization of linguistic expressions in all languages. But not all languages have the same types of "special treatment" for topical and focal elements. Thus, languages may differ in the set of distinctive Topic and Focus functions operative in their grammar. Just as in many other domains of grammatical articulation, however, it seems that languages choose their grammatically relevant distinctions in this area from a restricted universal set of possible distinctions.

13.3. Topic and topicality[3]

A discourse, taken in the wide sense of any kind of coherent text (a story, a monologue, a dialogue, a lecture, etc.), is "about" certain entities. For

---

3. For some of the points made in this section I am indebted to De Vries (1985) and to Hannay (1985a, 1985b).

example, this book is "about" Functional Grammar, this chapter is "about" pragmatic functions, and this subsection is "about" Topic and topicality. For those entities about which a certain discourse imparts information we may use the term Discourse Topic (D-Topic).[4] One discourse may have different D-Topics, some more central to the discourse than others. D-Topics may be hierarchically organized, as in the example given: the D-Topic "Topic and topicality" is part of the D-Topic "pragmatic functions", which in turn is part of the overall D-Topic of this book, "Functional Grammar". The notion of D-Topic should thus be interpreted relative to the stretch of discourse (book, chapter, section, paragraph, and ultimately the individual clause) under consideration. D-Topics may also be sequentially organized, as when different and possibly even unrelated D-Topics are treated one by one in a sequence of discourse episodes.

In an abstract sense we may think of the discourse as containing a "topic store" which is empty at the beginning of the discourse (unless the topic has been fixed in advance, as for a meeting or lecture), and which is gradually being filled with D-Topics as these are introduced into the discourse. Some D-Topics will be short-lived and disappear quickly, others will be more pervasive and kept alive all through the discourse.

If a discourse is to be about a certain D-Topic, that D-Topic will, at some point, have to be introduced for the first time. Such a first presentation of a D-Topic will be called a New Topic (NewTop); once the entity in question has been introduced, it can then be considered as a Given Topic (GivTop). Sometimes, given a certain GivTop, we may go on to talk about another Topic related to it "as if" it had been introduced before. For example, once we have introduced a certain party as a D-Topic, we may go on to talk about 'the music' as if it were a GivTop, as in:

(8)   *John gave a party last week, but* the music *was awful.*

This is warranted on the basis of the common knowledge that usually some music is played at parties, and that the music may be important for the atmosphere. In such cases, we shall call 'the music' a Sub-Topic (SubTop) of 'party'.[5] We can thus say that once a NewTop X has been introduced into the discourse, we can go on to talk, not only about X, but also about all SubTops

---

4. On the notion "discourse topic", cf. Brown—Yule (1983).
5. Prince (1981) uses the term "inferrables" for SubTops. The term Sub-Topic was introduced by Hannay (1985a, 1985b).

which may reasonably be assumed to be "available" to A on the basis of generally accessible pragmatic information, once X is available to him. Finally, it may be the case that there are special strategies through which a GivTop which has not been mentioned for a certain time in a stretch of discourse may be "revived" and re-established as a GivTop. Such an entity will be called a Resumed Topic (ResTop). In terms of these distinctions we can now ask the following questions concerning the "topicality strategies" available in a language:

(i) How is a NewTop first introduced into the discourse?
(ii) How is a D-Topic maintained, kept alive as a GivTop?
(iii) What kinds of SubTops may be associated with a given GivTop?
(iv) What kinds of strategies exist for re-introducing a GivTop as a ResTop?

These questions are considered in the following subsections.

13.3.1. Introducing a NewTop[6]

There are different construction types used for introducing NewTops into the discourse. These construction types show a high degree of uniformity across languages. First of all, use may be made of an explicit meta-linguistic statement about what is going to be the Topic of the ensuing discourse:

(9)   *I'm going to tell you a story about* an elephant called Jumbo.

In the second place, the object or second argument position is often used for the introduction of NewTops, typically in combination with a distinctive prosodic contour:

(10)   *In the circus we saw* an elephant called Jumbo.

When the NewTop is introduced through the first argument or the subject position, use is often made of existential or locative-existential constructions:

(11) a. *Once upon a time there was* an elephant called Jumbo.
     b. *Long ago, in the middle of the African jungle, there lived* an elephant called Jumbo.

---

6. For this section see Hetzron (1975), Givón (1978), and Hannay (1985b).

Another common strategy for introducing NewTops is through predicates which in some way or other designate a form of "appearing on the scene":

(12)   *Suddenly, right before our very eyes, there appeared* a huge elephant.

In all these examples the NewTop takes the form of an indefinite term. This is appropriate in situations in which S has no reason to assume that A is aware of the identity of the entity in question. It is not, however, a necessary property of NewTops: when S has reason to assume that the identity of the NewTop is known to A, he may well use a definite term to introduce it, as in:

(13) a.   *Yesterday in the pub I met* your sister Mary.
   b.   *Mind you, there's* the money issue *we have to reckon with.*
   c.   *Do you know who was there as well?* Our very own Prime Minister!

As we saw above NewTops combine properties from the dimensions of topicality and focality. They are topical in that they introduce *a topical entity* into the discourse, focal in that they *introduce* this entity into the discourse.

NewTop-introducing constructions display the following recurrent properties across languages:[7]

— Terms introducing NewTops have a strong preference for taking a relatively late position in the clause. Even in languages which normally place a Subject in initial position, NewTop Subjects typically take a later position, sometimes at the very end of the clause. Many languages, for example, have a characteristic opposition between:

(14) a.   The man (GivTop) [*was*] *in the house.*
   b.   *In the house* [*was*] a man (NewTop).

In such pairs it is often the constituent order which is the only differentiating factor, as in Russian:

(15) a.   *Čelov'ek v   dom'e.*
         man   in   house
   b.   *V   dom'e   čelov'ek.*
         in   house   man

---

7. Compare Hetzron (1975) for general discussion.

The preference of NewTops for non-initial position can also be seen at work in the following text, drawn from a tourist description of Oxford (boldface, italics, and capitals as in the original):[8]

(16) "The bridge over the lane connects the old and the new buildings of **Hertford College** [...]. On the corner of Catte St. opposite the Bodleian Library Extension stands the classical *Clarendon Building* [...]. Adjoining it in Broad St. is the splendidly restored **Sheldonian Theatre** [...]. Behind the Sheldonian lies the OLD SCHOOLS QUADRANGLE [...]. The building is now occupied by the **Bodleian Library** [...]"

We see in (16) that various strategies (VS order, passive constructions) conspire to bring the successive NewTops to a non-initial position.

— In certain languages, such as English and French, "presentative" constructions are characterized by "expletive" or "dummy" pronouns or adverbials taking the position which would otherwise be occupied by the Subject.

(17) a. A car *appeared on the horizon.*
b. There *appeared* a car *on the horizon.*
c. *On the horizon* there *appeared* a car.
(18) a. Un train passe *toutes les heures.*
    a train passes all the hours
b. Il *passe* un train *toutes les heures.*
    it passes a train all the hours
'Every hour a train passes.'

— Even where the NewTop at first sight seems to have Subj function, it often lacks certain properties criterial for Subjects in the language concerned. Thus, French has agreement in (19a), but not in (19b):

(19) a. *Les trois trains arrivaient.*
    the three trains arrived (plur.)
b. Il *arrivait* trois trains.
    it arrived (sing.) three trains
'There arrived three trains'

---

8. Stuart Rossiter ed., *England Blue Guide*. London: Ernest Benn 1972, pp. 268-269.

318   *Pragmatic functions*

Within our framework this could be interpreted as a sign that Subj assignment has not taken place, and that the term *trois trains* just has the semantic function Processed, together with the pragmatic function NewTop (cf. Vet 1981).

These various properties show that we will have to assign the pragmatic function NewTop to the relevant terms in the underlying clause structure, not only in order to describe the special pragmatic status of these terms, but also to trigger the various peculiarities of formal expression noted above.

13.3.2. Maintaining a D-Topic

Once a D-Topic has been introduced into the discourse as a NewTop, it can be treated as a Given Topic in the subsequent communication. Such a GivTop, however, must be "kept alive" through repeated references in subsequent predications. These repeated references create a kind of "topic chain" or "anaphoric chain" through the relevant part of the discourse. If that chain is broken through the intrusion of some other D-Topic, or because the last reference to the GivTop is too far removed, the D-Topic may have to be re-established, "revived" as it were, in the form of a Resumed Topic.

Strategies of Topic maintenance have been described in terms of "topic chains" (Dixon 1972), "identification spans" (Grimes 1975), and "topic continuity" (Givón ed. 1983). The intuitions behind these notions are basically the same: speakers apply strategies aimed at maintaining a GivTop as long as it is relevant to the communication; and languages provide various means for signalling that one is still talking about the same GivTop. What grammatical means do languages provide for maintaining Topic continuity? Let us mention the following:

(i) *Anaphoric reference*
A GivTop may be maintained through repeated anaphoric reference in subsequent predications. Anaphoric reference may take different forms, as exemplified in the following text:

(20)   *Yesterday I got a phone call from the tax inspector* (NewTop). He / The man / The joker *wanted me to come to* his *office, and* he / Ø *gave me the impression that I was in for some trouble.*

Thus, anaphoric reference may be established through an anaphoric personal pronoun (*he*) or possessive pronoun (*his*); through a term which specifies the class to which the GivTop belongs (*the man*); through an "epithet" (*the joker*) by which the Speaker provides a personal qualification of the GivTop; or through so-called "zero anaphora" (∅). Through each of these anaphoric devices, the GivTop is kept alive for further reference. Grimes (1975) has suggested that these types of anaphoric reference may be ordered on a scale from stronger (more explicit) to weaker (less explicit) anaphora, and uses this scale in defining his notion of "identification span": "... a series of identifications of the same participant [...] in which no identification is stronger than the one before it" (Grimes 1975: 92). According to this view, when (20) is continued with a stronger anaphoric reference, such as:

(21)   *Now*, this inspector *happens to be a good friend of my sister's* ...

this would by definition constitute the beginning of a new identification span.

However, the stronger anaphoric expression may also be a way of returning to a GivTop after ANOTHER GivTop has been mentioned. For a restricted type of discourse, Brown—Yule (1983: 174) showed that different strategies are used for referring to the last-mentioned GivTop vs. all GivTops introduced earlier. In their data, reference to an "earlier" GivTop was ALWAYS achieved by means of a full noun phrase. Note that there is an element of "topic resumption" (see 13.3.4. below) in this reference to "earlier" topics.[9]

(ii) *Syntactic parallelism*
In certain languages the maintenance of a GivTop through the discourse requires that it reappear in similar syntactic positions in subsequent predications. In Dyirbal, for example, a "topic chain" may be formed by explicitly introducing a NewTop, and then maintaining it by anaphoric reference through a whole series of clauses, all commenting on the same Topic (Dixon 1972: 71). A requirement on such topic chains is that in each subsequent clause the GivTop appear in a position in which it is marked by absolutive case, Dyirbal being an ergative language. Thus, it will appear as the sole argument of an intransitive predicate or as the second argument of a transitive predicate. In situations in which we would expect the GivTop to appear as the first argument of a transitive predicate (marked by the ergative), that predicate will be restructured through a rule of "antipassive" detransitivization, so that again the GivTop is marked by the absolutive case.

Note that in our interpretation of ergativity, as sketched in 11.6.2. above, we

---

9. In *TFG2*: chapter 10 we return to the matter of anaphora.

would interpret Dyirbal as a language of type II, i.e. a language with a "demarked" passive construction with no active counterpart. This means that we can still consider the absolutive term in a transitive predication as the Subj of the construction.[10] And if this interpretation is correct, the rule would be that the GivTop in Dyirbal has to be assigned the Subj function.

Such a correlation between GivTop and Subj is not at all unexpected. As De Vries (1985) puts it, the GivTop determines the "contextual" perspective from which the discourse is organized; the Subj determines the perspective from which the SoA is presented in the predication. It is natural, though not obligatory, for the two kinds of perspective to coincide: "In this way the narrator expresses on the level of sentence-grammar the dominant contextual perspective of the discourse" (De Vries 1985: 168).

A related phenomenon was found in Latin by Bolkestein (1985). Latin has a class of three-place predicates which can occur in two alternative constructions, without discernible difference in meaning. Compare the following constructions with the verb *aspergere* 'to sprinkle':

(22) a.   *Mensam aqua   aspergit.*
          table-acc water-abl sprinkle-3sg:pres
          'He sprinkles the table with water.'
     b.   *Aquam   mensae   aspergit.*
          water-acc   table-dat sprinkle-3sg:pres
          'He sprinkles water onto the table.'

Note that in (22a) *mensa* 'table' appears in the accusative, in (22b) *aqua* 'water'. Let us call this the Object term.[11] Both construction types can be passivized, but in both cases it is the Obj term rather than the "oblique" term which will appear as the Subj of the passive construction.

Bolkestein now demonstrates that the choice between the two constructions is co-determined by discourse factors in the following way: if the 'table' (or something related to it) is the GivTop of the preceding discourse, then (22a) (or its passive alternative) will be strongly preferred; if 'water' is the GivTop,

---

10. There are other arguments for this assumption. For example, relativization is restricted to absolutive terms, and would violate the general "Accessibility Hierarchy" (Keenan—Comrie 1977), unless the absolutive is interpreted as the Subj of the construction. Cf. Dik (1980, chapter 5).

11. Although it is doubtful whether in Latin the Obj function in the FG sense is relevant.

then (22b) will be strongly preferred. This is called "backward harmony" by Bolkestein. There is also evidence for "forward harmony": if either 'table' or 'water' is introduced as a NewTop, then again (22a) or (22b) (or their passive alternatives) will correspondingly be preferred. The choice of construction is thus strongly co-determined by the topicality of the entities involved.

Backward harmony need not consist in strict referential identity. It may also be monitored through the GivTop-SubTop relation, as in the following example:

(23) Folia   *comburunt.*   Cinerem   *aspergunt   vino.*
      leaves-acc   burn-3pl   ashes-acc   sprinkle-3pl wine-dat
      'The leaves they burn. The ashes they sprinkle into the wine.'

Here the burning of the leaves makes available the SubTop 'ashes'; and this SubTop is treated as an Obj. An example of "forward harmony" is the following:

(24) ...*consedit.*   Panem   *oleo*   *aspersit.*
      ...he-sat-down.   bread-acc   oil-abl   he-sprinkled.
          Deinde ∅   *comedit.*
          then   he-ate
      'He sat down. He sprinkled bread with oil. Then he ate (it).'

Even if the bread has not been mentioned before, it will nevertheless preferably be treated as an Obj if it is going to return as a GivTop in the ensuing context.

(iii) *Switch reference*
Some languages have a "switch reference" system which may lead to oppositions such as the following from Wambon (a Papuan language described by De Vries 1985):

(25) a. *Nukhe*   *oie*   *hetag-mbelo*   *topkeka-lepo.*
         I   pig   see-SS   flee-1sg:past:final
         'Seeing a pig, I fled', 'I saw a pig and fled.'
     b. *Nukhe*   *oie*   *hetakha-levo*   *topkeka-tbo.*
         I   pig   see-1sg:non-fut:DS   flee-3sg:past:final
         'When I saw the pig, it fled.'

These constructions end in "final verbs", marked for all the relevant Tense distinctions, preceded by "medial verbs" which have no or less elaborate Tense marking, but are distinguished for "same subject" (SS) or "different subject" (DS). As a first approximation we can say that these forms signal that the subject of the next verb will be the same (as in (25a)) or different (as in (25b)) from the subject of the current verb.

This formulation is not fully adequate, however, as was demonstrated by Reesink (1983, 1987), since there may be switches of subject which do not lead to DS marking. Thus, one might find a sequence of the following form:

(26)   *Mountain go-up-SS, deer hunt-SS, catch-SS, sun set-SS, home returned-I.*
'I went up the mountain hunting deer; I caught one and, when the sun set, I returned home.'

Note that, although there is a subject switch from 'I' to 'the sun', this is not marked by a DS medial form. The point here seems to be that the setting of the sun does not break the topic chain: the speaker is the topic of the whole chain, and the sunset is only mentioned as a background circumstance for the sequence of events in which the speaker was involved. This means that the DS/SS marking could better be glossed as follows:

(27)   DS: in the next verb there will be a shift to a different Topic;
        SS: in the next verb there will be no shift to a different Topic.

On this interpretation, then, switch reference is a mechanism for signalling topical (dis)continuity.

(iv) *Obviation*
Obviation (a strategy best known from the Algonquian languages) concerns a grammatical distinction among third person participants into "proximate", "obviative", and sometimes "second / further obviative". These distinctions are coded in nouns, pronouns, and cross-referential elements on the predicate. When a third person participant is first introduced into the discourse as a NewTop, it will occur in proximate form; other third person participants will be placed in the obviative. A participant remains in the proximate as long as it is the GivTop of a disourse. In his discussion of obviation in Menomini, Bloomfield (1962: 38) formulates this as follows:

> The proximate third person represents the topic of discourse, the person nearest the speaker's point of view, or the person earlier spoken of and

already known.

Keeping a third person participant in the proximate is thus a means of securing topic continuity in a text. And shifting between proximate and obviative signals topic discontinuity, as in the following example from Cree (Wolfart—Carroll 1981: 27):

(28) a. *Nâpêw   nîso atimwa   wâpamêw.*
       man-prox   two dog-obv   see-3sg:prox
       'The man saw two dogs.'
   b. *Atimwak   ê-pimipahtâcik.*
       dog-prox-pl run-3pl:prox
       'The dogs were running.'
   c. *Êkwa   nâpêw   atimwa   ê-pimitisahwât.*
       then   man-prox   dog-obv   follow-3sg:prox
       'Then the man followed the dogs.'

In (28b) the dogs are temporarily promoted to the status of main Topic; in (28c) they are pushed back again by the man. Thus, as Wolfart—Carroll comment, proximate / obviative shifts "... reflect changes in the topic of discussion or, when a story is told, the shifts in focus which move the actors on and off the stage."

13.3.3. Given Topic and Sub-Topic

Once a certain entity has been introduced into the discourse as a NewTop, we may treat not only that entity as a GivTop, but also those entities which may be inferred from it on the basis of our knowledge of what is normally the case in the world. These entities may be called Sub-Topics of the GivTop. We gave an example of this in (8) above:

(8)   *John gave* a party *last week, but* the music *was awful.*

Given our knowledge that music is normally one of the features of a party, we may go on to talk about 'the music' as if it had been introduced into the discourse, once 'the party' has been established as a GivTop. A SubTop may be defined as a Topic which may be legitimately inferred[12] from a GivTop on the basis of our knowledge of what is normally the case in the world. Hannay (1985b: 53) formulates the GivTop-SubTop relation in the following way:

(29)   SUBTOP FORMATION
        If an entity X has been activated in the given setting, then the speaker may present an entity Y as a sub-Topic entity, if Y R X, where R is a relationship of inference.
(30)   SPECIFICATION OF THE R RELATION
        R = part of, member of, subset of, instance of, copy of, aspect of, opposite of, projection of, associated with, ...

Interestingly, the GivTop - SubTop relation works both ways, in the following sense: if an entity is connected to a GivTop through any of the R relations in (30), it may be treated as a SubTop in the further discourse; on the other hand, if some entity is treated as a SubTop, the interpreter will assume that there is some R relation involved, even where this is not immediately apparent. Hannay (1985b: 54) gives the following example of this:[13]

(31)   *John and Bill came to see me yesterday.* Fred's *just bought a new car.*

Suppose that 'Fred' has not been mentioned yet in the preceding discourse. Then the Addressee will assume that 'Fred' is in some way associated with 'John and Bill', and conclude that their seeing the Speaker will have something to do with Fred's buying a new car. For another such example, consider the following (from Clark—Clark 1977: 97):

(32)   *Patience walked into a room.* The chandeliers *burned brightly.*

Clearly, when a 'room' is introduced into the discourse, A can hardly be assumed to be able to infer 'chandeliers' as a potential SubTop. Rather, S speculates on A's ability to reconstruct the link between the chandeliers and the room AFTER the former have been mentioned. As Clark—Haviland (1974, 1977) have argued, language users are able to do so by building "bridging

---

12. Cf. Prince (1981) on "inferrables".
13. From Werth (1984).

assumptions" in order to connect one topical entity to another. In the case of (32), A can give coherence to the discourse through the bridging assumption 'the chandeliers must have been in the room'.

Haviland—Clark (1974) demonstrated by psycholinguistic means that the construction of such bridging assumptions takes time. For example, it takes longer to assign an interpretation to (33b) than to (33a):

(33) a. *Mary got some* beer *out of the car.* The beer *was warm.*
 b. *Mary got some* picnic supplies *out of the car.* The beer *was warm.*

In the latter, not in the former case, A has to construct a bridging assumption to the effect that 'the beer must have been among the picnic supplies'.

13.3.4. Resuming a Given Topic

When an entity has been introduced into the discourse, but has not been mentioned for some time, it may have to be revived or re-established in the form of a Resumed Topic (cf. Givón 1978). This will especially be the case when several different Topics (say, A and B) have been introduced, and the discourse has continued for some time about A; a shift to B will then require some strategy through which B is brought back onto the stage of the discourse. Such a strategy typically consists of the following elements:

 (i) some indication that a shift is made from one GivTop to another,

 (ii) a relatively strong form of anaphorical reference ("strong" in the sense of Grimes (1975) mentioned above), and

 (iii) an explicit or implicit indication of the fact that the entity has been mentioned before. Consider the following example:

(34) *John had a brother Peter and a sister Mary. Peter ...* [considerable episode about Peter]. *Now,* John's sister Mary, *who I mentioned before ....*

In this example, *now* signals a change of Topic, *John's sister Mary* is a strong form of anaphora, and *who I mentioned before* is the explicit reference to the fact that the entity was introduced earlier in the discourse.

This ends our discussion of topic management and its grammatical manifestations. As De Vries (1985) has argued, more research into the phenomenology of topicality is required in order to get a fuller picture of the strategies that languages may use in this domain. It is to be expected that at

13.4. Focus and focality[14]

The pragmatic function of Focus pertains to the focality dimension of discourse. The focal information in a linguistic expression is that information which is relatively the most important or salient in the given communicative setting, and considered by S to be most essential for A to integrate into his pragmatic information.

The focal information will thus concern the changes that S wishes to bring about in the pragmatic information of A. Such changes may take different forms: S may wish to ADD pieces of information to A's pragmatic information, or he may wish to REPLACE some piece of information X which he assumes A possesses by some piece of information Y which he possesses himself. In either case, there must be some difference between the pragmatic information of S, and S's picture of the pragmatic information of A, in other words, between P_S and $(P_A)_S$. Typically, then, the focal information in a linguistic expression pertains to the difference between P_S and $(P_A)_S$, and the focal information is thus presented as being "new" to A. However, the information focused on is not always completely new to A. S may also focus on a piece of information judged to be already available to A, in order to put special emphasis on that piece of information. In such cases there will usually be implicit or explicit contrast between that piece of information and some other piece of information which is either presupposed, or explicitly presented in the context. Compare:

(35) A: *I've just bought a Peugeot.*
 B: *Did you buy a PEUGEOT???*
(36) *John and Bill came to see me. JOHN was NICE, but BILL was rather BORING.*

In (35) B focuses on *Peugeot*, though this has just been mentioned by A. Apparently, B finds this information surprising in relation to other information

---

14. For this section I have especially made use of Watters (1979), Dik et al. (1981), Bossuyt (1982), Hannay (1983), De Vries (1985), Moutaouakil (1984), and Thwing—Watters (1987).

that he may have expected. In (36) the constituents *John* and *Bill* are emphasized, although they have already been introduced and may thus be assumed to be Given Topics to A. The focusing is here due to the contrast between the two parallel statements about 'John' and 'Bill'.

Because of such usages as these we should not all too easily identify Focus with "information new to A".

When constituents which contain focal information behave in special ways on account of their focality, these constituents will be assigned the pragmatic function Focus; this function may be divided into different sub-functions, as we shall see below.

Cross-linguistically speaking, the Focus function may manifest itself through one or more of the following focalizing devices:

(i) *prosodic prominence*: emphatic accent on (part of the) focused constituent;

(ii) *special constituent order*: special positions for Focus constituents in the linear order of the clause;

(iii) *special Focus markers*: particles which mark off the Focus constituent from the rest of the clause.

(iv) *special Focus constructions*: constructions which intrinsically define a specific constituent as having the Focus function.

Examples of these various coding devices will be given in the further course of this chapter.[15]

Note that Focus may be expressed through, but is not to be equated with, "accent": prosodic prominence is one of the means (though a common one) through which Focus may be expressed (compare 18.2.5.2. below). In principle, however, there is a certain "trade-off" between the various coding devices mentioned in (i)-(iv): when Focus is expressed by any of (ii)-(iv), it is not necessarily also marked by prosodic prominence. This can be seen in the following way. Suppose we have a language with basic SVO order in which we want to express that John loves Mary (with Focus on Mary). We may then find such expressions as the following:

(37) a. *John love MARY.* [prosodic prominence on *Mary*]
 b. *MARY John love.* [special initial position for *Mary*]
 c. *John love FM MARY.* [a special Focus marker FM]
 d. *(it) (be) MARY (who) John love.* [a special Focus construction]

---

15. Focus constructions (such as cleft and pseudo-cleft constructions) will be discussed in *TFG2*: chapters 13-14.

Only in (37a) is prosodic prominence the ONLY expression device for Focus. In (37b-d), where Focus is already marked in other ways, we may indeed find that it is ALSO marked by prosodic prominence, but this is not necessary, and if it occurs the prosodic prominence may be less outspoken than in (37a). Nevertheless we can say that (37a-d) may achieve the same or similar effects in lending Focus to *Mary*. For reasons of typological adequacy, then, the pragmatic function of Focus must be distinguished from its possible manifestation in the form of prosodic prominence.[16]

13.4.1. Question-Answer pairs

It is easiest to illustrate the operation of Focus assignment with question-word questions and the answers given to such questions. Consider the following sequence:

(38) X: *Where is John going?*
　　Y: (a) *John is going to the* MARKET.
　　　　(b) *To the* MARKET.

Through his question, X signals (i) that he presumes that John is going somewhere, (ii) that he does not know where John is going, (iii) that he presumes that Y knows where John is going, (iv) that he wishes that Y should tell him where John is going.

The question can thus be compared to an "open form" of the following kind:

(39)　　*John is going to _____;*
　　　　Please fill in the blank.

In other words, a Q-word question is a means for signalling that one has some gap in one's information, and for requesting A to fill in this gap. It is clear that the question word (*where* in (38)) is the element which signals and identifies the gap in X's information, and thus pertains to the presumed difference between P_S and $(P_A)_S$. Therefore, the question word is the focal element in the

---

16. Interestingly, tone languages, which already use prosodic prominence for lexical and grammatical purposes, tend to use devices (ii)-(iv) rather than just accentuation for expressing Focus. For further discussion, see chapter 18.

question. Indeed, if a language has special strategies for the expression of Focus constituents, these strategies will typically be also used for question words.

Now consider the answers in (38). Through X's question Y now knows the nature of X's information gap. If Y possesses the requested information, and is prepared to share it with X, he may answer as in (38a) or (38b). In the case of (38b), Y provides just that information which is sufficient to fill X's information gap. It is evident that the constituent *to the market* as a whole pertains to the difference in pragmatic information between S and A, and will therefore be assigned Focus function.

In (38a), Y chooses to repeat the "open form" which has been handed to him through X's question. Here again, it is the constituent *to the market* which contains the focal information and may be assigned Focus function.

We shall represent a Q-constituent as (Qx_i), with a specification of the semantic function involved.[17] We can thus represent the question-answer sequence in (38) as:

(40) X: Int E_i: X_i: Pres e_i: Progr *go* [V] *(John)*$_{\text{AgSubjGivTop}}$ $(Qx_i)_{\text{DirFoc}}$
   Y: (a) Decl E_j: X_j: Pres e_j: Progr *go* [V] *(John)*$_{\text{AgSubjGivTop}}$ $(d1x_i:$ *market*$_N)_{\text{DirFoc}}$
   (b) Decl E_j: X_j: e_j: $(d1x_i:$ *market*$_N)_{\text{DirFoc}}$

The structure of (40(b)) is meant to express that, although Y only produces the term *to the market*, this term is nevertheless to be understood as representing a declarative speech act E_j, bearing on a proposition X_j, specified by an SoA e_j, specified by a predication of which only the term *to the market* is made explicit. The rest of that predication must be and can be reconstructed from the context, i.e. from the question posed. In this way, we avoid the deletion of specified material (cf. 1.6.1. above), while still accounting for the communicative status of the constituent *to the market*. The status of such answers as these is comparable to converting a query such as (41a) into (41b) through writing '51' in the blank space:

(41) a. Age: _____
   b. Age: _____51_____

Just as we do not have to say that writing '51' in (41) is a reduced form of

---

17. See *TFG2*: chapter 12.

writing 'My age is 51', so we do not have to say that answering 'To the market' is a reduction of 'John is going to the market'. If anything, the latter should rather be seen as an expanded form of the former.

We can now say that a Q-word question is an open predication in x_i, presented with interrogative illocution, and signalling a request from S to A to fill in the open position, marked by Q, with appropriate information.

13.4.2. Different types of Focus[18]

Certain languages have rather elaborate Focus systems, and use different formal strategies for different types of Focus. Such languages require a subdivision of the Focus function in order to trigger these different types of Focus. The main parameters for the subcategorization of Focus are:
— The "scope" of the Focus function, i.e. the question of what part of the underlying clause structure is placed in Focus;
— The "communicative point" of the focusing, i.e. the question of what pragmatic reasons underlie the assignment of Focus to the relevant part of the underlying clause structure.

13.4.2.1. Differences of scope. So far we have only given examples in which Focus was on one or more terms of the underlying predication. In fact, however, Focus may be assigned to any part of the underlying clause structure, as is clear from the following examples:

(42) a. *I prefer the GREEN car.*
    [Focus on restrictor]
  b. *I should like to have TWO cars.*
    [Focus on term operator]
  c. *John HASn't painted the house, he IS painting it right now.*
    [Focus on predication and predicate operators]
  d. *I didn't PAINT the house, I REpainted it.*
    [Focus on the predicate; on part of the predicate]

---

18. This section was strongly inspired by two detailed studies of Focus strategies in two African languages, by Watters (1979) and Thwing—Watters (1987), and by the studies of Moutaouakil (1984, 1989) on focusing strategies in Arabic.

As far as present information goes, the following differences in scope may lead to different focusing strategies:

(43)
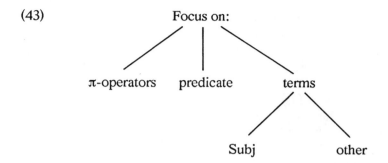

Thus, languages may have different focusing strategies according to whether Focus is placed on π-operators (in particular, on Tense, Mood, Aspect, and Polarity operators), on the predicate, or on terms; in the latter case, there may be a difference in strategy between focusing on the Subject or on other terms. Focus on the Polarity may be illustrated by the following examples:

(44) X: *Peter solved the problem.*
   Y: *He did NOT solve the problem.*
   X: *He DID solve the problem.*

13.4.2.2. Differences in communicative point. When Focus strategies are distinguished according to communicative point, the following distinctions may be relevant:[19]

(45)
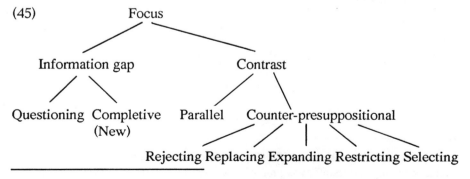

---

19. For the addition of Questioning and Rejecting Focus to earlier schemas see Moutaouakil (1989).

Thus, the communicative point of Focus assignment may either concern an information gap on the part of the speaker, or reside in some kind of contrast. In the former case the point may lie in the questioning of the information gap, or in the presentation of new information filling in such a gap. This is the case in the question-answer pairs discussed in 13.4.1. above. It applies not only to Q-word questions, but also to Yes/No-questions, in which case the Focus is on the truth value of the proposition. We may here speak of Questioning Focus and Completive Focus.

All other Focus types in (45) involve some kind of contrast between the Focus constituent and alternative pieces of information which may be explicitly presented or presupposed. "Parallel Focus" is assigned to corresponding constituents in parallel constructions, as in (36) above. In the other contrastive Focus types, the information presented is opposed to other, similar information which S presupposes to be entertained by A. These may be called cases of "counter-presuppositional" Focus.[20] The different subtypes mentioned in (45) may be clarified and distinguished from Questioning and Completive Focus as in Figure 7 (cf. Dik et al. 1981, Watters 1979).

Type of Focus	P_S	$(P_A)_S$	Expression
Questioning	????	X	????
Completive	X	????	X!
Rejecting	not X	X	not X!
Replacing	Y	X	(not X, but) Y!
Expanding	X and Y	X	also Y!
Restricting	X	X and Y	only X!
Selecting	X	X or Y	X!

Figure 7. Focus types in terms of communicative point

---

20. This is what Watters (1979) termed "counter-assertive" Focus. The term "counter-presuppositional" was preferred to this in Dik et al. (1981), because the information which S responds to need not have been asserted by A: it is sufficient that S supposes that A believes that information.

Let us consider these various types of Focus one by one.

(i) *Questioning Focus*
In the case of Questioning Focus S has an information gap for which he presumes A has a piece of information X. S will ask a Yes/No or a Question-word question.

(ii) *Completive Focus*
In the case of Completive Focus S (now: the answerer) has a specific piece of information X for which he presumes A has an information gap. S will fill in A's information gap with X.

(iii) *Rejecting Focus*
In the case of Rejecting Focus S presumes A has a piece of information X for which S has not-X. S corrects A's piece of information by rejecting it:

(46) A: *John bought apples.*
    B: *No, he didn't buy APPLES.*

(iv) *Replacing Focus*
In the case of Replacing Focus S presumes that A possesses some incorrect piece of information X, which is to be replaced by some correct piece of information Y:

(47) A: *John bought apples.*
    S: *No, he bought BANANAS.*

Rejecting Focus and Replacing Focus will often be combined, as in:

(48) A: *John bought apples.*
    B: (a) *No, he didn't buy APPLES, he bought BANANAS.*
       (b) *No, he bought BANANAS, not APPLES.*

(v) *Expanding Focus*
In the case of Expanding Focus S presumes that A possesses a correct piece of information X, but that X is not complete. S knows that there is at least one piece of information Y which it is also relevant for A to know. Consider the following example:

(49) A: *John bought apples.*
　　S: (a) *John not only bought APPLES, he also bought BANANAS.*
　　　 (b) *Yes, but he also bought BANANAS.*

(vi) *Restricting Focus*
In the case of Restricting Focus S presumes that A possesses a correct piece of information X, but also (incorrectly) believes that Y is the case. Consider the following example:

(50) A: *John bought apples and bananas.*
　　S: (a) *No, he didn't buy BANANAS, he only bought APPLES.*
　　　 (b) *No, he only bought APPLES.*

In a case of this type, then, S corrects the presumed pragmatic information of A by restricting a set of presumed items to those items which he considers to be correct values for the position involved.

(vii) *Selecting Focus*
S presumes that A believes that X or Y is correct, but does not know which. Usually, such a presupposition would be created through a disjunctive question of A's:

(51) A: *Would you like coffee or tea?*
　　S: *COFFEE, please.*

S thus selects a correct piece of information from a list of possibilities offered by A. Obviously, in this case too the relevant presupposition may be formed without a specific disjunctive question having been asked.

The examples given above are all cases of Focus with term scope. When other parts of the predication are in scope, we find the same subtypes. Compare the following examples with Focus on the predicate:[21]

---

21. In most languages it is not possible to straightforwardly question the predicate. This will be discussed in *TFG2*: chapter 12.

(52) a. Questioning Focus
   A: *What have you done with my money?*
  b. Completive Focus
   S: *I SPENT it.*
  c. Rejecting Focus
   A: *John grows potatoes.*
   S: *No, he doesn't GROW them.*
  d. Replacing Focus
   A: *John grows potatoes.*
   S: *No, he SELLS them.*
  e. Expanding Focus
   A: *John grows bananas.*
   B: *He also SELLS them.*
  f. Restricting Focus
   A: *It seems John grows and sells potatoes.*
   S: *No, he only SELLS them.*
  g. Selecting Focus
   A: *Are you going to rent or buy a car?*
   S: *I'm going to BUY one.*

13.4.3. The role of Focus in a grammar

In the preceding sections we have surveyed the various circumstances in which Focus function might be assigned to different parts of underlying clause structure. This might be considered a survey of the "etics" of focality. Another question is to determine the "emics" of focality, i.e. which distinctions must be integrated into a grammar to account for the different focalizing strategies found in a language (cf. De Vries 1985). When studying this question we find that Focus is probably relevant to the grammar of all languages, but that languages may differ in the way in which they "cut up the cake", and in the degree of detail required within the domain of Focus. These differences may be illustrated by brief descriptions of the Focus system of two languages which are rather far apart in this respect.

(i) *Focus in Wambon.*
The Focus system of Wambon, a Papuan language of Irian Jaya, was described by De Vries (1985). Wambon illustrates the fundamental unity of the different types of Focus, in the sense that it has one undifferentiated Focus

marker *-nde*, which marks constituents for different types of focality. It marks question words and the constituents answering these (Questioning and Completive Focus):

(53) A: *Jakhove   kenonop*-nde *takhim-gende?*
        they   what-Foc   buy-3pl:pres:final
        'What do they buy?'
   B: *Ndu*-nde *takhim-gende.*
        sago-Foc   buy-3pl:pres:final
        'They buy SAGO.'

It also marks the constituents involved in Rejecting and Replacing Focus:

(54) A: *Mbitemop   ndune   ande-tbo.*
        Bitemop   sago   eat-3sg:past:final
        'Bitemop ate sago.'
   B: *Woyo,   nekheve   ndu*-nde *e-nogma-tbo*
        no   he   sago-Foc neg-eat-3sg:past:final
        'No, he didn't eat SAGO,
        nekheve   ande-nde *ande-tbo.*
        he   banana-Foc eat-3sg:past:final
        he ate BANANAS.'

The same suffix can also be used to mark two GivTops which stand in contrast with each other:

(55) A: *Nombone   ndu-ngup   ande-ngup?*
        this   sago-and   banana-and
        'What about this sago and bananas?'
   B: *Wembane   ndu*-nde *takhima-tbo,*
        Wemba   sago-Foc buy-3sg:past:final
        'Wemba bought the SAGO,
        Karolule   ande-nde   *takhima-tbo.*
        Karolus   bananas-Foc buy-3sg:past:final
        Karolus bought the BANANAS.'

Wambon *-nde* is thus a general, multi-purpose Focus marker.

(ii) *Focus in Aghem.*
Aghem, a Grassfields Bantu language of Cameroon, as described by Watters

(1979), has a rich Focus system with a number of different strategies corresponding to differences in scope and communicative point. Aghem requires at least the following Focus types to be distinguished:

(56) FOCUS TYPES IN AGHEM
1. Questioning and Completive Focus
 1.1. On terms / predicate
 1.2. On polarity (π-operators)
2. Replacing Focus
 2.1. On terms / predicate
 2.2. On polarity (π-operators)
3. Restricting Focus

Being a tone language, Aghem does not use intonational prominence to express Focus. Instead, it uses different combinations of the following devices: (a) special constituent order, (b) a Focus marking particle, (c) a special Focus-bound Past tense marker, (d) a cleft construction.

The basic constituent ordering pattern of Aghem is as follows:

(57)   S Aux PØ V Pa O X

with designated positions for Subj (S), Auxiliary (Aux), Verb (V), Obj (O), and "other constituents" (X), and two "special positions" immediately before (PØ) and immediately after (Pa) the verb. The main rules for the expression of the different Focus types can now be summarized as follows:

(R1) Any Focus term, whether questioned or non-questioned, goes to Pa.
(R2) When the Focus term in Pa is not the Subj, then one or two Given Topic constituents (also non-Subj) may be placed in PØ. The resulting construction expresses Replacing rather than Completive Focus.
(R3) When the Focus term in Pa is the Subj, then there may be further Focus terms in X or PØ. This expresses multiple Completive Focus (*Who met who? JOHN met BILL.*). Multiple Focus is possible only if at least the Subj is in Focus.
(R4) When the Focus-bound Past marker is placed in Aux, this signals Focus on the polarity.
(R5) When in that condition all verbal complements are placed in PØ, so that the V is in final position, this signals Replacing rather than Completive Focus on the polarity (*John DID meet Bill*).

(R6) When the special Focus marker *nò* is placed after a constituent to the right of and including the verb, it adds the value "Replacing" to that constituent; if the constituent already has this value on other grounds, it adds the value "Restricting" (*Only JOHN met Bill.*).

(R7) The cleft construction is used only for Restricting Focus.

For further details on this intricate Focus system, I refer to Watters (1979). A similar system, confirming many of the distinctions made by Watters, is described for Vute in Thwing—Watters (1987). Note that, if better-known languages were analysed in comparable detail from the point of view of Focus, they might well turn out to have more intricate strategies than is commonly assumed.

14. Expression rules

14.0. Introduction

In the preceding chapters we have seen how fully specified underlying clause structures can be built up within the framework of FG. These clause structures should be such that they contain all the elements which are needed to specify the semantic content of the clause on the one hand, and the form in which it can be expressed on the other. In this chapter and the following we concentrate on the way in which the abstract underlying clause structures can be mapped onto actual linguistic expressions. This mapping will be effected by *expression rules*, which determine the form,[1] the order, and the intonation contour of the constituents, given their structural and functional status within the underlying structure of the clause.

We discuss the expression component of FG from a "productive" point of view, as if we were building a natural language generator which had actual linguistic expressions as its final output. It should be understood that in a full-scale model of the Natural Language User, the expression component should also be capable of operating in the reverse direction. Thus, in a natural language parser, it should be possible to implement the expression component in such a way that, given a linguistic expression, it is able to reconstruct the structure underlying that expression.

This two-directional usage of the expression component has been implemented in ProfGlot, a multilingual implementation of Functional Grammar in the programming language Prolog (Dik 1992). Although the discussion of the expression component in this and the following chapters is not cast in a computational format, it incorporates many ideas which have been developed through, and operationalized in, this computer implementation.

The discussion of the expression component is organized as follows:

Chapter 14: General properties of expression rules and their interrelations.

Chapter 15: The formal expression of terms, predicates, and other constituents under the influence of the various functions and operators which they

---

1. We restrict the notion "form" to the segmental form of constituents. All features pertaining to the suprasegmental, prosodic, or intonational form of linguistic expressions will be treated together in chapter 18.

carry in underlying clause structure.

Chapter 16/17: The nature of the expression rules which determine the order of constituents in the clause.

Chapter 18: The expression rules which determine the prosodic contour of the linguistic expression.

In the present chapter we discuss the following general features of the expression component: the interaction between the different types of expression rules (14.1.); the notions of productivity, rule, and regularity (14.2.); the principle of "lexical priority" (14.3.); the representation of irregular forms in the lexicon (14.4.); the place of morphology in the FG-model and the distinction between derivation and inflection (14.5.); and the general format of form-determining expression rules (14.6.).

14.1. Interactions between different types of expression rules

There are various interactions between expression rules of different types. Consider the possible relations between the (segmental) form of constituents and the order in which they appear. In a considerable number of cases, the form and the order of constituents can be defined independently: the form does not vary with the order, and the order does not vary with the form. Compare:

(1) a. *John saw a cat in the garden.*
    b. *In the garden John saw a cat.*

We see that the constituents have exactly the same segmental form in either order of constituents. In such cases where form and order are independent of each other, we could first determine the form and then the order, or first the order and then the form, without any observable difference in the final output.

In other cases, however, there is a dependency between form and order, such that either the order of constituents is co-dependent on their form, or the form of constituents is co-dependent on their order. Such cases require a "sandwich" application of expression rules, such that first certain aspects of the form of constituents are determined, then the ordering to the extent that it is form-dependent, and then again further aspects of the form which are order-dependent. Form-dependent ordering is involved when alternative orders of constituents depend on the form these constituents take. Consider the following example from French:

(2) a. *Jean voyait* le chat *dans le jardin.*
   'John saw the cat in the garden.'
   b. **Jean voyait* le *dans le jardin.*
   c. *Jean* le *voyait dans le jardin.*
   'John saw it in the garden.'

The object constituent must be preposed to the verb if it takes clitic form, but postposed when it takes the form of a full noun phrase. This means that it must at least be known whether the object takes clitic form before it can be placed in the correct position. Note that FG does not allow movement of constituents from one position to another, so that it is impossible to first generate (2b) and then derive (2c) from this through a rule of clitic movement. Rather, the information that a constituent takes the form of a clitic must be available when it is determined in which position that constituent is to be placed.

Order-dependent form specification is involved in a case such as the expression of the second person singular present tense form in Dutch:

(3) a. *Je* ziet *een kat in de tuin.*
   'You see a cat in the garden.'
   b. *In de tuin* zie *je een kat.*
   'In the garden you see a cat.'

Note that the verb takes a final ending -*t* when it follows, but not when it precedes the subject. This difference only holds for the second person singular. Here it seems intuitively clear that the formal difference is a consequence of the ordering, rather than the other way around. Similar order-dependent formal specification is involved in so-called "sandhi" and "liaison" phenomena, as in the following French example:

(4) a. *un grand homme* /õe-grãt-om/
   'a great man'
   b. *un homme grand* /õen-om-grã/
   'a big man'

Note that the article ends in /n/ and the adjective ends in /t/ when they precede a vowel-initial form, but not when this is not the case.

In such cases as these the order must have been fixed before the form can be determined. Note that since FG does not allow deletion of specific material, it is not possible to start with /õen/ and /grãt/ wherever they occur, and then apply /n/- or /t/-deletion when the next constituent starts with a consonant.

342   *Expression rules*

Also, such a description would be rather counterintuitive, since the INTRODUCTION of a consonant can be functionally understood as a means of avoiding or bridging a hiatus between two vowels, while the deletion of word-final consonants before consonant-initial words would seem to have no functional explanation.

In the ProfGlot program, the above considerations have led to the following design:

(5) (i) apply all form-determining rules except those of (iii),
 (ii) apply the ordering rules,
 (iii) apply the form-determining rules which are essentially dependent on order (such as sandhi rules).

After (5i) all information about the underlying clause structure is "forgotten", except that information which is necessary in order to trigger the ordering rules.

14.2. Productivity; rules and regularities

We make a basic distinction between forms which a speaker must learn and memorize as such if he is to be able to use them correctly, and forms which a competent speaker may form on his own account, even if he has never heard them before, and which will naturally be understood and accepted by a competent addressee. All expressions of the former type will be stored in the lexicon. Only expressions of the latter, productive type will be described by means of rules.

For example, if a speaker of English had not memorized the form *thought* as the past tense of *think*, he would never be able to correctly derive that form on his own account. Thus, the form *thought* must be stored in the lexicon as a "ready-made" past tense of the verb *think*. On the other hand, if a competent speaker of English has never heard the past tense of the verb *ingeminate*, he will nevertheless be able to correctly produce the form *ingeminated*, and no addressee will reject that form as being non-English. *Ingeminated* can be productively formed by general rule, and need not be stored in the lexicon. Rules thus capture "productive" processes, processes which speakers may apply in creating formations which they may never have heard before.

This formulation needs several qualifications. First, it may well be the case that a speaker knows a form as such, ready-made, even though he is also able to produce it by productive rule. It might well be, for example, that the plural form *books* is stored as such, and is not formed anew each time it is used. In a functional grammar of English, however, this form need not be stored, because it CAN be formed by general rule. The lexicon will thus contain those forms which a speaker must NECESSARILY know if he is to be able to use them correctly.

Second, speakers may incidentally use new expressions which are nevertheless not formed by productive rule. This is the case when new words are created which are not derivable by general rule (e.g. *punk, chip*), or when non-productive formations are incidentally extended to new creations (e.g. *cheeseburger, wash-o-matic*). Such formations, however, can be characterized as intentional innovations and will be recognized as incidental and often facetious additions to the lexicon. For this reason, the notion of productivity must include, as a defining feature, that the expressions formed by productive rule are such that their (potential) novelty remains unnoticed by both speaker and addressee.[2]

Third, if an expression, on the basis of these criteria, is stored in the lexicon, this does not mean that it may not display certain form-meaning correspondences with other, related forms. Consider the verbal pattern *begin-began-begun*. No speaker who has not learned that the past tense of *begin* is *began* could correctly and unintentionally create this form on his own account. Nevertheless, there is a series of verbs in English which have precisely the same pattern:[3]

(6)   *begin, drink, ring, shrink, sing, spring, stink, swim*

One could easily formulate a "rule" to capture the regular patterning of this group of verbs, as in:

(7)   present *-i-* : past *-a-* : past participle *-u-*

and define the verbs of (6) as input to this rule, so that the past tense and past participle forms would be correctly derived. This would appear to be all the more compelling since the pattern of (7) has historically extended to some verbs which originally had a different paradigm (such as *ring*), and since some speakers occasionally use forms such as *bring-brang-brung* which do not fall under this pattern.

---

2. For this point, see Schultink (1961: 113), Uhlenbeck (1978: 4).
3. See Quirk et al. (1972: 119).

Skousen (1975: 20), who otherwise restricts the notion of rule to those regularities which "speakers are accounting for", considers these two facts as sufficient reason to set up a synchronically productive rule for pattern (7). I do not follow him in this respect, since the pattern is not freely and unintentionally applicable to any verb with stem-vowel -*i*-, and since the occasional extensions have an incidental character, even if some of them have worked their way into the grammar of English. Note that even if the pattern of (7) is formulated in a "rule", this rule will have to be lexically governed in the sense that it requires a specification of just those verbs to which it applies. Our more restricted usage of the term "rule" entails that we do not accept rules that are lexically governed in this sense: each rule must be capable of being formulated without mention of the specific lexical items to which it may be applied.

I therefore assume that the verbs in (6) are stored in the lexicon together with their past tense and past participle forms, and that their common patterning constitutes a "regularity" within the lexicon. Regularities of this type usually go unnoticed,[4] but may occasionally be "abstracted" from the relevant forms, and then lead to incidental innovations of the type of *bring-brang-brung*.[5]

On the other hand, productive processes will be captured by means of rules in which no specific lexical items are mentioned. For example, the productive rule of past tense formation in English will get some such form as:

(8)   Past [pred [V]] = pred-ed

The input to this rule can in principle be any verbal predicate, and the output is regularly formed qua form and qua meaning. It is clear, however, that rule (8) may not apply to those verbs for which a non-productive past tense form

---

4. Note that native speakers are notoriously unable to enumerate such lists as (6).
5. It is possible that an element of hypercorrection plays a role in this abstraction process. In studying the production of inflectional forms of nonsense words, Berko (1958) found that children tend to follow the productive rule, whereas adults tend to extend non-productive patterns. Thus, when asked for the relevant forms of a verb like *gling*, almost all children come up with *glinged*, while adults strongly favour such forms as *glang* - *glung*. This difference might in part be an artefact of the test situation: adults might think that the answer will probably be "difficult" and non-obvious, while children would more spontaneously respond in terms of their developing knowledge of the language.

has been specified in the lexicon, otherwise we would get output such as *thinked and *maked. This undesired output can be avoided through a general principle of "lexical priority".

14.3. Lexical priority

The principle of lexical priority can provisionally be formulated as follows:

(9) Whenever a rule is encountered of the general form: M [X] = Y, where Y is the form of X under the operation M, first check the lexicon to see whether the M form of X is stored there ready-made. If so, select this form; otherwise apply the rule.

For example, under the entry for *think* we find the information Past = *thought*, and the choice of this form on account of lexical priority will block the operation of rule (8).

Note that children at a certain age tend to over-generalize such productive rules as (8), and produce *thinked* rather than *thought*. In our approach this might mean two different things: (i) the form *thought* is not yet, or no longer stored in the lexicon, or (ii) the principle of lexical priority is neglected.

14.4. The representation of non-productive forms

I will assume that if a predicate has irregular forms, these will be stored in a *paradigm* associated with this predicate. In the case of a predicate like *sing* this can be represented as follows:

(10) *sing* [V] $(x_1:\text{<anim>})_{Ag}$ $(x_2:\text{<song>})_{Go}$
paradigm(*sing*,[Past=*sang*,PaP=*sung*])

The paradigm thus informs us that the Past tense form of *sing* is *sang*, and the Past Participle *sung*. We can now implement the principle of lexical priority in such a way that when we need the Past tense form of *sing*, the ready-made form *sang* will be lifted out of its associated paradigm, which will then block the operation of rule (8). On the other hand, in the case of a regular verb there will be no associated paradigm, and the regular rule for Past tense formation will be applied.

In the simplest, most productive case, the predicate will have only a single form, from which all the other forms can be derived by rule. This applies, for example, to the verbal predicate *look*, and to nominal predicates such as *book*. At the other extreme we find a limited number of verbs for which almost all forms have to be specified in a paradigm. Thus, the verb *be* requires specification of the forms *be, am, are, is, was, were,* and *been*, each of them characterized for the grammatical circumstances in which they appear.

For each predicate the lexicon will thus contain the smallest and most simple set of forms from which all the other forms of the predicate can be derived by productive rule. These simplest forms may coincide with words, such as *sang* and *sung* in (10). Or they may take the form of stems which cannot by themselves be used as words, but serve as input to productive rules which derive words. Consider the opposition between *knife* and *knives*. The plural form cannot be directly derived from the singular by productive rule (this would yield **knifes*), nor can the singular be productively derived from the plural stem, since English has no productive rule of word-final consonant devoicing. It follows that both forms have to be specified in the lexicon. However, the plural form *knives* is not fully unpredictable: once we know that the plural stem is *knive-*, the plural form can be productively derived. The lexical entry for *knife* could thus take the following form:

(11)   *knife* [N]
       paradigm(*knife*,[pl=*knive-*])

The possibility that an unpredictable stem rather than a word is listed in the paradigm requires a slight modification of the principle of lexical priority as formulated in (9), in the following way:

(12) (i) if a ready-made *word* is found, select that word;
     (ii) if a ready-made *stem* is found, apply the relevant rule to that stem;
     (iii) otherwise, apply the rule to the basic form of the predicate.

There is reason to assume that the basic form of a predicate is always a stem, even though it may coincide with one or more forms which can also be used as words. Consider the basic form of the nominal predicate *book*. This form not only yields the singular form, but can also be used in compounds such as *bookstore, bookshelf, book-keeper,* etc. In these compounds, the basic form does not have the value "singular"; rather, it is neutral as to number. We must thus store the stem *book-* in the predicate frame, and formulate the following rule of singular noun formation, which turns the stem into a word of the same form:[6]

(13)   sg [pred [N]] = pred

Similarly, the word *look* can be the non-third person Present tense form of the verb, but also the imperative or the infinitive. We shall say that none of these forms is derived from any of the others: all of them are derived from the neutral stem *look-*, which also enters into such forms as *looked* and *looking*.

We thus reject the idea, advanced in Aronoff (1976), that all morphological rules should be word-based. We assume, on the contrary, that all such rules are stem-based, even in cases where the word formally coincides with the stem from which it is derived. In a language like English many words happen to coincide with stems. But in other languages, which have a more complex derivational and inflectional morphology, such formal identity is the exception rather than the rule. In a language such as Latin, for example, each verbal predicate may occur in some 250 different inflectional forms, none of which coincides with the stem from which they can be derived. For such a language, a word-based morphology breaks down immediately.

It may be objected to the present analysis of non-productive forms that it contains a certain amount of redundancy and does not make all the relevant generalizations. Consider again the form of the predicate *knife*:

(14)   *knife* [N]
         paradigm(*knife*,[pl=*knive*-])

What this representation does not express is that it is only in the final segment that there is any difference between the singular and the plural stem, and therefore no difference is made between such configurations as (14) and those in which there is nothing in common between different forms of the same predicate (as in *go* vs. *went*, which stand in a so-called "suppletive" relation to each other). This objection could be met by devising a more parsimonious representation for predicates such as (14), such that only the differences between the various forms of the predicate are specified, and no information is coded twice. This could, for example, be done as in:

---

6. This rule can be seen as an identity operation on the stem to yield the word in question.

(15)   paradigm(n a i f, [pl= ... v-])

And if we think of the forms of the predicate as being represented in some kind of phonological feature notation, a feature [+voice] would even be sufficient to differentiate the plural stem from the basic stem. In this way it is possible to list all the non-predictable forms of a predicate, while at the same time avoiding redundancy or underspecification of the similarities between the different forms.

14.5. The place of morphology in a Functional Grammar

Morphology is traditionally defined as dealing with the internal grammatical structure of words. What is the place of morphology, in this sense, within the model of FG (cf. Watters (1985))?

Morphological structure is not considered to be a unified phenomenon in FG: there is no single component in the grammar which deals with ALL and ONLY the word-internal grammatical structures. There is no component which deals with ALL aspects of word-internal grammatical structure because the information which may finally be mapped into the structure of words is judged to spring from different sources in the overall fabric of the grammar. And there is no component which deals with ONLY word-internal grammatical structure because the expression rules which serve to express certain features synthetically within a single word may also express such features analytically through a combination of words.

In order to clarify the issue, a first distinction must be made between complex words which can be productively formed and complex words which cannot be productively formed. Non-productive complex words will be listed in the lexicon. Consider a complex word such as *blackbird*. Within this word, two morphemes can be easily distinguished; but there is no rule through which this word could be productively formed (with this meaning). Therefore, the internal structure of this word is a matter of a regularity in the lexicon rather than of productive morphological rule.

In the case of productively formed words we can make a distinction between their abstract, underlying structure and their final surface form. The difference can be illustrated as follows:

(16)   ABSTRACT STRUCTURE   SURFACE FORM
        sg [book]   book
        pl [book]   book-s
        pres 3 sg [walk]   walk-s
        pres part [walk]   walk-ing
        ag nom [walk]   walk-er
        pl [ag nom [walk]]   walk-er-s

Thus, we can think of the abstract structure as consisting of certain operators (such as "singular", "plural", "past", "present participle", "agent nominalization"), applied to the basic forms of predicates as they are stored in the lexicon. I will assume that the relation between the abstract structure and the surface form is always mediated by the expression rules, which will thus take a general form such as:

(17)   Op [A] = B,
        where B is the form of A under the operation of the Operator(s) Op

The abstract structure of a complex word, however, may arise in different ways, and in different components of the grammar.

At this point we make a distinction between *predicate formation rules* and *inflectional rules*. Predicate formation rules serve to create predicate frames out of predicate frames. In (18), for example, an agent noun is derived from a verbal action predicate:

(18)   Input: pred [V,act] (args)
        Output: [ag nom [pred]] [N]

In *TFG2*: chapter 1 it will be argued that all predicate formation rules serve to create such abstract underlying structures. The form which these structures are going to take (e.g. the fact that [ag nom [walk]] is expressed as *walker*) will be determined by the expression rules. Predicate formation rules which create complex words may be derivational, as in *walker*; they may be compositional, as in *doorbell*; or they may combine the two formation principles, as in *doorkeeper*. But predicate formation rules may also create analytic derived predicates which consist of separate words. This can be illustrated with the formation of causatives, which may be expressed synthetically in one language (e.g. Turkish *öl-* 'die' vs. *öl-dür-* 'die-cause' = 'kill'), but analytically, by means of an auxiliary verb, in another (e.g. French *marcher* 'walk' vs. *faire marcher* 'let, make walk').

In the construction of underlying term and clause structures, derived predicate frames can be used in the same way as basic predicate frames. For example, term structure (19a) is built from the derived predicate [ag nom [walk]] just as term structure (19b) is built from the basic predicate *boy*:

(19) a.   (d pl x_i: [ag nom [*walk*]] [N])   -->   *the walkers*
     b.   (d pl x_i: *boy* [N])   -->   *the boys*

In the construction of these underlying term structures, various operators, such as "d" and "pl", will be applied to the basic or derived predicates in question. Through the inflectional expression rules, these operators will have their impact on the final form of the term, and again this impact may either be synthetic, as in (20a), or analytic, as in (20b):

(20) a.   pl [*boy*] = *boy-s*
     b.   d [*boy-s*] = *the boy-s*

Thus, inflectional rules may either lead to complex words, or to combinations of words. Only in the former case do they belong to morphology in the traditional sense. Whether inflectional rules result in synthetic or analytic expressions is in part a language-dependent matter. For example, English and Danish differ in analytic vs. synthetic expression of definiteness in such cases as:

(21) a.   d [*boy*] = *the boy*
     b.   d [*dreng*] = *dreng-en*

For similar differences in inflectional expression rules, consider the formation of the passive voice. In some languages, such as Latin, the passive voice is expressed synthetically (as in *amatur* '3 sg is loved'), while in others it is expressed analytically, as in English *is loved*. Even within the same language such differences may exist side by side. Thus, Latin has analytic expression of the passive in the Perfect, as in *amatus est* 'he has been loved'. Such differences as these demonstrate that a grammatical theory would lose in generalizing power and in typological adequacy if word-internal structure were treated as categorically different from word-external structure, and if an all too water-tight division were made between morphology and syntax.

The question of where morphology (in the sense of word-internal grammatical structure) is accounted for in FG can thus be answered as follows:

(i) Morphologically complex items are found in the lexicon if their formation is non-productive, i.e., if there is no productive rule through which the item, with this particular form and meaning, can be derived.

(ii) Morphologically complex items may result from the expression of productively derived predicates. The abstract form of such predicates is created in the predicate formation component; their concrete form is determined by the expression rules. These expression rules may be called derivational.

(iii) Morphologically complex items may result from the expression of various operators which have been applied to basic or derived predicates in the creation of underlying clause structures. The relevant expression rules may be called inflectional expression rules.

Neither the derivational nor the inflectional expression rules necessarily result in synthetic morphological structures. They may also create analytic combinations of separate words.

14.6. General format of form-determining expression rules

Consider the expression rules for productive plural formation in English. These rules may be formulated as follows:

(22) a. pl [pred [N]] = pred-/iz/
         if last phoneme of pred is sibilant.
         Otherwise,
     b. pl [pred [N]] = pred-/s/
         if last phoneme of pred is voiceless.
         Otherwise,
     c. pl [pred [N]] = pred-/z/

We can generalize this type of rule to the following format:

(23)   Operator [Operandum] = Value
            if Condition(s)

This rule schema says that a certain operator, when applied to some operandum, yields a value for the operandum if certain conditions hold. For example, the plural operator, when applied to *book-*, yields the value *book-s*, since the condition of (22b) holds. *Book-s* is the value of the nominal predicate *book-* under the operator plural; to put it more simply, *book-s* is the plural of *book-*.

As we shall see below, the operators which may play a role in expression rules of the general format of (23) do not coincide with the operators (Ω-operators and π-operators) which have been used to build up the underlying clause structure. The latter constitute only a proper subset of the full set of operators which may occur in (23). For that reason, we shall use the term "morpho-syntactic operators" (μ-operators) for the full set of operators which may occur in (23). "$\mu_1, \mu_2, ..., \mu_n$" will be used as variables ranging over individual morpho-syntactic operators.

We shall now assume that all form-determining expression rules can be cast in the format of (23). By studying the recurrent properties of such rules, we may eventually arrive at a general theory of the structure of the expression component. In order to achieve this, the following questions must be answered:

(i) What sorts of changes may be effected by μ-operators on their operandum? In other words, what sorts of differences may exist between Operandum and Value in (23)?

(ii) What sorts of μ-operators may play a role in expression rules?

(iii) What types of operanda can be distinguished, and what properties of these operanda are relevant to the operation of expression rules?

(iv) What sorts of μ-operator combinations may apply SIMULTANEOUSLY to a given operandum?

(v) What sorts of μ-operators may apply in sequence, and how can the expression component be organized so as to allow for this sequential application?

Let us consider these questions one by one.

14.6.1. Changes effected by expression rules

Expression rules may effect the following elementary changes in their operandum (in many expression rules, some of these changes will be effected simultaneously):

— A *full reduplication* of the operandum, for example if the plural of *foot* were *foot-foot*.

— A *partial reduplication* of the operandum, for example if the plural of *foot* were *foo-foot* or *foot-oot*.

— A *mutation* of the segmental form of the operandum. For example, a change in the quality of a consonant or vowel, as when the plural of *foot* is *feet*, or *voot*. Note that for such a mutation to be captured in an expression

rule, it must be a productive mutation.
— The introduction of an *auxiliary form*, e.g. an auxiliary verb, or an inflectible adposition (preposition or postposition). An auxiliary form is a (phonologically specifiable) form which is introduced by an expression rule and will be further processed by later expression rules.
— The introduction of a *terminal form*, i.e. an affix (a suffix, a prefix, or an infix, or any combination of these), a particle, or a non-inflectible adposition. Terminal forms will not be further processed by later expression rules.
— The introduction of an *auxiliary operator*. These are μ-operators which are introduced by some expression rule, and will then act as an operator in some later expression rules. The nature of these auxiliary operators will be discussed in the next section.

The meaning of the notions "auxiliary form" and "terminal form" will be further explained in 14.6.3. below.

14.6.2. Types of μ-operators

The different μ-operators may belong to the subtypes listed in (24):

(24) 1. *Primary μ-operators*: μ-operators which occur as such in underlying clause structure. These may be:
    1.1. Ω-operators (term operators);
    1.2. π-operators (predicate, predication, proposition, illocutionary operators);
    1.3. semantic, syntactic, and pragmatic functions.
2. *Auxiliary μ-operators*: these are μ-operators which do not occur in underlying clause structure (at least not in this particular position), but are introduced by expression rules in order to trigger later expression rules. Auxiliary μ-operators may be copies of primary μ-operators which occur in other positions in underlying clause structure; this may occur in the case of agreement relations.

Let us consider some properties of these two types of μ-operators.

(i) Primary μ-operators necessarily have semantic import: they contribute something to the overall content of the clause, and thus have a direct semantic interpretation. Note that for the purposes of the expression rules, the semantic, syntactic, and pragmatic functions are treated as μ-operators. For example, we may write:

(25) Ag[term] = *by* term
e.g. Ag[*the man*] = *by the man*
(26) Rec[term] = *to* term
e.g. Rec[*the man*] = *to the man*
(27) AgSubj[term] = term
e.g. AgSubj[*the man*] = *the man*
(28) RecObj[term] = term
e.g. RecObj[*the man*] = *the man*

(ii) Auxiliary μ-operators do not occur as such in the underlying structure of the clause, and thus have no unified semantic interpretation. They are introduced by expression rules, and may then trigger further expression rules, thus appearing and disappearing within the expression component.[7] As an example of an auxiliary μ-operator, consider the accusative case in a language such as Latin. A Latin noun normally has distinct accusative forms in both singular and plural. For example:

(29) *hort-* 'garden', acc sg *hortum*, acc pl *hortos*.

These accusative forms require expression rules of roughly the following form:

(30) a. acc sg[*hort-*] = *hort-um*
b. acc pl[*hort-*] = *hort-os*

Thus, we need "acc" as a μ-operator if we are to be able to define the correct forms of the noun. It is very difficult to maintain, however, that "accusative" should be a PRIMARY μ-operator, since the accusative serves a great number of different functions in Latin, which cannot be unified under one semantically interpretable label. Thus, the accusative may express the semantic functions of Goal, Direction, Distance, and Duration, it may appear in exclamations, it marks the Subject argument in the so-called *accusativus-cum-infinitivo* construction, and it appears on the complement noun of a great many prepositions. It must thus be assumed that the accusative has many different sources in underlying clause structure. All these sources, however, ultimately have the same effect on the form of the noun. This can be illustrated as follows:

---

7. Compare De Groot (1989) on the notions "primary" and "secondary trigger".

(31)   Go sg [*hort-*]   Dir sg [*hort-*]
         acc sg [*hort-*]   *ad* acc sg [*hort-*]
         hort-um   *ad hort-um*

Thus, the primary operator Goal is mapped onto acc, and the primary operator Direction is mapped onto the preposition *ad* + acc. From there onwards, rule (30a) expresses acc sg[*hort-*] as *hort-um*, no matter where the operator "acc" originates. The expression rules effecting such derivations can be formulated as in:

(32) a. Go[*hort-*] = acc[*hort-*]
     b. Dir[*hort-*] = *ad* acc[*hort-*]
     c. acc sg [*hort-*] = *hort-um*

We see here that the auxiliary μ-operator "acc" does not figure in underlying clause structure, but is introduced in various expression rules, which then "flow together" in the final rule which defines the effect of "acc" on the noun.

Auxiliary μ-operators can be more generally defined as those μ-operators which serve to express a variety of semantic relations, but have a unified formal effect on their operandum. The following items may provisionally be regarded as auxiliary rather than primary μ-operators:
— case distinctions, such as that exemplified by "acc" above;
— certain verbal categories which serve a variety of purposes, such as "infinitive", "present participle", "past participle", "indicative" and "subjunctive".[8]

(iii) Auxiliary μ-operators may be copies of primary μ-operators, as in the case of agreement relations. Let us consider the various problems involved in agreement relations by means of the simple example:

(33) a. *The boy walks.*
     b. *The boys walk.*

---

8. See Rijksbaron (1986) for arguments to the effect that no unified meanings can be attached to the Classical Greek "moods" indicative, subjunctive, and optative. This is because the meanings which are transmitted by these moods are co-determined by the subordinating conjunction with which they are combined, the wider context in which they appear, and even the type of discourse in which they are used.

We say that the present tense verb in English agrees with the Subject term at least in this sense that in order to determine the correct form for the verb *walks*, we need the information that the Subject is third person singular. The features "third person" and "singular" are intrinsic to the Subject term, in which they act as primary operators. But the information which they contain must in some way or other be made available to the verb, at or before the point at which the form of the verb is determined. This can in principle be achieved in two ways:

(34) a. By *copying*:
The potentially relevant agreement features are copied from the "source" of the agreement (in this case, the Subject term) to the "target" of the agreement (in this case, the predicate).
b. By *contextual retrieval*:
At the moment at which the form of the target of the agreement (in this case, the predicate) is to be determined, the context in which it occurs in underlying clause structure is searched for relevant agreement features.

The copying method runs the risk of creating a certain amount of redundancy, since features may be copied onto the target which later turn out to have no influence on its form. In our present example, if Number and Person of the Subject are copied onto the predicate, this information will usually be only relevant to the present tense third person singular form: all other forms can be defined by default, in the sense that if the relevant form is not to be specified as *walk-s*, it can be specified as *walk*. This could be remedied by only allowing those features to be copied to the target which will indeed have an influence on its form.

The contextual method may in this respect be preferable, since the context will only be searched by expression rules relevant to the target, if the contextual information is essential to these expression rules.

Although the two approaches are feasible, in the computational implementation as developed in ProfGlot (Dik 1992) it turned out that the copying method was easier to implement than the contextual retrieval method. For that reason I shall from here on assume that agreement relations are to be captured through the copying method. Copied agreement features will be placed between <..>. Furthermore, since the agreement features exert their influence in conjunction with the Tense operator, it is most expedient to copy the relevant features to that operator. In the case of our example I will thus assume the following sequence of events:

General format of form-determining expression rules 357

(35) *The man walk-s.*
UNDERLYING STRUCTURE:
a. Pres e_i: *walk* [V] $(d1x_i: man [N])_{AgSubj}$
COPYING YIELDS:
b. Pres <1,p3> e_i: *walk* [V] $(d1x_i: man [N])_{AgSubj}$
EXPRESSION RULE FOR THE PREDICATE:
Pres <1,p3> [pred [V]] = pred-*s*

Note that after copying, the relevant operators may occur twice in the clause structure. For example, in (35b) the operator "1" 'singular' occurs once as a term operator in the term structure for *the man*, and once as a copy on the predicate. The status of these two occurrences is not the same. As a term operator, "1" is a primary operator with semantic import: it indicates the number of men referred to. As a copied operator on the predicate, "1" has the status of an auxiliary operator: it helps to get the predicate in the correct form, given the nature of the Subject; but in this occurrence it has no semantic import: the agreement operator in no way signifies that the action of walking is singular rather than plural. It follows that the copying rule is not part of the rules for creating underlying structures, but of the expression rules which serve to express these structures. In chapter 15 we return in more detail to the question of agreement.

14.6.3. Types of operanda

The operanda of expression rules of type (23) will always consist of phonologically specified items of the object language. These may be predicates from underlying clause structure, or auxiliary forms introduced by the expression rules. This can be illustrated by means of the following simplified example:

(36) a. *John has walked.*
b. Pres <1,p3> Perf e_i: *walk* [V] $(d1x_i: John [N])_{AgSubj}$
c. (i)   Perf[pred [V]]= [*have* [V]] PaP[pred [V]]
(ii) PaP[pred [V]] = pred-*ed*
(iii) Pres <1,p3>[*have* [V]] = *has*

Rule (i) operates on the underlying verbal predicate *walk*, and introduces the auxiliary verb *have* plus the auxiliary operator PaP (Past Participle). The auxiliary operator turns *walk* into *walk-ed* in rule (ii). And rule (iii) specifies the operation of Pres on the auxiliary verb *have* introduced in rule (i).[9]

We can thus make a distinction between primary operanda, auxiliary operanda, and terminal forms. Primary operanda are predicates from the underlying clause structure. Auxiliary operanda are phonologically specified auxiliary forms which are introduced by expression rules, and then further treated by later expression rules. For example, the auxiliary verb *have* in example (36) above is an auxiliary operandum, first introduced by rule (36c(i)) and then further processed by rule (36c(ii)). Terminal forms are forms which are introduced by expression rules, but not further processed by expression rules. Terminal forms may be affixes, such as the ending *-ed* introduced in (36c(ii)), or words, such as *has* introduced in (36c(iii)).

The various types of elements distinguished here can be more formally defined in terms of the following rule schema:

(37)   Operator X [Operandum Y] = Value ...Z...

— α is a primary operandum iff there is a rule such that α = Y, but no rule such that α = Z.

— α is an auxiliary operandum iff there is a rule such that α = Z, and a further rule such that α = Y.

— α is a terminal form iff there is a rule such that α = Z, and no further rule such that α = Y.

In a similar way we can define the notions "primary operator" and "auxiliary operator" in terms of schema (37):

— μ is a primary operator iff there is a rule such that μ = X, and no rule such that μ = Z.

— μ is an auxiliary operator iff there is a rule such that μ = Z, and a further rule such that Z = X.

Certain intrinsic μ-features of the operandum may be essential to the operation of expression rules. Among these features we count the different classes into which predicates must be divided in terms of:

— categorial properties such as V, N, A, and possible subcategories of these;

— different declension classes for Ns and As and different conjugation classes for Vs; these are different subclasses of Ns, As, and Vs which have different inflectional paradigms.

— different gender classes of Ns; these are different subclasses of Ns which

---

9. Note that in a full statement of the rules, the form *has* will rather be selected from the predicate *have*, since it cannot be productively formed.

trigger different types of agreement in other constituents of the clause.

The relevance of these intrinsic μ-features may be exemplified by means of some examples from Latin. Consider the singular paradigms for *femina* 'woman' and *hortus* 'garden':[10]

(38)
	DECL I	DECL IIA
nominative	*femin-a*	*hort-us*
genitive	*femin-ae*	*hort-i:*
dative	*femin-ae*	*hort-o:*
accusative	*femin-am*	*hort-um*
ablative	*femin-a:*	*hort-o:*

We see that we get different case endings according as the noun belongs to declension class I (*femina*) or IIa (*hortus*). This means that the rules for specifying the case forms of nouns in Latin will have to take the intrinsic declension-features into account. This can be achieved by adding these features to the Type of the predicate, as in:

(39) a. dat sg [pred [N,I]] = pred-*ae*
     b. dat sg [pred [N,IIa]] = pred-*o:*

In many languages, declension classes and gender classes show considerable overlap. In Latin, for example, the great majority of Ns in declension class I are feminine, and in declension class IIa masculine. But the overlap is seldom complete. Thus, *poeta* 'poet' (declension I) is masculine, and *populus* 'poplar' (declension IIa) is feminine. This can be seen in agreement differences in Noun-Adjective combinations:

(40) a. *femin-ae bon-ae*   'to the good woman'
     b. *poet-ae bon-o:*   'to the good poet'
(41) a. *hort-o: bon-o:*   'to the good garden'
     b. *popul-o: bon-ae*   'to the good poplar'

From these examples we see that the inflection of the adjective is sensitive to the gender rather than to the declension class of the noun. In order to define the correct form of the adjective we must know: (i) the declension class of the adjective itself (an intrinsic A-feature), (ii) the gender of the N it modifies (an

---

10. V: indicates a long vowel of quality V.

agreement feature), (iii) the number of the term in which it occurs (a primary μ-operator), and (iv) the case in which it is to be expressed (an auxiliary μ-operator). For example, in order to get the form *bon-o:* in (40b) and (41a) we need the following rule:

(42)   dat sg <masc> [pred [A,I/II]] = pred-*o:*

From this example we see quite clearly that a variety of pieces of information, springing from different sources, may "flow together" in one expression rule to create the correct inflectional form.

14.6.4. Simultaneous application of μ-operators

Consider again rule (42), and compare the following forms of the Latin adjective:

(43) a.   dat sg <masc>   *bon-o:*
     b.   dat sg <fem>   *bon-ae*
     c.   dat pl   *bon-i:s*

Note that there is no single element of form which could be assigned to "dative", to "singular", to "plural", to "masculine", or to "feminine". For example, the ending *-o:* cannot be dissected into distinct formal elements symbolizing "dative", "singular", and "masculine". The endings give a "fused" or "portmanteau" expression of a combination of several different μ-operators. In other words, these μ-operators must be applied simultaneously to yield the correct form. If two μ-operators are to be applied simultaneously, they can be considered as a kind of "entry conditions" to a two-dimensional grid. Compare:

(44)

	sg	pl
nom	*hort-us*	*hort-i:*
gen	*hort-i:*	*hort-o:rum*
dat	*hort-o:*	*hort-i:s*
acc	*hort-um*	*hort-o:s*
abl	*hort-o:*	*hort-i:s*

In this grid, the information "gen pl" brings us unequivocally to the form *hort-o:rum*. We can now say that when n μ-operators apply simultaneously, they

General format of form-determining expression rules 361

bring us to the correct form in an n-dimensional grid.

The simultaneous application of μ-operators, yielding a form of fused or portmanteau expression, has been taken to be a defining feature of so-called "inflecting" as against "agglutinating" languages (in which in principle each operator has its own identifiable expression in the final complex word). Note that the difference between these two language types will be a matter of degree: the more rules there are which require the simultaneous application of μ-operators, the more "inflecting" the language is.

14.6.5. The sequential application of μ-operators

In many cases expression rules need not be ordered with respect to each other. For example, consider:

(45) a. d m [*girl* [N]] --->
     b. d [*girl-s*] --->
     c. *the girl-s*
(46) a. d m [*girl* [N]] --->
     b. *the* m [*girl* [N]] --->
     c. *the girl-s*

In derivation (45), the operator m is expressed before the operator d; in (46) the operators are expressed in reverse sequence. In English, this makes no difference for the final output. This is so because the expression of neither operator is dependent on the expression of the other.

However, compare the corresponding Swedish forms:

(47) a. *flick-a*   'girl'
     b. *flick-or*   'girl-s'
     c. *flick-or-na*   'girl-s-the' = 'the girl-s'

It is clear that we get the easiest application of expression rules in Swedish if it is assumed that "first" the plural operator attaches the plural ending, and "then" the definiteness operator adds the definite ending. Thus, the plural rule "feeds" the definiteness rule. The desired result could be achieved by ordering the operators in the term structure as follows:

(48)   d m [*flick* [N]]

and stipulating that the expression rules operate "centrifugally" from the inside to the outside, starting by defining the effect of m on *flick*, and then specifying the effect of d on *flick-or*.

For another example of such feeding order, consider example (36). The Perf operator there introduces the auxiliary verb *have*, and the Pres operator then operates on this auxiliary. Again, the desired effect can be achieved if the operators are ordered as in (36b), and applied centrifugally. This kind of organization is more generally found in the English verbal complex, as we shall see in chapter 15. For example, the following ordering of operators yields the correct output forms when applied in this manner:

(49) a.   Pres Perf Prog Pass [*kiss* [V]]
 b.   *has been being kissed*

In general we can say that two expression rules stand in a feeding order when one of them creates the operandum for the other. This is the case if the first rule creates the form to which the second rule attaches an affix or applies a mutation, or if the first rule introduces an auxiliary form or operator which will be further developed by the second rule.

It would now be interesting if the kind of ordering exemplified in (48) and (49a) could be shown to be more than just a way of getting the most elegant derivation of the final expression. In the next chapters, we shall therefore investigate the feasibility of the following assumptions:

(A1) The primary operators in underlying clause structure are ordered with respect to each other and with respect to their (lexical) operandum.

(A2) This ordering reflects their relative scope, in the sense that "inner" operators fall within the scope of "outer" operators. Thus m is in the scope of d in (48), and Prog is in the scope of Perf and Pres in (49a).

(A3) The expression rules operate centrifugally, starting with the operator closest to the operandum, and proceeding through the sequence of operators step by step.

(A4) If in a language L_1 the order of operators μ_1 and μ_2 is irrelevant to their expression, but in L_2 must be assumed to be μ_1 - μ_2, that order can be used for L_1 as well.

By developing the assumptions (A1)-(A4) we hope to arrive at a typologically adequate theory of operator order and scope, which at the same time will yield the most elegant expression results for particular grammars.[11] Some consequences of these assumptions will be discussed in the next chapter.

---

11. Ideas on correlations between semantically and formally relevant operator orderings were advanced in Foley—Van Valin (1984), Bybee (1985), and Hengeveld (1989). Some of these ideas will be discussed in more detail in the next chapters. Within a computational context these ideas have been further developed and implemented in ProfGlot (Dik 1992), as well as in a detailed study of verbal complexes in five languages (Dik 1994). An application of the latter to the Italian verbal complex is found in Rus (1992).

15. The operation of expression rules

15.0. Introduction

In this chapter we discuss in somewhat more detail how the various μ-operators may affect the form of terms, predicates, and the clause as a whole. We start with the expression rules which affect the form of terms (15.1.); in this connection we consider the expression of semantic, syntactic, and pragmatic functions (15.1.1.), some general properties of case marking systems (15.1.2.), the expression of term operators (15.1.3.), and the nature of agreement relations within terms (15.1.4.). We then turn to operators which affect the form of the predicate or the clause as a whole (15.2.); under this heading we consider the expression of Voice differences (15.2.1.), the effects of π-operators in general (15.2.2.), and more particularly the impact of Tense, Mood, and Aspect operators (15.2.3.), Polarity operators (15.2.4.), and Illocutionary operators (15.2.5.). In a final section (15.3.) we consider the nature of agreement relations at the clause level.

15.1. Expression rules affecting the form of terms

15.1.1. Semantic, syntactic, and pragmatic functions

Any term has a semantic function, and may have a syntactic and / or a pragmatic function. We thus get such function combinations as:

(1) a. Agent
    b. Agent + Subject
    c. Agent + Given Topic
    d. Agent + Subject + Given Topic

If these functions are formally coded in terms, this coding takes the form of adpositions (pre- or postpositions), case forms,[1] or combinations of

---

1. Case distinctions almost exclusively occur in the form of suffixes. For some speculation on why this should be so, see Kahr (1976) and Dik (1983b).

adpositions and case forms.

When a term has Subj or Obj function, the expression of this function typically "masks" or "neutralizes" the expression of the underlying semantic function. Compare English:

(2) a. Ag[*the man*]   = *by the man*
    b. AgSubj[*the man*]   = Ø *the man*
(3) a. Rec[*the man*]   = *to the man*
    b. RecObj[*the man*]   = Ø *the man*

In a case marking language such as Latin, we find the following expression devices:

(4) a. Ag[*vir*]   = *a* + abl[*vir*] = *a vir-o:* 'by man-abl'
    b. AgSubj[*vir*]   = nom[*vir*]   = *vir* 'man-nom'
(5) a. Go[*vir*]   = acc[*vir*]   = *vir-um* 'man-acc'
    b. GoSubj[*vir*]   = nom[*vir*]   = *vir* 'man-nom'

In both English and Latin we see that if a term has a semantic function only, this function is revealed in its form. But if it also has a syntactic function, it takes the most "neutral" marking available in the language (Ø in English, nominative case in Latin), and the underlying semantic function is no longer recoverable from the form of the term. This correlates with the fact that at the same time the Voice of the predicate now reveals something of the underlying semantic function of the Subj (and the Obj, in languages which have "Object voice" distinctions). For example, the passive in English at least reveals that the Subj is not a first argument, and will most probably be a Goal term. In languages which have more extensive Subj and Obj assignment possibilities, we find more Voice distinctions marked on the predicate, so that recoverability of the underlying semantic function of the Subj / Obj term is usually secured.

We can say, then, that the Subj / Obj assignment mechanism typically operates in such a way that the marking of the semantic functions of the relevant terms is shifted from the terms themselves to the predicate. Why this should be the case remains to be explained.

We saw in chapter 13 that pragmatic functions may be formally expressed in a variety of ways. When they are expressed in the segmental form of the term, this is typically done in the form of adpositions. Topic and Focus distinctions are not expressed in distinct case forms. The only known case form which expresses a pragmatic function is the not very common "vocative" case, which expresses the clause-external pragmatic function of Address.

When pragmatic functions are expressed in adpositions, this may have a "masking" effect on the expression of the underlying semantic and syntactic functions. Compare the following Japanese term expressions:

(6) a. Ag[*Taroo*] = *Taroo ni*
　　b. AgSubj[*Taroo*] = *Taroo ga* [**ni ga*]
　　c. AgSubjTop[*Taroo*] = *Taroo wa* [**ni ga wa, *ga wa*]
　　d. Go[*Taroo*] = *Taroo o*
　　e. GoSubj[*Taroo*] = *Taroo ga* [**o ga*]
　　e. GoSubjTop[*Taroo*] = *Taroo wa* [**o ga wa, *ga wa*]

(7)　　AgTop[*Taroo*] = *Taroo ni wa*

Note that the Subj marker neutralizes the expression of the underlying semantic function, and the Topic marker neutralizes the expression of the underlying syntactic and semantic function; but if the Agent has ONLY Topic function, as in (7), it gets its own expression (*ni*).

If a term has only a semantic function, this function will be coded in an adposition, a case form, or a combination of both. Typically, one adposition or case form will express different semantic functions, and sometimes one semantic function may be expressed in different adpositions or case forms, depending on the contextual conditions in which it occurs. For some examples of the latter phenomenon, consider the following expressions in English:

(8) a. The enemy destroyed the town.
　　b. The town was destroyed by the enemy.
　　c. The president deplored the enemy's destruction of the town.
　　d. The president deplored the destruction of the town by the enemy.
　　e. The president deplored the town's destruction.

If we assume that *the enemy* and *the town* have Agent and Goal function in all these constructions,[2] we must accept that the Agent is sometimes expressed by the preposition *by*, sometimes by genitive *-s*, and that the Goal is sometimes expressed by Ø, sometimes by genitive *-s*, and sometimes by *of*. Similar differences in adpositions / case forms are found in many languages. The mapping of semantic functions onto adpositions / case forms is thus in

---

2. This assumption will be defended in *TFG2*: chapter 7.

general not one-to-one, which implies that no unified non-disjunctive meaning can be assigned to these formal elements. This is the main reason for treating case distinctions as "auxiliary μ-operators".

15.1.2. Case marking

By case we understand systematic differences in the form of nominal and adjectival predicates and various types of term operators, corresponding (though not in a one-to-one way) to functional differences of the terms in which they occur. We thus take "case" in the traditional sense of morphological distinctions such as "nominative", "accusative", "dative", etc. which have some manifestation in the surface form of linguistic expressions. This excludes certain other current usages of the term "case":

— we do not identify "case" with "Deep Case Role / Relation" as introduced in Fillmore (1968): this notion covers underlying functional relations rather than expression categories. It coincides more or less with our notion of semantic function.

— we do not use "case" in such a way that adpositions, too, are seen as expressing case distinctions. We avoid this because we want to be able to study differences between adpositional and case marking, although we recognize that there is a certain "trade-off" between these expression devices.

— we do not use "case" in the sense of "abstract case" as in the theory of Government and Binding (Chomsky 1981). For example, in our approach there will be no case assignment unless this has some kind of impact on the formal expression of terms.

Case in our restricted sense is not a universal category of natural languages. There are languages which have no case distinctions whatsoever. In languages which do have case systems, the number of distinct cases may vary considerably, ranging from two (e.g. "nominative" vs. "oblique") to several dozen distinct cases. Beyond a certain point of around 7-8 case distinctions, the further complexity is typically created by a great number of finer and finer subdistinctions for indicating local and directional functions. In languages which go beyond this point we thus find separate cases for such relations as 'in X', 'into X', 'out of X', 'on X', 'onto X', 'off X', 'through X', 'under X', etc.

Apart from these finer subdistinctions in the local and directional domain, the following are the most common case distinctions found across languages. These are presented with their primary or most basic functions, on the understanding that each case usually has a variety of other usages.

(9)   NAME   PRIMARY FUNCTIONS
       Nominative languages
          1a. nominative (nom) A^1, Subj, citation form
          2a. accusative (acc) A^2, Goal, Obj
       Ergative languages
          1b. absolutive (abs)   Subj of intransitive, Obj of
                                    transitive V, citation form
          2b. ergative (erg)   Subj of transitive V
       All languages
          3. genitive (gen)   Possessor within term
          4. dative (dat)   Recipient
          5. instrumental (instr)   Instrument
          6. partitive (part)   Part-whole relation
          7. locative (loc)   Location
          8. ablative (abl)   Source
          9. allative (all)   Direction

For the differences between nominative and ergative languages, see section 11.6.2. above. If the theory sketched there is correct, the absolutive can historically be traced back to an earlier nominative, and the ergative to an earlier "agentive" case; the ergative is in many languages identical to the instrumental.

The main function of case distinctions is to express the underlying semantic functions of terms; some cases (typically nom / acc, or abs / erg) more primarily serve the expression of syntactic functions.

In view of the fact that one case may typically express different functions, it is in general not possible to identify a "common meaning" for a given case. Languages have a certain freedom in distributing the different functions to be expressed over the limited number of cases available, and even closely related languages may differ in their particular division of labour among the cases.[3] This may be understood by considering the functionality of case distinctions at a somewhat higher level of abstraction. We may then say that case distinctions serve two different purposes:

— they have a *characterizing* function: they characterize a term as having one of a limited set of possible semantic or syntactic functions, and

— they have a *distinguishing* function: they serve to keep terms with

---

3. This is demonstrated for a number of Australian languages in Dixon (1980: chapter 10).

different semantic / syntactic functions apart in the structure of the clause.

These two functions may be compared to the different uses of colour differences in geographical maps: the colours are used in a *characterizing* function to the extent that they symbolize some common property of the areas involved (e.g. green = 'forest', yellow = 'sand'); but they are used in a *distinguishing* function to the extent that they merely serve to keep two adjacent areas or countries apart. In a given atlas different colours are typically used in a mixture of characterizing and distinguishing functions. In such a situation the question: 'What is the meaning of green in this atlas?' makes no sense, since 'green' may have different meanings depending on the context of the particular map involved. Likewise, case systems are typically used in a partially characterizing, partially distinguishing function, and thus cases have different contextually dependent meanings.

Some aspects of this mixed characterizing / distinguishing function can be illustrated with some features of the Latin case system, as analysed by Pinkster (1984, 1985, 1988a). Pinkster argues that a distinction should be made between the case marking of arguments and of satellites. Satellite-marking cases can be said to express semantic functions (though not one-to-one), whereas the cases which mark arguments can to a high degree be predicted on the basis of the quantitative valency of the predicate. Consider the distribution of cases over the arguments of one-, two-, and three-place predicates in Latin:

(10)
	A_1, Subj	A^2	A^3
1-place	nom 100%		
2-place	nom 100%	acc 88.3%	
		dat 7.6%	
		abl 3.6%	
		gen 0.5%	
3-place	nom 100%	acc 100%	dat 70.3%
			abl 26.6%
			gen 1.7%
			acc 1.4%

Note the following features of this distribution: nom fully correlates with first argument (A^1) or Subj status, or both; second arguments of 3-place predicates are always expressed in acc, while for 2-place predicates this is so in the great majority of predicates; and dat and abl together take care of 96.9% of all third arguments. Further: two distinct arguments are hardly ever marked by the same case; a small minority of predicates with acc for both second and third argument form the only exception to this rule. To a very high degree, then, the nuclear argument cases serve to keep the different arguments apart, without necessarily expressing distinct semantic functions.

The cases which mark satellites do express semantic functions, but not in a fully unequivocal way. We do find constructions with a series of satellites, each with a different semantic function, but all marked by the same case. The following example from Caesar[4] is an extreme example of this: three semantically distinct satellites, all marked by the abl (note that one constituent is even discontinuous):

(11)   *incredibili   celeritate   MAGNO   SPATIO   paucis diebus*
        incredible   speed   great   distance few   days
                CONFECTO
                covered

'After a great distance had been covered (so-called "ablative absolute", expressing Circumstance) in a few days (Time within which) with incredible speed (Speed)...'

This would seem to be a curiously ineffective way of characterizing semantic functions, but it can be understood if we realize the following points:
— it is rare for such a series of terms in the same case to occur in one clause;
— the agreement relations within (11) show unambiguously which words go together to form the three constituents (there is no other way of parsing this sequence);
— the lexical content of the constituents helps a lot in identifying the semantic functions. For example, *paucis diebus* could not be interpreted with Speed function, nor could *incredibili celeritate* have the function of 'Time within which'.

Using a limited set of cases for a great variety of syntactic and semantic functions is thus a form of system economy which is bought at the price of occasional clashes such as that illustrated in (11).

It may now have become clear why we have given the status of "auxiliary μ-operators" to case distinctions (in our sense). Such distinctions cannot be primary μ-operators, present in underlying clause structure, because they do not have a unified semantic interpretation. On the other hand, we cannot immediately map the semantic function onto the final form of the noun, because the same case has many different origins, and has a variety of effects on the form of the noun, where these effects are co-dependent on the Number

---

4. *De Bello Gallico* 3:29:2.

of the term, and on the Declension of the noun in question. This, too, can be seen in (11), where we have seven words, all in the abl case, but marked by five different endings. The best way to capture this complex relationship thus seems to be to first map the semantic functions onto their respective cases, and then define the effect which these cases, in conjunction with other operators, have on the form of the operandum. This is achieved if cases are treated as auxiliary μ-operators in the way exemplified in section 14.6.2. above.

15.1.3. The expression of term operators

With respect to the expression of term operators we shall here restrict our attention to Definiteness, Number, and Demonstratives, since these may have a variety of effects on the form of different constituents in the term phrase, and may interact with each other in various ways. Consider, for example, the underlying term structure of a term such as *these grey elephants*:

(12)   (d prox m x_i: *elephant* [N]: *grey* [A])

The expression of such a term structure would be a comparatively simple matter if each term operator had its own distinct expression, without affecting the form of the restrictors or interacting with each other. We would then get expressions such as:

(13)   *the this more elephant grey*

This, however, is typically not the way in which term operators are expressed. Compare the reflection of the term operators in the correct English form of the term:

(14)

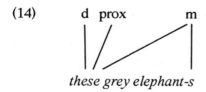

We see here that plurality is coded (i) in the affix on the nominal predicate, (ii) in the form of the demonstrative, whereas definiteness is coded in the demonstrative, together with proximity and plurality.

Languages differ from each other in the way in which the different term operators are reflected in the various constituents of the term phrase. Compare the following expressions in four languages:

(15)   English   Dutch
 i 1   *a pretty girl*   *een mooi meisje*
 d 1   *the pretty girl*   *het mooi-e meisje*
 i m   *pretty girl-s*   *mooi-e meisje-s*
 d m   *the pretty girl-s* *de mooi-e meisje-s*

        Swedish   Latin
 i 1   *en vack-er flick-a*   *puell-a pulchr-a*
 d 1   *den vack-ra flick-an*   *puell-a pulchr-a*
 i m   *vack-ra flick-or*   *puell-ae pulchr-ae*
 d m   *de vack-ra flick-or-na*   *puell-ae pulchr-ae*

In English, the form of the noun varies with Number, whereas the adjective is invariable. In Dutch, the adjective has a different form in the indefinite singular (at least, with this class of nouns), and thus needs information on Definiteness and Number for its formal specification. The same is true for Swedish, where the noun, in addition to Number, also expresses Definiteness. In Latin there is no formal expression of Definiteness,[5] but Number is marked both on the noun and the adjective, which further "agrees" with the noun in Gender and Case.

15.1.4. Agreement within terms

Agreement obtains between two constituents when the formal expression of one of them (say, B) depends on some independently varying property (say, Gender) of the other constituent (A). In such a case we say that B agrees with A in Gender. A may be called the "Source", B the "Target" of the agreement relation, and Gender would (in this case) be the category of A to which B is sensitive (cf. Moravcsik 1978):

---

5. Nevertheless it must probably be assumed that terms are marked for Definiteness, since there are ordering differences which seem to correlate with the d/i distinction.

(16)   *Target*   *Source*   *Category*
        B   agrees with   A   in   Gender

For example, when B is an adjective and A a noun, Gender agreement will lead to different forms of the adjective according as A is masculine, feminine, neuter, or has any other relevant Gender (or "class") distinctions in the language in question.

Agreement relations mainly obtain in two distinct domains: the domain of the term phrase, and the domain of the clause. One distinguishing feature is that the category Person is only relevant at the clause level (Lehmann 1982b). Clause level agreement will be discussed in 15.3. below.

At both levels I shall give a more restricted interpretation to "agreement" than is usual in the linguistic literature (cf. Moravcsik 1978, Lehmann 1982b). In the first place, for reasons set forth in section 6.6. above, agreement is distinguished from cross-reference, which obtains in such constructions as (17a-c), if the bracketed constituents can be left out without affecting grammaticality:

(17) a.   (*the man*) *he-sings*.
      b.   (*the man*) *his-hat*
      c.   (*the chair*) *it-on*

In such cases the term phrase is regarded as an apposition to the pronominally marked constituent: the pronominal marking is a matter of independent choice rather than an automatic consequence of the presence of some property in the term.

In the second place I impose the requirement that the agreement "Category" should be inherent in the Source. Gender is a good example of this: Gender is an intrinsic μ-feature of the type of the nominal predicate, and when other constituents in the term are sensitive to this feature, they must "inherit" it from the Noun. This, however, does not apply to Number, Case, and Definiteness: these represent operators which apply to the whole term, and which may more or less independently be coded on different constituents of the term phrase. Consider a term structure such as:

(18) $(d1x_i: man [N]: big [A])_{Rec}$

Let us suppose that the Recipient function is coded in the dative on both the noun and the adjective, so that we get:

(19)   man-dat big-dat
        'to the big man'

This situation is typically described as "agreement" in Case between adjective and noun. This suggests, however, that "Case" is somehow inherent in, or first assigned to, the N, and only secondarily "inherited" by the adjective. This is not correct, for the following reasons:
  — in some languages there is clear evidence that the case marker is attached to the whole term phrase rather than to the noun or any other constituent. Thus, we find:

(20) a.   [*man*]dat
     b.   [*man big*]dat

Note that we have reason to assume this type of structure when the case marker attaches to the final element of the term, no matter what category this element belongs to. This kind of case marking is found in Basque and Persian (Lehmann 1982b: 204). It must be added that it is difficult, in such a situation, to maintain that the dative marker is a case marker rather than a postposition.
  — there are situations in which case is not marked on the noun, but is marked on a modifier of the noun. In such a situation we find:

(21)   *big*-dat *man*   'to the big man'

In such a construction it would be very unnatural to say that the modifier inherits its case from the noun, although the noun itself does not show it. This kind of case marking occurs, according to Lehmann (1982b), in Rushi (a Pamir language); in German noun phrases of certain types, such as *dieser Frau* 'this-gen woman = of this woman', it is only the determiner which reveals the case of the whole term. Lehmann (1982b) takes the point of view that the term "agreement" should be used only for those constructions in which the noun is overtly marked for case. This implies that there is agreement in German *dieses Mannes* 'this-gen man-gen = of this man', but not in the phrase *dieser Frau*. The question then arises, of course, from which source the adjective gets its case-marking in the latter construction.

However, even if the noun is marked for case, it does not seem correct to say that it is the "Source" of the case marking, and that the other case-marked constituents of the term phrase "inherit" their case from the noun. We should rather say that noun and modifiers may each be sensitive to the semantic or syntactic function of the whole term. The case in which this function is expressed is then "distributed", in various ways, over the different constituents of the term. When both noun and modifiers are marked for case, it may seem as if the modifier inherits its case from the noun, but in fact it is independently sensitive to the case which marks the whole term.

What has been said about Case above also applies to Number and Definiteness. None of these categories is inherent in the noun, and none of them is necessarily expressed on the noun. For example, Number is marked on the whole term according to the pattern of (20) in Yucatec, and in many noun phrases in French it is only the modifiers which reveal Number (Lehmann 1982b). Similar constructions occur in Limbu (Tibeto-Birmese).[6]

As for Definiteness, we saw in (15) that this operator may be expressed on the noun, and may also have impact on the form of the adjective, as in Swedish. Again, however, we find languages in which Definiteness is only expressed in one or more modifiers of the noun. Thus, Serbo-Croatian has such oppositions as:

(22) a. *mlad student*   'a young student'
    b. *mlad-i student*   'the young student'

in which the form of the adjective is the only sign that the term is definite or indefinite. Another example is Nkore-Kiga, a Bantu language described in Taylor (1985). Again, Definiteness is not marked on the noun, but does appear on the adjective and other restrictors:

(23) a. *ekitabo kirungi*
      book   good   'a good book'
    b. *ekitabo e-kirungi* 'the good book'

In such cases as these it would be strange indeed to say that the adjective agrees with the noun in definiteness, since the noun does not express this operator in the first place.

If the point of view taken in the preceding is correct, Gender correspondences are the only genuine example of agreement relations within terms. We speak of Gender when nominal predicates must be divided into a number of different classes (ranging from a minimum of two to a whole range of distinct noun classes as found, for example, in the Bantu languages), because of the different requirements which these classes impose on the

---

6. Jadranka Gvozdanović, pers. comm.

formal specification of the other constituents with which they are combined. Such Gender classes typically have SOME semantic motivation, but are based for the greater part on rather arbitrary divisions within the full class of nominal predicates, such that in general the Gender has to be learned for each noun.

Consider Latin, which has three noun classes traditionally referred to as "masculine", "feminine", and "neuter", with such effects as the following:

(24) a. *Puella* (fem) *pulch*-ra *laudat*-a *est*.
      girl   pretty   praised   is
      'The pretty girl has been praised.'
   b. *Puer* (masc) *pulch*-er *laudat*-us *est*.
      'The pretty boy has been praised.'
   c. *Mare* (neut) *pulch*-rum *laudat*-um *est*.
      'The pretty sea has been praised.'

We see here that both the adjective within the term, and the passive participle in the predicate, have to agree in Gender with the head noun of the term.

In section 14.6.3. above we saw how this kind of agreement can be described: the Gender feature is assigned to the type of the noun as an intrinsic μ-feature, and copied onto those target constituents which are sensitive to it. The copied (and thus, auxiliary) Gender operators will then locally co-determine the form of the agreeing constituents.

15.2. Expression rules affecting the predicate

We now turn to expression rules which may affect the form of the predicate. Under this heading, we discuss the treatment of Voice distinctions and the influence of the different π-operators.

15.2.1. Voice distinctions

We saw in chapters 10 and 11 that Voice distinctions are treated in terms of differential assignment of Subj and Obj function to the terms within the predication. In English, the predicate is only sensitive to Subj assignment: if Subj is assigned to any argument other than the first argument A^1, the predicate must be expressed in passive form. Otherwise, we get the active form of the predicate. The expression rules specifying the form of the predicate must thus be made sensitive to Subj assignment. Let us first consider the simple case of an active-passive opposition such as that between:

(25) a. *Mary kissed John.*
    kiss [V] (*Mary*)$_{AgSubj}$ (*John*)$_{Go}$
 b. *John was kissed by Mary.*
    kiss [V] (*Mary*)$_{Ag}$ (*John*)$_{GoSubj}$

In (25b), but not in (25a), we require the passive form of the predicate. This can be achieved by assigning an auxiliary operator Pass 'passive' to the predicate when Subject has been assigned to a non-first argument, and then formulating the expression rules as follows:

(26) a. Pass[pred [V]] = [*be* [V]] PaP[pred [V]]
 b. PaP[pred [V]] = pred-*ed*

Rule (26a) introduces the passive auxiliary *be*[7] and adds the auxiliary μ-operator PaP (past participle) to the predicate. This operator will turn the predicate into the correct form through rule (26b). In the case of (26b), this will thus lead to the following derivation:

(27) a. Pass[*kiss* [V]]
 b. [*be* [V]] PaP[*kiss* [V]]
 c. [*be* [V]] *kiss-ed*

In certain languages, such as German and Dutch, the choice of passive auxiliary is co-dependent on the presence of other π-operators. Thus, Dutch has *zijn* 'be' in the Perfect passive, *worden* 'become' otherwise. Compare:

(28) a. *Jan   is   door   iedereen   geprezen.*
      John   is   by   everybody   praised
      'John has been praised by everybody.'
 b. *Jan   wordt   door   iedereen   geprezen.*
      John   becomes by   everybody   praised
      'John is praised by everybody.'

---

7. In Dik (1983a) I showed that it is also possible to have (25a) just introduce the operator PaP, and then leave the introduction of *be* to the rule of copula support discussed in 8.3.

Expression rules affecting the predicate 379

This difference can be captured by formulating the expression rules in the following way:

(29) a. Perf Pass[pred [V]] = [*zijn* [V]] PaP[pred [V]]
    b. Pass[pred [V]] = [*worden* [V]] PaP[pred [V]]

(29a) will apply first, otherwise (29b); if neither rule applies, the predicate remains unaffected. (29a) is an example of the simultaneous application of two μ-operators.

This mechanism of Voice expression can be just as easily applied to languages which give *morphological* expression to the passive. Consider the following examples from Swahili (Ashton 1947, Vitale 1981):

(30) a. *Juma   a-li-m-pig-a   Hamisi.*
       Juma   he-Past-him-hit-Ind   Hamisi
       'Juma hit Hamisi.'
    b. *Hamisi   a-li-pig-w-a   na Juma.*
       Hamisi   he-Past-hit-Pass-Ind   by Juma
       'Hamisi was hit by Juma.'

The rule introducing the passive suffix *-w-* can be formulated as follows:

(31)   Pass[pred [V]] = pred-*w*- [V]

This rule creates a passive "stem" which can then be input to further expression rules.

Languages which have extensive Subj assignment possibilities often have different corresponding "passives"; typically, each of these passives takes care of some semantic functions to which Subj has been assigned (see 10.4.2. above). In Tagalog, for example, the relevant relations are as follows:

(32)   Voice   *To be chosen when*
           Active   Subj = A_1
           Passive-1   Subj = Go
           Passive-2   Subj = Rec / Loc
           Passive-3   Subj = Ben / Instr

Given these relations, auxiliary operators Pass1, Pass2, or Pass3 can be added to the predicate when the Subject assignments as indicated in the right-hand column of (32) have been effected.

Certain languages have Voice distinctions corresponding not only to Subj assignment, but also to Obj assignment. Again, Swahili can be taken as an example of this phenomenon. Compare the following constructions:

(33) a. *Hamisi a-li-m-pik-i-a   Juma   chakula.*
      Hamisi   he-Past-him-cook-Appl-Ind Juma   food
      'Hamisi (AgSubj) cooked Juma (BenObj) some food (Go).'
  b. *Juma   a-li-pik-i-w-a   chakula   na   Hamisi.*
      Juma   he-Past-cook-Appl-Pass-Ind food   by   Hamisi
      'Juma (BenSubj) was cooked some food (Go) by Hamisi (Ag).'

where "Appl" ('applicative') represents the element in the predicate which signals that a Beneficiary (or some later semantic function in the Semantic Function Hierarchy) has been assigned Subj or Obj function. The relevant Voice markings can be displayed as follows:

(34)
	A^1	Go	Ben
Subj	Ø	-w-	-i-w-
Obj		Ø	-i-

The relevant expression rules can be formulated by adding an auxiliary operator Appl to the predicate when either Subj or Obj has been assigned to the Beneficiary or some later semantic function; the auxiliary operator Pass will be added whenever Subj has been assigned to some non-first argument. The effects of these auxiliary operators can then be formulated as follows:

(35) a.   Appl[pred- [V]] = pred-*i*- [V]
    b.   Pass[pred- [V]] = pred-*w*- [V]

In the case of (33b) we have BenSubj; therefore, Appl will be added to the predicate, and *-pik-* will be turned into *-pik-i-* through rule (35a); and Pass will be added to the predicate as well, so that *-pik-i-* will be turned into *-pik-i-w-* through (35b).

15.2.2. The effects of π-operators

In chapters 9 and 12, following Hengeveld (1987, 1988, 1989), we distinguished four types of π-operators, which can be briefly characterized as follows:

(36) π_1 further specifying the quality of the nuclear State of Affairs;
        π_2 quantifying the SoA and locating it with respect to temporal, spatial, and cognitive dimensions;
        π_3 expressing an attitude of the Speaker with respect to the propositional content;
        π_4 specifying or modifying the illocutionary force of the clause.

It is clear that these operators have wider and wider scope as we proceed from π_1 through π_4. In their relation to the predicate they can be ordered as follows:

(37) $\pi_4 \, \pi_3 \, \pi_2 \, \pi_1$ pred

This hierarchical, semantically interpretable order is relevant to the expression of π-operators in the following sense. Building on results of Foley—Van Valin (1984) and Bybee (1985), Hengeveld (1989) formulated the following principle:

(38)   The preferred order for the expression of π-operators is:
        $\pi_4 \, \pi_3 \, \pi_2 \, \pi_1$ pred
   or: pred $\pi_1 \, \pi_2 \, \pi_3 \, \pi_4$

According to this principle, then, the hierarchical relationships among the π-operators are iconically mapped onto the surface structure of the predicate phrase. Obviously, principle (38) only predicts the preferred order of expression when the elements manifesting the π-operators either all precede or all follow the (stem of the) predicate. This is not always the case. In English, for example, the Past tense is expressed in a suffix, while the other π-operators are expressed in auxiliary verbs which precede the predicate. And in some of the Swahili examples given above, we saw that the Past tense is expressed in a prefix, while the Indicative / Subjunctive distinction is coded in a suffix. Perhaps it is possible, however, to generalize across these different orderings in the following way:

(39)   [π_4 [π_3 [π_2 [π_1 [pred] π_1] π_2] π_3] π_4]

where this schema would be interpreted as being compatible not only with the orders given in (38), but also with such orders as:

(40) a.   [π_4 [π_3 [.. [.. [pred] π_1] π_2] ..] ..]
     b.   [.. [.. [π_2 [.. [pred] π_1] ..] π_3] π_4]

This would then mean that (39) could be taken as a general schema for the preferred expression of π-operators even in those languages in which these may be expressed on two sides of the predicate. At the same time, this schema would define the preferred order of applying the expression rules, if we accept the assumptions (A1)-(A4) formulated in 14.6.5. above. In chapter 16 we will identify the type of ordering displayed in (39) as being due to a principle of "Centripetal Orientation".

Rather than continuing this general discussion here, I shall concentrate on the way in which a fragment of the English verbal complex can be most economically captured by expression rules. In doing so, I concentrate on the interaction between Tense, Aspect, Infinitive, Participle, and Passive. Mood distinctions are left out of account because of the complexities involved.[8] Negation will be discussed in 15.2.3., and Illocution in 15.2.4.

The relevant fragment of the English verbal complex can be captured in terms of the following array of μ-operators, to be applied from right to left in the order given:

(41) $\left\{\begin{array}{l}\text{Pres / Past} \\ \text{Inf}\end{array}\right\}$ (Perf) (Progr) (Pass) [pred [V]]

Progr and Perf are aspectual operators which may or may not be present. For each predication, a choice must have been made between Pres / Past or Infinitive, where the latter may be interpreted as a choice for −Tense. Pres, Past, Perf, and Progr are primary μ-operators: they occur in the underlying clause structure, and have a unified semantic interpretation. Pass is an auxiliary operator, introduced when Subj has been assigned to some non-first argument. Inf is also an auxiliary operator, introduced under certain more complex conditions.[9]

Schema (41) defines a great number of different possible combinations of operators, each with their own effect on the formal specification of the verbal complex. The rules defining these effects can be formulated as follows:[10]

---

8. In the computational implementations of the English verbal complex discussed in Dik (1992, 1994) the full interaction between the relevant operators has been captured.

9. For the idea that Inf is an operator in complementary distribution with Tense (Pres/Past), see Dik (1983a).

10. Passive and progressive *be* are here introduced as auxiliaries for the expression of the operators Pass and Progr. In Dik (1983a) it has been shown that there is a feasible alternative in which all occurrences of *be* are introduced through

(42) (R1) Pass[pred [V]] = [*be* [V]] PaP[pred [V]]
      (R2) Progr[pred [V]] = [*be* [V]] PrP[pred [V]]
      (R3) Perf[pred [V]] = [*have* [V]] PaP[pred [V]]
      (R4) (i) Pres <1 p3>[pred [V]] = pred-*s*
            (ii) Pres [pred [V]] = pred
      (R5) Past[pred [V]] = pred-*ed*
      (R6) Inf[pred [V]] = *to* pred
      (R7) PaP[pred [V]] = pred-*ed*
      (R8) PrP[pred [V]] = pred-*ing*

These rules must obviously be conditioned by the principle of "lexical priority", as defined in 14.3. Thus, most forms of *be* and *have* will be lifted out of their respective paradigms before the rules of (42) get a chance to apply.[11] The status of these auxiliary verbs is special in this sense that they are not selected from the lexicon but introduced through expression rules such as (R1), (R2), and (R3), whereas the paradigms containing their irregular forms do occur in the lexicon.

Let us now see how the rules of (42) operate on a maximal expansion of operators such as:

(43) Pres <1,p3> Perf Progr Pass [*call* [V]] (*John*)$_{Ag}$ (*Bill*)$_{GoSubj}$

When this structure is input to the rules of (42) we will get the following derivation of the verbal complex:

(44) a. Pres <1,p3> Perf Progr[*be* [V]] PaP[*call* [V]] (by (R1))
     b. Pres <1,p3> Perf[*be* [V]] PrP[*be* [V]] PaP[*call* [V]] (by (R2))
     c. Pres <1,p3>[*have* [V]] PaP[*be* [V]] PrP[*be* [V]] PaP[*call* [V]]
        (by (R3))
     d. Pres <1,p3>[*have* [V]] PaP[*be* [V]] PrP[*be* [V]] *call-ed* (by (R7))
     e. Pres <1,p3>[*have* [V]] PaP[*be* [V]] *be-ing call-ed* (by (R8))
     f. Pres <1,p3>[*have* [V]] *been be-ing call-ed* (by lexical priority)
     g. *has been be-ing call-ed* (by lexical priority)

---

the rule of copula support.

11. Note that if all the unpredictable forms are listed in the paradigms, the actual productive rules can remain rather simple.

The full input structure will thus be expressed as:

(45)   Bill has been being called by John.

It will be clear that the order of the operators in (44) and the convention of applying the rules in a "centrifugal" fashion are essential to the proper operation of these rules. We can now ask whether this order of operators, which in the first instance was dictated by descriptive convenience, can also be interpreted in terms of semantic scope relations. This seems to be the case, at least inasfar as the operator order is not incompatible with the distinctions which we have made among the π-operators. Pass, the innermost operator, has to do with the presentation of the SoA; the Progr operator tells us that the SoA was going on at a particular moment, and was analysed as a $π_1$ operator in 9.1.2. above; the Perf operator (a $π_2$ operator) places the whole SoA in the past and signals that it has some kind of current relevance; and the Pres tense (also a $π_2$ operator) indicates that the point of current relevance is the moment of speaking (in contrast to *had been being called*, where it would be some moment in the past). It thus seems to be the case that, as we proceed from the inner to the outer operators, they have less and less to do with the inner constitution of the SoA, and more and more with the location of the whole SoA with respect to a reference point in time.

However, further research on a number of different languages is required to establish whether semantic scope and descriptive convenience do in fact define the same order of operators in a significant majority of languages.[12]

15.2.3. The expression of polarity

The polarity opposition (positive / negative) can be captured by $π_2$-operators[13] Pos and Neg, where Pos will usually go unexpressed, unless it is focused on. Compare Dutch:

---

12. See Hengeveld (1989) for some suggestive discussion, and Dik (1992, 1994) for a development of the present ideas within a computational context.

13. In *TFG2*: chapter 8 it will be argued that there are reasons of distinguishing different types of negation, corresponding to the different layers of underlying clause structure. Such differences are disregarded here.

(46) A: *JAN heeft het gedaan.*
John has it done
'JOHN did it.'
B: *Jan heeft het NIET gedaan.*
John has it not done
'John did NOT do it.'
A: *Hij heeft het WEL gedaan*
he has it Pos done
'He HAS done it.'

Although Neg has the whole predication in its scope, it is typically expressed as part of, or in close association with the predicate. This was shown in a study by Dahl (1979) on the expression of negation in around 240 languages, which yielded the following results:

(47) THE EXPRESSION OF NEG   PERCENTAGE[14]
  1. morphologically as part of the predicate   45.0
  2. morphologically in an auxiliary verb   16.7
  3. by a separate negative particle
     a. in preverbal position   12.5
     b. in pre-auxiliary position   20.8
     c. in position before verbal group   2.1
     d. in postverbal position   1.2
     e. in post-auxiliary position   3.7
  4. by a separate negative particle
     a. in sentence-initial position   0.4
     b. in sentence-final position   4.2

Note that only in the cases 4a-b (4.6%) does the negative particle orient itself to the sentence as a whole rather than to the predicate. The FG representation for negated predications would seem to be appropriate in this respect:

(48) a. *John did not buy the book.*
 b. Neg Past e_i: *buy* [V] *(John)*$_{AgSubj}$ *(the book)*$_{GoObj}$

This representation expresses that Neg takes the whole predication in its

---

14. The percentage runs above 100% because a number of languages have more than one expression type for negation.

scope, but is nevertheless rather closely associated with the predicate, just like the Tense operator Past.

Note that we do not use the operator Neg for such constructions as:

(49)   *John has bought no books.*

Rather, we regard (49) as containing a zero-quantified term, as represented in:

(50)   Past e_i: *buy* [V] (*John*)$_{AgSubj}$ (Øx_i: *book* [N])$_{GoObj}$

where the zero-quantifier indicates that the set of books (which one might think John might have bought) was in fact empty. There will thus be no equivalent to so-called "Neg Incorporation" in such constructions as (49).[15]

15.2.4. The expression of illocutionary operators

Illocutionary operators may have a variety of effects on the expression of the clause. Sometimes they only affect the intonation, as in:

(51) a.   *John is not coming.*   [Decl]
     b.   *John is not coming?*   [Int]

Or they affect the ordering of constituents (and the intonation), as in:

(52) a.   *John is not coming.*   [Decl]
     b.   *Is John not coming?*   [Int]

Illocutionary operators, however, may also affect the *form* of constituents, and will thus have to trigger form-determining expression rules. Consider:

(53) a.   *Did John buy the book?*
     b.   *Give that book to me!*

In (53a) we need the operator Int, and in (53b) we need the operator Imp in order to properly define the form of the predicate.

Although illocutionary operators take the whole clause in their scope, their

---

15. See Brown (1985) and Kahrel (1987), and *TFG2*: chapter 8.

overt expression generally "lands" in, or close to the predicate. This is most clearly the case in the Imperative, for which most languages use a special verbal form which, moreover, is typically identical to the stem of the verb. This kind of expression requires a rule of the form:

(54)   Imp[pred [V]] = pred

This rule yields the correct form of the Imperative in English and many other languages. Note that if a grammar distinguishes between "indicative", "subjunctive", and "imperative" mood, this should not be taken to imply that all these moods relate to the same level in underlying clause structure. Indicative and subjunctive will typically be triggered by π_2 (objective modality) and π_3 (subjective modality) operators and have the status of auxiliary operators, whereas imperative mood is triggered by the illocutionary (π_4) operator Imp, which has the status of a primary operator.

As for (53a), note that in English the interrogative operator, when no other auxiliary verb has been introduced, will have to trigger a rule of *do*-support, which would have the effect of turning (55a) into (55b):

(55) a. Int [Past [*buy* [V] (*John*)$_{Ag}$ (*the book*)$_{Go}$]]
     b. Int [Past [*do* [V]] Inf [*buy* [V]] (*John*)$_{Ag}$ (*the book*)$_{Go}$]

Note that *do*-support simultaneously introduces the auxiliary operator Inf(initive); Past[do [V]] will yield *did* (through lexical priority), and Inf[buy [V]] will yield *buy*.

Illocutionary operators may also be "spelled out" in special illocutionary particles; these particles are typically used for marking interrogatives (declaratives being the most unmarked sentence type, and imperative usually being coded in the verb), and usually take a position close to the verb. Japanese, for example, has a clause-final interrogative particle *ka*, as in:

(56) a. *Taroo   wa   Hanako ni   tegami   o   kaita   ka?*
         Taro   Top   Hanako Rec   letter   Go   write-Past   Int
         'Did Taro write a letter to Hanako?'

Note that leaving out *ka* we get the corresponding declarative. This particle also marks question-word questions and embedded questions.

Serbo-Croatian has a Yes / No interrogative marker *li*, which behaves like a clitic and therefore takes its place in the clitic cluster in clause-second position. Compare:

388   *The operation of expression rules*

(57) a. *Idete   u   školu.*
         you-go   to   school
         'You are going to school.'
     b. *Idete   li   u   školu?*
         you-go   Int   to   school
         'Are you going to school?'

The particle *li* is also used to introduce embedded Yes / No questions. For more detailed treatment of questions I refer to *TFG2*: chapter 12.[16]

15.3. Agreement at the clause level

There are two forms of agreement which commonly occur at the clause level:

(58)   TARGET   SOURCE   AGREEMENT PROPERTIES
     a.   predicate A^1, A^2, A^3 Person, Number, Gender
                         Subj, Obj
     b.   anaphor   antecedent   Person, Number, Gender

Agreement between the predicate and one or more terms must be distinguished from "cross-reference", in which the predicate is independently marked for one or more pronominal terms, and nominal terms can be added to the verbal complex as appositions (see 6.6. above). We thus get patterns such as:

(59)   CROSS-REFERENCE
     a.   *The man he-walks.*
           'The man walks.'
     b.   *He-walks.*
           'He walks.'
(60)   AGREEMENT
     a.   *The man walks.*
     b.   **Walks.*

In the case of agreement, as in (60a), the agreement marker has no independ-

---

16. For some generalizations concerning the occurrence of interrogative particles, see Greenberg (1963), Ultan (1969), and Sadock—Zwicky (1985).

ent semantic import, but is simply a mechanical consequence of the verb being combined with a Subj term that has certain properties (viz. third person singular). The rule specifying this kind of agreement in English can be formulated as follows:

(61)   Pres <1 p3>[pred [V]] = pred-*s*

in which <1 p3> indicate the features copied from the Subject term.

Agreement between anaphor and antecedent is involved in such cases as:

(62)   When   I   left, nobody saw   me
                he   him
                the men   them
                the woman   her
                the car   it

It is evident that the anaphorical element takes different forms, depending on the Person / Number / Gender properties of the antecedent. The rules effecting this could have some such form as:

(63) $(Ax_i:<1\ p3\ masc>)_{Subj} = he$

in which (Ax_i) is the anaphorical term variable, and the features <1 p3 masc> have been copied from the antecedent term.

Note that the upshot of our treatment of agreement in 15.1.4. and here can be summarized as follows:

— There is a basic difference between agreement within terms, and agreement at the clause level.

— Only intrinsic properties of Source constituents can trigger agreement.

— Within terms, the head noun is the only Source constituent, and Gender is the only agreement category.

— At clause level, only terms trigger agreement, and Number, Person, and Gender are the only agreement categories. Note that Number is not intrinsic to the head noun within a term, but is intrinsic to the term as a whole. Therefore, it can figure as an agreement category at clause level.

— Apparent examples of Case, Number, and Definiteness agreement within terms are better regarded as being due to simultaneous expression of the relevant operators on different constituents of the term phrase, for reasons specified in 15.1.4.

16. Principles of constituent ordering

16.0. Introduction

As pointed out at several points in the preceding chapters, the abstract clause structures underlying linguistic expressions are regarded as unordered, at least in the sense that the order in which the various underlying constituents are given is not judged to be directly relevant for the linear order in which they finally appear in linguistic expressions.

Underlying clause structures are to be seen as relational structures ("networks"), in which the relational status of constituents is coded in their functional labels, whereas various scope differences are coded through bracketing. This is also true of the internal structure of terms. A term structure does have a certain ordering, but this ordering expresses semantic relations and does not necessarily correlate with surface linear order. For example, the term structure in (1) may be mapped onto such different linear orders as (2a-c):

(1)   (d 2 x_i: *elephant* [N]: *grey* [A])
(2) a. *the two grey elephants*
     b. *the two elephants grey*
     c. *elephants grey two the*
         etc.

In order to arrive at actual linguistic expressions, then, we need rules which assign positions to the constituents of the underlying structure in the linear sequences in which they can actually appear. These rules will be called *placement rules*. Both within and across languages, placement rules obey certain principles which constrain the possible sequences of constituents, and the possible combinations of such sequences in different domains. For example, a language may have prepositional (*on the table*) rather than postpositional (*the table on*) ordering at the phrase level, and this may correlate with VSO vs. SOV ordering at the clause level. The latter type of correlation was discovered by Greenberg (1963), and was termed "cross-categorial harmony" by Hawkins (1982, 1983). For both types of constraints we must try to formulate *constituent ordering principles*, which together approximate as closely as possible the different arrays of ordering patterns found in natural languages.

In this chapter we first make some preliminary remarks on the FG treatment of constituent ordering (16.1.); then, we formulate the idea of a "multifunctional" theory of constituent ordering (16.2.); in 16.3. we introduce a number of auxiliary notions, needed for the proper formulation of constituent ordering principles; in 16.4. we formulate a number of such principles, divided over more general and more specific principles. In the present chapter we simply present, explain, and exemplify the principles. Discrepancies, anomalies, counterexamples, and other complications will be discussed in chapter 17.

16.1. Some preliminary remarks

We start with some general remarks on the treatment of constituent ordering in FG, and on how it differs from other approaches to the problem.[1]

(i) *Placement rules are expression rules*. Placement rules are regarded as part of the expression component of a functional grammar: constituent order serves as one of the means through which relations and functions of underlying clause structure can be formally expressed. By regarding placement rules as an expression device, we can demonstrate the functionality of constituent ordering: alternative orderings may express certain distinctions between underlying clause structures. Some languages make more extensive use of this expression device than other languages, just as languages may differ in the amount of information they code in the form of constituents. Moreover, there is a certain degree of "trade-off" between these expression devices: roughly, the more information is coded in the form of constituents, the less is expressed in the order, and *vice versa*. This again shows that form and order together do the job of expressing the relevant underlying relations, with additional support from the prosodic contour differences to be discussed in chapter 18.

(ii) *Placement rules are not movement rules*. Placement rules are not rules which "move" a constituent from one specified position to another. Rather, they assign a position to a constituent which has no position yet, and in this sense "add" the feature of ordering to underlying unordered structures. Placement rules thus map underlying networks onto surface sequences (see 3.2.2. above).

---

1. For a detailed comparison of the treatment of constituent ordering in FG and some other theories, see Siewierska (1988).

Some preliminary remarks

The avoidance of movement rules in FG has an important consequence: constituents must be carried to their final position "in one go": once the constituent has been assigned a position, it cannot be moved to any other position in the sequence. This implies that all sorts of differences which have traditionally been described in terms of "reordering", "inversion", "permutation", etc., will have to be captured through alternative placements which are sensitive to differences in the underlying clause structure. For a very simple example, consider:

(3) a. *John is ill.*
 b. *Is John ill?*

In describing the order of (3b) we will not start with the order in (3a), to be reordered by some rule of "Subject-Verb Inversion". Rather, we start from a structure of roughly the form:[2]

(4) Int $[X_i: [is [V] ill [A] (John)_{\emptyset Subj}]]$

and formulate placement rules such that, given a structure such as (4), the verb will be immediately placed in front of the Subject. In order to do so, we could start with an ordering pattern or "template"[3] consisting of four labelled positions:

(5) 1 2 3 4

and formulate placement rules which put *John* in 2, *ill* in 4, and *is* in 1 if the clause carries the illocutionary operator Int, and otherwise in 3. In this way, it is directly expressed that this ordering difference is a function of the illocutionary status of the clause.

 (iii) *Constituent ordering is not a deep property of languages.* This approach implies that constituent ordering is not a "deep" property of natural languages, but a more superficial expressive device which, to a greater or lesser extent, can be used to code underlying relations into surface sequences. This has some important consequences:

— Since order is not a deep property, underlying clause structures for

---

 2. This structure has already undergone a number of form-determining rules, such as copula support and verb agreement.
 3. For the term "template" as used in this context, see Connolly (1983, 1986).

different languages need not differ in constituent ordering. This adds to the crosslinguistic validity of the notion "underlying clause structure", and to the typological adequacy of the theory.

— Since order is not a deep property of natural languages, there is no reason for there to be only a single "basic" order for a given language. The FG approach to constituent ordering is fully compatible with the co-existence of different patterns or templates, to be used in different conditions and for different purposes.

— Since order in not a deep property, there is no "deep" split between languages with relatively fixed and languages with relatively "free" word order patterns. So-called free word order languages from our point of view are languages in which placement rules carry less of the functional load of expressing the relevant underlying relations.

(iv) *There are no free word order languages*. A true free word order language would be a language in which, for a given set of constituents, all possible permutations of these constituents would not only be grammatical, but also communicatively equivalent to each other. Such languages do not exist, because:

— there are no languages which do not exclude at least certain sequences of constituents at some level;

— even where different sequences exist side by side, there will usually be some significant difference between them (for example, a difference in the pragmatic functions of the constituents).

Even in so-called free word order languages, then, we need placement rules in order to account for these facts.

16.2. Towards a multifunctional theory of constituent ordering

Since Greenberg's pioneering study of constituent ordering typology (1963) there has been a tendency to discuss constituent order in terms of a small number of simple principles dividing all languages into two or three basic types. Greenberg himself discussed his data in terms of the three basic types VSO, SVO, and SOV, although he was careful to add that this division was based on "... the relative order of subject, verb, and object in declarative sentences with nominal subject and object", on the assumption that "the vast majority of languages have several variant orders but a single dominant one"

(Greenberg 1963: 76).[4] Although Greenberg's trichotomy was thus based on a small, though important domain of constituent ordering, later authors tended to hypostatize such labels as VSO, SVO, SOV into names of supposedly unified, holistic language types, much as "isolating", "agglutinating", and "inflecting" were once used in morphological typology. This trichotomy breaks down on the fact that SVO languages, in contrast to VSO and SOV languages, do not constitute a unified type: very few constituent order correlations can be inferred from the knowledge that a language has SVO order.

Greenberg's three-way typology was further simplified into a dichotomy of VO vs. OV languages in the work of Vennemann (1972, 1973, 1974) and Lehmann (1973). Vennemann motivated his two types in terms of a principle of "natural serialization", which says that languages either choose the order Operand-Operator (as in VO languages), or Operator-Operand (as in OV languages), where "Operator" and "Operand" range over a variety of "modifying" vs. "modified" constituents at different levels of structure.

However, if the VO-OV opposition is taken as the only explanatory principle, only about 50% of all languages turn out to be true to one or the other type: all other languages must then be considered as mixtures of these types, or as being on their way from the one type to the other. The main reason for this is, again, that SVO is not a unified type, and can therefore not be joined into one type with VSO.[5]

Rather than blaming so many languages for not conforming to a simple principle, we assume that the principle is too simple to account for the actual complexity of the facts. This means that either the principle is incorrect, or interacts with other principles in determining the actual arrays of ordering patterns found in natural languages. I shall here take the latter course, and assume that constituent ordering patterns should be described and explained in terms of a number of interacting and possibly competing principles and preferences. This is what I understand by a "multifunctional" theory of constituent ordering.[6]

---

4. Siewierska (1988: 8-14) argues that the "basic" order as defined by Greenberg need not be the "dominant" one in terms of text frequency; nor need it be the "unmarked" order in given contextual conditions.

5. See Comrie (1981), Mallinson—Blake (1981), Hawkins (1979, 1980, 1982, 1983), and Siewierska (1988) for extensive discussion of the problems involved.

6. For similar approaches, see Steele (1975), Keenan (1979), Hawkins (1983). Note that the assumption of potentially conflicting tendencies may explain the lack of stability which occasions historical changes in constituent ordering. This is aptly

A multifunctional theory of constituent ordering is based on the following assumptions:

(A1) The actual constituent ordering patterns found in a language are the resultant of a number of interacting principles.

(A2) Each of these principles is in itself functionally motivated: it is a "natural" principle with respect to some parameter of "naturalness".

(A3) But two such principles do not necessarily define the same ordering preference. One principle may, for good reasons, prefer the order AB while another may, for equally good reasons, prefer BA.

(A4) Therefore, no language can conform to all the ordering principles at the same time and to the same degree.

(A5) The actual "solution" for constituent ordering in a given language will thus contain an element of compromise, and will to that extent be characterized by a certain amount of "tension".

(A6) Shifts in the relative force of the different principles may lead to (sometimes radical) changes in constituent ordering.

(A7) Where such changes relieve tension with respect to one principle, they may create new tension with respect to another.

(A8) There is consequently no optimal, stable solution to the constituent ordering problem.

16.3. Some auxiliary notions

In order to be able to formulate a multifunctional theory of constituent ordering as specified in (A1)-(A8) above, we need a number of auxiliary notions in terms of which the ordering principles can be formulated. In the first place, we must distinguish different domains of constituent ordering. The most important domains are (i) the clause (main or subordinate) as a whole, (ii) the term phrase, (iii) the adjectival phrase (= an adjectival restrictor plus its possible modifiers).

---

expressed by Steele (1975: 243): "If the order of elements is, at least in part, a function of strategies which may conflict, word order change may be the result of ever-changing resolutions of conflicts". The multifunctional approach has also been described in terms of the notion "competing motivations": certain principles motivate an ordering A-B, others an ordering B-A, and the two motivations are thus in competition with each other, a competition which may be won by either the one or the other principle. See Croft (1990).

The constituents to be ordered in the different domains are distinguished into the following types:

(6)   1.   lexical constituents
            1.1. heads
            1.2. dependents
      2.   grammatical constituents
            2.1. relators
            2.2. operators
                  2.2.1. ω-operators (term operators)
                  2.2.2. π-operators

Each domain in principle contains a (lexical) head.[7] The head is the central constituent of the domain, and acts as the point of orientation for the other constituents (dependents, relators, operators) in the domain. The heads of the different domains are the following:

(7)   DOMAIN   HEAD
      clause   main predicate (typically V)
      term phrase   first restrictor (typically N)
      adjectival phrase   adjective (A)

In each domain, the area in front of the head will be called the "Prefield"; the area after the head the "Postfield":

(8)   _____Prefield_____[head]_____Postfield_____

The area opposite a given field will be called the "Counterfield" of that field.

The dependents in a given domain are all the lexical constituents of that domain other than the head. The most important types of dependents are:

---

7. In earlier writings I used the term "center" for what is here called the "head". The present notion of "head" should not be equated with other uses of this notion. In particular, relators and operators are not treated as heads in the present approach.

(9)   DOMAIN   DEPENDENTS
      clause: — arguments, satellites;
      term phrase: — arguments, satellites (if any);
                              (i) non-first restrictors:
                              (ii) adjectival restrictors
                              (iii) possessive term predicates
                              (iv) other term predicates
                              (v) verbal restrictors (including relative clauses and participials);
      adjectival phrase: — arguments (if any), including standard of comparison;
                            — degree adverbials

For the various dependents which may occur in adjectival phrases, compare:

(10) a.   *fond of* cheese (argument)
     b.   *taller than* Peter (argument, standard of comparison)
     c.   extremely *cold* (degree adverbial)

The class of relators contains those grammatical elements which serve to link two constituents together, and/or to mark the function(s) of a constituent as specified in underlying clause structure. Relators may mark a relation of coordination or a relation of dependency. In the former case we speak of *coordinators*. Coordinators link two or more relata of equal rank, without forming a constituent with any of them. The resulting structures can be represented as:

(11)   [relatum] R [relatum]

Relators which mark a relation of dependency comprise (i) adpositions, (ii) case markers, (iii) subordinating elements (= either independent subordinating particles or subordinating affixes). These relators link a dependent constituent to a head. They form one constituent with one of their relata, usually with the dependent. This can be represented as follows:

(12)   [dependent[R]]...[head]...[[R] dependent]

We can now say that a dependent is placed either in the Prefield or in the Postfield of its domain, and may be linked to its head by a relator.

16.4. Constituent ordering principles

We are now ready to formulate a number of constituent ordering principles which together should approximate as closely as possible the actual ordering patterns found in individual languages.

Note that a number of things are uncertain with respect to these principles, their mutual interaction, and their relative "strength". Also, none of these principles has absolute validity: to all of them, exceptions can be found. The general idea behind the principles is, however, that they should reduce the number of stipulations required for defining the constituent ordering of individual languages. For example, in most languages Subjects precede Objects in the unmarked order of the clause. By formulating this as a general principle, we need not stipulate it again and again for those individual languages in which it applies. At the same time, languages with apparent Object-Subject order can be more closely scrutinized as to whether they present genuine or only apparent counterexamples to the principle. If they are genuine counterexamples, their "marked" character in this respect may be stipulated individually. When there is no such individual stipulation, the general default principle will apply. Various exceptions to, and conflicts between, the principles formulated here will be discussed in chapter 17.

We divide the constituent ordering principles into general and specific principles. The idea is that the general principles are reflected in the specific principles, and the specific principles in the actual constituent ordering patterns of individual languages.

16.4.1. General principles

(GP1)   *The Principle of Iconic Ordering.*[8]
Constituents conform to (GP1) when their ordering in one way or another iconically reflects the semantic content of the expression in which they occur.

The following would be examples of iconic ordering:

(i) The ordering of clauses in a text will, in the unmarked case, reflect the order of the events which they describe. The same is true of coordinated clauses. Subordinate clauses with the meaning 'after X' will more commonly

---

8. On iconicity as a factor in syntactic organization, see Haiman ed. (1985).

precede the main clause; those with the meaning 'before X' will more commonly follow the main clause:

(13) a. unmarked: *After John had arrived, the meeting started.*
    b. marked: *The meeting started after John had arrived.*
(14) a. unmarked: *The meeting started before John arrived.*
    b. marked: *Before John arrived, the meeting started.*

(ii) Conditional clauses most commonly precede the main clause, no matter what constituent ordering type the language belongs to (Greenberg 1963):

(15) a. unmarked: *If you are hungry, you must eat.*
    b. marked: *You must eat if you are hungry.*

Greenberg already explained this by saying that the "condition" is in some sense conceptually prior to the consequent.

(iii) Purpose clauses commonly follow the main clause, no matter what constituent ordering type the language belongs to:

(16) a. unmarked: *John went to the forest in order to catch a deer.*
    b. marked: *In order to catch a deer, John went to the forest.*

Again, the "purpose" of an action is in some sense something that can be realized only after the action has been carried out.[9]

(iv) It has been argued that the different "priority hierarchies" discussed in 2.4. play a role in constituent ordering, in the sense that what is closer to the "deictic centre" (what is more familiar, closer to the pragmatic information of S) comes earlier in the linear sequence (Allan 1987, Siewierska 1988).

Various further examples of iconic ordering will be encountered below.

(GP2)   *The Principle of Linear Ordering*
          Constituents conform to (GP2) when their linear order is fixed, no matter which position they take relative to the head.

Thus, the constituents x, y, z obey (GP2) if we find the following patterns (where H is the head):

---

9. Compare Thompson (1984) on purpose clauses in English, and Wakker (1987) on Classical Greek.

(17)   xyzH, xyHz, xHyz, Hxyz

Note that we can generalize across these patterns in terms of the ordering xyz, which is independent of H.

Linear ordering may be iconic (as in some of the examples discussed under (GP1)), but it may also be due to other factors, such as ease of production or comprehension.

(GP3)   *The Principle of Centripetal Orientation*
        Constituents conform to (GP3) when their ordering is determined by their relative distance from the head, which may lead to "mirror-image" ordering around the head.

Thus, the constituents x, y, z display centripetal orientation if we find such patterns as:

(18)   zyxH, zyHx, zHxy, Hxyz

Note that we can generalize across such patterns in terms of the ordering schema zyxHxyz. The relevant patterns could also be represented as follows:

(19)

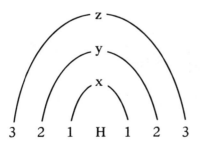

```
            z
          y
        x
3   2   1   H   1   2   3
```

In this schema, the vertical column represents the hierarchical relations among the constituents; we could now say that x takes position 1, y position 2, and z position 3, no matter whether they precede or follow the head. Note that this predicts the following possible orderings for the constituents in (19):

(20) | | 3 | 2 | 1 | H | 1 | 2 | 3 |
|---|---|---|---|---|---|---|---|
| a. | z | y | x | H | | | |
| b. | z | y | | H | x | | |
| c. | | y | x | H | | | z |
| d. | z | | x | H | | y | |
| e. | z | | | H | x | y | |
| f. | | y | | H | x | | z |
| g. | | | x | H | | y | z |
| h. | | | | H | x | y | z |

We may hypothesize that centripetal orientation of constituents reflects the closeness of the bond between the dependents and the head, and the scope relations among the dependents. Thus, centripetal orientation will always be a matter of iconic ordering.

(GP4) *The Principle of Domain Integrity*[10]
Constituents prefer to remain within their proper domain; domains prefer not to be interrupted by constituents from other domains.

Exceptions to (GP4) will be described in terms of "displacement": constituents may exceptionally be displaced to a position outside their own domain (see chapter 17).

(GP5) *The Principle of Head Proximity*[11]
Constituent ordering rules conspire to keep the heads of different domains as closely together as possible.

For example, (GP5) would define (21a) as preferred to (21b):

(21) a. *the very* young man sneezed *suddenly*
 b. young *very* man *the suddenly* sneezed

In (21a) the three heads are contiguous, in (21b) they are separated by

---

10. The formulation of this principle is due to Jan Rijkhoff (work in progress).
11. This principle was formulated by Rijkhoff (1986). In his view this principle can be used to capture a number of phenomena which otherwise require separate principles.

intervening material. Rijkhoff (1986) argues that a number of ordering phenomena may be understood as strategies for avoiding or reducing such intervening material. See below, under (GP8) and (SP8).

(GP6)   *The Principle of Functional Stability*
Constituents with the same functional specification are preferably placed in the same position.

For example, (GP6) is responsible for the fact that in most languages which have Subject and/or Object assignment it makes sense to speak of a characteristic Subject and Object position.

(GP7)   *The Principle of Pragmatic Highlighting*
Constituents with special pragmatic functionality (New Topic, Given Topic, Completive Focus, Contrastive Focus) are preferably placed in "special positions", including, at least, the clause-initial position.

(GP7) implies that constituents may be placed in positions other than their basic position for pragmatic reasons. (GP7) may override such principles as (GP6) and even (GP4): in the latter case, a constituent is "displaced" from its proper domain for pragmatic reasons.

(GP8)   *The Principle of Cross-domain Harmony*
Each language has a certain degree of consistency in either using Prefield or Postfield ordering across the different ordering domains.

Thus, if we find (a certain degree of) Prefield ordering at the clause level, we may also expect (a certain degree of) Prefield ordering at the level of the term phrase and the adjectival phrase. The principle of "harmony" across different domains was formulated by Greenberg (1963), and underlies the idea of a "Natural Serialization Principle" as formulated by Vennemann (1972). In Hawkins' (1983) formulation, however, the principle includes the idea that if the clause domain is in some respects "less" Prefield/Postfield, the term domain will likewise have a lesser degree of field consistency.

Rijkhoff (1986, 1987) tries to explain this type of relative harmony by means of his Principle of Head Proximity (GP5) above. For example, a consistent Prefield language (of the "rigid" subtype) will have ordering patterns of the form:

(22)   — — N — — N V

in which — — indicate the dependents of the N, which will remain in their Prefield position since otherwise the N head would be separated from the V head. In languages of the "non-rigid" Prefield type, in which certain terms can be placed after the V, we would get patterns of the form:

(23)   — — N V — — N

In such a pattern, the postverbal N would be separated from the V head by the intervening dependents. Therefore, Rijkhoff hypothesizes that in the non-rigid, but not in the rigid subtype of Prefield languages, there will be a tendency to place some dependents of the N in postnominal position, so that the distance between the V head and the postnominal N head is minimized:

(24)   — N — V — N —

Rijkhoff finds some confirmation for this hypothesis, but there are counterexamples both ways. For that reason, we just present (GP5) as one possible principle, while still retaining some other principles which, if the correlations were perfect, could be seen as being entailed by it.

(GP9)   *The Principle of Increasing Complexity*
        There is a preference for ordering constituents in an order of increasing complexity.

This principle, which can be seen as an instantiation of GP2, was first formulated by Behaghel (1932) as the "Gesetz der Wachsenden Glieder" ('law of increasing parts') (see H. Dik 1988). It can be illustrated as follows:

(25) a. preferred: [–] [—] [——] [———] [———]
     b. non-preferred: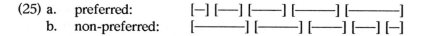

As we shall see below, (GP9) may counteract certain other principles, in particular (GP6): although constituents with the same functional "profile" prefer to be placed in the same position, this preference may be overridden by differences in internal complexity between such constituents. Complexity in this sense is often referred to as "heaviness" (Mallinson—Blake 1981: 157; Hawkins 1983).

16.4.2. Specific principles

(SP1)   A language makes a basic choice between Prefield or Postfield ordering of dependents with respect to their heads.

This is a more specific formulation of (GP8). If (SP1) were the only principle determining constituent ordering, there would be just two distinct language types, parallel to the OV-VO distinction made by Vennemann and Lehmann, with the following ordering patterns:

(26)   PREFIELD   POSTFIELD

boy book girl give   give *boy book girl*
              'the boy gives the book to the girl'
boy book   book *boy*
              'the book of the boy'
brown book   book *brown*
              'the brown book'
fast running boy   boy *running fast*
              'the fast running boy'
extremely cold   cold *extremely*
              'extremely cold'
Peter taller   taller *Peter*
              'taller than Peter'

In actual fact, however, (SP1) is often counteracted and interfered with by other principles, so that only about 50% of all languages belong to one or the other of these "consistent types". Such languages may be called "Prefield languages" and "Postfield languages". Even for the other languages, however, we can start from these two types in order to understand how the different variant types may be interpreted.

(SP2)   The Subject position precedes the Object position.

(SP2) defines the following basic patterns for Prefield and Postfield languages:

(27) a.   Prefield: S O V   *man tree cut*
     b.   Postfield: V S O   *cut man tree*

Thus, we can say that Subject and Object have linear orientation (see (GP2) above), independently of their position with respect to the predicate. (SP2) is functionally motivated, and can be interpreted as one form of "iconic" linear ordering (cf. (GP1)). This can be understood in the following way. We have interpreted the functions Subj and Obj in terms of a notion of "perspective": the Subj function marks that term which designates the entity from whose point of view the SoA is presented; the Obj function marks a secondary vantage point relevant to the presentation of the SoA (see 10.2.). On that interpretation of Subj/Obj, (SP2) is certainly a "natural" principle: it would be rather strange for a language to systematically prepose the Obj to the Subj, where the Obj marks the secondary, and the Subj the primary vantage point.

It should be noted, however, that we do not assume that Subj and Obj assignment are relevant to all languages. We restrict the claim of (SP2) to those languages in which we assume that Subj *and* Obj assignment are relevant operations, according to the criteria discussed in 10.4.1. (SP2) therefore embodies no claim for languages in which Subj/Obj are not both relevant in this respect. In this light we shall consider the claim that certain languages have basic Object-Subject order in section 17.1. below.

(SP3) Relators have their preferred position
 (i) in between their two relata;
 (ii) at the periphery of the relatum with which they form one constituent (if they do so).

For coordinators, (SP3) defines the following preferred and non-preferred orderings:

(28) a. Preferred: [relatum] R [relatum] *John* and *Peter*
 b. Non-preferred: [relatum] [relatum] R *John Peter* and
  R [relatum] [relatum] and *John Peter*

Non-coordinating relators mark a dependent as being linked to some head. For these relators, (SP3) defines the following preferred and non-preferred orderings:

(29) a. Preferred: [[dependent] R]...[head]
  [head]...[R [dependent]]
 b. Non-preferred: [R [dependent]]...[head]
  [head]...[[dependent] R]

Non-coordinating relators may be: (i) adpositions, (ii) case markers, (iii) subordinating elements (i.e. subordinating words or subordinating affixes). We may distinguish the different applications of patterns (29a) according to the domain in which they operate (cf. Limburg 1983, 1985).

In the domain of the predication, (SP3) defines the following preferred markings of arguments and satellites in relation to the V:

(30)   PREFIELD   POSTFIELD
        postposition   preposition
        case suffix   case prefix

(31)   PREFIELD PREFERRED PATTERN
        John-nom car-with Amsterdam-to went

(32)   POSTFIELD PREFERRED PATTERN
        went nom-John with-car to-Amsterdam

It must be noted that case prefixes are exceedingly rare. Thus, although the relators in Prefield patterns may well have the status of case suffixes, the relators in Postfield patterns typically are independent or possibly proclitic words (i.e. prepositions).[12]

(SP3) also applies to embedded constructions in their relation to the main V. In this case it predicts that preverbal embedded clauses will tend to be marked finally, whereas postverbal embedded clauses tend to be marked initially:[13]

(33)   PREFIELD PREFERRED PATTERN
        John-nom [Peter-nom arrived-when] house-to went
        'John went home when Peter arrived'

(34)   POSTFIELD PREFERRED PATTERN
        went nom-John to-house [when-arrived nom-Peter]

Within the domain of terms, (SP3) defines the preferred way in which restrictors will be linked to the head noun. Thus, if restrictors have any relator at all, this will preferably be a final marker if the restrictor is in the Prefield, and an initial marker if it is in the Postfield. This may be illustrated with the preferred patterns for possessors, adpositional restrictors, and relative constructions

---

    12. See the discussion in Kahr (1976) and Dik (1983b).
    13. Compare Dik (1983b), Kahrel (1985) for other manifestations of these preferences.

(where RM = Relative Marker):

(35) PREFIELD PREFERRED PATTERNS
1. *man-of house*
   'house of the man'
2. *garden-in chair*
   'chair in the garden'
3. *[chair-on sit-RM] man*
   'man sitting on a chair'

(36) POSTFIELD PREFERRED PATTERNS
1. *house of-man*
2. *chair in-garden*
3. *man [RM sit on-chair]*

In the domain of adjectival phrases, (SP3) predicts preferred patterns such as:

(37) PREFIELD PREFERRED PATTERNS
1. *John-than taller*
   'taller than John'
2. *students-of smartest*
   'smartest of the students'

(38) POSTFIELD PREFERRED PATTERNS
1. *taller than-John*
2. *smartest of-students*

It is clear that (SP3) has strong predictive power with respect to a variety of construction types. As far as data are available now, all the predictions of (SP3) are correct in at least a strong statistical sense. However, violations of preferred relator positions may arise through the interactive competition between different ordering principles. Some of the resulting conflicts will be discussed in chapter 17.[14]

(SP4) There is a universally relevant clause-initial position P1, used for special purposes, including the placement of constituents with Topic or Focus function.

Together with (SP1) and (SP2) this gives us the following basic patterns:

---

14. See Limburg (1983, 1985) for more detailed discussion of (SP3).

(39) a. Prefield: P1 S O V
     b. Postfield: P1 V S O

All languages may be supposed to use P1 for special purposes, though not necessarily in the same way. The general pattern for the uses made of P1 is as follows:

(i) Languages often have designated categories of constituents which must be placed in P1 (P1-constituents);

(ii) If P1 is not occupied by some P1-constituent, it may be used for constituents with (Given)Topic or Focus function.

Some usages of P1 will be exemplified in chapter 17. Languages may have other "special positions" than P1. These will also be discussed in chapter 17.

(SP5)   Since the Subject is the prime GivenTopic candidate, it will often be placed in P1.

Principle SP5 may lead diachronically to a reinterpretation of P1 as the unmarked Subject position.

Compare, in this light, the following patterns:

(40)   PREFIELD   POSTFIELD
       P1 S O V   P1 V S O
       S   O V   S V   O

When the Subj-GivTop is placed in P1 in Prefield languages, this has little effect on the resulting order of constituents. Thus, a reinterpretation of P1 as the basic Subj position will not create a different ordering pattern in Prefield languages. In Postfield languages, on the other hand, this reinterpretation process (due to a kind of markedness shift) may lead to a new pattern SVO; since P1 is claimed to be universally relevant, a new P1 position must be added to this pattern, yielding P1SVO. In that pattern, an over-exploitation of P1 will not lead to a different ordering. Thus, it is in fact only V-initial languages which are sensitive to the type of reinterpretation mentioned in (SP5). Indeed, VSO languages always have SVO as an alternative order (Greenberg 1963: 79): they are intrinsically under a certain pressure to develop into SVO languages.[15]

On the other hand, many alleged SVO languages are better interpreted as

---

15. For the historical development involved, see Dik (1980: chapters 7-8).

P1VSO languages with a strong tendency to place the Subj in P1. We can see this by comparing English and Dutch, both at first sight SVO languages:

(41) a. *John stays in Amsterdam until December.*
b. *Jan blijft in Amsterdam tot december.*
(42) a. *Until December John stays in Amsterdam.*
b. *Tot december blijft Jan in Amsterdam.*
(43) a. *In Amsterdam John stays until December.*
b. *In Amsterdam blijft Jan tot december.*

There are two relevant differences between English and Dutch:

(i) Dutch much more often has non-Subject constituents in P1 than English; correspondingly, the constructions of (42) and (43) are less "marked" than they are in English (see 2.5.1 above).

(ii) when a non-Subject is placed in P1 in Dutch, the Subj itself appears in postverbal position. For this reason, Dutch can be described in terms of a P1VSO pattern, whereas English requires a P1SVO pattern.

(SP6)   The Prefield is universally less hospitable to complex material than the Postfield; Prefield languages may thus be expected to possess strategies for relieving the Prefield of excessive complexity.

Whereas (SP4) predicted that Postfield languages will often place constituents in the Prefield P1 position, (SP6) predicts that Prefield languages will often tend to place certain constituents in the Postfield. It may be supposed, however, that the reasons for these two cases of "Counterfield placement" are rather different. Placement in P1 is mainly triggered by pragmatic factors: the initial position is used to "highlight" a constituent which has special pragmatic significance in the clause. The reason underlying (SP6), on the other hand, is supposed to be the tendency to avoid excessive complexity in the Prefield (i.e., too much complex material before the head is reached).

With respect to (SP6) we must distinguish between "strict" Prefield languages, which allow no constituents after the head, and more liberal Prefield languages, which do allow such constituents. We can also express this by saying that liberal Prefield languages allow a certain amount of "leaking" of constituents beyond the head.[16]

---

16. The difference between strict and more liberal SOV languages was made by Greenberg (1963). The term "leaking" is due to Ross (1973).

There is some reason to believe that diachronically leaking may progressively allow more and more constituents to be placed in the Postfield, in such a way that an initial Prefield pattern may finally yield a dominant SVO order:

(44) a. P1 S O X V
     b. P1 S O   V   X
     c. P1 S   V O X

If this presumed development were to occur, the final product would be a Prefield-derived SVO language, i.e. an SVO language which still has a number of Prefield properties. For example, in a pattern such as (44a) we expect postpositional marking of the terms. Suppose, now, that we find an SVO language with patterns such as:

(45)   *man kill tiger gun-with*

Then, the postpositional marking of the instrumental term in the Postfield may be taken as a Prefield trait, and the language may be supposed to be the result of the development sketched in (44). Such languages do indeed occur rather frequently. Note that the postposition in (45) is in non-preferred position in relation to (SP3). Further developments might create a prepositional marking on such Postfield terms. For discussion of such reorganizations, see 17.5.2.

The upshot of these various principles is that SVO languages in fact come in two types: Postfield-derived, with placement of the Subj in P1 according to principles (SP4) and (SP5); and Prefield-derived, due to leaking of constituents beyond the V. This squares with the fact that the class of SVO languages is typologically not uniform: unlike SOV and VSO languages, SVO languages do not allow solid predictions with respect to constituent order correlations in other domains.

(SP7)   Other things being equal, constituents prefer to be placed in an order of increasing complexity, which is defined as follows:
  (i) clitic < pronoun < noun phrase < adpositional phrase < subordinate clause;
  (ii) for any category X: X < X co X;
  (iii) for any categories X and Y: X < X [sub Y].
  (co = coordinating element, sub = subordinating element)

This principle, a more specific formulation of (GP9), was termed "LIPOC" (language-independent preferred order of constituents) in Dik (1978a: ch. 9). The present formulation of this principle differs in some respects from the earlier one: it has been adapted to fit in with the other ordering principles presented in this chapter.

(SP7) is intended to account for the fact that in most languages there are situations in which we find constituents either earlier or later in the sequence than would be expected on the basis of their functional profiles. To a considerable extent, such deviations from expected ordering may be understood in terms of the following two tendencies:

(46) (i) constituents which are relatively less complex than other constituents of similar function tend to occur earlier in the linear sequence;
 (ii) constituents which are relatively more complex than other constituents of similar function tend to occur later in the linear sequence.

For an example, consider the following French examples:

(47) a. *Jean a donné le livre à son frère.*
 John has given the book to his brother
 'John has given the book to his brother.'
 b. *Jean l' a donné à son frère.*
 John it has given to his brother
 'John has given it to his brother.'
 c. *Jean a dit à son frère qu' il est malade.*
 John has said to his brother that he is ill
 'John has said to his brother that he is ill.'

In (47a) the nominal Goal constituent *le livre* is in the basic position for such Goals, in a pattern of the form:[17]

(48)   P1   S   V   A²   X

In (47b), on the other hand, the clitic pronominal element *le* is placed in preverbal position, whereas the subordinate clause which functions as Goal in (47c) appears in clause-final position.

According to (SP7) these are not idiosyncratic facts about French: the principle predicts that such complexity-monitored order variations may be

---

17. French has no Object assignment.

expected in languages, and also in which direction these variations will go.

(SP8) π-operators prefer expression in
    (i) the Counterfield;
    (ii) the second position in the clause.

Consider an auxiliary verb as the manifestation of a π-operator.[18] (SP8) predicts the following preferred positions for such an auxiliary:

(49)   PREFIELD   POSTFIELD
      P1 S   O V Aux   P1 Aux   V S O
      P1 Aux   S O V

Note that (SP8)(ii) adds no further preferred pattern for Postfield languages, since Aux is already in clause-second position on the basis of Counterfield placement; in Prefield languages, however, (SP8)(ii) does add an extra pattern, in which the Aux takes the same position as in Postfield languages.

Placement of Aux in clause-second position has been described as a form of "cliticization" (Steele 1977, Hock 1982). If it is true that only clitic auxiliaries tend to undergo this shift, then this phenomenon may be subsumed under LIPOC (SP7). However, it is questionable whether "weakening" of the auxiliary to a clitic is a necessary condition for this type of placement.

The preference of Aux-like elements for clause-second position may explain certain historical developments which, in the last instance, may lead to a shift from SOV to SVO order (Steele 1977, Garber 1980, Hock 1982). The scenario would be as follows:

(50)   Stage 1: S   O   X V Aux
      Stage 2: S   Aux O X V
      Stage 3: S   Aux O V X
      Stage 4: S   Aux V O X

Placement of Aux in clause-second position leads to a discontinuity of the verbal complex in Stage 2 (which is the present-day stage of Dutch and German main clauses); this would be followed by a tendency to re-unite the verbal complex through progressively placing constituents after the V (such

---

18. Compare Greenberg (1963) and Steele (1975) for the preferred positions of auxiliaries.

postposing is optional in Dutch for prepositional phrases); the end result at Stage 4 is a Prefield-derived SVO language with reunited verbal complex (this would be the present-day stage of English).

Hock (1982) argues that some such process has taken place in the Germanic and the Slavic languages, and Garber (1980) interprets the constituent ordering variations in a number of West African languages as representing different stages of (50). Thus, the following example from Tyebara (Gur) illustrates a Stage 3 construction:

(51) mìi à gé le lòno ni
     I Fut them put water in
     'I shall put them in water'

Note that the postpositional marking in the Postfield reveals the Prefield origin of the constituent. Such marking is a widespread phenomenon in the Gur and Mande languages of Western Africa.[19]

(SP9) π-operators prefer centripetal orientation according to the schema: $\pi_4\ \pi_3\ \pi_2\ \pi_1$ [stem] $\pi_1\ \pi_2\ \pi_3\ \pi_4$

This principle, formulated by Hengeveld (1989), says that the mutual ordering of π-operators iconically reflects their scope differences. See 15.2.2. above.

(SP10)   Term operators prefer the Prefield.

Hawkins (1983) found the following distribution of "demonstratives" (Dem, including articles) and "numerals" (Num) in postpositional and prepositional languages (postpositional strongly correlates with Prefield, prepositional with Postfield ordering):

---

19. There is a question here as to what triggers what in this postulated development: does Aux-placement in clause-second position trigger "leaking" (Hock 1982), or does "leaking" trigger the shift of Aux (Rijkhoff 1987)? Crucial to this question is whether languages of Stage 2 can be found: with Aux in second position, but without leaking. Rijkhoff had no languages of this type in his sample of 22 Prefield languages.

(52)

	DemN	NDem	NumN	NNum
postpositional:	75.9	24.1	70.0	30.0
prepositional:	49.4	50.6	65.7	34.3
overall:	62.6	37.4	67.8	32.2

These data show that both Dem and Num have a rather strong preference for Prefield position. In the case of Num, this preference is hardly influenced by the Prefield/Postfield character of the language; in the case of Dem the preference for Prefield position increases by about 13% in Prefield languages, and decreases by the same percentage in Postfield languages. Note that our principles provide no explanation for Postfield placement of Dem and Num in Prefield languages (24.1% and 30.0%, respectively).

(SP11)   Dem, Num, and Adj prefer centripetal orientation according to the schema: Dem Num Adj N Adj Num Dem.

The facts concerning this type of ordering are as follows: if Dem, Num, and Adj all precede the N, they are always ordered according to (SP11); if they all follow the N, the mirror-image ordering of (SP11) is the most frequent ordering (cf. Greenberg 1963, Hawkins 1983). We return to some of the complications involved in term phrase ordering in chapter 17.

(SP12)   Relative constructions prefer the Postfield.

Hawkins' data are here as follows:

(53)

	RelN	NRel
postpositional:	61.4	38.6
prepositional:	00.9	99.1
overall:	31.1	68.9

Most remarkable here is the fact that Postfield languages will hardly ever have their relative constructions in the Prefield; on the other hand, there is a rather strong tendency for Prefield languages to have them in the Postfield. This could be interpreted as due to the impact of LIPOC (SP7) at the term phrase level. A more detailed look at the typology of relative constructions will reveal, however, that prenominal and postnominal RCs differ not only in position, but also in internal organization. For example, prenominal RCs are typically non-finite and do not contain relative pronouns. These features of RCs will be discussed in *TFG2*: chapter 3.

The internal ordering of term phrases displays more variation than could be captured by a few simple principles. We return to some of the problems involved in the next chapter.

17. Constituent ordering: problems and complications

17.0. Introduction

The general and specific ordering principles formulated in the preceding chapter go a long way towards explaining the actual constituent ordering patterns found in individual languages. To most of these principles, however, real or apparent counterexamples may be found; certain constituent ordering phenomena are not accounted for by the principles; and complications may arise through the mutual interaction between competing principles. In this chapter, we consider a number of such problems and complications. In 17.1. we discuss languages which are said to have Object-Subject order, against the prediction of (SP2). Section 17.2. further discusses the status and the usage of the "special position" P1, and shows that languages may have other such "special positions", usually with a certain "division of labour" with respect to pragmatic functionality. Section 17.3. considers a number of difficult facts concerning ordering within term phrases. In 17.4. we consider some cases of "displacement", by which a constituent is placed outside its proper domain, against (GP4), the principle of Domain Integrity. Section 17.5., finally, discusses some cases in which ordering according to one principle may lead to violation of some other principle.

17.1. Object-Subject languages

Certain languages are described in the literature as having a basic order in which the Object precedes the Subject (VOS, OVS, or OSV).[1] The number

---

1. The best documented language with alleged OVS order is Hixkaryana (Derbyshire 1977, 1979, 1981). Derbyshire—Pullum (1979) made a special study of "OS" languages, presenting 8 candidates for OVS (including Hixkaryana), and 4 for OSV status. Many of these languages belong to the Amazon area, and many of them have not been extensively described. The case for OSV languages in particular is not yet very strong. See also Pullum (1981) on the problem. Howell (1983) describes another Carib language, Wajana, as OVS. Romero-Figueroa (1985) presents Warao as an OSV candidate. Keenan (1978) is a special study on Subject-

of these languages is quite small, so that even if they are genuine counterexamples to (SP2), such counterexamples amount to no more than about 1% of the world's languages. Thus, (SP2) in any event has a very high degree of statistical validity. Nevertheless, genuine counterexamples to this principle would present a problem to the FG interpretation of Subject and Object, for the general interpretation of Subj and Obj in terms of primary and secondary perspective could hardly be upheld in languages in which the Obj systematically precedes the Subj. As I have argued in Dik (1980: 136-150), however, it is doubtful whether the languages which have been claimed to have O-S order do indeed present genuine counterexamples to (SP2). Consider the following points:

(i) In many of these languages it can be shown that Object assignment in the FG sense is not distinctively relevant. This means that what is called "object" is in fact the second argument A^2. The counterexamples then reduce to cases of VA^2S, A^2VS, and A^2SV order. These are not in contradiction with (SP2).

(ii) In many of these languages even Subj assignment in the FG sense is not relevant. This means that the counterexamples reduce to cases of VA^2A^1, A^2VA^1, and A^2A^1V. Again, these orders are not excluded by (SP2).

(iii) In some of the relevant languages there are indications that the "subject" is, or was originally, a Tail constituent (a final constituent which falls outside the clause proper, cf. 13.1. above). Consider the following constructions:

(1) a. *The rich man bought the house.*
    b. *He-bought the house, the rich man.*

(1b) might arise as a variant of (1a) in an SVO language. If, for some reason, (1b) became the normal clause order through a process of "markedness shift" (see 2.5.3. above), the result would be a language with apparent VOS order in which, however, the position of pronominal subjects might reveal its original SVO character. There is indeed evidence in a number of alleged OS languages that such a process of markedness shift may at least have played a historical role in the creation of the uncommon constituent order.[2]

---

final languages, presenting 8 candidates (including Malagasy and Fiji) for VOS status.
  2. Compare Dik (1980) for more detailed discussion, and Derbyshire (1981) for the possible role of the demarking of original Tail constituents in creating OVS order.

If Subj/Obj assignment is not relevant to a given language, and (SP2) is thus irrelevant to that language, the question arises what the preferred orders are of A^1 and A^2 in relation to the V and to each other. There is some reason to believe that the following (tentative) principle may be involved in this case:

(SP2*) The preferred ordering of A^1 and A^2 in relation to the V is determined by the principle of Centripetal Orientation (GP3) as: A^1 A^2 V A^2 A^1.

(SP2*) would define the following preferred orders for languages without Subj/Obj assignment:

(2) a. A^1 A^2 V   ["SOV"]
    b. A^1 V A^2 ["SVO"]
    c. A^2 V A^1 ["OVS"]
    d.   V A^2 A^1 ["VOS"]

Principle (SP2*) could be interpreted as pointing to the fact that, when Subj/Obj assignment is not relevant to a language, there is a closer bond between A^2 and V than between A^1 and V. Some evidence for this may be found in the Carib languages (to which Hixkaryana belongs): these languages may be described in terms of the general pattern:

(3) A^1 [A^2 V] A^1

in which the A^2 precedes the V and forms a closely-knit unit with it, while the A^1 may either precede or follow this combination. In Hixkaryana it is common for A^1 to follow the V, although it may also precede the [A^2 V] unit; in other Carib languages, the order A^1 [A^2 V] dominates; these languages are accordingly described as "SOV".

If (SP2) and (SP2*) together account for the preferred orders of the V and its most central arguments, then there will be no room for "OSV" languages. Perhaps this is not a bad result, since the evidence for the existence of such languages is the weakest of all.

17.2. Special positions

In (SP4) of the preceding chapter it was claimed that all languages have a special clause-initial position P1 which is used for special purposes. These special purposes include (i) placement of constituents which *must* be placed in P1; (ii) placement of constituents with special pragmatic significance. In this section we consider in more detail how the P1 position is exploited (with special reference to Dutch constituent ordering); and we consider other special positions which languages may use for similar purposes.

17.2.1. The uses of P1

Languages differ in the ways in which and in the degree to which they exploit the P1 position. In order to clarify the uses of P1 by means of a concrete example, let us look at the uses of P1 in Dutch. Dutch constituent ordering is rather remarkable in the following three respects:
— the basic position of the Subj in main clauses may be claimed to be postverbal, although the most frequent surface order is S V ...;
— Dutch has distinct ordering patterns for main and for subordinate clauses;
— in main clauses the verbal complex (i.e. the finite verb Vf and the non-finite verb Vi) may be discontinuous: Vf...Vi.
Some of these properties can be captured by assuming the following ordering patterns (templates) for main and subordinate clauses:

(4) a. main: P1 Vf S O X Vi
    b. subordinate: P1   S O X {Vf Vi}/{Vi Vf}

Note that, subject to certain constraints, the Vf in the subordinate clause may be placed before or after the Vi. Note further that the position of the Vf is the major difference between main and subordinate clause ordering. Obviously, the two templates could be collapsed in the following way:

(5)   P1 Vf[main]   S O X Vf[sub] Vi Vf[sub]

The Vf would then be placed in Vf[main] in the expression of main clauses, and in one of the Vf[sub] positions otherwise.

X in these various patterns stands for non-Subj, non-Obj constituents ("oblique" arguments, satellites) which will need further differentiation in a full description of Dutch constituent ordering.[3] In such a fuller account of Dutch constituent ordering, some further X-positions will be required.

The various uses made of P1 in Dutch can be formulated in the following rules:

(6)   (R0)   P1 must contain one and only one constituent.
        (R1)   Place P1-constituent in P1, where P1-constituent = question word,[4] subordinator, or relative pronoun.
        (R2)   else, place constituent with GivTop, SubTop or Foc function in P1 (optional).
        (R3)   else, place X in P1, where X = some satellite or a dummy element.

In main clauses the only potential type of P1-constituent to which reference is made in (R1) is a Q-word. Thus, if there is a Q-word, this must be placed in P1 (unless the question is an echo question). If the Q-word is in P1, no other constituent can take that position:

(7) a.   *Waarom heb je dat boek gekocht?*
        why   have   you that book bought
        'Why have you bought that book?'
    b.   **Waarom dat boek heb je gekocht?*
        why   that book have you bought

Note that in accordance with template (5), the Subj appears in post-Vf position. If the Q-word itself happens to be Subj or Obj, the post-Vf S or O position will remain empty:

(8) a.   *Wie heeft [S] dat boek gekocht?*
        who   has   that book bought
        'Who has bought that book?'

---

3. In ProfGlot (Dik 1992) an overall template of some 16 positions is used for some seven languages.

4. Since question words are assumed to have intrinsic Focus, one might ask why P1-placement of Q-words is not left to (R2). However, P1-placement of Q-words is obligatory (except in echo questions), whereas it is optional for Focus constituents. Obviously, the intrinsic Focus of Q-constituents may have contributed to their being treated as P1-constituents.

b. *Wat   heb   je   [O] gekocht?*
   what   have   you   bought
   'What have you bought?'

Although multiple questions are possible in Dutch, only one Q-constituent may be placed in P1:

(9) a. *Wie   heeft   welk   boek   gekocht?*
       who   has   which   book   bought
       'Who has bought which book?'
    b. **Wie   welk   boek   heeft   gekocht?*
       who   which   book   has   bought[5]

If there is no Q-constituent in the main clause, the P1 position may be used for Topic or Focus constituents:

(10) A: *Heb   je   dit   boek   gelezen?*
        have   you   this   book   read
        'Have you read this book?'
     B: *Nee,   dit   boek*[GivTop]   *heb   ik   niet   gelezen.*
        no   this book   have   I   not   read
        'No, I haven't read this book.'
(11) A: *Welk   boek   heb   je   gelezen?*
        which book   have   you   read
        'Which book have you read?'
     B: *DIT BOEK*[Foc]   *heb   ik   gelezen.*
        this book   have   I   read
        'I read THIS BOOK.'

There are situations in which neither (R1) nor (R2) leads to a constituent being placed in P1. In such conditions, some other constituent will be placed in P1, since, as stipulated in (R0), P1 must be filled (and thus the Vf must be in clause-second position in main clauses). This will happen above all in two conditions:

---

5. (28b) can be used as a kind of echo question in the sense of '(You ask me) who has bought which book?', but in that case the construction may be interpreted as exemplifying the subordinate clause pattern.

(i) in constructions in which a NewTop is introduced, as in:

(12) a. *Er heeft een man voor je opgebeld.*
 there has a man for you called
 'A man called to speak to you.'
 b. *Vanmorgen heeft (er) een man voor je opgebeld.*
 this-morning has there a man for you called
 'This morning a man called to speak to you.'

As we saw in 13.3.1, NewTop constituents are not usually placed in clause-initial position. In Dutch they normally occupy their basic "pattern position". Thus, the Subject *een man* is placed in S position in (12a-b), and if nothing else were done, the P1 position would remain empty. Two strategies are followed to prevent this: in (12b) a temporal satellite is placed in P1; in (12a) a dummy adverb *er* (= weak 'there') occupies the P1 position.

Note that the dummy *er* optionally also occurs in (12b). This shows that this element is not ONLY a P1 place-holder. However, Haiman (1974) has demonstrated that such elements as *er* arose, in various Germanic languages, as mere P1-dummies. In some of these languages, in different conditions and at different times, these dummies came to be integrated into the construction so that they could also be used outside the P1 position. This happened in the Dutch construction (12b) but not, for example, in the German equivalent:

(13) a. *Es hat ein Mann für dich angerufen.*
 b. *Heute morgen hat (*es) ein Mann für dich angerufen.*

Satellites placed in P1 on account of (R3) are typically satellites of place, time, or circumstance, i.e. satellites which specify features of the setting in which the described SoA took place.

(ii) The second condition in which (R3) operates is when clausal Subjects are placed in clause-final position on account of LIPOC (SP7). Compare:

(14) a. *Dat je niet kunt komen is jammer.*
 that you not can come is a pity
 'That you cannot come is a pity.'
 b. *Het is jammer dat je niet kunt komen.*
 it is a pity that you not can come
 'It is a pity that you cannot come.'

In (14a) the clausal Subj is placed in P1. In (14b) it is placed in clause-final position, and the dummy *het* 'it' takes the P1 position. The same element appears in Subj position when some other constituent is placed in P1:[6]

(15)   *Daarom is   het   jammer dat je   niet kunt   komen.*
        therefore is it   a pity that you not can   come
        'Therefore it is a pity that you cannot come.'

Subordinate clauses use the template (4b), with the Vf-Vi complex in final position, as is evident from examples (14)-(15). Subordinate clauses almost always have a P1-constituent (subordinator or relative pronoun). The subordinator is exemplified by *dat* 'that' in (14)-(15). Relative pronouns likewise go to P1, as in:

(16)   *de   man   die   deze   auto   heeft gekocht*
        the man   who   this   car   has   bought
        'the man who bought this car'

The P1 position in subordinate clauses will thus usually be occupied by a P1-constituent; placement of Top or Foc constituents in P1 is therefore excluded.[7]

17.2.2. Special positions other than P1

The claim that P1 is universally used as a "special position" does not exclude the possibility that languages may have other such special positions inside the ordering template, used for similar purposes, possibly even with a certain degree of specialization as to the kinds of constituents which they may accommodate. Indeed, such further special positions have been postulated for

---

6. In ProfGlot (Dik 1992) a specific treatment of the appearance of such dummies has been implemented: a first Subj placement rule checks whether the Subj has the form of a subordinate clause; if so, that Subject is optionally or obligatorily "extraposed" to one of the last positions in the template. At the same time, the dummy *het* is left in the Subj slot and will from that moment on be treated as "the" Subject by later Subject placement rules.

7. There are some alternative ways of creating some kind of "pragmatic articulation" in subordinate clauses. See Dik (1981) for some discussion.

a number of languages. Consider the following examples:

Hungarian
De Groot (1981b) analysed Hungarian as a language in which Subj and Obj function play no distinctive role, and in which constituent ordering can be described in terms of the following template:

(17)   P1   P∅   V   X

which is used in the following ways:
— P1 can harbour one or more Topic constituents;
— P∅ can harbour just one Focus constituent;
— constituents with neither Topic nor Focus function go to X.

Turkish
Van Schaaik (1983) argues that Turkish has the following template:

(18)   P1 A^1 X   Y   P∅   V

in which:
— P1 can be used for Topic constituents;
— P∅ is used for Focus constituents;
— A^1 is used for first arguments, X for satellites, and Y for A^2 and A^3 terms, when these constituents have no special pragmatic function.

Serbo-Croatian
Dik—Gvozdanović (1981) and Gvozdanović (1981) argued for a template of the form:

(19)   P1   CL   P∅   V   X

where CL is a strongly defined clause-second position used for a variety of clitics (pronominal, verbal, and clausal clitics all flock together into this position), whereas constituents with Topic or Focus function go to P1 or P∅; terms with no particular pragmatic function are placed in the postverbal position X.

Arabic
Moutaouakil (1984, 1985) argues that constituent ordering in Arabic can be described in terms of the following template:

(20)   P1 PØ V S O X

In this template:
— P1 and PØ can each contain only one constituent;
— subordinators obligatorily go to P1;
— one Q-constituent or constituent with Contrastive Focus obligatorily goes to PØ;
— SubjTop can only go to S; otherwise a Top constituent may optionally be placed in PØ, unless this position is occupied by some other constituent.

Aghem
Watters (1979) analysed Aghem in terms of the following template:

(21)   P1 S Aux   PØ V Pa O X

with a special postverbal position Pa used for Focus constituents. See 13.4.5. for a summary of the uses of pattern (21).

Polish
Siewierska (1988: 125-127) described Polish as having a clause-final position PØ, used for Focus constituents. Similar clause-final Focus positions have been claimed to be used in Czech (cf. Kim 1988b) and Bulgarian (Stanchev 1988).

Although only a few languages have been described in any detail in this respect, their ordering patterns nevertheless allow for some tentative generalizations:
(i) such multiple special positions typically occur in languages in which the Subj/Obj system is not, or only weakly developed. The explanation for this is that Subj and Obj are typically tied to specific positions, such that the Subj position precedes the Obj position. If Subj/Obj are not relevant in a language, constituent ordering will be mainly determined by pragmatic factors. In such languages, we typically find more "freedom" of constituent ordering, or rather a richer array of pragmatically monitored "special positions" and a richer set of rules for exploiting these positions.
(ii) the most common "extra position" is the position immediately before the Verb.[8] Languages which have this position typically use it for Focus

---

8. Compare Kim (1988a) for general discussion.

constituents, while using P1 for Topic placement. Such languages thus have two special positions in the Prefield; constituents without special pragmatic function end up in the Postfield.

(iii) a restricted number of languages use the clause-final position for Focus placement. In the languages which have been claimed to have a clause-final Focus position, however, this position is not used for Q-words (except in echo questions). Siewierska (1988: 125) describes the clause-final position in Polish as that position which takes items in focus IN THE UNMARKED CASE. Further research will have to show whether such clause-final positions are also used for marked placement of pragmatically salient items. If not, the clause-final position could be described as a position which lends a certain "natural" relief to that constituent which happens to end up in it.

(iv) exceptionally, the immediately postverbal position Pa may be used for special purposes. Note, however, that this position is only used for Focus constituents. In *TFG2*: 14.2 it will be suggested that this position is not a genuine "special position" of the simplex clause, but rather reflects an alternative "Cleft" or "Pseudo-cleft" organization of the clause. The constructions in question would then not correspond to (22a), but rather to (22b):

(22) a. *Has this book written who?*
    b. *The one who has written this book (is) who?*

Note that in (22b) *who* can be interpreted as being in predicate position rather than in postverbal (or post-predicate) Focus position.

The conclusion is that special positions are typically found in the Prefield; if the postverbal instances of special positions can be explained in other ways, as suggested under (iii) and (iv) above, then we can even say that special positions are always found in the Prefield.

17.3. Constituent ordering within term phrases

In chapter 16 we formulated some tentative principles concerning constituent order within term phrases. These principles certainly do not account for all the actual patterns found in this domain. There is much more variation in term phrase ordering than would be expected on the basis of these principles. This variation, however, is not random: although in many languages constituents within term phrases do not appear in their expected Prefield or Postfield positions, the ways in which they deviate from these expected positions dis-

428 *Constituent ordering: problems and complications*

play a degree of orderliness which asks for further explanatory principles. This has been most clearly demonstrated by Hawkins (1983), who also formulated some tentative explanatory principles in order to make sense of the rather chaotic data at the term level.

17.3.1. Applicability of the principles to the term domain

Let us first consider to what extent the various principles formulated in chapter 16 have explanatory value with respect to term phrase ordering.

(SP1) Prefield/Postfield choice
(SP1) and, more generally, the principle of Cross-domain Harmony (GP7), does have a certain degree of explanatory power at the term level. This is most clearly the case for the placement of Possessor constituents, which strongly correlates with the Prefield/Postfield character of the language:

(23)   Prefield: Possessor - Head
        Postfield: Head - Possessor

This correlation holds for about 82% of all languages.

The Prefield/Postfield parameter is also relevant to the placement of relative constructions (RCs), in the sense that Prefield RCs are almost exclusively found in Prefield languages. In general, however, RCs prefer the Postfield (SP12).

We return to the effect of the Prefield/Postfield parameter in 17.3.2. below.

(SP2*) A^1/A^2 ordering
Subj and Obj assigment are not applied within the domain of nominal terms in FG, so that (SP2) is not relevant at this level. Nominal predicates may have arguments, however, and some evidence for the centripetal principle (SP2*) may be found at the term level. Consider such constructions as the following:

(24) a. *the marching of the soldiers*
     b. *the capturing of the plane by the hijackers*

It has been argued that nominalizations such as (24a-b) can be understood in terms of a tendency to formally adjust the expression of verbal predications within the domain of a term to the prototypical format of nominal terms (Dik 1985a). One step in this adjustment is the use of Possessor expression for one of the arguments of the nominalized predicate. In one-place predicates it is the A^1 which is so adjusted; in two-place predicates, however, it is typically the A^2, as in (24b). This points to a closer bond between A^2 and predicate than between A^1 and predicate, and the typical order of the arguments in (24b) could be interpreted as being due to a centripetal ordering preference according to the pattern $A^1 \; A^2 \; V \; A^2 \; A^1$. This would make us expect that nominalizations may take the ordering $A^1 \; A^2 \; V$ in Prefield languages. This happens to be true in Tamil (Asher 1982), Kobon (J. Davies 1981), and Imbabura Quechua (Cole 1982), but I know of no systematic typological survey relevant to this question.[9]

(SP3) The placement of relators
This principle is strongly operative at the term level. Such orderings as the following exemplify strongly preferred patterns:[10]

(25) a. *John's car*   car of John
     b. *garden in chair*   chair in garden
     c. *mother to letter*   letter to mother
     d. *laughing man*   man who laughs
     e. *four-footed animal*   animal with four feet
     f. *Viennese sweets*   sweets from Vienna
     g. *presidential address*   address by the president

In about 80% of all languages, a prenominal Possessor is finally marked, a postnominal Possessor initially marked (Limburg 1985).

(SP4) Special positions
This principle, and the more general principle of Pragmatic Highlighting (GP7) is much less influential at the term phrase level than at clause level. There is apparently less reason to assign special pragmatic significance to

---

9. In both Tamil and Kobon the arguments retain the form which they also have in verbal clauses. This is also the case in Imbabura Quechua, where, however, we find an optional feature which points to a closer bond between A^2 and V: when the Goal of a nominalized complement appears immediately before the V, its accusative marker may be left out, so that the bare stem of the noun is in immediate contact with the V. This process is described as a form of noun incorporation by Cole (1982: 37).

10. Here and elsewhere in this chapter I use a kind of "pseudo-English" to exemplify patterns which are commonly found (or not found) across languages.

parts of term phrases than there is to parts of the clause. The order of constituents within a term is usually rather fixed, and there is little room for pragmatically significant alternatives. There are exceptions to this, however.

One example is Babungo (Schaub 1985) in which all nominal dependents (including possessors and demonstratives) occur in the Postfield, but EMPHATIC possessors and demonstratives may be placed in prenominal position. Such a situation could well be described by means of a pattern of the form:

(26)   P1   N   X

where P1 is the first position in the term phrase, used for special pragmatic purposes, in this case for Focus.

A second example is Latin, according to the analysis given in De Jong (1983). According to this analysis nominal dependents are placed in the Postfield in the unmarked case, but may be preposed for various pragmatic reasons, such as Contrastive Focus, GivenTopic, and SubTopic highlighting.

(SP6) Lower degree of hospitality of the Prefield
This principle is relevant at the term level, as is evident from such facts as the following:

(i) relative clauses have a preference for the Postfield.

(ii) sometimes less complex modifiers may be preposed, but more complex modifiers must be placed after the noun:[11]

(27) a.   *an interesting book*
     b.   *a book interesting for readers of any age*

(iii) a rather specific, but telling rule from Mam (a Mayan language, England 1983: 145): the adjective precedes if there are no other modifiers (demonstrative, numeral, negative element) in front of the noun; otherwise the adjective follows. This clearly suggests that there is "limited space" in the Prefield.

(SP7) LIPOC: increasing complexity
This principle is relevant at the term level (cf. Siewierska 1988: 43-47). For example, RCs not only prefer the Postfield, but also preferably occupy the

---

11. Compare Siewierska (1988: 43-47).

final slot in the term phrase. Alternatively, they may even get "extraposed" (displaced) out of the term phrase altogether into some later position in the clause, as in:

(28)   *I met a girl last week in Paris who had the most beautiful eyes I have ever seen.*

We return to the relevance of LIPOC at the term level below.

(SP10) Preference of term operators for the Prefield.
(SP11) Centripetal orientation of Dem, Num, and Adj with respect to the N.
(SP12) Preference of RCs for the Postfield.

These principles do have some explanatory power with respect to preferred term phrase ordering, but they leave many facts unexplained. Let us consider some of these facts.

17.3.2. Hawkins' facts and their explanation

The placement of term phrase constituents was most extensively studied by Hawkins (1983), who considerably extended Greenberg's (1963) data base with respect to the order of Dem, Num, Gen ("genitive" or Possessor) and Rel with respect to the head Noun. Starting from the theoretical assumption that all determiners and modifiers might be expected to occur in either the Prefield or the Postfield, Hawkins found two kinds of deviations from this theoretically expected pattern: quantitative deviations (e.g., in a postpositional or Prefield language we nevertheless find 42% adjectives in the Postfield), and hierarchical "priorities" (e.g. in a prepositional or Postfield language we never find the Adj in the Prefield unless Dem and Num also occur in the Prefield).[12] Hawkins' findings can be summarized as in the following diagram:

---

12. Hawkins' data are based on a division into "postpositional" and "prepositional" languages; however, this division strongly correlates with Prefield and Postfield organization, respectively.

(29) | | PREFIELD | | | POSTFIELD | | | |
|---|---|---|---|---|---|---|---|
| | (postpositional) | | | (prepositional) | | | |
| Poss | Dem | Adj | N | Dem | Adj | Poss | Rel |
| 5.9 | 24.1 | 42.0 | | 49.4 | 31.5 | 11.9 | 0.9 |
| | Num | Rel | | Num | | | |
| | 30.0 | 38.6 | | 65.7 | | | |

This diagram should be read as follows:

(i) The constituents are presented in their expected positions at the basis of Pre/Postfield ordering. The percentage underneath each constituent type indicates the degree of deviation from the theoretical expectation. For example, in Prefield languages we find postnominal Possessors in only 5.9% of all languages.

(ii) The order of the constituent types indicates a partial hierarchy according to which they may deviate from the theoretical assumption. Thus, in a Prefield language Adj/Rel are the first to be expected in the Postfield, then Dem/Num, and finally Poss.

Hawkins tries to make sense of these data in terms of two explanatory hierarchies: "Heaviness" (= increasing complexity = LIPOC), and "Mobility":

(30) HEAVINESS HIERARCHY:
Dem/Num < Adj < Poss < Rel
(31) MOBILITY HIERARCHY:
Adj/Dem/Num > Poss/Rel

The Heaviness hierarchy is used to explain the deviation from Postfield placement in Postfield languages: the less "heavy" a constituent, the greater its liability to appear in the Prefield even in Postfield languages. However, if constituents "defect" from the Postfield in the order defined by the Heaviness hierarchy, we should expect the reverse order in Prefield languages. The order of deviations to the Postfield should then be:

(32) Rel > Poss > Adj > Dem/Num

In fact, however, the order of defection in this case is:

(33) Rel/Adj > Dem/Num > Poss

It is this discrepancy which Hawkins tries to explain through interference with the Mobility Hierarchy (31). This hierarchy says that Adj/Dem/Num more easily defect from their field than Poss/Rel. In Postfield languages, Heaviness and Mobility define the same order of defection. In Prefield languages, however, the interference of Mobility keeps Poss longer in the Prefield than would be expected on the basis of Heaviness. For Rel, Hawkins has to assume that Heaviness outweighs Mobility in both cases, so that it is the first constituent type to defect to the Postfield, and the last to defect to the Prefield.

17.3.3. Discussion of Hawkins' explanation

It is questionable whether Hawkins' explanation brings us much closer to an understanding of the facts of diagram (29). Note the following points:

(i) The explanation is based on the initial theoretical assumption of full Prefield/Postfield consistency. This assumption, however, leads to rather strange results in the case of Dem and Num which, as we saw in (52) of chapter 16, have a rather strong preference for the Prefield (62.6% and 67.8%, respectively). This is especially so in the case of Num, the placement of which is hardly sensitive to the Prefield/Postfield parameter: if we assume that Num should theoretically appear in the Postfield in Postfield languages, we find that this is actually true in only one out of three of these languages. Rather than explain why Num defects from this theoretical assumption so often, we should question the theoretical assumption as such. This is what we have done by assuming that term operators have other placement preferences than term dependents, and basically prefer a position in the Prefield. That Dem and Num may appear in the Postfield in Postfield languages in 50.6 and 34.3% of all cases can then be attributed to the influence of the Postfield parameter. What we do not explain in this way is why 24.1% Dem and 30.0% Num appear in the Postfield even in Prefield languages.

(ii) If the factor "heaviness" is involved, this factor should operate across the board, in the same way for Prefield and Postfield languages. This is true for Rel, which hardly ever leaves the Postfield in Postfield languages, but shows 38.6 % defection from the Prefield in Prefield languages. But it is not the case for Poss, which shows the highest degree of "field loyalty", and is the last constituent type to appear in the Postfield in Prefield languages. Hawkins' factor "Mobility" does not add much explanatory power, since it is in fact a restatement of the facts of diagram (29).

(iii) With respect to "Heaviness", Adj is not convincingly more heavy than Num, nor is Poss, when expressed adjectivally, convincingly more heavy than Adj. This throws further doubt on the relevance of this parameter.

(iv) Hawkins' explanation does not account for a number of facts concerning the mutual ordering of term constituents. It has been known since Greenberg (1963) that, when all of Dem, Num, and Adj precede the noun, they always occur in this order. However, when all these constituents follow the noun, a frequent (though not universal) order of these constituents in the Postfield is the mirror image of the Prefield ordering:[13]

(34)　　Dem Num Adj N Adj Num Dem

This type of Postfield ordering is incompatible with the linear order imposed by "heaviness"; rather, it points to a certain degree of "centripetal orientation", which we have captured in (SP11) of the preceding chapter. This type of orientation suggests that the organization of term phrases is not only determined by linear, but also by hierarchical parameters.

Apart from the kind of mirror-image ordering of (34), there are some further facts which point to centripetal orientation in term phrases:

— Though, as we saw above, the Adj has little preference for Prefield or Postfield position, it does seem to have a strong preference for being contiguous with the Noun. In most languages, in other words, Adj-Noun combinations can be described in terms of the schema:

(35)　　...............Adj N Adj..................

— When several adjectives are combined in a non-coordinate way, their order is usually fixed, as in:

(36)　　*beautiful fast red car*

It has been argued that such adjectives are ordered in such a way that the adjective designating the most "intrinsic/permanent/unchangeable" property is closest to the noun (cf. Clark—Clark 1977: 474). Hetzron (1978) distinguished a great number of semantic subcategories of adjectives, and suggested that the adjective is closer to the noun the more "objective" the property which it indicates. This was confirmed for Latin by Risselada (1984). In other words, the following ordering might be expected in Prefield and Postfield languages:

(37)　　*beautiful fast red car red fast beautiful*

---

13. Compare Hawkins (1983: 119), Siewierska (1988: 44).

If it is true that the order of Dem, Num, and Adj is determined by centripetal orientation rather than by some such linear principle as "heaviness", it may be concluded that differences in the semantic status and the scope of term dependents may be more important than their internal complexity.

Though we do not find Hawkins' explanations convincing, it must be added that our own principles, as formulated in chapter 16, leave many of the relevant facts unexplained. The following facts concerning term phrase ordering do not follow from these principles:

(i) why should Dem and Num appear in the Postfield in Prefield languages?

(ii) why should Adj only occur in the Prefield in Postfield languages when Dem and Num likewise occur in the Prefield? And why should the other precedence relations of diagram (29) be as strong as they are?

(iii) what kind of principle could explain the ordering N Dem Num Adj which is found in the Postfield as a frequent alternative to N Adj Num Dem?

(iv) what explains the remarkable "field loyalty" of Poss?

Rather than speculate about these questions, I shall leave them unanswered as they stand.

17.3.4. Some conclusions

Constituent ordering within term phrases is a difficult area for linguistic theory, for three reasons: (i) there is a greater amount of crosslinguistic variation here than in some other domains, (ii) there is less crosslinguistic data available than on other domains, (iii) fewer convincing or at least promising explanatory principles have been advanced. At least the following points have emerged from the discussion in the preceding sections:

(i) Num has a rather strong preference for the Prefield.

(ii) The placement of Num is hardly sensitive to the Prefield/Postfield parameter.

(iii) The placement of Dem, Poss, Adj, and Rel is codetermined by the Prefield/Postfield parameter.

(iv) Rel has a strong preference for the Postfield. This preference can be understood in terms of LIPOC ("Heaviness").

(v) Centripetal orientation is an important factor in term phrase ordering. This suggests that semantic status and scope relations among term phrase constituents may be more important in monitoring constituent ordering than linear principles connected with internal complexity.

17.4. Displacement phenomena

Principle (GP4) of chapter 16 said that constituents prefer to be placed within their proper domains, and that domains prefer not to be interrupted by constituents from other domains. Both within and across languages, we find a number of systematic exceptions to this principle, in which a constituent or part of a constituent is "displaced" outside its proper domain. In this section we consider some examples of the different forms in which such displacement manifests itself, and some factors which might condition its occurrence.[14]

Four types or "degrees" of displacement may be distinguished:

(i) Pure displacement: a constituent is placed in some position outside its proper domain; the resulting construction is otherwise identical to the construction without displacement.

(ii) Displacement + adjustment to the host domain: a constituent is placed outside its proper domain, and is in some way formally adjusted to the requirements of the "host domain" in which it ends up.

(iii) Displacement + adjustment of the source domain: a constituent is displaced outside its proper domain, and its "source domain" is formally expressed in a different way than if the constituent were not displaced.

(iv) "Raising": a constituent is displaced outside its proper domain by virtue of Subj or Obj assignment from a higher domain into a lower domain.

These various types of displacement can be illustrated with the following examples:[15]

(38) a. *John believed [that the enemy-nom had blown up the bridge-acc].*
    b. *The enemy-nom John believed [that had blown up the bridge-acc].*

This is a case of pure displacement: the term *the enemy* is placed in the domain of the matrix clause without any further adjustment of the construction. Note that (38b) could be described in terms of placing a constituent of an embedded clause in the P1 position of the matrix clause; this would presumably be done for pragmatic reasons.

(39)   *The enemy-acc John believed [that had blown up the bridge-acc].*

---

14. For general discussion of such displacement phenomena within the context of FG, see Bolkestein et al. (1981).
15. Again I use "pseudo-English" to illustrate these phenomena.

In this case the displaced term is formally adjusted to the requirements of the matrix domain: it is assigned accusative case, "as if" it were a Goal argument of the matrix verb *believe*.

(40)   *The enemy*-nom *John believed [to have blown up the bridge*-acc*]*.

Here the source domain of the displaced term gets non-finite (infinitival) expression, as a corollary to the displacement: one might connect this with the fact that the Subj has been displaced out of the subordinate domain, and that the lack of a Subj in that domain leads to non-finite expression.

Typically, the source domain will be adjusted in this way only when the displaced constituent is adjusted in the way exemplified in (39). It remains to be determined, however, whether this is a necessary condition for adjustment of the source domain.

(41) a.   *The enemy*-nom *was believed by John [to have blown up the bridge*-acc*]*.
     b.   *The bridge*-nom *was believed by John [to have been blown up by the enemy]*.

These examples cannot be described in terms of displacement plus formal adjustment, since that would not explain why the matrix verb is realized in passive rather than active voice. If these voice differences are accounted for in terms of alternative Subj assignment, we must assume that exceptionally the Subj function relevant to the matrix verb *believe* has been assigned to the Subj of the embedded clause, rather than to the embedded clause as a whole. This yields the FG interpretation of "Raising" phenomena, as discussed in 11.5.[16]

Displacement, in its various guises, may be attributed to a defeat of the principle of Domain Integrity (GP4) by certain other principles, the most important of which would seem to be the principle of Pragmatic Highlighting (GP7) and the principle of Increasing Complexity (GP9), (SP7).

Pragmatic Highlighting is involved when the displaced constituent is placed in some "special position" of the host domain on account of its pragmatic functionality. This factor is especially clear in cases of displacement of Q-words, a widespread phenomenon in languages which do place Q-words in special positions, especially if the special position is P1:

---

16. See also Dik (1979) on the treatment of Raising phenomena in FG.

(42) a. *Who did John believe [had blown up the bridge]?*
b. *What did John believe [the enemy had blown up]?*

This kind of displacement of Q-words is so widespread that it might well be taken as the source of displacement phenomena in non-interrogative clauses. Underlying this would be the preference for using the same format for Q-word questions and their corresponding answers:

(43) a. *What did John believe [the enemy had blown up]?*
b. *The bridge John believed [the enemy had blown up].*

The strategy should thus be to find out what pragmatic factors might explain the displacement phenomena in these cases.[17]

Increasing Complexity is involved when the displacement can be interpreted as a means of reducing the complexity of constituents in the position in which these occur. The clearest case is provided by so-called "Extraposition from NP", as in:

(44) a. *John met [a man who tried to sell him a second-hand car] yesterday.*
b. *John met [a man] yesterday [who tried to sell him a second-hand car].*

The displacement of the relative clause from the complex term relieves that term of the excessive complexity which creates difficulties in the non-final position in which it occurs in (44a).

Note that displacement for pragmatic reasons will bring constituents to "special positions" which are typically found towards the front end of the clause, whereas displacement for complexity reasons will typically bring constituents towards the end of the clause. Even in the latter case, however, pragmatic factors may also be involved: thus, Guéron (1980) argued that Extraposition from NP is restricted to presentative constructions in which (in

---

17. There is a reasonable amount of evidence that such pragmatic factors are involved. For example, De Groot (1981a) analysed displacement phenomena in Hungarian in terms of the rule that a Topic term may be displaced out of a Topic embedded clause, and a Focus term out of a Focus embedded clause; in each case, the displaced constituent will be placed in the Topic or Focus position of the higher clause.

our terminology) the NP has NewTopic function, and both the NP as such and the extraposed constituent contain focal information (Siewierska 1988: 41).

17.5. Interactions between the ordering principles

In the preceding sections we have already encountered some examples of interactions or "competition" between different ordering principles: situations in which a principle A "wins out" over another principle B, and may thus create A-preferred orders which are non-preferred with respect to B.

Obviously, a multifunctional theory of constituent ordering as advocated here has an inherent danger of "vacuity" or "explanation after the fact": the danger is that we set up a principle A and, if the facts do not conform to A, call in a principle B in order to explain solely the violations of principle A.

Explanations of this type are strengthened if:

(i) violations of principle A lead to orderings which are clearly "marked" either within or across languages, or both;

(ii) violations of principle A can be understood in terms of the operation of INDEPENDENTLY MOTIVATED principles B, C, etc.

(iii) violations of principle A may be shown to be followed by adjustments which serve to reduce the violation.

Some examples of these various situations will be discussed now.

17.5.1. Preposings in Postfield languages

If we start from a consistent Postfield language, all preposings of constituents to the verbal (Aux V) complex may create conflicts with some of the principles governing Postfield languages. Such preposings may first of all be due to the principle of Iconic Ordering (GP1). Consider:

(45)   *If will tell John the truth will cry Mary.*

This construction, while conforming to the iconicity principle in respect to the preferred position of conditional clauses, has at least two non-preferred properties: the subordinate clause is in initial rather than in final position (non-preferred with respect to LIPOC), and the subordinator *if* is in non-preferred position with respect to the Relator Principle (SP3). However, we do find the following variants in different non-related languages:

(46) a. *If will tell John the truth,* then *will cry Mary.*
b. *Should tell John the truth,* (then) *will cry Mary.*

Thus, the conditional protasis may be placed in initial, extra-clausal position (as in (46a)); this position is arguably less sensitive to LIPOC; it may be resumed by an element such as *then*, which may be interpreted as a kind of relator; and/or a language may have variants of conditional protases without initial subordinator. Note that if the latter feature is interpreted as a strategy for avoiding the non-preferred relator position, we would not expect such variants in the Postfield. At least for some languages this expectation is borne out. Compare Dutch:

(47) a. *Mocht   Jan   komen, bel   me dan   even.*
        might   John   come   call me then   moment
        'Should John come, please give me a ring'
   b. **Bel   me   dan   even,   mocht   Jan   komen.*
        call   me   then   moment   should   John   come
   c. **Bel   me   even,   mocht   Jan   komen.*
        call   me   moment   should   John   come

The second source of preposings in Postfield languages is placement of constituents in P1 position. Compare:

(48) a. *Will go John to London.*
b. *To where will go John?*
c. *To London will go John.*

Again, the preposition *to* is in non-preferred position in (48b-c). Especially in the case of Q-words (for which P1 in many languages is the unmarked position), however, we do find phenomena which can be interpreted as strategies for avoiding the non-preferred relator position. Consider the following constructions:

(49) a. *Where will go John?*
b. *Where-to will go John?*
c. *Where will go John to?*

In (49a) we have a Q-word without relator; in (49b) we have an exceptional postposing of what elsewhere appears as a preposition; in (49c) the preposition is "stranded" in the Postfield.

It may not be immediately convincing to propose that preposition stranding should be interpreted as a strategy for avoiding a non-preferred relator position. The prediction is, however, that no "postposition stranding" will occur in Prefield languages. Compare:

(50) a. *John London to go will.*
  b. *Where to John go will?*
  c. **Where John to go will?*

Preposings in Prefield languages do not create any problems with respect to the Relator principle. Therefore, we do not expect (50c); and indeed, no examples of this kind of postposition stranding seem to be on record.

Note that postposing constituents in general creates no conflicts in Postfield languages. We may therefore expect those principles which tend to carry constituents to later positions in the linear order to freely operate in Postfield languages.

17.5.2. Postposings in Prefield languages

In Prefield languages, the situation is just the other way around: preposing constituents to P1 position in general creates no conflicts; placing constituents after the verbal complex (V Aux) does create such problems. Compare:

(51) a. *John London to go will friend visit for.*
  b. *John London to go will he friend visit want because.*
  c. *John London to go will friend with.*

The tendency to postpose constituents might be due to the Iconicity Principle (51a), to LIPOC (51b), or to "leaking" (51c), which itself may be due to avoidance of excessive complexity in the Prefield, or to other factors as discussed above. Each of these postposings leads to conflicts with the Relator principle. Perhaps this is the reason why many Prefield languages (of the "rigid" type) disallow any such postposing. In such languages, embedded clauses will be placed in the Prefield, but at the same time they will typically get some kind of non-finite realization:

(52) a. *John [friend visiting for] London to go will.*
  b. *John [friend visiting wanting because] London to go will.*

The pervasive non-finite realization of embedded clauses in the Prefield may be due to the fact that non-finite (participial, nominalized) constructions are less sensitive to LIPOC than finite subordinate clauses.[18]

If it is assumed that leaking and/or placement of Aux in clause-second position may cause a shift from SOV to SVO (see the discussion under (SP8) in chapter 16), then it must also be assumed that a shift from postposition to preposition is part of this process:

(53) a. *John friend with London to go will.*
 b. *John will London to go friend with.*
 c. *John will go London to friend with.*
 d. *John will go to London with friend.*

Such a shift may have taken place in the Romance and the Germanic languages, if it is assumed that these originate in Prefield (SOV) patterns.

---

18. See Dik (1978a: chapter 9) for discussion of this point.

18. Prosodic features

18.0. Introduction

There are three essential aspects of the form of linguistic expressions which are taken care of by the expression rules: (i) the segmental form of constituents (see chapters 14–15), (ii) constituent ordering (chapters 16–17), and (iii) the prosodic properties of linguistic expressions. In this chapter we discuss these prosodic properties. We shall say that a linguistic expression gets or is assigned a *prosodic contour*, which is composed of three main features: *tone*, *accent* and *intonation*. In 18.1. we discuss the main properties of these features, and the general form of the prosodic contours which they are used to create. Then, we consider the different functions of prosody, indicating, in each case, how that particular function could be accounted for in terms of the model of FG (18.2.). Finally, we consider how these different functions interact in producing the final prosodic contour of the linguistic expression, and how prosodic contours could be generated through expression rules, given the various relevant features of the underlying clause structure (18.3.).[1]

18.1. Prosodic contours

The same string of phonological segments may be expressed with different prosodic contours, as in:

(1) a. *John left the COUNtry*
     b. *John left the COUNtry/*
     c. *JOHN left the country*
     d. *JOHN left the country/*

---

1. The study of the forms and functions of prosodic contours is a very complicated matter, of which this chapter only gives a first and sketchy impression. The most important distinctive feature of this sketch is that an attempt is made to view the prosodic contour of an utterance as the compositional expression of a number of different-level properties of the underlying clause structure. For a recent discussion of the many problems involved in the study of prosody, see Cruttenden (1986).

These expressions, in which small capitals provisionally indicate accent-bearing syllables, and \ and / a falling or rising terminal intonation, have clearly different meanings, corresponding to the systematic differences in prosodic contour. That they have different meanings implies that there must be differences in their underlying clause structures; and that these meanings are expressed by different prosodic contours means that there must be expression rules which map the underlying semantic differences onto differences in prosody.

By *prosodic contour* we mean the over-all "melody" with which the linguistic expression is produced. For our present purposes we identify the *domain* across which prosodic contours range with the clause. One clause typically has a unified prosodic contour, although within such a contour different subcontours may be distinguished. Constituents which fall outside the structure of the clause ("extra-clausal constituents", such as Themes, Parentheses, Tails, and the like, to be treated in *TFG2*: chapter 17) are typically "set off" from the prosodic contour of the clause proper by some kind of intonational inflection (cf. Cruttenden 1986: 75-80). Consider:

(2) a. *Well* \, *John* /, *I* THINK *we can start the proceedings* \
 b. JOHN /, (*Peter's brother* /), *seems to have* LEFT \
 c. JOHN *seems to have* LEFT *London* \ *Peter's* BROTH*er I mean* \

In the following we leave these extra-clausal constituents out of account.

The main components of which prosodic contours are made up are *tone*, *accent* and *intonation*. The study of prosody is complicated by the fact that these three components use the same primary medium of expression: differences in "pitch" (tone level) with which the linguistic expression is pronounced. Apart from these primary pitch features, there may be concomitant features of loudness, preciseness of articulation, duration and rhythm. These features, however, play a subordinate role in the constitution of prosodic contours.

18.1.1. Tone

The feature of *tone* is confined to so-called "tone languages". In such languages, each syllable is characterized by an intrinsic "pitch profile", which in many cases is distinctive for the lexical identity of predicates. These tone differences then play the same role as distinctive differences between segmental phonemes. For that reason, such distinctive tones are often called "tonemes". Tonemes can be distinguished into *level tones* (e.g. High, Low, Mid) and *contour tones*, in which there is a change in pitch level; contour tones may be *simple* (e.g. a Rise, a Fall) or *complex* (e.g. a Rise-Fall, or a Fall-Rise). Maddieson (1978) formulates the following universal with respect to the cooccurrence of these tone types:

(3)   Level > Simple Contour > Complex Contour

I.e., languages never have complex contour tones unless they have simple contour tones; and they never have simple contour tones unless they have level tones.

Contour tones may be distinguished in terms of the tone levels at which they start and at which they end up. In some respects contour tones resemble diphthongs in segmental phonology, in that they can only be described in terms of "movement" through articulatory or auditory "space". Note, however, that even in systems with level tones, these are not produced at absolute pitch levels, but at pitch levels which are "high" or "low" relative to one another. This means that even in such systems, it is the *transition* from one level to another rather than the pitch level as such which signals the different tones.

The distinctive nature of tonemes can be illustrated with the following examples from Mandarin Chinese (Hyman 1975a: 214), where we find:

(4) a.   /ma/ + High tone   = 'mother'
    b.   /ma/ + High-Rise tone = 'hemp'
    c.   /ma/ + Fall-Rise tone = 'horse'
    d.   /ma/ + High-Fall tone = 'scold'

Tone patterns may also be distinctive on polysyllabic predicates. For example, a language may distinguish bisyllabic predicates in terms of tone pattern, as in Igbo (Hyman 1975a: 213):

(5) a.   AK-WA (H-H) = 'crying'
    b.   AK-wa (H-L) = 'cloth'
    c.   ak-WA (L-H) = 'egg'
    d.   ak-wa (L-L) = 'bed'

The tone which characterizes a syllable in a tone language is an intrinsic property of that syllable. This does not mean that a High tone syllable will always be pronounced on a High tone; but it will always be pronounced on a certain tone level in relation to surrounding syllables, where this tone level will be either High, or a modification of High: modifications of intrinsic tones come about through assimilation and dissimilation rules and other tone-affecting processes which come into play when constituents are strung together in linguistic expressions.

18.1.2. Accent

In contrast to tone, accent is not an intrinsic feature of syllables, but a "holistic" property of larger constituents: words, phrases, clauses, or even whole sentences. Accent consists in the relative perceptual prominence of one syllable over the other syllables of such a larger constituent. Accent can and must also be distinguished from intonation. For example, (1a) and (1b) can be said to have the same accent, but different intonation; (1a) and (1c) can be said to have the same intonation, but different accent.

Accent is a "perceptual" rather than a "phonetic" notion. The perceptual difference relevant to accent has no straightforward one-to-one relation to phonetic distinctions in the sound wave. There must be certain phonetic distinctions, but these may be different in both kind and degree in different circumstances. On the other hand, certain obvious phonetic distinctions will either not be perceived at all, or not perceived as constituting a difference in accent. In this respect, the situation is comparable to the case of segmental phonological units.

Accent is a phonetically "composite" notion. Its main exponent consists in relative differences in pitch, but there may be subsidiary differences involved, so that accented and non-accented syllables may have a whole range of differences:

(6)   +ACCENT   −ACCENT
          Pitch change   No Pitch change
          Louder   Less Loud
          Longer   Shorter
          More tense   Less tense
          Fuller articulation   Reduced articulation

It is generally agreed that a change of pitch is the main component of accent. We cannot simply say "high pitch" vs. "low pitch", since there must be a crucial difference in pitch with surrounding syllables in order for accent to be established. For example, if accent were a matter of (relatively) high pitch, then a series of syllables pronounced at the same relatively high pitch level should all count as carrying accent, as in:

(7)   BA-BA-BA-BA-
        ba-ba-ba

In fact, however, it is very well possible to have such a sequence with only some of the high-pitched syllables carrying accent, as in:

(8)   BA-ba-ba-BA-
        ba-ba-ba

The reason for this is that it is the *changes* in pitch which have an accent-creating value. A change in pitch may be a Rise or a Fall in pitch. Rise and Fall are thus the two most important accent-creating pitch features.

Although pitch is the most important factor expressing accent, it is not the only factor. This can be seen by pronouncing a sequence of syllables in a fully monotonous way, or whispering it; though no pitch changes are involved in these conditions, we are still able to convey an impression of accentual differences. We do this by making use of the concomitant features mentioned in (6): Loudness, Duration, and "Tenseness of articulation". More "tense" means "pronounced with greater muscular effort"; this feature is closely related to full / reduced articulation: less effort in pronunciation correlates with less "precise" articulation. Less precise articulation means that the articulatory movements are reduced and the articulatory organs travel shorter distances; auditorily this easily leads to a degree of blurring and merging of different segments. Thus, the vowels in non-accented syllables will often display a certain degree of "syncretism", with the neutral central schwa as the common "target".[2] It will be clear that if such reduced articulation has become an invariant feature of the non-accented syllable, then the other features mentioned may be less essential for creating the "accent" impression.

Accent is a matter of *relative* perceptual differences. The actual level of the pitch change may be widely different for different speakers, and even for the same speaker in different positions in the prosodic contour; nevertheless, the pitch movement may create the same accentual impression.

Since accent, like tone, is primarily expressed through pitch differences, accent languages may have minimal pairs which are phenomenologically difficult to distinguish from similar pairs in tone languages. Compare:

---

2. See, for example, Koopmans-Van Beinum (1980).

(9)   Igbo   English
    a. AK-wa 'cloth'   CON-struct (noun)
    b. ak-WA 'egg'   con-STRUCT (verb)

Nevertheless, there are important differences between such pairs:
    (i) a word in an accent language can never have more than one "peak" or "High"; thus, there can be no distinctive oppositions involving High-High or Low-Low patterns. This is what Hyman (1975a) called the "culminative" character of accent as opposed to tone;
    (ii) the so-called accentuated syllable of a word in an accent language need not actually carry "the" accent when it is used in a linguistic expression. Compare:

(10) A: *Shall we go to the MARket to buy some baNAnas?*
     B: *I don't LIKE the bananas they sell on the market.*

In (10A) there will be accents on *market* and *bananas* as indicated by the small capital print. But in (10B) these same words need not have any kind of accentual prominence at all.
    In tone languages we can say that syllables "have" a certain (intrinsic) tone. In accent languages it would seem to be more appropriate to say that a given syllable may or may not receive the accent, provided that, in the wider context of occurrence, there is an accent to receive in the first place. Instead of saying that a word such as *market* "has" an accent on the first syllable, we should rather say that the first syllable is the "characteristic accent position" (CAP) of the word, that is, the position which will function as the "landing site" for the accent if an accent is to be assigned to the word. If we follow this course, we avoid the counterintuitive claim that in an expression such as (10B), all constituents except *like* have "lost" their accents.

18.1.3. Intonation

Whereas tone and accent characterize designated syllables or constituents, intonation stretches across the whole linguistic expression. The pattern created by the distribution of tones and accents is necessarily part of the intonation. On the other hand, the intonation has certain "holistic" features which are independent of the tonal and accentual structure: in (1a), the final Fall independently symbolizes the declarative illocution of the expression. And there may be clause-internal pitch inflections which do not create accents, but rather "articulate" the whole clause into distinct sections. This means that intonation cannot be reduced to tonal and accentual distribution. For that reason it is expedient to use the term "prosodic contour" for the combined effect of tone, accent and intonation, plus other potentially relevant features such as rhythm and pause structure.

18.1.4. The form of prosodic contours

Much about the precise structure of prosodic contours in uncertain, many different analytic systems are in use, and there may be marked differences between different languages and even dialects. Nevertheless, the following general picture may be assumed to have some measure of general validity.[3]

The prosodic contour consists of a series of Rises and Falls in pitch, embroidered on a "pitch range" defined by a lower-level "baseline" and an upper-level "topline". The pitch range shows a natural gradual decline ("declination", "downdrift") from beginning to end through the prosodic contour. At the same time, the pitch range gradually narrows towards the end. Certain languages may require a third or even more "reference lines" in between the baseline and the topline. At the end of each unified prosodic contour, the baseline will be "reset" at its initial value. The last syllable of a prosodic contour will generally be pronounced longer than would otherwise be the case. The contour as a whole may be followed by a pause. The extent of the final pitch Fall or Rise, the degree of lengthening of the final syllable, and the length of a pause, if any, may be indicative of the communicative importance of that particular break in the ongoing discourse.

---

3. In this section I use some elements of the theory on prosodic contours as developed by the research group of the Institute of Perception Research, Eindhoven, The Netherlands: see, for example, Cohen—'t Hart (1967), 't Hart—Cohen (1973), and 't Hart—Collier (1975). A recent comprehensive discussion is found in 't Hart—Collier—Cohen (1990). This theory was developed through a method of resynthesizing stylized intonation patterns for Dutch and English utterances, such that the stylized patterns were accepted as natural prosodic contours by native speakers. It must be added here that the Eindhoven group restricts its attention mainly to the form of prosodic contours, and pays little attention to the complex form-function relations. Such attention is required, however, if a functional account of prosodic contours is to be developed. For various of the points touched upon here, see also Bolinger (1978), Vaissière (1983) and Cruttenden (1986).

450 *Prosodic features*

Rises and Falls come in four main kinds: Lexical (L), Accent-creating (A), Intonational (I), and Bridging (B).

— Lexical pitch movements may be intrasyllabic or intersyllabic. Intrasyllabic L-movements are the contour tones mentioned in 18.1.1 above. Intersyllabic L-movements are those movements which are necessary when two non-identical syllabic level tones occur in sequence. They might also be called B-movements typical of tone languages.

— Accent-creating pitch movements cover a substantial part of the nucleus (usually, the vowel) of the syllable on which accent is to be conferred. They can be divided into:

(11) a. A-Rise   ╱   a Rise in pitch "towards" the acccent-bearing syllabic nucleus (represented from here on by a little black block;
     b. A-Fall   ╲   a Fall in pitch "from" the accent-bearing syllabic nucleus;
     c. A-Rise/Fall ╱╲ = a combination of A-Rise and A-Fall on the accent-bearing syllabic nucleus.

Other things being equal, an A-Rise will usually occur early in the clause, an A-Fall later in the clause. If no intermediate movements occur, the result is a so-called "hat pattern" of the following form:

(12)   ─────╱▪   ▪╲─────

This "hat pattern" is, according to the Eindhoven-group, a typical recurrent feature of prosodic contours. The distance between the Rise and the Fall may vary, with the A-Rise/Fall in (11c) as the logical minimum (the "pointed hat").

Intonational pitch movements do not create accents. Their main inflection does not cover the nucleus of the syllable. Inside the clause they act as boundary markers, at the end they serve to express illocutionary and other communicative distinctions. They come in two main forms:

(13) a. I-Fall   ╲
     b. I-Rise   ╱

I-Fall cannot very well be realized from the baseline; I-Rise cannot well be realized from the topline. In such conditions these movements may either lead to a little extra fall or rise, or be neutralized. Sometimes a third I-inflection is recognized: a non-rising, non-falling level tone, which would be a third type of boundary marker. However, this could also be seen as absence of I-Fall and I-Rise at an "I-relevant position", i.e. a position where such I-movements might in principle occur.

— Bridging pitch movements have no distinctive role of their own: they are auxiliary movements which serve to clear the way for a new Rise or Fall:

(14) a. B-Fall connects two subsequent A-Rises: /▀   /▀
     b. B-Rise connects two subsequent A-Falls: ▀\   ▀\

The B-movements do not orient themselves to the syllable nucleus, nor to any special position in the clause: they simply connect two Rises or Falls. The reason for their occurrence is that there cannot be unlimited series of Rises or Falls, since these would break through the topline and the baseline, respectively.

It follows that B-movements need not be coded in the representation of a prosodic contour. Consider the following representation of a prosodic contour:

(15)   It was a /▀VERy pleasant /▀JOURney \

It will be clear that between the A-Rise on *very* and the A-Rise on *journey*, there must be a B-Fall in order to regain impetus for the second rise.[4]

It may thus be assumed that the most important ingredients for prosodic contours are L-, A-, and I-Rises and -Falls. Note that it is not excluded that tone languages, alongside L-movements, also have A- and I-movements. But it seems true that either L or A will usually be dominant. Thus, a tone language could be defined as a language in which L-movements are dominant, and an accent language as one in which A-movements are dominant.

---

4. Note that in a system which uses three rather than two reference lines, there may be a Rise from Low to Mid, followed by a Rise from Mid to High; likewise, a Fall from High to Mid, followed by a Fall from Mid to Low. In such a system there would also be room for distinguishing "small" Rises or Falls (across half of the pitch range), and "big" Rises or Falls (across the whole pitch range). It is sometimes assumed that Dutch has a prosodic system with only two reference lines, whereas British English uses three (De Pijper 1983).

18.2. The functions of prosody

We saw that the prosodic contour of an utterance is structurally composite in the sense that it may be built up of different partially independent elements: the tones, the accents, the intonation, and also the rhythm and the pause distribution. Functionally, the prosodic contour is composite as well: it potentially combines a number of different functions, such that the exponents of these functions are in a sense "superimposed" on each other, in the following way. In a sequence such as:

(16) A: *Who is missing?*
      B: *JOHN is missing.*

there will be accent on *John* in (16B), as the expression of the Completive Focus on that constituent. It might be, however, that (16B) is pronounced with great anxiety or anger. This will lift the whole expression to a higher pitch level, but it may also entail a higher Rise and a deeper Fall for the constituent *John* with respect to the rest of the utterance. The actual prosodic contour is then a compositional function of the separate contributions of Completive Focus and "Emotion". Note that this compositional function is not additive: the combined effect will not usually be interpretable as the sum of each of the separate effects.

In order to arrive at a better understanding of the various functions which potentially contribute to the final form of the prosodic contour, it is useful to consider these functions one by one. In doing so, we will also consider how these various functions can be accounted for within the model of FG.

18.2.1. Distinctive function

As we saw in 18.1.1. above, tonemes have a distinctive function in differentiating distinct predicates consisting of the same segmental material. In languages having such tonemic differences, these will have to be coded in the form of the predicate in the lexicon. The same applies to distinctive tonal patterns on polysyllabic predicates, unless such different patterns could be predicted by general rule. For example, if it is the case in some language that all intransitive verbs have a tonal pattern Low-High, then this could be stated once and for all for this whole category by general rule. That rule could then either be used to add the tonal pattern to the relevant verbal predicates, or as a redundancy rule which would reduce the "cost" of the individual stipulation of tonal patterns in the lexicon.

In accent languages, there is sometimes a limited and marginal class of "minimal pairs" which are differentiated solely by their characteristic accent position (CAP). This is the case in such English pairs as (9) above. In such cases the CAP will likewise be coded in the lexical predicates, unless it can be predicted by general rule. For example, if in a language all nouns had a pattern ■ — and all verbs derived from these nouns a pattern — ■, then the noun pattern could be taken care of by a general (redundancy) rule (if N, then ■ —), and the verb pattern could be captured in the predicate formation rule deriving verbs from nouns. But usually, in languages which make distinctive use of patterns of this kind, the distribution of these patterns does not have such an overall predictability. Thus, distinctive tonal and accentual patterns will typically be a matter of lexical stipulation.

18.2.2. Characterizing function

Even when accentual patterns do not have distinctive function, any predicate will usually have a CAP. Consider a predicate such as English *ba-na-na*. It is not necessarily the case that there is any accent on this predicate. However, if the predicate *ba-na-na* comes in the scope of an accent-allotting device, then the accent will fall on the second syllable (*ba-NA-na*) rather than on the first or the last. For this reason, the predicate will usually be listed in some such form (e.g. *ba'nana*) that it is clear that the second syllable is the designated recipient of the accent.

From Bolinger (1978) we may cite the following generalizations concerning the position of the CAP:

(17) a. In most languages, predicates have a fixed CAP.
 b. In most languages for which (17a) is true, the CAP can be predicted by general rule.
 c. In about half of the languages for which (17b) is true, that position is the penultimate (one before last) syllable.
 d. In most languages in which (17b) is true, but (17c) is false, the position is an extreme (i.e. initial or final) syllable.

With Hyman, Bolinger explains these facts as follows: (i) the penultimate syllable is the easiest to have a "Fall from" (⌐\), while still leaving room for a final Fall or Rise relevant to the terminal intonation; (ii) the initial syllable is the easiest to have a "Rise towards" (/ˆ); (iii) the terminal syllable is easy to have a "Fall from", although it does not leave room for a further terminal Fall / Rise (one may thus presume that languages having terminal CAP will find some other way of still adding the terminal intonation).

With respect to the treatment of CAP there are two relevant considerations: on the one hand, the CAP is an intrinsic feature of the predicate, and would thus be expected to be coded in the lexicon; on the other hand, to the extent that the CAP is predictable by general rule, such a rule could be formulated to uniformly assign characteristic accent positions to predicates in the lexicon. Perhaps the best solution for this kind of situation is to assume that the CAP is coded with each predicate in the lexicon, but that there are redundancy rules which capture the predictable features of this position.

18.2.3. Predicate formation (derivation and composition)

Predicate formation rules may affect the prosodic structure of the input predicate in different ways:

(i) In tone languages there may be predicate formation rules which affect only the toneme of the input predicate. This would be the case, for example, in a rule which took High tone transitive predicates as input and delivered the corresponding Low tone predicate with intransitive value (e.g. *pa*-H = 'open (trans.)', *pa*-L = 'open (intrans.)').

(ii) Likewise, a predicate formation rule might affect only the CAP of the input predicate. For example: con-STRUCT (V) ---> CON-struct (N), if this were a productive predicate formation rule in English.

(iii) More commonly, a predicate formation rule may add a derivational affix, while at the same time affecting the tone or the CAP of the input predicate. In English, for example, certain derivational affixes "attract" the accent position, others "shift" the accent position inside the input predicate. Compare PIC-ture ---> picturESQUE, and CURious ---> curiOSity (cf. Cruttenden 1986:20). Note that in our FG framework we would accept such "attraction" and "shift" only to the extent that it could be described by productive rule. Otherwise, the relevant relationship would have to be coded in the lexicon, with possible regularities covered by redundancy rules.

(iv) A phenomenon which appears to be restricted to tone languages is that the tone of an affix may be defined as "opposite" to the tone of the last syllable of the predicate to which it attaches: e.g. when that last syllable is High, the affix is Low; when the last syllable is Low, the affix is High (see Maddieson 1978 for discussion and examples of this kind of tonal "polarity").

(v) In the formation of compounds, there will usually be two input predicates, each with their own CAP (e.g. WATer + CARrier), whereas the output compound predicate will only have one CAP (e.g. WATer carrier).[5] To the extent that such compounding, and its effect on accentual position, is productive, it will have to be taken care of by the predicate formation rule. Otherwise, it will be coded in the lexicon.

18.2.4. Inflectional expression rules

For inflectional expression rules, the same things can be said as in the preceding section. Inflectional rules may have the same kinds of effects on the input predicate (the μ-operandum in the sense of chapters 14 and 15) as predicate formation rules.

18.2.5. Pragmatic functions

Pragmatic functions, as discussed in chapter 13 above, typically have impact on the prosodic contour of the linguistic expression. However, there is no necessary connection between pragmatic functions and prosodic contour features. Pragmatic functions may be expressed by: (i) special segmental markers (usually particles), (ii) special positions to be assigned to constituents with pragmatic functions, (iii) special construction types connected with a particular distribution of pragmatic functions, and (iv) prosodic features. It is possible for pragmatic functions to be expressed by only (i)-(iii), without any special effect on the prosodic contour. For some tone languages, it is reported that this is the case (e.g., Watters 1979 on Aghem), although, again, this is not a necessary feature of tone languages. In languages in which pragmatic functions do have impact on prosodic contour, this may occur together with other expression features, or the prosodic pattern may be the only expression device. In the former case, the prosody is obviously less essential to the communication than in the latter case. Compare the following examples from English:

---

5. Or a main CAP on one syllable, a secondary CAP on another.

(18) a. *JOHN bought the book*\
   b. *John bought the BOOK*\
(19)   *John DID buy the book*\

In (18a-b) the prosodic structure is the only indication of the pragmatic function distribution. Therefore, if the prosodic pattern is removed, this distribution is not expressed. In (19), on the other hand, the polar contrastive Focus on the predicate is signalled twice: once by the use of the supportive auxiliary *did*, and once by the accentual prominence of this auxiliary. If we take off the prosody, as in:

(20)   *John did buy the book.*

the sentence is still unambiguous with respect to its pragmatic function assignment.

From the above considerations it will be evident that "Focus" and "accentual prominence" cannot be identified with each other. Focus is an abstract function defined in terms of the informational status of the constituent in question within the discourse. It may, but need not be expressed in accentual prominence, and if it is, the relationship between Focus and Accent need not be one-to-one. On the other hand, accentual prominence may be used to express features other than Focus. We therefore need rules and principles which relate the underlying pragmatic functions to features of the prosodic structure, depending on the expressive conventions of the language in question.[6] Nevertheless, we can say a number of general things concerning the prosodic effects of pragmatic functions in those cases in which they have such effects. In discussing this relationship, we follow the order in which the pragmatic functions were introduced in chapter 13 above.

18.2.5.1. Topicality. In 13.3. different types of Topic were distinguished. Their potential impact on the prosodic contour are considered here.

New Topic: we saw that NewTops are typically introduced through some non-initial position in the clause. The general rule will be that the NewTop constituent captures the most prominent accent of the expression. Inside that constituent it will be distributed to characteristic accent position(s) of the

---

6. In this view of the relationship between Focus and Accent, we follow Gussenhoven (1983, 1985), except that we postulate a richer array of underlying pragmatic functions, as discussed in chapter 13.

constituent. Compare:

(21) a. *In the circus we saw an /˘ELephant*
     b. *In the circus we saw an /˘ELephant called /˘JUMbo*
     c. *There is a /˘HAIR in my soup*

Note that the accent does not distribute to all constituents of the NewTop. For example, *called* in (21b) and *soup* in (21c) remain without accent. I return to this point below.

Given Topic: a GivTop will have no accentual prominence (unless contrasted to some other GivTop). It may even take the form of Zero Anaphora, and will often be realized in a clitic pronoun. Such pronouns by definition cannot have accentual prominence.

Sub-Topic: SubTops will typically have some degree of accentual prominence, as in:

(22)   (*Mary got some picnic supplies out of the car ...*)
        The /˘BEER was /˘WARM

There are two explanations for why SubTops behave differently from GivTops: (i) SubTops, although they can be understood in terms of contextual information, have not been mentioned as such in the preceding context, and their individual identity is thus "new" to the discourse; (ii) As the notion of SubTop suggests, there are often other potential SubTops of the same GivTop. In (22), for example, the beer is only one of the picnic supplies. Thus, SubTops have something "new" and something "contrastive", which is apparently sufficient for them to qualify for accentual prominence.

Resumed Topics: these will typically also have a degree of accentual prominence (which may go hand in hand with a stronger form of anaphora), since they are intended as "reminders" to the Addressee concerning entities which, though they have been mentioned before, may have shaded into the background of his pragmatic information.

18.2.5.2. Focality. In 13.4.2.2. we distinguished different types of Focus in terms of differences in communicative "point". We now consider these different Focus types in terms of their potential impact on the prosodic contour.

We made a first distinction between Focus types which concern an information gap (Questioning Focus when the information gap is questioned, and New (or Completive) Focus for constituents which are intended to fill an information gap), and Focus types which in one way or another concern a contrast between the item focused on and some alternative item which is either explicitly mentioned or presupposed. Let us consider the former type first.

Questioning Focus: Q-word questions universally contain a questioned constituent which marks the information gap. Across languages, Q-constituents are treated in three main ways: (i) they are placed *in situ*, in the normal position for the corresponding non-questioned constituent; (ii) they are placed in a "special position" (most commonly, the initial P1 position); (iii) they are placed in the Focus position of a special Focus construction; in this case, they can again be placed *in situ* or in a special position (most commonly, P1).[7] This yields the following most frequent patterns for Q-word questions:

(23) a. *John met Peter* where?
    b. Where *did John met Peter?*
(24) a. *It is* where *(that) John met Peter?*
    b. Where *is it (that) John met Peter?*

In all these constructions, the nature of the information gap is clearly signalled by segmental means. But the constructions differ in the number of special features setting off the Q-word question from the normal declarative:

(25)

	(23a)	(23b)	(24a)	(24b)
Q-word	+	+	+	+
Special Position	-	+	-	+
Special Construction	-	-	+	+

In none of these cases are prosodic features needed to mark the special status of the Q-constituent or the Q-word question as a whole. This explains why it is that Q-word questions usually do not have the rising terminal intonation which is otherwise almost universally present in interrogatives (cf. Bolinger 1978). On the other hand, we may presume that prosodic features may play a complementary role in the expression of Q-word questions, the fewer the segmental markings of the special status of the question in the sense of (25). In other words, we hypothesize that Q-constituents will have some degree of prosodic prominence above all in constructions of type (23a), less prominence in (23b) and (24a), and least prominence in (24b).

---

7. This subject will be more extensively discussed in *TFG2*: chapter 12.

Completive Focus in answers / statements: Completive Focus constituents in answers to Q-word questions and in statements volunteered to fill in a presumed gap in the Addressee's information occur in patterns similar to those of (23)-(24). In many languages an answer to a Q-word question will have the same pattern as the question. Thus, we find such Completive Focus declaratives as the following:

(26) a. *John met Peter* in London.
 b. In London *John met Peter.*
(27) a. *It is* in London *(that) John met Peter.*
 b. In London *is it (that) John met Peter.*

In these declaratives there is obviously no Q-word to mark the special nature of the relevant constituent, and in general there is no segmental marker on the Completive Focus constituent signalling something like: 'this is the constituent intended to fill your information gap'. Thus, when we take stock of the segmental marking of these constructions, we find:

(28)

	(26a)	(26b)	(27a)	(27b)
Special Position	-	+	-	+
Special Construction	-	-	+	+

In general, then, the segmental marking of Completive Focus declaratives is weaker than that of Q-word questions. Correspondingly, we expect a more pronounced role for prosodic features, especially in the case of constructions of type (26a), which would otherwise carry no information leading the Addressee to the Completive Focus constituent. Indeed, constructions of type (26a) will, in English, typically have a strong main accent on the Completive Focus constituent, so that we get contrasts such as those between:

(29) a. Where *did John meet Peter?*
 b. *John met Peter in /*LONdon \
(30) a. Who *did John meet in London?*
 b. *John met /*PEter in London \

As with Q-word questions, we expect a less pronounced role for prosodic features to the extent that there are more segmental clues pointing towards the Completive Focus constituent.

To the above we must add the following two notes: first, in most languages the normal answer to a Q-word question will consist of only the Completive Focus constituent:

(31) a. Where *did John meet Peter?*
 b. In London.

Since in such a case there is no mistake as to which constituent has Completive Focus, we expect a less outspoken need for prosodic prominence on the answer.

The second note is that some languages do have segmental markers which are added to Completive Focus constituents in declaratives. Such markers often originate from earlier Focus constructions which have been demarked and have lost most of their segmental distinctives in the process. Again, we expect a certain trade-off with prosodic prominence in such constructions.

Contrastive Focus was divided into Parallel Focus and Counter-presuppositional Focus. Parallel Focus is involved in such constructions as:

(32) John *bought* a book, *and* Mary *bought* a magazine.

In such constructions there are typically two or more pairs of constituents such as (*John, a book*) and (*Mary, a magazine*), which are contrasted to each other. For this type of contrast it is immaterial whether the constituents involved present new or given information. Parallel Focus constructions typically have a rather pronounced prosodic pattern in which all the constituents from the relevant pairs get rather strong accent:

(33) /ˑJOHN bought a /ˑBOOK, and /ˑMARy bought a /ˑMAGazine \

Counterpresuppositional Focus constituents explicitly or implicitly reject and correct a (presumed) presupposition on the part of the Addressee. The Speaker not only wishes to add something to A's pragmatic information, but also to further specify, change, or correct something in A's information. Probably for this reason, Counterpresuppositional Focus constructions seem to have the most outspoken prosodic prominence patterns in many languages.

For all the cases in which the pragmatic function of a constituent is expressed in an accent on that constituent, it need not be the case that all parts of the constituent in question receive the accent. In most cases, there will be only one accent on the whole constituent, selected according to the expression rules of the language in question. The problems involved in the formulation of such rules have been most insightfully discussed by Gussenhoven (1983, 1985, cf. also Gussenhoven—Bolinger—Keijsper 1987) and Baart (1987). For some examples, consider the following:

(34)   A: *What happened?*
       B: /⁻*JOHN*son died\
(35)   A: *Who died?*
       B: /⁻*JOHN*son died\

In (34B), the whole combination of subject and predicate is in Focus. Nevertheless, only the Subject takes the accent. This is also the case in (35), where only the Subject itself is in Focus. The prosodic outcome is thus the same, although the distribution of pragmatic functions is different. Such examples as these show, once again, that there is no one-to-one relation between Focus assignment and accent distribution. Gussenhoven (1983, 1985) shows that the question of which constituent(s) of an expression in Focus will receive the accent is codependent on a number of syntactic, semantic, and pragmatic factors, and proposes a formal mechanism for handling the distribution of accents under different Focus assignments. Baart (1987) gives a detailed analysis of Dutch accent placement from a similar point of view.

18.2.6. Articulation of the clause

In 18.1. we saw that a prosodic contour most often coincides with a clause, and that extra-clausal constituents are typically "set off" from the clause by an intonational inflection. Within the clause, however, similar I-inflections may serve to "articulate" the clause into different subcontours. The I-movements involved in this articulation may be called "medial" I-movements (mI-Rise, mI-Fall), as opposed to "terminal I-movements" (tI-Rise, tI-Fall) which round off the clause as a whole.[8] As opposed to tI-movements, mI-movements necessarily have an element of "openness", suggesting that there is "more to come".

Inflections of type mI will typically be found, first of all, between the simple clauses that make up one compound or complex clause (cf. Cruttenden 1986: 76), as in:

---

8. Cohen—'t Hart (1967: 188) already demonstrated that a very slight shift in the location of a Fall may turn a medial I-Fall into a terminal one.

(36) a.   He RAN to the STATion / and CAUGHT the TRAIN \
     b.   Because he RAN to the STATion / he CAUGHT the TRAIN \

Although the mI-Rise in these cases separates the simple clauses from each other, and thus creates subcontours within the over-all prosodic contour, we nevertheless regard the whole complex or compound clause as the domain of the full prosodic contour, because the initial clauses in (36a-b) have different final intonation from what is found when they are used on their own as a complete statement. Compare:

(37)   A: *How did he manage to catch the train?*
       B: *He RAN to the STATion* \
           Because he RAN to the STATion \

The mI-Rises in (36a-b) thus serve to create an internal "punctuation" within the complex / compound clause.

mI-inflections may also occur within simple clauses, for example at the boundary between subject and predicate, or between predicate and object (Cruttenden 1986: 76):

(38) a.   *Mr. WHITE / wants to KNOW / whether ....*
     b.   *I quite LIKE HIM / but I LOATHE / and deTEST / his FATHer* \

Note that in (38b) the mI-Rises go hand in hand with the accentuation which is typical of Parallel Focus.

18.2.7. Illocutionary operators

Terminal I-movements typically serve to express the Illocutionary operators which characterize the clause as a whole. This is most markedly the case if the intonation is the only means for identifying the illocution, as in:

(39) a.   *His FATHer was a PAINter* \
     b.   *His FATHer was a PAINter* /

In this example, the tI-Fall signals "Declarative", whereas the tI-Rise signals "Interrogative". As will be argued in *TFG2*: chapter 11, we may regard (39b) as a declarative clause which is converted into an interrogative by means of the tI-Rise. This conversion yields the typical communicative effect of a confirmation question.

When an interrogative is also signalled by segmental means, the tI-movement becomes less important to the achievement of the communicative effect:

(40) a. *Was his FATHer a PAINTer /*
b. *Was his FATHer a PAINTer *

Both of (40a-b) will be interpreted as questions. The intonational difference, however, again creates a communicative effect, in that (40a) is a more "open" interrogative than (40b). In Question-word questions which, as we saw in 18.2.5.2. above, are sufficiently marked by segmental means, differences in tI-movements may again create communicative variations on the interrogative illocution.

Though it is not necessary for a language to use tI-movements for illocutionary purposes, such usage is quite widespread (cf. Bolinger 1978), and if a language has such differences, the tI-Rise is typically associated with "interrogative", and the tI-Fall with "declarative" and "imperative".

18.2.8. Conventionalized pragmatic effects

An elusive area of prosodic functionality is the use of prosodic means to express or create special conventionalized pragmatic effects. Certain prosodic inflections may sound "polite" or "impolite", "arrogant" or "modest", "friendly" or "unfriendly", "ironic" or "sarcastic". To the extent that such effects are conventionalized in a language, they should somehow be coded in the underlying clause structure. The most plausible way of doing this would be to code them in auxiliary operators at the π_4 level, which serve to modify the basic illocution of the clause. They can be compared to "mitigating" and "reinforcing" operators in the sense of Hengeveld (1989), for which certain languages also have segmental means. Little is known about the relation between such illocutionary modifiers and their prosodic expression, except that such functions of prosody seem to occur, in one way or another, in most languages.[9]

---

9. See e.g. Halliday's (1970b: 331) discussion of the use of prosodic means in the expression of reservation in English.

18.2.9. Emotional expression

Equally elusive is the usage of prosodic means for expressing personal emotions. This function of prosody is likewise found in all languages, and it has an "iconic" character in that "extravert" emotions such as anger or indignation will lead to a general heightening of the prosodic contour, a widening of the "pitch range", and a corresponding increase in the differences between peaks and valleys in the prosodic contour, whereas "introvert" emotions such as sorrow and disappointment will have the reverse effect. Compare:

(41) a. *I don't LIKE this at ALL, he said indignantly.*
b. *I don't LIKE this at ALL, he said almost inaudibly.*

We can easily imagine the difference in prosody between what he said in (41a) and (41b). But is difficult to formulate more specific rules and principles concerning the expression of emotions by prosodic means.

18.3. Generating prosodic contours

Given the various forms and functions of prosodic features as discussed in the preceding sections, we can now envisage a procedure for compositionally building up the final prosodic contour of a linguistic expression, starting from the information contained in the underlying clause structure. Such a procedure may consist of the following steps:[10]

Step 1. *Determining the characteristic accent positions (CAPs).*
The CAPs of basic predicates will be coded in the lexicon, at least to the extent that they are not predictable by general rule. If they are predictable, they will either be assigned to basic predicates by CAP-assigning rules; or they will be captured by redundancy rules.

The CAPs of productively derived predicates will be defined by the relevant predicate formation rules. The CAPs of inflected forms will be determined by the relevant formal expression rules. In both cases, only those CAPs will have to be determined which differ from the CAPs of the basic input predicates.

---

10. In this sketch, tone languages are left out of account.

Step 2. *The effect of pragmatic functions*.
The accents determined by pragmatic functions will be mapped in the form of A-movements (A-Rises / Falls) onto the CAPs of the constituents which carry these pragmatic functions. Rules and conventions of accent distribution will make sure that the A-movement "lands" on the correct CAP within these constituents.

Step 3. *I-movements*.
Medial I-movements are placed at clause-internal boundaries; terminal I-movements are placed at the end of the clause, depending on the illocutionary operators present in underlying clause structure, and on the extent to which these operators are already reflected in the form and / or the order of the constituents.

We now have a series of Rises and Falls on the segmental material of the linguistic expression, where A-Rises / Falls coincide with CAPs, and I-Rises / Falls occur in between or after CAPs.

Step 4. *Determining the pitch range*.
To determe the pitch range we may start from a "normal form" consisting of a gradually declining baseline, a somewhat more strongly declining topline at neutral distance from the baseline, plus possible reference lines in between. Certain conventionalized pragmatic effects (e.g. expressing surprise) and features of emotional expression (e.g. anger) may affect the neutral pitch range in two different ways: they may shift the topline up or down, thus widening or narrowing the pitch range; or they may shift the whole pitch range up, thus leading to an overall higher pitch delivery.[11]

Step 5. *Mapping the expression into the pitch range*.
The segmental material of the linguistic expression, provided with A- and I-movements, may now be mapped into the pitch range. If these movements are full Rises and Falls, they may be coded as connecting baseline and topline; if they are partial Rises and Falls, they will connect the baseline or topline to some reference line.

The mapping of A- and I-movements into the pitch range may involve some "compression" in the following sense: between two successive full Rises,

---

11. The former shift creates a difference in "key", the latter a difference in "register" in the terminology of Cruttenden (1986: 129-130).

there must be a return to the baseline; between two successive full Falls there must be a return to the topline.

Step 6. *Inserting B-lines*.
All the A- and I-movements within the pitch range may now be connected with bridging lines (B-lines). These may run parallel to the reference lines, for example when a full Rise is connected with a subsequent full Fall; the result will be the "hat pattern". Or they may be B-movements, as defined in 18.1.4. above.

The result of these six steps should now result in a perceptually acceptable and pragmatically adequate prosodic contour for the linguistic expression as a whole.

I fully realize that it is much easier to formulate some procedure such as the above than to actually implement it in a satisfactory way. Nevertheless, something in the order of complexity of this procedure is required if justice is to be done to the manifold functions which the final prosodic contour of the linguistic expression may compositionally fulfil.

First steps towards an application of the ideas set forth in this chapter to Modern Chinese have been set by Van den Berg (1990, 1991). Van den Berg clearly demonstrates that the final prosodic contour of a Chinese sentence must be created as a compositional function of the (four) lexical tones, the pragmatically monitored accents, and the illocutionary-sensitive intonation features. This implies that in the final prosodic contour the initial lexical tones may appear in many different actual phonetic manifestations.

References[1]

Allan, Keith
    1977   "Classifiers", *Language* 53: 285-311.
    1987   "Hierarchies and the choice of left conjuncts (with particular attention to English)", *Journal of Linguistics* 23: 51-77.

Allen, Barbara J.—Donald G. Frantz
    1977   Passive in Southern Tiwa. [Paper.]
    1978   "Verb agreement in Southern Tiwa", *Berkeley Linguistic Society* 4: 11-17

Aronoff, Mark
    1976   *Word formation in generative grammar*, Cambridge, Mass.: MIT Press.

Asher, R.E.
    1982   *Tamil*. (Lingua Descriptive Studies 7). Amsterdam: North-Holland.

Ashton, E.O.
    1947   *Swahili grammar (including intonation)*. London: Longman.

Austin, J.L.
    1962   *How to do things with words*. Cambridge, Mass.: MIT Press.

Auwera, Johan van der
    1981   "Tagalog *ang* - an exercise in universal grammar", in: S. Daalder—M. Gerritsen (eds.), *Linguistics in The Netherlands 1981*, 127-139. Amsterdam: North-Holland.

Auwera, Johan Van der—Louis Goossens (eds.)
    1987   *Ins and outs of the predication*. Dordrecht: Foris.

Awbery, G.M.
    1976   *The syntax of Welsh; a transformational study of the passive*. Cambridge: Cambridge University Press.

Baart, Joan L.G.
    1987   *Focus, syntax, and accent placement*. Dordrecht: Foris.

Bach, Emmon—Robert T. Harms (eds.)
    1968   *Universals in linguistic theory*. New York: Holt, Rinehart and Winston.

Bartsch, Renate
    1972   *Adverbialsemantik*. Frankfurt a/M: Athenäum.
    1976   *The grammar of adverbials*. Amsterdam: North-Holland.

Bartsch, Renate—Theo Vennemann
    1972   *Semantic structures*. Frankfurt a/M.: Athenäum.

---

1. *WPFG* = Working Papers in Functional Grammar, available from IFOTT, University of Amsterdam, Spuistraat 210, NL-1012 VT Amsterdam.

Behaghel, O.
    1932   *Deutsche Syntax; eine geschichtliche Darstellung. Band IV: Wortstellung, Periodenbau.* Heidelberg: Carl Winter.

Bell, Sarah J.
    1974   Some notes on Cebuano and Relational Grammar. [Paper, MIT, Cambridge, Mass.]
    1983   "Advancements and ascensions in Cebuano", in: Perlmutter (ed.), 143-218.

Berg, Marinus E. van den
    1990   Chinese stress and intonation: a model and some data. [Paper, University of Leyden.]
    1991   "Lexical tone and syntactic stress in Chinese: phonetic mapping in Functional Grammar", *Proceedings of the International Conference on Chinese Linguistics*, Wuhan: 208-215.

Berko, Jean
    1958   "The child's learning of English morphology", *Word* 14: 150-177.

Berlin, Brent—Paul Kay
    1969   *Basic color terms; their universality and evolution.* Berkeley: University of California Press.

Bloomfield, Leonard
    1933   *Language.* New York: Holt.
    1962   *The Menomini language.* New Haven: Yale University Press.

Boas, Franz
    1911   "Introduction to the *Handbook of American Indian Languages*", 1-83. Washington: Smithsonian Institution.

Boër, Steven E.—William G. Lycan
    1980   "A performadox in truth-conditional semantics", *Linguistics and Philosophy* 4: 71-100.

Bolinger, Dwight
    1978   "Intonation across languages", in: Greenberg (ed.), vol. 2, 471-524.

Bolkestein, A. Machtelt
    1980   *Problems in the description of modal verbs; an investigation of Latin.* Assen: Van Gorcum.
    1983   "Genitive and dative possessors in Latin", in: Dik (ed.), 55-91.
    1985   "Discourse and case marking: three-place predicates in Latin", in: C. Touratier (ed.), *Syntaxe et Latin*, 191-225. Aix en Provence: Université de Provence.
    1991   "Causally related predications and the choice between parataxis and hypotaxis in Latin", in: R. Coleman (ed.), *New studies in Latin linguistics*, 427-451. Amsterdam: Benjamins.

Bolkestein, A. Machtelt—Henk A. Combé—Simon C. Dik—Casper de Groot—Jadranka Gvozdanović—Co Vet
    1981   *Predication and expression in Functional Grammar.* London: Academic Press.

Bolkestein, A. Machtelt—Rodie Risselada
1985 "De tekstuele funktie van valentie: Latijnse drieplaatsige predikaten in kontekst", in: Dik (ed.), 161-176.
Bolkestein, A. Machtelt—Casper de Groot—J. Lachlan Mackenzie (eds.)
1985a *Syntax and pragmatics in Functional Grammar*. Dordrecht: Foris.
1985b *Predicates and terms in Functional Grammar*. Dordrecht: Foris.
Bossuyt, Alain
1982 Aspekten van de geschiedenis van de negatieve zin in het Nederlands. [Ph.D. dissertation, Free University Brussels.]
1983 "Historical Functional Grammar: an outline of an integrated theory of language change", in: Dik (ed.), 301-325.
Bresnan, Joan—Sam A. Mchombo
1987 "Topic, pronoun, and agreement in Chichewa", *Language* 63: 741-782.
Brigden, Nigel
1984 "Towards a Functional Grammar of aspect in Finnish", in: De Groot—Tommola (eds.), 179-198.
Brown, D. Richard
1984 An outline of a theory of pragmatic information and illocutionary operators. [Paper, SIL Nairobi.]
1985 "Term operators", in: Bolkestein—De Groot—Mackenzie (eds.) (1985b), 127-145.
Brown, Gillian—George Yule
1983 *Discourse analysis*. Cambridge: Cambridge University Press.
Bunt, Harry
1985 *Mass terms and model-theoretic semantics*. Cambridge: Cambridge University Press.
Bybee, Joan
1985 *Morphology; a study of the relation between meaning and form*. Amsterdam: Benjamins.
Carnap, Rudolf
1937 *The logical syntax of language*. London: Routledge & Kegan Paul.
1956 *Meaning and necessity; a study in semantics and modal logic*. Chicago: Phoenix.
Cate, Abraham P. ten
1985 *Aspektualität und Nominalisierung*. Frankfurt a/M: Peter Lang.
Chafe, Wallace L.
1968 "Idiomaticity as an anomaly in the Chomskyan paradigm", *Foundations of Language* 4: 109-125.
1970 *Meaning and the structure of language*. Chicago: University of Chicago Press.

Chomsky, Noam
  1957 *Syntactic structures*. The Hague: Mouton.
  1965 *Aspects of the theory of syntax*. Cambridge, Mass.: MIT Press.
  1981 *Lectures on Government and Binding*. Dordrecht: Foris.
Chung, Sandra
  1976 "An object-creating rule in Bahasa Indonesia", *Linguistic Inquiry* 7: 41-87.
  1978 *Case marking and grammatical relations in Polynesian*. Austin: University of Texas Press.
Chung, Sandra—William A. Seiter
  1980 "The history of raising and relativization in Polynesian", *Language* 56: 622-638.
Chung, Sandra—Alan Timberlake
  1985 "Tense, aspect, and mood", in: Shopen (ed.), vol. 3, 202-258.
Clark, Eve V.
  1978 "Locationals: existential, locative, and possessive constructions", in: Greenberg (ed.), vol. 4, 85-126.
Clark, Herbert H.—Eve V. Clark
  1977 *Psychology and language; an introduction to psycholinguistics*. New York: Harcourt Brace Jovanovich.
Clark, H.H.—S.E. Haviland
  1974 "Psychological processes and linguistic explanation", in: D. Cohen (ed.), *Explaining linguistic phenomena*, 91-124. Washington: Hemisphere.
  1977 "Comprehension and the given-new contract", in: R.O. Freedle (ed.), *Discourse production and comprehension*, 1-40. Norwood, N.J.: Ablex Publishing.
Claudi, Ulrike—Bernd Heine
  1985 "From metaphor to grammar: some examples from Ewe", *Afrikanische Arbeitspapiere (Köln)* 1: 17-54.
Clayre, Iain F.C.S.
  1973 "A preliminary note on focus and emphasis in Melanau - a language of coastal Sarawak", *Lingua* 31: 237-269.
Cohen, A.—J. 't Hart
  1967 "On the anatomy of intonation", *Lingua* 19: 177-192.
Cole, Peter
  1982 *Imbabura Quechua*. Amsterdam: North-Holland.
Cole, Peter (ed.)
  1981 *Radical pragmatics*. New York: Academic Press.
Cole, Peter—Jerry L. Morgan (eds.)
  1975 *Speech acts*. (Syntax and Semantics 3). New York: Academic Press.
Cole, Peter—Jerrold M. Sadock (eds.)
  1977 *Grammatical relations*. (Syntax and Semantics 8). New York: Academic Press.

Comrie, Bernard
   1976   *Aspect*. Cambridge: Cambridge University Press.
   1978   "Ergativity", in: Lehmann (ed.), 329-394.
   1981   *Language univerals and linguistic typology*. Oxford: Blackwell.
   1985   *Tense*. Cambridge: Cambridge University Press.
Connolly, John H.
   1983   "Placement rules and syntactic templates", in: Dik (ed.), 247-266.
   1986   "Testing Functional Grammar placement rules using Prolog", *International Journal of Man-Machine Studies* 24: 623-632.
Connolly, John H.—Simon C. Dik (eds.)
   1989   *Functional Grammar and the computer*. Dordrecht: Foris.
Craig, Colette
   1992   "Classifiers in a functional perspective", in: Fortescue—Harder—Kristoffersen (eds.), 277-301.
Craig, Colette (ed.)
   1986   *Noun classes and categorization*. Amsterdam: Benjamins.
Croft, William
   1990   *Typology and universals*. Cambridge: Cambridge University Press.
Cruttenden, Alan
   1986   *Intonation*. Cambridge: Cambridge University Press.
Dahl, Östen
   1970   "Some notes on indefinites", *Language* 46: 33-41.
   1971   "Nouns as set constants". *Gothenburg Papers in Theoretical Linguistics* 3.
   1979   "Typology of sentence negation", *Linguistics* 17: 79-106.
Davies, John
   1981   *Kobon*. Amsterdam: North-Holland.
Davies, William D.
   1981   "Choctaw subjects and multiple levels in syntax", in: Hoekstra—Van der Hulst—Moortgat (eds.), 235-271.
Derbyshire, Desmond C.
   1977   "Word order universals and the existence of OVS languages", *Linguistic Inquiry* 8: 590-599.
   1979   *Hixkaryana*. Amsterdam: North-Holland.
   1981   "A diachronic explanation of the origin of OVS in some Carib languages", *Journal of Linguistics* 17: 35-45.
Derbyshire, Desmond C.—Geoffrey K. Pullum
   1981   "Object-Initial languages", *International Journal of American Linguistics* 47: 192-214.
Des Tombe, Louis
   1976   "Competence and performance", in: G. Koefoed—A. Evers (eds.), *Lijnen van taaltheoretisch onderzoek*, 111-141. Groningen: Tjeenk Willink.

Dik, Helma
- 1988 Het onderwerp onderwerp van onderzoek: constituentenvolgorde en subjectuitdrukking in Xenophons Hellenica. [Paper, Department of Greek, University of Amsterdam.]

Dik, Simon C.
- 1975a *Universal quantifiers in Dutch*. Lisse: Peter de Ridder Press.
- 1975b "The semantic representation of manner adverbials", in: A. Kraak (ed.), *Linguistics in The Netherlands 1972-1973*, 96-121. Assen: Van Gorcum.
- 1978a *Functional Grammar*. Amsterdam: North-Holland. (3rd printing 1981, Dordrecht: Foris).
- 1978b *Stepwise lexical decomposition*. Lisse: Peter de Ridder Press. (Available through *WPFG*).
- 1979 "Raising in a Functional Grammar", *Lingua* 47: 119-140.
- 1980 *Studies in Functional Grammar*. London/New York: Academic Press.
- 1981 "Embedded Themes in spoken Dutch: two ways out", in: Bolkestein—Combé—Dik—De Groot—Gvozdanović—Rijksbaron—Vet, 113-124.
- 1983a "Auxiliary and copula *be* in a Functional Grammar of English", in: F. Heny—B. Richards (eds.), *Linguistic categories: auxiliaries and related puzzles*, vol. 2, 121-143. Dordrecht: Reidel.
- 1983b "Two constraints on relators and what they can do for us", in: Dik (ed.), 267-298.
- 1985a "Formal and semantic adjustment of derived constructions", in: Bolkestein—De Groot—Mackenzie (eds.) (1985b), 1-28.
- 1985b "Progress in linguistics", in: T. Hägerstrand (ed.), *The identification of progress in learning*, 115-139. Cambridge: Cambridge University Press.
- 1986 "On the notion 'functional explanation'", *Belgian Journal of Linguistics* 1: 11-52 (= *WPFG* 11).
- 1987a "Linguistically motivated knowledge representation", in: M. Nagao (ed.), *Language and artificial intelligence*, 145-170. Amsterdam: North-Holland.
- 1987b "Generating answers from a linguistically coded knowledge base", in: G. Kempen (ed.), *Natural language generation; new results in artificial intelligence, psychology and linguistics*, 301-314. Dordrecht: Nijhoff.
- 1987c "Copula auxiliarization: how and why?", in: Harris—Ramat (eds.), 53-84.
- 1987d "A typology of entities", in: Auwera—Goossens (eds.), 1-20.
- 1989a "Towards a unified cognitive language", in: F.J. Heyvaert—F.Steurs (eds.), *Worlds behind words; essays in honour of Prof.Dr. F.G. Droste on the occasion of his sixtieth birthday*, 97-110. Leuven: Leuven University Press.
- 1989b "Idioms in a computational Functional Grammar", in: M. Everaert—E.J. van der Linden (eds.), *Proceedings of the First Tilburg Workshop on Idioms*, 41-55. Tilburg: ITK.
- 1990 "Some developments in Functional Grammar: predicate formation", in: F.Aarts—T. van Els (eds.), *Contemporary Dutch Linguistics*, 58-79. Washington: Georgetown University Press.

1992   *Functional Grammar in Prolog; an integrated implementation for English, French, and Dutch*. Berlin: Mouton de Gruyter.
1994   "Computational description of verbal complexes in English and Latin", in: Elisabeth Engberg-Pedersen—Lisbeth Falster Jakobsen—Lone Schack Rasmussen (eds.), *Function and expression in Functional Grammar*, 353-383. Berlin: Mouton de Gruyter.
Dik, Simon C.—Helma Dik—Inge Genee—Joris van den Hauwe—Rob de Jong—Harke Jan van der Meulen—Marijke de Roeck—Carla Zijlemakers
1989   Specific and generic reference in FG. [Paper, Institute for General Linguistics, University of Amsterdam.]
Dik, Simon C.—Jadranka Gvozdanović,
1981   "Subject and Object in Serbo-Croatian", in: Hoekstra—Van der Hulst—Moortgat (eds.), 21-39.
Dik, Simon C.—Kees Hengeveld—Elseline Vester—Co Vet
1990   "The hierarchical structure of the clause and the typology of satellites", in: Nuyts—Bolkestein—Vet (eds.), 25-70.
Dik, Simon C.—Maria E. Hoffmann—Jan R. de Jong—Sie Ing Djiang—Harry Stroomer—Lourens de Vries
1981   "On the typology of Focus phenomena", in: Hoekstra—Van der Hulst—Moortgat (eds.), 41-74.
Dik, Simon C. (ed.)
1983   *Advances in Functional Grammar*. Dordrecht: Foris.
1985   *Valentie in Funktionele Grammatika*. (Tijdschrift voor Taal- en Tekstwetenschap 5:2).
Dixon, Robert M.W.
1972   *The Dyirbal language of North Queensland*. Cambridge: Cambridge University Press.
1980   *The languages of Australia*. Cambridge: Cambridge University Press.
Donnellan, Keith
1971   "Reference and definite descriptions", in: D.D. Steinberg—L.A. Jacobovits (eds.), *Semantics: an interdisciplinary reader in philosophy, linguistics and psychology*. Cambridge: Cambridge University Press.
Dowty, David R.
1979   *Word meaning and Montague Grammar; the semantics of verbs and times in Generative Grammar and Montague's PTQ*. Dordrecht: Reidel.
Dryer, Matthew S.
1983   "Indirect Objects in Kinyarwanda revisited", in: Perlmutter (ed.), 129-140.
Duranti, Alessandro
1977   "Contributi delle lingue Bantu alla teoria della Grammatica Relazionale", *Rivista di Grammatica Generativa* 1.

Eijk, Jan van
    1981   *Cuystwí malh Ucwalmícwts (Teach yourself the Indian language)*. Mount Curry, B.C.: The Ts'zil Publishing House.
    1985   The Lillooet language. [Ph.D. dissertation, University of Amsterdam.]
Eijk, Jan van—Thom Hess
    1986   "Noun and verb in Salish", *Lingua* 69: 319-331.
England, Nora C.
    1983   *A grammar of Mam, a Mayan language*. Austin: University of Texas Press.
Ertel, S.
    1977   "Where do the subjects of sentences come from?", in: S. Rosenberg (ed.), *Sentence production; developments in research and theory*, 141-168. Hillsdale, N.J.: Lawrence Erlbaum.
Estival, Dominique—John Myhill
    1988   "Formal and functional aspects of the development from passive to ergative systems", in: M. Shibatani (ed.), *Typological studies in language*.
Ferguson, Charles A.
    1971   "Absence of copula and the notion of simplicity: a study of normal speech, baby talk, foreigner talk, and pidgins", in: Dell Hymes (ed.), *Pidginization and creolization of languages*, 141-150. Cambridge: Cambridge University Press.
Fillmore, Charles
    1968   "The case for case", in: Bach—Harms (eds.), 1-88.
    1971   "Types of lexical information", in: D.D. Steinberg—L.A. Jakobovits (eds.), *Semantics, an interdisciplinary reader in philosophy, linguistics, and psychology*, 370-392. London: Cambridge University Press.
Firth, J.R.
    1957   *Papers in Linguistics 1934-1951*. London: Oxford University Press.
Foley, William A.—Robert D. Van Valin, Jr.
    1984   *Functional syntax and universal grammar*. Cambridge: Cambridge University Press.
Fortescue, Michael—Peter Harder—Lars Kristoffersen (eds.)
    1992   *Layered structure and reference in a functional perspective*. Amsterdam: Benjamins.
Fraser, Bruce
    1970   "Idioms within a transformational grammar", *Foundations of Language* 6: 22-42.
Frege, Gottlob
    1892   "Ueber Sinn und Bedeutung". *Zeitschrift für Philosophie und Philosophische Kritik* 100(1892): 25-50.
Garber, Anne
    1980   "Word order change and the Senufo languages", *Studies in the Linguistic Sciences* 10: 45-55.

García, Erica C.
   1975   *The role of theory in linguistic analysis; the Spanish pronoun system.* Amsterdam: North-Holland.
Gary, Judith Olmsted—Edward L. Keenan
   1977   "On collapsing grammatical relations in universal grammar", in: Cole—Sadock (eds.), 83-120.
Givón, Talmy
   1976   "Topic, pronoun, and grammatical agreement", in: Li (ed.), 151-188.
   1978   "Definiteness and referentiality", in: Greenberg (ed.), vol. 4, 291-331.
   1979   *On understanding grammar.* New York: Academic Press.
   1984   *Syntax; a functional-typological introduction.* Vol. 1. Amsterdam: Benjamins.
Givón, Talmy, (ed.)
   1983   *Topic continuity in discourse: a quantitative cross-linguistic study.* Amsterdam: John Benjamins.
Goossens, Louis
   1985   "Modality and the modals: a problem for Functional Grammar", in: Bolkestein—De Groot—Mackenzie (eds.) (1985b), 203-217.
   1987a   "Modal shifts and predication types", in: Auwera—Goossens (eds.), 21-37.
   1987b   "The auxiliarization of the English modals", in: Harris—Ramat (eds.), 111-143.
Greenbaum, Sidney
   1969   *Studies in English adverbial usage.* London: Longmans.
Greenberg, Joseph H.
   1963   "Some universals of grammar with particular reference to the order of meaningful elements", in: Greenberg (ed.), 73-113.
   1966   *Language universals.* The Hague: Mouton.
   1978   "How does a language acquire gender markers?", in: Greenberg (ed.), vol. 3, 47-81. Stanford: University Press.
Greenberg, Joseph H. (ed.)
   1963   *Universals of language.* Cambridge, Mass.: MIT Press
   1978   *Universals of human language.* 4 volumes. Stanford: University Press.
Grice, H.P.
   1975   "Logic and conversation", in: Cole—Morgan (eds.), 41-58.
Grimes, Joseph H.
   1975   *The thread of discourse.* The Hague: Mouton.
Groot, Casper de
   1981a   "Sentence intertwining in Hungarian", in: Bolkestein—De Groot—Mackenzie, 41-62.
   1981b   "The structure of predicates and verb agreement in Hungarian", in: S. Daalder—M. Gerritsen (eds.), *Linguistics in The Netherlands 1981*, 149-158. Amsterdam: North-Holland.

1983a "On non-verbal predicates in Functional Grammar: the case of possessives in Hungarian", in: Dik (ed.), 93-122.
1983b "Typology of States of Affairs", in: H. Bennis—W.U.S. van Lessen Kloeke (eds.), *Linguistics in The Netherlands 1983*, 73-81. Dordrecht: Foris.
1984 "Totally affected; aspect and three-place predicates in Hungarian", in: De Groot—Tommola (eds.), 133-151.
1985 "Predicates and features", in: Bolkestein—De Groot—Mackenzie (eds.) (1985b), 71-84.
1986 "Hongaren en Nederlanders smeren niet hetzelfde", in: E. Mollay (ed.), Németalföldi-Magyar kontrasztiv filológiai tanulmányok, 4-18. Budapest: Elte.
1989 *Predicate structure in a Functional Grammar of Hungarian*. Dordrecht: Foris.

Groot, Casper de—Machiel Limburg
1986 "Pronominal elements: diachrony, typology, and formalization in Functional Grammar", *WPFG* 12.

Groot, Casper de—Hannu Tommola (eds.)
1984 *Aspect bound; a voyage into the realm of Germanic, Slavonic, and Finno-Ugrian aspectology*. Dordrecht: Foris.

Guéron, J.
1980 "On the syntax and semantics of PP extraposition", *Linguistic Inquiry* 11, 636-678.

Gussenhoven, Carlos
1983 "Focus, mode, and the nucleus", *Journal of Linguistics* 19: 377-417.
1985 "Two views of accent: a reply", *Journal of Linguistics* 21: 125-138.

Gussenhoven, Carlos—Dwight Bolinger—Cornelia Keijsper
1987 *On accent*. Bloomington, Ind.: Indiana University Linguistics Club.

Gvozdanović, Jadranka
1981 "Word order and displacement in Serbo-Croatian", in: Bolkestein—Combé—Dik—De Groot—Gvozdanović—Rijksbaron—Vet, 125-141.

Haiman, John
1974 *Targets and syntactic change*. The Hague: Mouton.

Haiman, John (ed.)
1985 *Iconicity in syntax*. Amsterdam: Benjamins.

Hale, Kenneth
1970 "The passive and ergative in language change: the Australian case", in: S. Wurm—D. Laycock (eds.), *Pacific-linguistic studies in honor of Arthur Capell*, 757-81. Canberra: Pacific Linguistics C-13.
1973 "A note on Subject-Object inversion in Navajo", in: B. Kachru (ed.), *Issues in Linguistics*, 300-309. Urbana: University of Illinois Press.

Halliday, M.A.K.
1970a "Language structure and language function", in: J. Lyons (ed.), *New horizons in linguistics*, 140-165. Harmondsworth: Penguin.
1970b "Functional diversity in language, as seen from a consideration of modality and mood in English", *Foundations of Language* 6: 322-361.
1973 *Explorations in the functions of language*. London: Arnold.
1985 *An introduction to Functional Grammar*. London: Arnold.
Hannay, Michael
1983 "The Focus function in Functional Grammar: questions of contrast and context", in: Dik (ed.), 207-223.
1985a "Inferrability, discourse-boundness and sub-Topics", in: Bolkestein—De Groot—Mackenzie (eds.) (1985a), 49-63.
1985b *English existentials in Functional Grammar*. Dordrecht: Foris.
Hannay, Mike—Elseline Vester (eds.)
1990 *Working with Functional Grammar. Descriptive and computational applications*. Dordrecht: Foris.
Harris, Martin—Paolo Ramat (eds.)
1987 *Historical development of auxiliaries*. Berlin: Mouton De Gruyter.
Harris, Zellig S.
1951 *Methods in structural linguistics*. Chicago: University of Chicago Press,
't Hart, J.—A. Cohen
1973 "Intonation by rule: a perceptual quest", *Journal of Phonetics* 1: 309-327.
't Hart, J.—R. Collier
1975 "Integrating different levels of intonation analysis", *Journal of Phonetics* 3: 235-255.
't Hart, J.—R. Collier—A. Cohen
1990 *A perceptual study of intonation; an experimental-phonetic approach to speech melody*. Cambridge: Cambridge University Press.
Haverkate, Henk
1979 *Impositive sentences in Spanish; theory and description in linguistic pragmatics*. Amsterdam: North-Holland.
Haviland, S.E.—Herbert H. Clark
1974 "What's new? Acquiring new information as a process of comprehension", *Journal of Verbal Learning and Verbal Behavior* 13, 512-521.
Hawkins, J.A.
1978 *Definiteness and indefiniteness: a study in reference and grammaticality prediction*. London: Croom Helm.
1979 "Implicational universals as predictors of word order change", *Language* 55: 618-648.
1980 "On implicational and distributional universals of word order", *Journal of Linguistics* 16: 193-235.
1982 "Cross-category harmony, X-bar and the predictions of markedness", *Journal of Linguistics* 18: 1-35.

1983 *Word order universals*. New York: Academic Press.
Hawkinson, Annie—Larry Hyman
    1974 "Hierarchies of natural topic in Shona", *Studies in African Linguistics* 5: 147-170.
Hengeveld, Kees
    1986 "Copular verbs in a Functional Grammar of Spanish", *Linguistics* 24: 393-420.
    1987 "Clause structure and modality in Functional Grammar", in: Van der Auwera—Goossens (eds.), 53-66.
    1988 "Illocution, mood, and modality in a Functional Grammar of Spanish", *Journal of Semantics* 6.3/4: 227-269.
    1989 "Layers and operators in Functional Grammar", *Journal of Linguistics* 25.1: 127-157 (= *WPFG* 27 (1988)).
    1990 "Semantic relations in non-verbal predication", in: Nuyts—Bolkestein—Vet (eds.), 101-122.
    1992a "Parts of speech", in: Fortescue—Harder—Kristoffersen (eds.), 29-55.
    1992b *Non-verbal predication; theory, typology, diachrony*. Berlin: Mouton de Gruyter.
Hetzron, Robert
    1975 "The Presentative Movement, or why the ideal order is V.S.O.P.", in: Li (ed.), 345-388.
    1978 "On the relative order of adjectives", in: H. Seiler (ed.), *Language universals*, 165-184. Tübingen: Gunter Narr.
Hewitt, B.G.
    1979 *Abkhaz*. Amsterdam: North-Holland.
Hock, Hans Henrich
    1982 "Aux-cliticization as a motivation of word order change", *Studies in the Linguistic Sciences* 12: 91-101.
Hoekstra, Teun—Harry van der Hulst—Michael Moortgat (eds.)
    1981 *Perspectives on Functional Grammar*. Dordrecht: Foris.
Hohepa, Patrick
    1969 "The accusative-to-ergative drift in Polynesian languages", *Journal of the Polynesian Society* 78: 295-329.
Howell, Kenneth J.
    1983 "Object initial languages and their implications for word order universals", *Proceedings of the 13th International Congress of Linguists*, 941-945. Tokyo.
Huddleston, R.
    1970 "Some remarks on Case Grammar", *Linguistic Inquiry* 1: 501-511.
Hyman, Larry M.
    1975a *Phonology; theory and analysis*. New York: Holt, Rinehart and Winston.
    1975b "On the change from SOV to SVO: evidence from Niger-Congo", in: Li (ed.), 113-147.

Hymes, Dell
1972   "On communicative competence", in: J.B. Pride—J. Holmes (eds.), *Sociolinguistics*, 269-293. Harmondsworth: Penguin.

Isačenko, A.V.
1962   *Die russische Sprache der Gegenwart, I: Formenlehre*. München: Hueber.

Itagaki, Nobuya—Gary D. Prideaux
1983   "Pragmatic constraints on subject and agent selection", in: Dik (ed.), 329-342.
1985   "Nominal properties as determinants of Subject selection", *Lingua* 66: 135-149.

Jackendoff, Ray
1972   *Semantic representation in generative grammar*. Cambridge, Mass.: MIT Press.
1975   "Morphological and semantic regularities in the lexicon", *Language* 51: 639-671.

Jakobson, Roman
1936   "Beitrag zur allgemeinen Kasuslehre", *Travaux du Cercle Linguistique de Prague* 6: 240-288.

Janssen, Theo M.V.
1989   "Towards a universal parsing algorithm for Functional Grammar", in: Connolly & Dik (eds.), 65-75.

Johnson, David E.
1974   "On the role of grammatical relations in linguistic theory", *Chicago Linguistic Society* 10: 269-283.
1977   "On relational constraints on grammar", in: Cole—Sadock (eds.), 151-178.

Johnson-Laird, Philip N.
1983   *Mental models*. Cambridge: Cambridge University Press.

Jong, Jan R. de
1981   "On the treatment of Focus phenomena in Functional Grammar", in: Hoekstra—Van der Hulst—Moortgat (eds.), 89-115.
1983   "Word order within Latin noun phrases", in: H. Pinkster (ed.), *Latin linguistics and linguistic theory*, 131-141. Amsterdam: Benjamins.

Kahr, J.C.
1976   "The renewal of case morphology: sources and constraints", *Working Papers on Language Universals* 20: 107-151.

Kahrel, Peter
1985   "Indirect questions and relators", in: Bolkestein—De Groot—Mackenzie (eds.) (1985b), 165-181.
1987   "On zero terms and negative polarity", in: Auwera—Goossens (eds.), 67-76.

Kampers-Manhe, Brigitte
   1985   "Le subjonctif dans la relative: une question de champs", in: H. Bennis—F. Beukema (eds.), *Linguistics in The Netherlands 1985*, 67-75. Dordrecht: Foris.

Karttunen, Lauri
   1976   "Discourse referents", in: McCawley (ed.), 363-387.

Keenan, Edward L.
   1972a "On semantically based grammar", *Linguistic Inquiry* 3: 413-461.
   1972b "Relative clause formation in Malagasy (and some related and not so related languages)", in: Peranteau—Levi—Phares (eds.), 169-189.
   1975   "Some universals of passive in Relational Grammar", *Chicago Linguistic Society* 11: 340-350.
   1976a "Remarkable subjects in Malagasy", in: Li (ed.), 247-301.
   1976b "Towards a universal definition of 'subject'", in: Li (ed.), 303-333.
   1978   "The syntax of subject-final languages", in: Lehmann (ed.), 267-327.
   1979   "On surface form and logical form", *Studies in the Linguistic Sciences* 8: 1-41.

Keenan, Edward L.—Bernard Comrie
   1977   "Noun phrase accessibility and universal grammar", *Linguistic Inquiry* 8, 63-99.

Keizer, M. Evelien
   1991   "Referring in Functional Grammar: how to define reference and referring expressions", *WPFG* 43.
   1992   "Predicates as referring expressions", in: Fortescue—Harder—Kristoffersen (eds.), 1-27.

Kiefer, Ferenc
   1968   "A transformational approach to the verb *van* 'to be' in Hungarian", in: J.W.M. Verhaar (ed.), *The verb 'be' and its synonyms*, vol. 3, 53-85. Dordrecht: Reidel.

Kim, Alan Hyun-Oak
   1988a "Preverbal focussing in type XII languages", in: M. Hammond—E. Moravcsik—J. Wirth (eds.), *Studies in syntactic typology*, 148-171. Amsterdam: Benjamins.
   1988b Two levels of functional linear order in Functional Grammar. [Paper read at the 3rd International Conference on FG, Amsterdam.]

Kinkade, M. Dale
   1983   "Some evidence against the universality of 'noun' and 'verb'", *Lingua* 60: 25-39.

Kirsner, Robert S.
   1979   *The problem of presentative sentences in Modern Dutch*. Amsterdam: North-Holland.

Kisseberth, Charles W.—Mohammad Imam Abasheikh
1977 "The object relationship in Chimwi:ni, a Bantu language", in: Cole—Sadock (eds.), 179-218.
Kölver, Ulrike
1982 "Klassifikatorkonstruktionen in Thai, Vietnamesisch und Chinesisch; ein Beitrag zur Dimension der Apprehension", in: Seiler—Lehmann (eds.), 160-185.
Koopmans-van Beinum, F.J.
1980 *Vowel contrast reduction; an acoustic and perceptual study of Dutch vowels in various speech conditions*. Amsterdam: Academische Pers.
Kraak, A.—W.G. Klooster
1968 *Syntaxis*. Culemborg: Stam.
Kučanda, Dubravko
1984 "On Subject assignment in Serbo-Croatian within the framework of FG", *Lingua* 64: 99-114.
Kuhn, Thomas S.
1962 *The structure of scientific revolutions*. Chicago: University of Chicago Press.
Kuipers, Aert H.
1968 "The categories verb-noun and transitive-intransitive in English and Squamish", *Lingua* 21: 610-626.
Kuno, Susumu
1973 *The structure of the Japanese language*. Cambridge, Mass.: MIT Press.
1976 "Subject, theme, and the speaker's empathy - a reexamination of relativization phenomena", in: Li (ed.), 417-444.
Kuno, Susumu—Etsuko Kaburaki
1977 "Empathy and syntax", *Linguistic Inquiry* 8: 627-672.
Kwee Tjoe Liong
1979 "a68-fg(3); simon dik's funktionele grammatika geschreven in algol68, versie no. 03", *Publications of the Institute of General Linguistics*, 23. University of Amsterdam.
Lakoff, George
1966 Stative adjectives and verbs in English. [Report NSF-17, The Computation Laboratory, Harvard University.]
Laudan, Larry
1977 *Progress and its problems; towards a theory of scientific growth*. London: Routledge and Kegan Paul.
Lee, Ernest W.
1964 "Non-focus verbs in Maguindanao", *Oceanic Linguistics* 3: 49-57.
Lehmann, Christian
1982a *Thoughts on grammaticalization; a programmatic sketch*. Cologne: AKUP 48.

1982b "Universal and typological aspects of agreement", in: Seiler—Stachowiak (eds.), 201-267.
1987 "Towards a typology of clause linkage", in: John Haiman—Sandra Thompson (eds.), *Clause combining in discourse and syntax*. Amsterdam: Benjamins.

Lehmann, Winfred P.
1973 "A structural principle of language and its implications", *Language* 49: 47-66.

Lehmann, Winfred P. (ed.)
1978 *Syntactic typology; studies in the phenomenology of language*. Sussex: Harvester Press.

Leuven-Zwart, Kitty van
1984 *Vertaling en origineel; een vergelijkende beschrijvingsmethode voor integrale vertalingen, ontwikkeld aan de hand van Nederlandse vertalingen van Spaanse narratieve teksten*. Dordrecht: Foris.

Levinson, Stephen C.
1983 *Pragmatics*. Cambridge: Cambridge University Press.

Li, Charles N. (ed.)
1975 *Word order and word order change*. Austin: University of Texas Press.
1976 *Subject and Topic*. New York: Academic Press.
1977 *Mechanisms of syntactic change*. Austin: University of Texas Press.

Li, Charles N.—Sandra A. Thompson
1976 "Subject and topic: a new typology of language", in: Li (ed.), 457-489.

Limburg, Machiel J.
1983 "The parameter preposition/postposition in word order typology", in: H. Bennis—W.U.S. van Lessen Kloeke (eds.), *Linguistics in The Netherlands 1983*, 149-158. Dordrecht: Foris.
1985 "On the notion 'relator' and the expression of the genitive relation", in: Bolkestein—De Groot—Mackenzie (eds.) (1985b), 147-163.

Lyons, John
1967 "A note on possessive, existential, and locative sentences", *Foundations of Language* 3: 390-396.
1968 *Introduction to theoretical linguistics*. Cambridge: Cambridge University Press.
1977 *Semantics*. Two volumes. Cambridge: Cambridge University Press.

Mackenzie, J. Lachlan
1981 "Functions and cases", in: Hoekstra—Van der Hulst—Moortgat (eds.), 299-318.
1983 "Nominal predicates in a Functional Grammar of English", in: Dik (ed.), 31-51.
1987 "The representation of nominal predicates in the fund", *WPFG* 25.

Maddieson, Ian
1978 "Universals of tone", in: Greenberg (ed.), vol. 2, 335-365.

Mallinson, Graham—Barry J. Blake
    1981   *Language typology; cross-linguistic studies in syntax.* Amsterdam: North-Holland.
Manley, Timothy M.
    1972   *Outline of Sre structure.* Hawaii: Oceanic Linguistics Special Publication 12.
Maslov, Yuri
    1978   *Voprosy sopostavitel'noj aspektologii.* Leningrad: Izdatel'stvo Leningradskogo Universiteta (Engl. transl.: *Contrastive studies in verbal aspect*. Heidelberg: Groos 1985).
Matthews, W.K.
    1953   "The ergative construction in modern Indo-Aryan", *Lingua* 3: 349-371.
McCawley, James D.
    1968   "The role of semantics in a grammar", in: Bach—Harms (eds.), 125-169.
McCawley, James D., (ed.)
    1976   *Notes from the linguistic undergound (Syntax and Semantics 7).* New York: Academic Press.
McKaughan, Howard
    1962   "Overt relation markers in Maranao", *Language* 38: 47-51.
    1969   "Topicalization in Maranao: an addendum", *Working Papers in Linguistics, University of Hawaii* 11: 129-141.
Miller, George A.
    1969   "A psychological method to investigate verbal concepts", *Journal of Mathematical Psychology* 6: 169-191.
Mirikitani, Leatrice
    1972   *Kapampangan syntax.* Hawaii: Oceanic Linguistics Publication 10.
Moravcsik, Edith A.
    1978   "Agreement", in: Greenberg (ed.), vol. 4, 331-374.
Moravcsik, Edith A.—Jessica Wirth (eds.)
    1980   *Current approaches to syntax (Syntax and Semantics 13).* New York: Academic Press.
Moutaouakil, Ahmed
    1984   "Le Focus en Arabe: vers une analyse fonctionnelle", *Lingua* 64: 115-176.
    1985   "Topic in Arabic: towards a functional analysis", in: Bolkestein—De Groot—Mackenzie (eds.) (1985a), 75-89.
    1986   "Towards an adequate representation of illocutionary forces in Functional Grammar", *WPFG* 10.
    1989   *Pragmatic functions in a Functional Grammar of Arabic.* Dordrecht: Foris.
Mulder, Hotze
    1988   "Non-accusative second arguments of two-place verbs in Ancient Greek", in: A. Rijksbaron—Mulder—Wakker (eds.), *In the footsteps of Raphael Kühner*, 219-238. Amsterdam: Gieben.

Myhill, John
　1988　"Variation in Spanish clitic climbing", *Georgetown University Round Table on Languages and Linguistics 1988*.
Naylor, Paz Buenaventura
　1975　"Topic, focus, and emphasis in the Tagalog verbal clause", *Oceanic Linguistics* 14: 12-79.
Nichols, Johanna
　1986　"Head-marking and dependent-marking grammar", *Language* 62: 56-119.
Nuyts, Jan
　1988　Aspekten van een kognitief-pragmatische taaltheorie; een poging tot een bijdrage aan de theorievorming over de kognitie van natuurlijke taal. [Ph.D. dissertation, University of Antwerp.]
Nuyts, Jan—A. Machtelt Bolkestein—Co Vet (eds.)
　1990　*Layers and levels of representation in language theory*. Amsterdam: Benjamins.
Nuyts, Jan—Georges de Schutter (eds.)
　1987　*Getting one's words into line*. Dordrecht: Foris.
Okombo, Duncan Okoth
　1983　"Alpha vs. Non-Alpha: some observations on the position of semantic functions on the SFH", in: Dik (ed.), 143-154.
Olbertz, Hella
　1989　"Periphrastic Aspect in Spanish", *WPFG* 32.
Orlandini, A.
　1983　"Une analyse sémantique et pragmatique des pronoms indéfinis en latin", in: H. Pinkster (ed.), *Latin linguistics and linguistic theory*, 229-240. Amsterdam: Benjamins.
Payne, John R.
　1980　"The decay of ergativity in Pamir languages", *Lingua* 51: 147-186.
Peranteau, Paul M.—Judith N. Levi—Gloria C. Phares (eds.)
　1972　*The Chicago which hunt: Papers from the relative clause festival*. Chicago: Chicago Linguistic Society.
Peres, Joao Andrade
　1984　*Elementos para uma gramática nova*. Coimbra: Livraria Almedina.
Perlmutter, David M.
　1980　"Relational Grammar", in: Moravcsik—Wirth (eds.), 195-229.
　1981　"Functional Grammar and Relational Grammar: points of convergence and divergence", in: Hoekstra—Van der Hulst—Moortgat (eds.), 319-352.
　1982　"Syntactic representation, syntactic levels, and the notion of subject", in: P. Jacobson—G.K. Pullum (eds.), *The nature of syntactic representation*, 283-340. Dordrecht: Reidel.
Perlmutter, David M. (ed.)
　1983　*Studies in Relational Grammar 1*. Chicago: University of Chicago Press.

Perlmutter, David M.—Paul M. Postal
- 1983 "Towards a universal characterization of passivization", in: Perlmutter (ed.), 3-29.

Perlmutter, David M.—Carol G. Rosen (eds.)
- 1984 *Studies in Relational Grammar 2*. Chicago: University of Chicago Press.

Philippaki-Warburton, Irene
- 1985 "Word order in Modern Greek", *Transactions of the Philological Society 1985*: 113-143.

Pijper, Jan Roelof de
- 1983 *Modelling British English intonation*. Dordrecht: Foris.

Pike, Kenneth L.
- 1967 *Language in relation to a unified theory of the structure of human behavior*. The Hague: Mouton.

Pinkster, Harm
- 1972 *On Latin adverbs*. Amsterdam: North-Holland.
- 1983 "Tempus, Aspect and Aktionsart in Latin (recent trends 1961-1981)", in: H. Temporini—W. Haase (eds.), *Aufstieg und Niedergang der Römischen Welt*, vol. II:29, 270-319. Berlin: De Gruyter.
- 1984 *Latijnse syntaxis en semantiek*. Amsterdam: B.R. Grüner.
- 1985 "Latin case and valency grammar", in: C. Touratier (ed.), *Syntaxe et Latin*, 163-189. Marseille: Lafitte.
- 1988a *Lateinische Syntax und Semantik*. Tübingen: Francke Verlag.
- 1988b "Non-accusative second arguments of two-place verbs in Latin", *Cuadernos de Filología Clásica*.

Platero, Paul R.
- 1974 "The Navajo relative clause", *International Journal of American Linguistics* 40: 202-246.

Prince, Ellen F.
- 1981 "Towards a taxonomy of given/new information", in: Cole (ed.), 223-256.

Pullum, Geoffrey K.
- 1981 "Languages with object before subject: a comment and a catalogue", *Linguistics* 19: 147-155.

Quirk, Randolph—Sidney Greenbaum—Geoffrey Leech—Jan Svartvik
- 1972 *A grammar of contemporary English*. London: Longmans.

Rando, R.—D.-J. Napoli
- 1978 "Definites in *there*-sentences", *Language* 54: 300-313.

Reesink, Ger P.
- 1983 "Switch reference and topicality hierarchies", *Studies in Language* 7: 215-246.
- 1987 *Structures and their functions in Usan, a Papuan language of Papua New Guinea*. Amsterdam: Benjamins.

Reichenbach, Hans
- 1947 *Elements of symbolic logic*. New York: Free Press.

Reichling, Anton J.B.N.
   1963   "Das Problem der Bedeutung in der Sprachwissenschaft", *Innsbrucker Beiträge zur Kulturwissenschaft* 19.
Rijkhoff, Jan
   1986   "Word order universals revisited: the principle of Head Proximity", *Belgian Journal of Linguistics* 1: 95-125. (= *WPFG* 14).
   1987   "Word order tendencies in two prefield subtypes", in: Nuyts—De Schutter (eds.), 1-15.
   1988   "A typology of operators; towards a unified analysis of terms and predications", *WPFG* 29.
   1989   "The identification of referents - a procedural model", in: Connolly—Dik (eds.), 229-247.
   1990   "Toward a unified analysis of terms and predications", in: Nuyts—Bolkestein—Vet (eds.), 165-192.
   1991   "Nominal aspect", *Journal of Semantics* 8: 291-309.
   1992   The noun phrase; a typological study of its form and structure. [Ph.D. dissertation, University of Amsterdam.]
Rijksbaron, Albert
   1976   *Temporal and causal conjunctions in Ancient Greek*. Amsterdam: Hakkert.
   1986   "The pragmatics and semantics of conditional and temporal clauses; some evidence from Dutch and Classical Greek", *WPFG* 13.
Risselada, Rodie
   1984   "Coordination and juxtaposition of adjectives in the Latin NP", *Glotta* 62: 202-231.
Robins, R.H.
   1968   "Basic sentence structures in Sundanese", *Lingua* 21: 351-358.
Romero-Figueroa, A.
   1985   "OSV as the basic word order in Warao", *Lingua* 66: 115-134.
Ross, John R.
   1967   Constraints on variables in syntax. [Ph.D. dissertation, MIT, Cambridge, Mass.]
   1970   "On declarative sentences", in: R. Jacobs—P. Rosenbaum (eds.), *Readings in English transformational grammar*, 222-272. Waltham, Mass.: Ginn.
   1973   "The penthouse principle and the order of constituents", in: Claudia Corum—T. Cedrik Smith-Stark—Ann Weiser (eds.), *You take the high node and I'll take the low node*, 397-422. Chicago Linguistic Society.
Rus, Thomas
   1992   L'espressione del complesso verbale in una grammatica funzionale computazionale dell'Italiano. [M.A. thesis in Italian, University of Amsterdam.]
Russell, Bertrand
   1905   "On denoting", *Mind* 14: 479-493.

Sadock, Jerrold M.—Arnold M. Zwicky
  1985 "Speech act distinctions in syntax", in: Shopen (ed.), Vol.I, 155-196.
Sapir, Edward
  1921 *Language; an introduction to the study of speech*. New York: Harcourt, Brace and Company.
  1949 *Selected writings in language, culture, and personality*, (ed.) by D.G. Mandelbaum. Berkeley: University of California Press.
Schaaik, Gerjan van
  1983 A functional analysis of aspects of Turkish grammar. [M.A. thesis in General Linguistics, University of Amsterdam.]
Schachter, Paul
  1976 "The subject in Philippine languages: Topic, Actor, Actor-Topic, or none of the above?", in: Li (ed.), 491-518.
  1977 "Reference-related and role-related properties of subjects", in: Cole—Sadock (eds.), 279-306.
Schaub, W.
  1985 *Babungo*. London: Croom Helm.
Schuchardt, Hugo
  1895 "Ueber den passiven Charakter des Transitivs in den kaukasischen Sprachen", *Ber. Ak. Wien, Phil.-hist. Klasse*, 133:1.
Schultink, H.
  1961 "Produktiviteit als morfologisch fenomeen", *Forum der Letteren* 2: 110-125.
Schutter, George de—Jan Nuyts
  1983 "Towards an integrated model of a Functional Grammar", in: Dik (ed.), 387-404.
Searle, John
  1969 *Speech acts; an essay in the philosophy of language*. Cambridge: Cambridge University Press.
Seiler, Hansjakob—Christian Lehmann (eds.)
  1982 *Apprehension; das sprachliche Erfassen von Gegenständen, Teil I: Bereich und Ordnung der Phänomene*. Tübingen: Gunter Narr.
Seiler, Hansjakob—Franz Josef Stachowiak (eds.)
  1982 *Apprehension; das sprachliche Erfassen von Gegenständen, Teil II: Die Techniken und ihr Zusammenhang in Einzelsprachen*. Tübingen: Gunter Narr.
Serzisko, Fritz
  1982 "Temporäre Klassifikation; ihre Variationsbreite in Sprachen mit Zahlklassifikatoren", in: Seiler—Lehmann (eds.), 147-159.
Seuren, Pieter A.M.
  1969 *Operators and nucleus*. Cambridge: Cambridge University Press.

Shopen, Timothy (ed.)
    1985   *Language typology and syntactic description.* Vol. 1: Clause structure, vol. 2: Complex constructions, vol. 3: Grammatical categories and the lexicon. Cambridge: University Press.

Sie Ing Djiang
    1988   The syntactic passive in Bahasa Indonesia; a study in Government-Binding theory. [Ph.D. dissertation, University of Amsterdam.]

Siewierska, Anna
    1988   *Word order rules.* London: Croom Helm.

Silverstein, Michael
    1976   "Hierarchy of features and ergativity", in: R.M.W. Dixon (ed.), *Grammatical categories in Australian languages*, 112-171. Canberra: Australian Institute of Aboriginal Studies.

Skousen, Royal
    1975   *Substantive evidence in phonology.* The Hague: Mouton.

Smith, Neil V.
    1975   "On generics", *Transactions of the Philological Society 1975*: 27-48.

Smyth, R.H.—G.D. Prideaux—J.T. Hogan
    1979   "The effect of context on dative position", *Lingua* 47: 27-42.

Sommers, F.
    1965   "Predicability", in: M. Black (ed.), *Philosophy in America*, 262-281. London: Allen & Unwin.

Sridhar, S.N.
    1976a   "Dative subjects", *Chicago Linguistic Society* 12: 582-593.
    1976b   "Dative subjects, rule government, and Relational Grammar", *Studies in the Linguistic Sciences* 6: 130-151.

Stanchev, Svillen
    1988   Some pragmatic aspects of constituent order in Bulgarian. [Paper read at the 3rd International Conference on Functional Grammar, Amsterdam.]

Steele, Susan
    1975   "On some factors that affect and effect word order", in: Li (ed.), 197-268.
    1977   "Clisis and diachrony", in: Li (ed.), 539-579.

Steen, Gerard
    1985   "Grammar and metaphor; the consequences of an anomaly", *WPFG* 3.

Strawson, P.F.
    1971   *Logico-linguistic papers.* London: Methuen.

Stroomer, Harry
    1987   A comparative study of three Southern Oromo dialects in Kenya. [Ph.D. dissertation, University of Leyden.]

Taylor, C.
    1985   *Nkore-Kiga.* London: Croom-Helm.

Tesnière, Lucien
    1959   *Eléments de syntaxe structurale.* Paris: Klincksieck.

Thompson, Sandra A.
    1984   "Grammar and written discourse: initial vs. final purpose clauses in English", *Nottingham Linguistic Circular* 13: 157-185.
Thwing, Rhonda—John Watters
    1987   "Focus in Vute", *Journal of African Languages and Linguistics* 9: 95-121.
Trithart, Lee
    1975   "Relational Grammar and Chicewa subjectivization rules", *Chicago Linguistic Society* 11: 615-624.
Trubetzkoy, N.S.
    1939   *Grundzüge der Phonologie*. Prague: Travaux du Cercle Linguistique de Prague 7.
Tweehuysen, Rolandt
    1988   Verbale suffigering (s-vorm) in het Zweeds. [M.A. thesis in General Linguistics, University of Amsterdam.]
Uhlenbeck, E.M.
    1978   *Studies in Javanese morphology*. The Hague: Martinus Nijhoff.
Uit den Boogaart, P.C., (ed.)
    1975   *Woordfrequenties in geschreven en gesproken Nederlands*. Utrecht: Oosthoek, Scheltema en Holkema.
Ultan, Russell
    1969   "Some general characteristics of interrogative systems", *Working Papers on Language Universals* 1: 41-63.
Vaissière, Jacqueline
    1983   "Language-independent prosodic features", in: A. Cutler—D.R. Ladd (eds.), *Prosody: models and measurements*, 53-66. Berlin: Springer.
Van Valin, Robert D.
    1985   "Case marking and the structure of the Lakhota clause", in: J. Nichols—A. Woodbury (eds.), *Grammar inside and outside the clause*, 363-413. Cambridge: Cambridge University Press.
Vendler, Zeno
    1967   *Linguistics in philosophy*. Ithaca, NY: Cornell University Press.
Vennemann, Theo
    1972   "Analogy in generative grammar: the origin of word order", *Proceedings ICL* 11, vol. 2: 79-83. Bologna: Mulino.
    1973   "Explanation in syntax", in: J. Kimball (ed.), *Syntax and Semantics* 2: 1-50. New York: Academic Press.
    1974   "Topic, subject and word-order: from SXV to SVX via TVX", in: J.M. Anderson—C. Jones (eds.), *Historical Linguistics*, vol. 1, 339-376. Amsterdam: North-Holland.
Verkuyl, H.J.
    1972   *On the compositional nature of the aspects*. Dordrecht: Reidel.

Vester, Elseline
   1983   *Instrument and Manner expressions in Latin*. Assen: Van Gorcum.
   1985   "Latin relative clauses and the notion of specificity", in: H. Bennis—F. Beukema (eds.), *Linguistics in The Netherlands 1985*, 197-203. Dordrecht: Foris.
   1987   "A representation of Latin relative clauses", in: Auwera—Goossens (eds.), 153-162.

Vet, Co
   1980   *Temps, aspects, et adverbes de temps en français contemporain*. Genève: Droz.
   1981   "Subject assignment in the impersonal constructions of French", in: Bolkestein—Combé—Dik—DeGroot—Gvozdanović—Rijksbaron—Vet, 143-163.
   1983   "Possessive constructions in French", in: Dik (ed.), 123-140.
   1986   "A pragmatic approach to Tense in Functional Grammar", *WPFG* 16.

Vitale, Anthony J.
   1981   *Swahili syntax*. Dordrecht: Foris.

Vries, Lourens de
   1983   "Three passive-like constructions in Indonesian", in: Dik (ed.), 155-173.
   1985   "Topic and Focus in Wambon discourse", in: Bolkestein—De Groot—Mackenzie (eds.) (1985a), 155-180.

Vygotsky, L.S.
   1962   *Thought and language*. Cambridge, Mass.: MIT Press.

Wackernagel, Johann
   1892   "Ueber ein Gesetz der indogermanischen Wortstellung", *Indo-Germanische Forschungen* 1(1892): 333-436.

Wakker, G.C.
   1987   "Purpose clauses in Ancient Greek", in: Nuyts—De Schutter (eds.), 89-101.

Walle, Lieve van der
   1990   "Semantic functions and subject assignment revisited. Evidence from Classical Sanskrit", in: Hannay—Vester (eds.), 87-102.

Watters, John R.
   1979   "Focus in Aghem: a study of its formal correlates and typology", in: L. Hyman (ed.), *Aghem grammatical structure*, 137-197. Los Angeles: University of Southern California.
   1985   "The place of morphology in FG: the case of the Ejagham verb system", in: Bolkestein—De Groot—Mackenzie (eds.) (1985b), 85-104.

Weinreich, Uriel
   1966   "Explorations in semantic theory", in: T.A. Sebeok (ed.), *Current trends in linguistics* 3: 395-477. The Hague: Mouton.
   1969   "Problems in the analysis of idioms", in: J. Puhvel (ed.), *Substance and structure of language*, 23-81. Berkeley: University of California Press.

Werth, Paul N.
   1984   *Focus, coherence and emphasis*. London: Croom Helm.
Wolfart, H.C.—J.F. Carroll
   1981   *Meet Cree; a guide to the Cree language*. Edmonton: University of Alberta Press.
Work group on FG
   1981   "On the Functional Grammar of teaching verbs", in: Hoekstra—Van der Hulst—Moortgat (eds.), 203-231.
Zavala, R.M.
   1989   "Los sistemas clasificadores en el Kanjobal de San Miguel Acatan", *Function* IV, Guadalajara.

Index of languages

Abkhaz 156
Aghem 336, 337, 426, 455
Arabic 330, 425
Babungo 430
Bantu 36, 156, 264, 265, 272, 274, 282, 336, 376
Basque 375
Bulgarian 426
Carib 417, 419
Cebuano 256, 267, 272, 274
Chicewa 282
Chimwi:ni 267, 282
Chinese 61, 173, 445, 466
Chinook 156
Cree 323
Czech 426
Danish 16, 17, 350
Dholuo 120, 254
Dutch 33, 42, 43, 46, 82, 83, 92, 151, 170, 176, 178, 202-204, 207-212, 244, 267, 298, 341, 373, 378, 384, 410, 413, 414, 420-423, 440, 449, 451, 461
Dyirbal 287, 319, 320
English 16, 17, 21, 33, 35, 36, 42, 43, 46, 78, 82, 83, 92-94, 99, 116, 119, 150, 151, 178, 180, 186, 189, 190, 196, 198, 199, 202-204, 208, 212, 216, 220, 224, 229, 244, 248, 255, 258-260, 262, 264, 265, 267, 268, 273, 275, 288, 298, 317, 342-344, 346, 347, 350, 351, 356, 361, 362, 366, 367, 372, 373, 377, 381, 382, 387, 389, 400, 410, 414, 429, 436, 448, 449, 451, 453-455, 459, 463
Fiji 418
French 82, 83, 85, 154, 155, 178, 190, 209, 317, 340, 341, 349, 376, 412
German 87, 262, 298, 375, 378, 413, 423
Germanic 414, 423, 442
Greek 178, 186, 276, 277, 279, 305, 355, 400
Gur 414
Hixkaryana 417
Igbo 445, 448
Japanese 36, 134, 135, 267, 367, 387
Kalagan 267, 272
Kanjobal 167
Kannada 116, 117
Kapampangan 267
Kinyarwanda 267, 272, 282
Kobon 429
Latin 154-156, 187, 190, 207-209, 277, 297, 305, 320, 347, 350, 354, 359, 360, 366, 370, 373, 377, 430, 434
Lillooet 182, 183, 195
Luganda 265, 267, 272
Maguindanao 267
Malagasy 267, 272, 418
Mam 430
Mande 414
Maranao 256, 257, 267
Mayan 430
Melanau 267
Menomini 322
Navajo 34-36
Pamir 375
Persian 375
Polish 426, 427
Quechua 429

Romance 442
Rushi 375
Russian 190, 316
Salish 182, 195
Sanskrit 267
Serbo-Croatian 187, 254
Spanish 38, 93, 147, 200, 303
Sre 267
Sundanese 267
Swahili 265, 267, 272, 282-284, 379-381
Swedish 361, 373, 376
Tagalog 267, 268, 272, 288, 379
Tamil 429
Turkish 296, 349, 425
Tyebara 414
Vute 338
Wajana 417
Wambon 321, 335, 336
Warao 417
Welsh 240

Index of names

Abasheikh 265, 266, 274, 282
Allan 36, 40, 143, 277, 400
Allen 36
Aronoff 347
Asher 429
Ashton 265, 266, 379
Austin 3, 299, 300
Auwera 256
Awbery 241
Baart 461
Bartsch 169, 298
Behaghel 404
Bell 256, 266, 272, 274
Berg 466
Berko 344
Berlin 31
Blake 395, 404
Bloomfield 3, 122, 322
Boas 156
Boër 305, 307
Bolinger 449, 453, 458, 461, 463
Bolkestein 190, 209, 241, 256, 305, 320, 321, 436
Bossuyt 14, 326
Bresnan 156
Brigden 106, 108
Brown 11, 31-33, 40, 45, 128, 140, 169-171, 174-176, 188, 198, 310, 314, 319, 386, 405
Bunt 139, 141
Bybee 54, 363, 381
Carnap 3, 97
Carroll 323
Cate 222
Chafe 103, 105, 122
Chomsky 3, 6, 13, 22, 368
Chung 241, 264, 266, 286, 295
Clark 11, 14, 134, 209, 324, 325, 434
Claudi 240

Clayre 266
Cohen 449, 461
Cole 429
Collier 449
Comrie 29, 40, 41, 64, 106, 108, 110, 221-223, 237, 238, 252, 256, 260, 286, 320, 395
Connolly 393
Craig 138, 167, 168
Croft 178, 396
Cruttenden 443, 444, 449, 454, 461, 462, 465
Dahl 133, 134, 190, 385
Davies 250, 429
Derbyshire 417, 418
Des Tombe 14
Dik 2, 4, 7, 14, 57, 58, 70, 93, 99, 103, 104, 106, 138, 140, 143, 176, 188, 199, 209, 218, 230, 232, 240, 248, 254, 256, 265, 281, 286, 320, 326, 332, 339, 356, 363, 365, 378, 382, 383, 385, 404, 407, 410, 412, 418, 421, 424, 425, 429, 437, 442
Dixon 287, 318, 319, 370
Donnellan 189
Dowty 106, 108, 110
Dryer 265, 266, 274, 282
Duranti 265
Eijk 182, 195
England 317, 430
Ertel 36
Estival 286
Ferguson 198
Fillmore 100, 117, 120, 122, 124, 265, 368
Firth 3
Foley 50, 54, 160, 241, 256, 363, 381
Frantz 36

Fraser 103, 104
Frege 135
Garber 413, 414
García 36
Gary 265, 266, 274, 282
Givón 158, 256, 315, 318, 325
Goossens 93, 241
Greenbaum 66, 67, 297, 304, 306
Greenberg 27, 44, 144, 388, 391, 394, 395, 400, 403, 410, 411, 413, 415, 431, 434
Grice 128, 185
Grimes 318, 319, 325
Groot 106, 108, 118, 120, 152, 156, 157, 187, 209, 223, 254, 276, 354, 425, 438
Guéron 438
Gussenhoven 456, 461
Gvozdanović 158, 254, 376, 425
Haiman 399, 423
Hale 35, 36, 286
Halliday 3, 463
Hannay 130, 212, 213, 216, 313-315, 324, 326
Harris 3
Hart 449, 461
Haverkate 303
Haviland 324, 325
Hawkins 7, 185, 391, 395, 403, 404, 415, 428, 431-435
Hawkinson 36, 39
Heine 240
Hengeveld 50, 54, 55, 64, 82, 146, 149, 160, 161, 193, 200, 201, 215, 216, 218, 232, 241-243, 293, 295, 296, 303, 304, 363, 381, 385, 414, 463
Hess 195
Hetzron 213, 315, 316, 434
Hewitt 156
Hock 413, 414
Hogan 255
Hohepa 286

Howell 417
Huddleston 119
Hyman 36, 39, 157, 445, 448, 453
Hymes 3, 5
Itagaki 255, 279
Jackendoff 103, 122, 265
Jakobson 41
Janssen 24
Johnson 129, 265, 266, 268, 461
Johnson-Laird 129
Jong 55, 302, 430
Kaburaki 36, 39, 252
Kahr 365, 407
Kahrel 386, 407
Kampers-Manhe 190
Karttunen 130, 184, 190
Kay 31
Keenan 41, 252, 260, 265, 266, 272, 274, 282, 285, 320, 395, 417
Keijsper 461
Keizer 55, 82, 131, 136, 146, 215
Kiefer 198
Kim 426, 427
Kinkade 195
Kirsner 36
Kisseberth 265, 266, 274, 282
Klooster 203
Kölver 144
Koopmans-van Beinum 447
Kraak 203
Kučanda 254
Kuhn 2
Kuipers 195
Kuno 36, 39, 252, 266
Kwee 81
Lakoff 105
Laudan 2
Lee 266
Lehmann 54, 93, 138, 374-376, 395, 405
Leuven-Zwart 102
Levinson 306

Li 173, 282, 283, 379, 380, 388
Limburg 152, 156, 157, 407, 408, 429
Lycan 305, 307
Lyons 55, 106, 136, 143, 167, 178, 190, 209, 211, 232, 241, 306
McCawley 100
McKaughan 257, 266
Mackenzie 63, 121, 207
Maddieson 445, 455
Mallinson 395, 404
Manley 266
Maslov 221
Matthews 287
Mchombo 156
Miller 100
Mirikitani 262, 266, 273
Moravcsik 374
Moutaouakil 55, 302, 326, 330, 331, 426
Mulder 276, 277
Myhill 38, 286
Napoli 212
Naylor 266, 268
Nichols 156
Nuyts 14
Okombo 120, 254
Olbertz 93
Orlandini 188
Payne 287
Peres 55, 302
Perlmutter 119, 249, 250, 274, 276
Philippaki-Warburton 178
Pijper 451
Pike 3
Pinkster 87, 88, 106, 112, 188, 245, 277, 297, 305, 370
Platero 34-36
Postal 274
Prideaux 255, 279
Prince 130, 314, 324
Pullum 417
Quirk 273, 343

Rando 212
Reesink 322
Reichenbach 54, 233
Reichling 12
Rijkhoff 130, 138, 145, 146, 159, 161, 162, 165, 166, 184, 219, 402-404, 414
Rijksbaron 305, 355
Risselada 256, 434
Robins 266
Romero-Figueroa 417
Rosen 249
Ross 150, 305, 411
Rus 363
Russell 185
Sadock 388
Sapir 3, 94, 126
Schaaik 425
Schachter 256, 266, 288
Schaub 430
Schuchardt 286
Schultink 343
Schutter 14
Searle 3, 127, 299, 300
Seiler 138
Seiter 286
Serzisko 144
Seuren 160
Sie Ing Djiang 195
Siewierska 36, 40, 277, 392, 395, 400, 426, 427, 430, 431, 434, 439
Silverstein 36
Skousen 344
Smith 178, 188
Smyth 255
Sommers 149
Sridhar 116
Stanchev 426
Steele 395, 396, 413
Steen 94
Strawson 184
Stroomer 165

Taylor 377
Tesnière 87
Thompson 173, 400
Thwing 326, 330, 338
Timberlake 241, 295
Trithart 265, 282
Trubetzkoy 41
Tweehuysen 104
Uhlenbeck 343
Uit den Boogaart 33
Ultan 388
Van Valin 50, 54, 156, 160, 241, 256, 363, 381
Vendler 52, 54, 105, 176, 292
Vennemann 169, 395, 403, 405
Verkuyl 105, 106, 109
Vester 106, 108, 110, 112, 114, 188, 190, 218, 232
Vet 54, 106, 108, 114, 209, 218, 232, 235, 318
Vitale 266, 282, 379
Vries 256, 313, 320, 321, 325, 326, 335
Vygotsky 5
Wakker 400
Walle 266, 267
Watters 326, 330, 332, 337, 338, 348, 426, 455
Weinreich 96, 97, 103
Werth 324
Wolfart 323
Yule 40, 128, 310, 314, 319
Zavala 167
Zwicky 388

Index of subjects

ablative *see* case
abstractness 16, 23
accent 443, 444, 446-448, 450, 456, 460
  culminative character of *see* characteristic accent position
accent language 451, 453
accessibility 41, 150, 247, 278-280
Accomplishment 144
accusative *see* case
Action 105, 114-115, 307
action-predicate 86
active languages 123
active—passive 26, 34, 64, 248-250, 259-271, 275, 284-289, 320, 366, 377-380, 437
Activity 114-115
adequacy
  descriptive 12-13
  explanatory 12-13
  pragmatic 13, 310
  psychological 13-14, 57-58
  standards of 12-15
  typological 14-15, 16-17, 80, 187-188, 350, 362-363, 394
address 49, 311, 367
adjectival phrase 396-398, 408
adjectival predicate 193-197
adjective 193, 359-360, 415, 431-435
adposition 365-368, 407, 442
adposition stranding 440-441
adpositional predicate 206-208
affix 186-188, 407, 454
Agent 105, 118-119, 254-255, 259-260, 287-289
agglutination 361

agreement 154-158, 355-357, 359-360, 373-377, 388-389
  source of 356, 373-375, 389
  target of 356, 373-374
Aktionsart 105, 106, 221, 241
allative *see* case
analytic—synthetic 348-351
anaphora 82-83, 294, 318-319, 389
  zero 82
anaphorical operator 83, 234-235, 294-295
animacy 94, 115
animacy hierarchy 36-37
antecedent 388-389
antipassive 319
applicative 264, 282, 380
apposition 156, 374, 388
appositional language 156-158
apprehension 138
argument 50-51, 86-90 271-280, 398
  first 118-120, 252, 275-279, 370, 418-419, 428-429
  second 120-122, 252, 273-277, 370, 418-419, 428-429
  third 120-122, 277, 370
article 16-17, 186-188, 205-208
articulation, reduced 446-447
Aspect 105-106, 200, 221-225, 241, 382-384
  internal—external 225
aspectual verb 111
aspectuality 138, 163, 221-222
attitudinal disjunct 66, 297
attitudinal satellite 297-299
attributive clause 151-152
attributive function 194-197, 207-208

attributive phrase 151-152
auxiliary operandum 357-360, 455
auxiliary verb 353, 383, 413-414, 441-442
availability 130-131, 184-186, 214, 315

backgrounding 322
Beneficiary 113-114, 229, 254-255, 264, 282-283, 380
boundary marker 450
bridging assumption 324-325

cardinal number 139, 169
case 207, 368-372, 374-376, 389
    ablative 231, 371-372
    absolutive 284-287, 369
    abstract 368
    accusative 276-277, 284-287, 354-355
    allative 231, 369
    dative 117, 229, 276
    deep 117, 368
    ergative 284-289, 369
    genitive 207, 431
    see possessor
    instrumental 285
    locative 369
    nominative 284-286
    partitive 369
    vocative 49, 366
case marker 398, 407
category 24-27, 193-197, 358
Cause 244-245
centripetal orientation 401-402, 414-419, 428, 429, 434-435
Change 114-115
characteristic accent position 71, 448, 453-456, 464-465
chômeur 249
Circumstance 243-244
class inclusion 204-206, 214
classifier 143, 164
    mensural 143, 166-168
    sortal 143-144, 164-166
clause 49-55, 292, 310-311, 388-389, 396-400, 444, 461-462
    main—subordinate 49, 420
clause structure 49-55
    fully specified 68
cleft construction 327, 427
clitic 341, 387-388, 407, 412, 413, 425, 457
clitic climbing 38-39
closed predication 81
Collection 140-142
collective noun 142, 164-165
colour terms 31-33, 42
commissive 113
communication 5
communicative competence 5, 7, 58
communicative functions 6
communicative intention 8-9, 11, 57
communicative setting 311
Company 229
competence 5-6
composition 348, 454
comprehension model 13
computational implementation 1, 7, 58, 103, 104, 339, 382
conative aspect 224
condition 305
conditional clause 400, 439
conjugation class 358
constituent ordering 68, 70, 80, 340, 391-442
    domain of 396-398
    multifunctional theory of 394-396, 439
    principles of 391, 394-396, 399-415
constituent ordering in terms 427-435
constituent ordering template 70-71, 393, 420, 425-426
content words 159

Index of subjects 501

contextual information 6, 10
Continuous aspect 225
contrast 326, 336
   see Focus
control 112-115, 227-231
controller 121
converse relation 251
coordinator 398, 406
copula 196-202, 205-206
copula support 198-202
core predication 51-52, 64-65,
   217-219, 275
count noun 164
counterfield 397
cross-categorial harmony 391
cross-domain harmony 403, 428
cross-reference 156-158, 374, 388
current relevance 240
cut-off point 32, 268

dative see case
dative movement 249
declarative 301-303, 462-463
declension class 358-360
definiteness 16-17, 132, 180,
   183-189, 204-206, 210, 212-214,
   255, 316, 372-374, 376, 389
definiteness hierarchy 37-38
deictic centre 40, 181, 400
deletion 19, 197, 306, 329, 341
demonstratives 180-183, 372,
   414-415, 430-435
demonstrative systems 182
demotion 249
dependencies 56
dependent 397-398, 430, 433
derivation 220, 347, 349-351
designating 131
direct object 249-250
direct—inverse construction 34-35
Direction 120-123, 231, 273-274
directive 113
discourse 309-338, 449

discourse coherence 324-325
discourse referent 184
Discourse Topic see Topic
displacement 402, 435-438
Distributive aspect 236
domain integrity 402, 435, 437
do-support 199, 387
downdrift 449
dummy adverb 210-214, 317, 422
dummy pronoun 317, 424
Duration 109
dynamicity 107-108, 112, 228,
   230-231
dynamism 114-115

Egressive aspect 25, 240
embedded clause 407, 441-442
emotion 464, 465
empathy 40, 252
ensemble 139-140, 170
   domain 171
   referent 171
   universal 171
ensemble noun 142-145, 163-165
entity 129-130
   first-order 55, 136-137, 147,
     215-216, 232-234
   fourth-order 55, 136-137
   second-order 55, 136-137, 214-
     216, 232-236
   third-order 55, 136-137
   zero-order 55, 136-137, 147,
     215-216
   typology of 136-147, 163-164,
     215
epithet 319
ergative see case
ergativity 123, 284-289, 319, 369
event 54, 107, 111-112
exclamative 301-302
existence 129, 214, 285

existential construction 209-212, 315
  definiteness restriction on 212
  entity existential 216
  state of affairs existential 216
existential-locative construction 211-212, 315
Experience 115-117
Experiencer 116-117, 119
expressibility 150-151
expression rules 49, 61, 62, 68, 339-466
  centrifugal aplication of 384
  form-determining 68-70, 340-342, 351-363, 386, 464
  order-determining 340-342
  see placement rule
expressiveness 44
extended predication 52, 65, 217
extra-clausal constituent 49, 310-311, 444
extraposition 430, 438

fact 54
  possible 52
feeding order 362
filtering 21-22
focality 68, 312, 326-338, 438, 457-461
Focus 289, 313, 326-338, 408-409, 421, 422, 425-427, 438, 456
  communicative point of 330-335
  completive 331-333, 335-338, 403, 459-460
  contrastive 331-335, 403, 426, 430, 456, 460
  counter-presuppositional 331-335, 460
  expanding 331-335
  new see focus, completive
  parallel 332, 460
  questioning 331-337, 457-458
  rejecting 331-337
  replacing 331-338
  restricting 331-335, 337-338
  scope of 330-331
  selecting 331-335
Focus and accent 456
Focus construction 327, 336-338
Focus marker 327, 335-338
Force 118-119
foregrounding 256-257
form words 159
formal paradigm 2-3
formal syntax 2
free word order 394
frequency 32-33, 36, 44, 268
Frequentative aspect 236
function 25-27, 369-372
  see pragmatic, semantic, syntactic function
functional explanation 4
functional logic vi
functional paradigm 3-8
functional stability 403
fund 58-62

gender 85, 96, 152-153, 358-360, 373-374, 376-377, 389
gender hierarchy 37
generative semantics 23, 101-102
generator 14, 24, 56, 339
generic operator 177-178
generic reference 176-178, 191
genitive see case, possessor
given—new 11, 312-313
Given Topic see Topic
Goal 120-124, 254-255, 287-289, 412
grammatical relations 249-250
grammaticalization 93, 240, 256

Habitual aspect 236-237
head 397, 428
Head—Modifier
  see Modifier—Head

head of term 134-136, 151-152, 194-197
head proximity 402-403
heaviness *see* increasing complexity
hierarchy 30-34
hyperonym 143

iconicity 253
iconic ordering 399-400, 402, 406, 439, 441
identification 130, 184, 204-206, 214
idiom 59, 103-104
illocution 299-307, 448
  basic 301-302, 463
illocutionary act variable 55, 66, 292
illocutionary conversion 302-304
illocutionary force 53, 299-304
illocutionary frame 53, 299
illocutionary intention 301
illocutionary modifier 304, 311, 463
illocutionary operator 53, 66-67, 71, 300-304, 386-388, 462-463, 465
illocutionary particle 387-388
illocutionary satellite 53, 66-67, 304-307
  see satellite, level 4
imperative 56, 113, 301-302, 386-387, 463
imperfective *see* perfective
implicature 185-186
inclusive reference 185-186
incorporation 429
increasing complexity 404, 411-412, 430-435, 437-438
indefinite pronoun 189-190
indefiniteness 183-189, 203-206, 210, 212-214, 316
indicative 190, 355
indirect object 249-250
individual 140-142
inferrable 89-90, 130-131, 323

infinitival complement 261
infinitive 84, 355
inflection 166, 220, 347, 349-351, 361, 455
information gap 328-335, 457-459
information, shared 10
Ingressive aspect 220, 225, 240
Initiator 311
innateness 6-7
Instrument 113-114, 123-124, 230, 264-265
instrumental *see* case
instrumental nature of language 3
intention *see* communicative intention
interpretation 8-9, 11
  special strategies of 95
interrogative 301-303, 386-388, 462-463,
interrogative particle 387
intonation 443, 444, 446, 448-449, 450-451
irregular forms 345-348
Iterative aspect 111, 236

knowledge, mutual 10-11
knowledge base 57

language acquisition 6-7
language change 32, 268
language universals 7, 27-30
  implicational 28-29
  statistical 28-29
layering of the clause 50-55, 217-218, 271-272, 291-292
leaking 410-411, 414, 441
left-dislocation 157
lexical decomposition 23
lexical item 58-59
lexical priority 345
lexicon 59, 452-454, 464
liaison 341
linear ordering 80, 400-401, 406

linguistic insecurity 32, 268
linguistic relativity 94, 126
LIPOC 411-413, 423, 430-432, 435, 439, 441-442
Location 88, 120-122, 214-215, 243, 272-274
   inner 273-274
   outer 272-274
locative
   General Locative 273
   Terminus Locative 273
   see case
locative construction 209-212
logic 17
logical form 17, 97, 168

μ-operator *see* morpho-syntactic operator
Manner 88, 226-228, 230, 298, 304-307
markedness 41-47, 212, 439
   - of constructions 41-43, 266
   - of oppositions 43-44
markedness shift 44-47, 281-289, 418
mass 139
mass noun 139, 141, 144, 163
maxim of quantity 128
meaning 12, 368-370
meaning definition 59, 78, 97, 99-103
meaning postulate 59, 78, 97-99, 102
measure 139
measure function 169-170
member 138-139
mental image 98
mental model 129-130
metaphor 94
metaphorical interpretation 95
misunderstanding 9
mobility 432-433

modality 241
   deontic 242
   epistemic 242
   experiential 242, 297
   evidential 242, 296
   inferential 241
   inherent 241
   objective 242, 296
   quotative 242, 297
   reportative 242, 297
   subjective 242-243, 296, 297
mode of action *see* Aktionsart
mode of being *see* Seinsart
Modifier—Head 134-136, 151-152
momentaneousness 111-112
Mood 241
   objective 296
morphology 348-351
   stem-based—word-based 347
morpho-syntactic feature 358-360, 374, 377
morpho-syntactic operator 69, 351-363, 382-384
   auxiliary 69, 353-357, 371-372, 378-380, 382, 387
   primary 353-354, 357, 382, 387
   sequential application of 361-363
movement of constituents 20-21, 80, 341, 392-393
movement verb 85, 93

natural language 5-8
natural language user 1, 339
   capacities of 1-2
   model of 1, 4
natural serialization 403
negation 385-386, 430
neutralization 44
New Topic *see* Topic
Nominal Aspect 138
nominal predicate 193-197, 202-206
nominalization 196, 288-289, 293, 428-429

nominative *see* case
non-verbal predicate 193-216
noun 142-146, 202-204, 359-360, 415, 453
nuclear predication 51, 63, 78, 217-219
number 152-153, 356, 372-374, 376, 389
number function 169-170
numeral 143, 414-415, 430-435
numerator 172

object *see* subject—object
object assignment 249-250, 254, 258, 271-289, 412, 418, 436
object—subject order 417-419
object voice 264, 366
obviation 322-323
obviative *see* proximate—obviative
open predication 61, 80-81, 132-133, 148, 330
operators 51, 159-161, 397
    order of 361-363, 381-382, 384, 414
    scope of 161-163, 362, 381, 384, 414
order of constituents *see* constituent ordering
ordinator 178-180

π-operator 199-200, 380-384, 413
    see predicate, predication, proposition, illocutionary operator
P1-constituent 409
P1-position 408-411, 413, 419-426, 430, 436-437, 440-441, 458
PØ-position 425-426
paradigm 2, 4, 84, 345-348
parallel processing 58
parser 14, 24, 56, 339
participial construction 261
participle 355, 357, 378-379

partitive 173-174, 176
    see case
passive *see* active—passive
Path 231-232, 273
Patient 122
Perfect aspect 110-111, 238-240, 382-384
Perfective/Imperfective aspect 220-225
performance 5
performative 300
    explicit 300, 306
    implicit 300, 306
performative analysis 305-307
permutation 20, 393
    see movement of constituents
person 153, 356, 389
person hierarchy 36-37
personal pronoun 152-153, 186-188
perspective 27, 64-65, 247-268, 277-278, 406, 418
    basic 250-254, 277
Perspectival aspect 221, 238-241
Phasal aspect 221, 225, 240-241
pitch 444, 448-451
pitch fall 447, 449-451, 453-454, 462-463, 465
pitch movement 450-451
    accent-creating 450-451
    bridging 451, 464
    intonational 450-451
    medial 461-462, 465
    terminal 461, 462-463, 465
    lexical 450-451
pitch range 449, 451, 464, 465
pitch rise 447, 449-451, 453-454, 462-463, 465
placement rule 70-71, 210, 391-392
plural marking 43, 143, 351
polarity 384-386
politeness 46-47, 152, 463
portmanteau expression 263, 360-361

Position 114-115
Positioner 118-119
possessive predicates 208-209
possession 208-209, 214
Possessor 208-209, 428-435
Possible Fact 52, 136-137, 291-294
postfield 397-398, 403, 405-415, 427, 428-435, 440
postfield language 405, 409, 413, 415, 431-435, 439-441
postposition *see* adposition
pragmatic adequacy *see* adequacy
pragmatic function 26-27, 68, 71, 213-214, 254, 255-257, 278, 309-338, 366-367, 455-461
pragmatic function hierarchy 37
pragmatic highlighting 403, 429-430, 437
pragmatic information 5, 9, 128, 131, 301-302, 311-312, 326, 460
pragmatics 7-8
pragmatic space 40-41, 181
Prague school 3
predicability 149-150
predicate 50-51, 58-61, 193-197, 377-388, 453-454
   abstract 23, 97
   basic 21, 59
   derived 21, 59, 61, 204-206
   type of *see* Type
predicate formation 21, 59, 93, 219-220, 259, 349-351, 453, 454-455, 464
predicate frame 59, 78-82
predicate operators 51, 63-64, 162
predicate satellite 51, 64
   see satellite, level 1
predicate variable 55, 62-63, 82-83
predicating 127
predication operator 51-52, 65, 162, 236-243
predication satellite 51-52, 65
   see satellite, level 2

predicative function 194-197, 202-203, 207-208
prefield 397-398, 403-415, 426-427, 428-435
prefield language 405, 409, 413, 415, 431-435, 440-442
   liberal 410
   strict 410, 441
preposition *see* adposition
presentative construction 213, 317, 438
presupposition 100, 460
priorities 34-41, 279, 400
Process 114-115, 119
Processed 118-119
pro-drop 155
   see adposition
production model 13-14, 57-58
productivity 343
ProfGlot 4, 14, 104, 339, 356, 363, 420, 424
Progressive aspect 110-111, 201-202, 220, 225, 240, 382-384
prominence 253-254
promise 113
promotion 249
pronoun *see* personal pronoun
proper noun 141, 164, 186-188
property 137, 146
property assignment 205-206, 214
proposition 52, 65, 242-243, 291-299,
propositional content variable 55, 66, 294-295
proposition operator 52, 66, 243, 295-296
proposition satellite 52, 66
   see satellite, level 3
prosodic contour 68, 71, 309, 443-446
   domain of 444
   functions of 450-466
prosodic prominence 327-328

Prospective aspect 93, 238-240
proximate—obviative 322-323
pseudo-passive 248
psychological adequacy
  see adequacy
Purpose 244, 305
purpose clause 400

Quality 231
Quantificational aspect 162, 222, 236-237
quantifier 168-176
  absolute 171-175
  partitive 176
  proportional 172-175
  relative 171-175
  universal 168, 175-176
  zero 386
quantification 169-170
question
  disjunctive 334
  multiple 422
  see interrogative
question—answer pair 328-330
question-word question 328-330, 421-422, 437-438, 440, 458-460

raising 261, 280-281, 436-437
  subjet raising 280-281
reality 124-126, 129-130, 185
Reason 244, 305
Recipient 120-123, 254-255, 262, 264, 282-284
recursion 62
redundancy rule 86, 454, 464
reduplication 352
Reference 120-122
reference 127-131, 146-147, 184-186, 188-191
  constructive 130-131, 184
  identifying 130-131, 184
referent 127-131, 147, 185
reflexivization 260

regularity 344-345
relation 137
Relational Grammar 249-250, 265
relational hierarchy 250
relative clause 190, 415, 424, 428, 430-433, 438
  headless 293
relativization 196, 253, 260-261, 320
relator 397-398, 406-408, 429, 439-441
representation, simplification of 62-63, 83, 84
request 113
research tradition 3
restrictive—non-restrictive 147-148
restrictor 62, 133-136, 147-152, 398
Result 244
Resumed Topic see Topic
right-dislocation 157
root 84
rule 342-345

sandhi 341-342
Sapir—Whorf hypothesis 94, 126
satellite 51, 86-90, 113-114, 398, 421, 423
  implied 227-228
  level 1 87, 225-232, 271-274, 278
  level 2 87, 88, 235-236, 243-245, 271-274, 278
  level 3 87, 226, 292, 297-299
  level 4 87, 245, 292, 304-307
  see predicate, predication, proposition, illocutionary satellite
Seinsart 138, 163-164
selection restriction 59, 91-97
semantic content 12
semantic function 26-27, 59, 117-126, 254-255, 258, 364-365, 368-372

semantic function hierarchy 37, 262-280
semantics 7-8
Semelfactive aspect 236
sentence type 300-304
series of entities 178-180
set 138-141
set nouns 145, 163
set theory 138-139
setting 89, 128
simplification of representation *see* representation
situation 107
situational information 6, 10
size function 170-171
social interaction 3, 5
Source 120-123, 231, 273-274
spatial entity 137
specific reference 188-191
speech act 53, 137, 299-307
speech act theory 300-301
speech act variable *see* illocutionary act variable
Speed 108, 231
State 114-115, 119
state of affairs 51-52, 105, 124-126, 136-137, 292-294
  typology of 105-117
state of affairs noun 233-234
state of affairs variable 55, 64, 101, 232-236
stem 84, 346-348
stepwise lexical definition 99-101
structure-changing operation 19-21
style disjunct 67, 297, 304
subcategorial conversion 141-142, 145
Subject assignment 248-250, 254, 256-289, 378-379, 418-419, 436-437
Subject—Object 64-65, 247-289, 320-321, 366, 403, 418, 425, 426, 437

Subject—Object order 405-406, 417-419
Subject—Object position 409, 420-421, 423, 426
subject—verb inversion 393
subordinator 398, 407, 421, 424, 440
subjunctive 190, 355
substitution 20
Sub-Topic *see* Topic
SVO languages 394-345, 409-411, 413-414, 418, 441
switch reference 321-322
syncretism 447
syntactic function 26-27, 64-65, 367, 369-371
syntactic function hierarchy 37
syntax, autonomous 8

tag 303, 311
Tail 311, 418, 444
telicity 108-111, 112
temporality 237
tendency 29-30
Tense 200, 237-238, 240, 382-384
  absolute 237
  relative 237
term 50-51, 55, 132-136, 365-377, 396-398, 407-408, 427-435
  basic 61
  derived 55, 61
term formation 61, 148
term operator 61, 132, 159-163, 372-376, 433
  localizing 162, 180-191, 218-219
  qualifying 161-162, 163-166, 218-219
    collectivizing 165-166
    individualizing 165-166
  quantifying 162, 166-180, 218-219
term predicate formation 197, 204-208

Index of subjects 509

term structure 61-62, 132-136
term variable 132, 216
terminal form 351, 358
Theme 444
Time 243, 272-274
tone 443, 444-446, 448
   contour 445
   level 445, 450
tone languages 444-446, 451, 452-455
toneme 445, 452-453
tone polarity 454
Topic 313-325, 408-409, 422, 425-426, 438
   Discourse Topic 314, 318-323
   Given Topic 213-314, 252, 255-256, 314, 323-325, 403, 409, 421, 430, 457
   New Topic 213-214, 252, 312, 314-318, 403, 438, 456-457
   Resumed Topic 315, 325, 457
   Sub-Topic 314, 323-325, 421, 430, 457
topicality 68, 312-325, 456-457
topic chain 318
topic continuity 318, 322, 323
topic maintenance 318-323
transformation 19-21
Transformational Grammar 13, 17, 18, 122, 249

translation 102-103
Type 67, 77, 84-85, 96, 138, 359
typological adequacy *see* adequacy
typological frequency 32, 268
typological hierarchy 266, 278
typology of entities *see* entity
typology of SoAs *see* state of affairs

underlying clause structure 49-55
use of language 5-6

valency 59, 78-79, 89-90
   qualitative 79
   quantitative 79
valency reduction 90, 259
vantage point 65, 244
   see perspective
verb 193-197, 452-453
verbal complex 363, 382-384, 420, 424, 439, 441
verbal interaction 3-4, 8-12, 302
vocative *see* case
voice 248, 257, 263-264, 275, 366, 377-380
   see active—passive

word—stem 346-348
word order *see* constituent ordering

Zero semantic function 118-119